IN SEARCH OF THE
BIG BANG

IN SEARCH OF THE
BIG BANG

Quantum Physics and Cosmology

JOHN GRIBBIN

BANTAM BOOKS
TORONTO · NEW YORK · LONDON · SYDNEY · AUCKLAND

IN SEARCH OF THE BIG BANG: QUANTUM PHYSICS AND COSMOLOGY
A Bantam Book / April 1986

New Age and the accompanying figure design as well as the statement "a search for meaning, growth and change" are trademarks of Bantam Books, Inc.

Illustrations by Neil Hyslop.

Library of Congress Cataloging-in-Publication Data
Gribbin, John R.
  In search of the big bang.

Bibliography: pg. 393
Includes index.
*1. Big bang theory. 2. Cosmology. 3. Particles
(Nuclear physics) 4. Quantum theory. I. Title.*
QB991.B54G75   1986   523.1'8   85–48112
ISBN 0-553-34258-4 (pbk.)

Bantam Books are published by Bantam Books, Inc. Its trademark, consisting of the words "Bantam Books" and the portrayal of a rooster, is Registered in U.S. Patent and Trademark Office and in other countries. Marca Registrada. Bantam Books, Inc., 666 Fifth Avenue, New York, New York 10103.

PRINTED IN THE UNITED STATES OF AMERICA

O   0 9 8 7 6 5 4 3 2

Credit must be given to observation rather
than theories, and to theories
only insofar as they
are confirmed by the observed facts.
Aristotle

The more I see, the more I see there is to see.
John Sebastian

ACKNOWLEDGMENTS

The roots of this book go back a long way, to the birth of my fascination with science in the early 1950s. I cannot quite recall which author first introduced me to the mystery and wonder of the universe, but I know that it must have been either Isaac Asimov or George Gamow, since I began reading the books of both of them so long ago that I literally cannot remember ever being without them. And it was not just science, but specifically the mystery of the origin of the Universe that fascinated me from the outset. Thanks to Gamow and his fictitious "Mr. Tompkins" I cut my intellectual teeth on the Big Bang model of the origin of the Universe, and although later on I learned of the steady state hypothesis, it has always been the idea of the Big Bang, the idea that there was a definite moment of creation when the Universe came into being, that held my fascination. It never occurred to me that I might make a career out of studying such deep mysteries, or writing about them. Indeed, I scarcely appreciated that being an astronomer, let alone a cosmologist, was a viable job for anyone, let alone myself, until 1966. Then, just before taking my final undergraduate examinations at Sussex

University, I discovered that Bill (now Sir William) McCrea was about to establish a research center in astronomy on the campus.

That discovery changed my life. First it led to a swift change of direction from a planned period of postgraduate research in particle physics to a year working for an M.Sc. in astronomy in McCrea's group. Then I moved on to Cambridge, becoming a very junior founding member of another new astronomy group, Fred (now Sir Fred) Hoyle's Institute of Theoretical Astronomy, as it then was. For reasons I have never quite fathomed myself, I somehow became sidetracked into working on problems involving very dense stars (white dwarfs, neutron stars, pulsars, and X-ray sources) for my thesis and never did do any real research in cosmology. But while in Cambridge I met Hoyle himself, Jayant Narlikar, Martin Rees, Geoffrey and Margaret Burbidge, Stephen Hawking, William Fowler, and many other eminent astronomers who were deeply immersed in problems of literally cosmic significance. I learned from them what research at this level was really like, and I learned, too, that I could never hope to achieve anything of comparable significance myself. So I became a writer, reporting on new developments not just in cosmology and astronomy but also across the sciences, keeping in touch with new developments even though I was not involved in making those new developments.

When cosmology made a great leap forward in the 1980s, it came about through a marriage with particle physics, the line of work I had abandoned so lightly in 1966. After initially struggling to cope with new developments that seemed to be appearing faster than I could write about them, I had an opportunity to catch up by attending as an observer a joint meeting organized by the European Southern Observatory and CERN, the European Centre for Nuclear Research, in Geneva in November 1983. There, participants from both sides of the fence discussed the links between particle physics and cosmology. It was that meeting, and the fact that I convinced myself that I could understand *most* of what was going on there, that convinced me I could tackle writing this book. Following the meeting, I was able to straighten out my ideas and improve my understanding of the new idea of inflation, the key to understanding the modern version of Big Bang cosmology, in correspondence with Dimitri Nanopoulos of CERN and with two of the founders of the inflationary hypothesis, Alan Guth of MIT and Andrei Linde in Moscow.

As I write these words in the summer of 1985, it looks as if science has achieved, in outline at least, a complete understanding of how the universe as we know it came into being and how it grew from a tiny seed, via the Big Bang, into the vastness we see about us. Martin Rees of Cambridge University has put the importance of the new work clearly in perspective. At that meeting in Geneva in November 1983, he commented that when asked if the Big Bang was a good model of the Universe we live in, he used to say, "It is the best theory we've got." That was indeed a very cautious endorsement. But now, he said in Geneva, if asked the same question he would reply, "The Big Bang model is more likely to be proved right than it is to be proved wrong." Coming from Rees, one of the most cautious of modern cosmologists, who makes no claim lightly, this is a much stronger endorsement of the Big Bang, and amply sufficient justification for me to proceed in writing this book!

The fact that I can understand the physics underlying these new ideas is a tribute to the skills of teachers going back to my school days and to the universities of Sussex and Cambridge; to be alive at a time when such mysteries are resolved, and to be able to understand how they have been resolved, is the greatest stroke of fortune I can imagine. Maybe new mysteries will emerge to disturb the present picture, and the completeness of our understanding of the moment of creation will prove to be an illusion. But the picture today is satisfyingly complete, and I hope I can share with you, through this book, the wonder of its completeness, and of the search that led to a successful theory of the creation, less than sixty years after the discovery that the Universe is expanding and that, therefore, there must indeed have been a moment of creation.

If I succeed at all in holding your attention, that is largely because the story is so fascinating that only the most inept of storytellers could fail to make it interesting. It is also thanks to Asimov and Gamow, who first told an earlier version of the tale to me; to Bill McCrea, who by appearing on the campus at Sussex University showed me that cosmologists were real people and that I might work alongside them; to Fred Hoyle, who established an institute where briefly it was possible for me to mingle with cosmologists of the first rank; to CERN, for inviting me to attend the first ESO/-CERN symposium, and to *New Scientist,* for sending me there to report the meeting. Once the book was under way, I received direct help from Alan Guth and Andrei Linde, from Dimitri Nanopoulos, and from Martin Rees in Cambridge and Jayant Narlikar at the Tata Institute in Bombay. Bill McCrea found time in a busy life to read the first two parts of the book in draft and correct some of my historical misconceptions, while Frank Close of Oxford University carried out a similar task on the chapters dealing with particle physics, and Martin Rees tactfully pointed out the places where my understanding of the new ideas in cosmology was still inadequate. No doubt some errors remain. These are entirely my responsibility. If you spot one, let me know and I will do my best to correct it in future editions of the book. But I hope that they are few enough, and minor enough, not to mar your enjoyment of the story of the search for the ultimate cosmic truth, the origin of the Universe itself.

John Gribbin
June 1985

CONTENTS

PART THREE:

. . . AND BEFORE

THE METAPHYSICAL UNIVERSE

People have always wondered about the mystery of creation. How did the Universe, as we now call it, come into being? *Why* does the Universe, or the world, exist? And how is it that we are here to wonder about such things? Such questions were for thousands of years the province of philosophers and theologians. Even when the foundations of modern science were laid four or five centuries ago, it was accepted that some questions were outside the province of science. Newton, for example, sought to explain the behavior of things within the Universe as it exists; he did not try to explain how or why the Universe came to exist in the first place. But today science is encroaching onto the territory of the philosophers. Modern physics—quantum physics—is on the track of answers to the ultimate questions, the nature of reality, the nature of life, and the origin of the entire Universe.

Has science become philosophy, or has philosophy become science? Whichever way you view it, the distinction between the two has become blurred and is far less real than most scientists or philosophers themselves acknowledge today. This is surprising, since the philosophi-

cal study now being subsumed by physics is the deepest
and most profound area of philosophical study, metaphysics, which dates back to the great work of Aristotle more
than two thousand years ago. So although this is a book
about the modern ideas of astronomy and physics concerning the origin of the Universe, its birth in a cosmic
fireball called the Big Bang, it seems appropriate to set the
scene by going back to Aristotle and taking a quick look at
the puzzles metaphysicians have been pondering for
centuries.

Aristotle was born in Macedonia, in northern Greece,
in 384 B.C. His father was the court physician to Amyntas
III, the king of Macedonia and grandfather of the boy who
became Alexander the Great. When Aristotle was in his
early forties, he served for a time as tutor to the teenage
Alexander, at the invitation of Philip II, Alexander's father.
But Aristotle's fame today does not rest upon his position
in the Macedonian court. Among his many scientific and
philosophical writings, two are particularly relevant to
the modern search for an understanding of the nature of the
universe. One, the *Physica*, deals with the nature of the
world as we perceive it. The other, *Metaphysica* (literally
meaning "what comes after physics"), is an inquiry into
what Aristotle called "being as such," the underlying truths
responsible for the world being as we perceive it.

By contemporary standards, both treatises would be
regarded as philosophical works, but the distinction Aristotle was trying to make between the world we see, or
measure with our scientific instruments, and the underlying reality is an important one that strikes to the heart of
modern physics. The study of "being as such" became
known as metaphysics among Aristotle's followers. Philosophers down the centuries have regarded it as the most
fundamental science, a search for a comprehensive understanding of reality as a whole.

This scarcely squares with the popular image of metaphysicians as the stereotypical philosophers who are more
concerned with splitting hairs than with any real investigation of the nature of the Universe. The metaphysician who
wonders whether a tree, or a house, has any real existence
when nobody is looking at it, is seen by most of us lesser
mortals as something of a joke. But the joke is on us, for

the twentieth-century discoveries of physics, that most hard-nosed and objective of sciences, have led inexorably to the conclusion that at the fundamental level of sub-atomic particles such as electrons and protons, things really *don't* have any "real" existence when they are not being monitored.

This concern with the ultimate nature of reality is the first of three great roots of metaphysics. The metaphysician is concerned to know just how accurate a picture of the real world our sense impressions provide. Our senses respond to impressions they receive from the world outside, and our brains interpret those sense impressions as indicating, perhaps, that there is a tree in the garden. But the only things that my brain can ever have direct knowledge of are sense impressions; all my "knowledge" about trees is secondhand, filtered through my senses and into my brain. So which is the more real—the sense impressions or the trees? I don't intend to address the traditionally philosophical side of that question here, but the discussion is remarkably similar to the discussion among physicists in the 1920s, and since, concerning the "reality" of the world of subatomic particles that we probe with our experiments. Nobody has ever even seen an electron, say, or an atom. We deduce that there are things we call electrons and atoms because whenever we carry out certain experiments we get results that are consistent with the existence of atoms and electrons. But what we actually "know" are sense impressions of readings on meters, or of lights flickering on a screen, not even direct sense impressions of the particles we believe we are investigating. Ernst Mach, the famous physicist who, among other things, lent his name to the number by which we measure the speed of an aircraft, summed the position up in his book *Science of Mechanics* in 1883: "Atoms cannot be perceived by the senses; like all substances they are things of the thought . . . a mathematical *model* for facilitating the mental reproduction of the facts."

Fifty years later, in his book *The Nature of the Physical World*, another great physicist, Sir Arthur Eddington, also pondered about the nature of this reality reported to us by our scientific instruments. A desk, he pointed out, appears to our senses to be a solid object with an impres-

sive physical reality. Yet our beloved laws of physics tell us
that the results of experiments probing into the structure
of matter can only be interpreted as meaning that your
desk is mostly empty space and actually consists of a
collection of tiny atoms, separated from one another by
relatively huge empty spaces. A single grain of sand in the
center of the Albert Hall would be less lonely than an atom
in your desk separated from its neighbors. The "solid reality" of your desk is mostly invisible electromagnetic forces
holding the atoms together. Is the solid desk of your sense
impressions any more, or any less, real than the atoms
that our scientific investigation tells us it is made of? All
this is puzzling enough. But there is worse to come.

When physicists tried to probe the exact nature of the
electrons and other particles of which atoms are made,
they found the very concept of a "real" particle slipping
away from them. To explain the behavior of electrons,
protons, and the rest, they had to develop, in the 1920s, a
new sort of physics, quantum physics. Quite literally, "what
comes after physics" is quantum physics; and, serendipi-
tously, quantum physics is just what you need to resolve
the puzzles of metaphysics. In this new world of particle
physics it turned out that particles and waves are two
aspects of the same thing. Light, which was thought of as
an electromagnetic wave, had now to be thought of also as
a stream of particles, called photons; electrons, previously
regarded as particles, like little hard billiard balls, now had
to be thought of also as smeared-out waves. Worse still,
when they tried to apply their new understanding of quantum physics to *predicting* the behavior of electrons, or
other objects, in an experimental setup, the physicists of
the 1920s found that it was impossible, except on a statistical basis. In quantum physics, nothing tells you where
an electron is, or what it is doing, when you are not
looking at it. All you can do, if you make a measurement of
some property of an atom and get the answer A, is calculate the probability that next time you measure the same
thing you will get answer B. Even then there is a definite
probability that you will actually get a different answer, C,
when you do the experiment!

This state of affairs is as unsatisfactory as it sounds—so
much so that most scientists and engineers today ignore it

and continue to pretend that electrons are little, hard, predictable billiard balls, even though the equations they use to design lasers, or nuclear reactors, depend fundamentally on the bizarre laws of quantum physics worked out in the 1920s. Quantum physics has provided the "answer" to the first of the three great metaphysical puzzles. It says, as I have spelled out in my book *In Search of Schrödinger's Cat,* that nothing is real, in the everyday meaning of the term.

So quantum physics tackles the fundamental puzzle of what things do when you are not looking at them, and whether they are really real even if you are looking at them. The second of the three great metaphysical puzzles concerns the origin and nature of life, and this, too, can now be understood in terms of quantum physics, which lays the ground rules for the interactions between atoms that allow molecules such as DNA, the double-helical life molecule itself, to exist. As with the puzzle of the nature of reality, the links between quantum physics and the mystery of life require a whole book of their own, and I addressed these issues in *In Search of the Double Helix.* Neither of these puzzles will get much further discussion here, because now I want to tackle the third and greatest of the metaphysical puzzles: Why should anything exist at all? Where does our world, the Universe, come from?

Although nobody appreciated it at the time, the ground rules of quantum physics, being discovered in the 1920s, also provide an insight into this third mystery. It has taken sixty years for physics to catch up with the metaphysical implications of those discoveries, and it has only been in the 1980s that science has, for the first time ever, come up with a satisfactory explanation not just of how the Universe got to be the way we see it today, but also of how it came into existence in the first place. Since the 1950s, the "best buy" among cosmological theories has been that the Universe began in a Big Bang, an outburst from a state of very high density and very high temperatures. But how did the Big Bang itself come into existence? That is the question now being answered, and in this book I hope to show you how the answer is being arrived at. But the search for an understanding of the Big Bang followed two separate paths from the 1920s onward, paths that have only recently converged on this answer. The quantum physicists went on their way, investigating the nature of the world of atoms and particles, but seldom, if ever, raising their eyes to the heavens and considering whether their world could tell us anything significant about the existence of the world at large. Meanwhile, the astronomers were following another path, but one no less closely linked with the musings of metaphysicians than the quantum physicists' puzzle of the nature of reality.

From Plato to Kant and up to date philosophers have mused on the nature of space and time. Admittedly this is a lesser puzzle than the puzzle of reality, or of the origin of everything, but it is also one that strikes closer to home. We all know of the need to define both place and time to label an event precisely—it is no good arranging to meet someone "under the clock at six" if you don't say which clock, or arranging to meet under a specific clock at a specific location without saying what time you will be there. But are space and time any more real than atoms and electrons? Or are they just artifacts of our perceptions? The man who tried to establish a framework for understanding both space and time, and their interrelationships, in scientific terms was Albert Einstein; and in so doing he set scientists on the trail that was to lead them to the Big Bang.

PART ONE

EINSTEIN'S UNIVERSE

The most incomprehensible thing about the universe
is that it is comprehensible.

Albert Einstein

CHAPTER ONE

THE REALM OF THE NEBULAE

The Universe in which we live is a huge and almost empty place. Bright stars, like our Sun, huddle together in groups called galaxies, which may contain a trillion (million million) stars. Some idea of how distant the stars are from each other can be gained by looking up at the dark night sky and realizing that each of the tiny pinpricks of light we see represents a star and that each of these stars is intrinsically about as bright as our Sun. When we look up at the night sky on the darkest, moonless night, far away from the city lights, we can see no more than two thousand stars with the naked eye. The faint band of light we call the Milky Way is all that marks the rest of our island in space, the combined glow of millions upon millions of stars too faint and too far away to be seen separately except with the aid of a telescope.

And yet, that Milky Way Galaxy of stars is itself no more than an island in space, a dot on the cosmic landscape. Just as there are millions upon millions of stars in our Milky Way Galaxy, so there are many millions of other islands in space, other galaxies, scattered across the Universe, separated from each other by distances hundreds of thousands of times greater than the size of the whole Milky Way.

To a cosmologist, someone who studies the nature and evolution of the whole Universe, a galaxy is just about the smallest thing worthy of consideration. To a human being, living on one small planet circling an ordinary star in the backwoods of a run-of-the-mill galaxy, a galaxy—our Milky Way—is just about the largest thing we can have knowledge of with our own senses, and then only with one of them, sight.

The best modern scientific understanding of the Universe reveals that it was born in fire, a Big Bang of creation some fifteen billion years ago. Cosmologists can now explain how the Universe got from a superhot, superdense fireball into the stage we see today, with island galaxies separated from one another by vast gulfs of space. They can, thanks to the very latest work by researchers such as Stephen Hawking at Cambridge, at least suggest how and why the Big Bang itself occurred. And they can provide us with at least an outline guide to the ultimate fate of the Universe. This understanding of the origin and fate of the entire Universe, of everything that exists and of which we can have knowledge, is the theme of this book. But none of this understanding could have been achieved without the discovery that our Milky Way is just one ordinary galaxy among millions. The scientific search for an understanding of the origin of our Universe—the search for the Big Bang—really began when other galaxies, beyond our Milky Way, were first unequivocally identified as comparable collections of stars to our own Galaxy.* And that firm identification was made only in the 1920s.

Cosmology is very much a science of the twentieth century. But like all of twentieth-century science, its roots go back to the speculations of natural philosophers and metaphysicians of old.

---

*Astronomers commonly use the convention of giving an initial capital letter to our Galaxy, the Moon that orbits the Earth, our Sun and Solar System, and so on. Other moons, galaxies, and the rest are not so honored. I shall follow this convention; "Galaxy" means "the Milky Way," while "galaxy" means any one of the millions of islands of stars across the Universe.

AN ORIGINAL THEORY

To the ancient Greeks and Romans, the Earth was both the center of the Universe and its most important constituent. Although Greek philosophers had a fair grasp of the distance to the Moon, it was only with the advent of the telescope in the seventeenth century that anyone began to comprehend the great remoteness of the stars. Galileo was the first person to use a telescope for astronomical observations, and he was surprised to discover that even with the aid of his telescope's magnifying power the stars still appeared only as points of light, not as spheres like the Sun and planets. This could only mean that they were very much farther away than the Sun and planets. He also found a multitude of stars visible through the telescope but unseen to the unaided human eye, and his telescope revealed the Milky Way itself to be made up of swarms of individual stars. At the same time, in the early seventeenth century, that Galileo was opening a new observational window on the Universe, Johannes Kepler was developing the basis of a theoretical understanding of our own backyard, the Solar System. His discovery of a relationship between the time it takes for a planet to orbit once around the Sun and the average distance of that planet from the Sun led, by the 1670s, to a reasonably accurate estimate of the distance from the Earth to the Sun, which we now know to be about 150 million kilometers. Kepler's observations also provided one of the foundations for Isaac Newton's study of gravity.

It took 150 years for astronomers to refine and improve both their observations and their theories to the point where accurate distances to a few stars were first estimated, in the late 1830s. Such estimates, and those of the twentieth century, provide a crucial stepping-stone in measuring the scale of the Universe, right out to the most distant galaxies. But even before the distances to the stars were known accurately, the revolutionary discoveries of the seventeenth century provided a new view of the Universe, on a vastly greater scale than the old vision of a series of crystal spheres surrounding the Earth and extending out a little beyond the orbit of Saturn. In the eighteenth century, a few philosophers interpreted these new discoveries in terms of a picture, an imaginary model, of the Milky Way and its place in the Universe. That model is surprisingly close to modern thinking and fueled debate among astronomers and philosophers for the best part of two centuries.

Credit for the new theory of the Universe—the first modern cosmological theory—belongs to Thomas Wright of Durham, England. Wright was an English philosopher, born in 1711. Like most thinkers of his era, he spread his interests over a wide variety of subjects, including astronomy. He was the son of a carpenter, and his interest in astronomy was kindled by his childhood teacher. But his formal education was curtailed by a serious speech impediment and for a time he ran wild, becoming, he tells us in his journal, "much addicted to sport." At thirteen he was apprenticed to a clock- and watchmaker, where he stayed for four years but spent all his spare time studying astronomy, encouraged by his mother but violently opposed by his father, who did everything he could to prevent these studies, including burning young Thomas's books. During his turbulent early adult years, Wright tried his hand at the sailor's life, quitting after a violent storm during his first voyage, set up as a tutor of mathematics at Sunderland, was involved with a scandal concerning a clergyman's daughter, taught navigation to seamen, and then in the 1730s began to achieve success and prosperity (after some initial trials and tribulations with dishonest publishers and a failed attempt to produce an almanac) as a tutor and consultant to the aristocracy. The speech impediment, if it still existed, was no longer a handicap to this confident and self-assured young man. He would survey a grand estate (or a modest one), hold private classes in natural philosophy, mathematics, or navigation, and along the way began to publish successful books and broadsheets. By 1742, his reputation was such that Wright was invited to become professor of navigation at the Imperial Academy in St. Petersburg, at a salary of £300 a year; he declined the post after failing to get the proposed salary increased to £500 per annum. So it was as a successful, educated (if largely self-educated), and reasonably well-known philosopher of his day that Thomas Wright published, in 1750, a work entitled *An Original Theory or New Hypothesis of the Universe*. This is the work for which he is remembered today, with a place in the history of science important enough for the book to have been reprinted, in facsimile form, in 1971.

In the early seventeenth century, a hundred years after Galileo's revolutionary discoveries, it was widely accepted among natural philosophers that the stars must be distant bodies that shine with their own light, like the Sun, and not because (like the Moon) they reflect the light from the Sun. Since telescopes could not show the stars as discs, they must be very far away indeed. Many, but not all, of Wright's contemporaries would argue that since the brightest object we know is the Sun, therefore the best guess we can make about the stars is that they are comparably bright objects set at suitably remote distances from us. Some speculated that the apparent randomness of the pattern of stars in the sky was simply due to us being embedded within a system whose pattern and structure could be seen only from outside—like the shape of a forest concealed from someone inside the forest, who sees only a seemingly random distribution of trees in all directions.

In earlier works, described by Michael Hoskin in his introduction to the 1971 edition of *An Original Theory,* Wright considered the Universe (as we would now call it) like a sphere or globe filled with stars and described how an observer sitting on a planet like the Earth orbiting one of those stars would see nearby stars bright and clear; others farther away too faint to be resolved without the aid of a telescope; and still others, yet more distant, so faint that they appear only as a band of light circling the sky. The description begins to fit the Milky Way, except, as Wright realized later if not sooner, that if we are surrounded on all sides by an even distribution of stars, the whole sky should appear to glow like the band of the Milky Way. By 1750, in *An Original Theory,* Wright had hit on the reason why the Milky Way appears as a band across the sky. We must imagine the stars, he says, "all moving the same Way, and not much deviating from the same

Plane, as the Planets in their heliocentric Motion do around the solar Body." In other words, our Sun is but one star in a great swarm that fills a flat disc, not a spherical volume of space. When we look along the disc, toward the center around which all the stars orbit, we see the profusion of stars that together form the band of light we call the Milky Way. But when we look out of the thin disc upward or downward into the depths of space, we see only a few nearby stars and no band of light because there are no very distant stars to see. In fact, Wright's vision of the star system was more like the rings of Saturn, with a central gap, than a solid disc of stars. And, to be honest, his speculations about the nature of the Milky Way did not form what he regarded as the most important of his contributions to science and philosophy, since his main interests concentrated on topics that would today be regarded as primarily the province of religion. Indeed, what seems with hindsight to be Wright's deepest insight of all appears almost as an aside, tossed away in a summing up at the end of his book. Having offered an explanation for the appearance of the Milky Way, he went on to speculate on what might lie outside this island in space. What we now call the Galaxy Wright called the Universe, or the Creation, and he imagined all the stars with their own families of planets, sidereal systems like our own Solar System. "As the visible Creation is supposed to be full of sidereal Systems and planetary Worlds," he wrote, "so on, in like manner, the endless Immensity is an unlimited Plenum of Creations not unlike the known Universe." In other words, Wright imagined the immensity of space beyond our Milky Way Galaxy to be populated by other galaxies like the Milky Way. And he even suggested that faint patches of light on the sky, called nebulae, visible with the aid of telescopes but unresolved into stars, "may be external Creation[s] [galaxies], bordering upon the known one, too remote for even our Telescopes to reach."

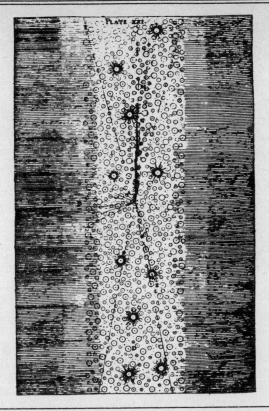

Figure 1.1/ Thomas Wright's representation of the Milky Way as a disc of stars, from *An Original Theory,* published in 1750.

With these words, Wright lit a spark of understanding concerning the nature of our Galaxy and of the Universe, a spark that was gradually fanned into a flame, initially through the work of another philosopher, Immanuel Kant, and another astronomer, William Herschel.

A NEBULAR HYPOTHESIS

Kant is best known as a philosopher, one of the first rank, whose teaching has had an influence on all philosophical thinking of the past two hundred years. But even so, it is surprising to find his entry in the *Encyclopaedia Britannica* scarcely mentioning his interest in astronomy. Even more surprisingly, there is no mention at all of Kant's early work *General History of Nature and Theory of the Heavens,* which was published in 1755. Greatly influenced by Wright's *An Original Theory,* which had appeared five years before, in his own *Theory of the Heavens* Kant presented speculations about the nature of the Universe that are both much clearer than Wright's ideas and bear an almost prescient resemblance to the present picture of the Universe based on twentieth-century observations. Kant never performed experiments or observations, and from time to time over the years he has been derided as an "armchair scientist" who simply speculated about the meaning of discoveries made by others. If only there were a few more armchair scientists like him—and like Einstein, who also relied solely on brainpower, not on any practical skills.

Kant was born in what was then Königsberg, East Prussia (now Kaliningrad, in the Soviet Union), in 1724. His surname came from a Scottish immigrant called Cant, his grandfather, who settled there and Germanicized his name; Immanuel Kant's father was a saddlemaker, and the boy himself was the fourth of eleven children in a poor family, the oldest child to survive to maturity. His parents were devout Lutherans, and it was through the influence of their pastor that young Immanuel took the first steps toward a formal education. Indeed, in 1740 he enrolled at the University of Königsberg as a theological student; but it was courses in mathematics and physics that caught his fascination and to which he devoted most of his attention. He was by then set upon an academic career, but when his father died in 1746, Immanuel had to leave the university and work as a private tutor—by no means uncongenial employment, since his three employers over the span of the next nine years were all influential society families who introduced him to a new way of life and circle of acquaintances. During this period Kant made the longest journey of his life, traveling sixty miles to the town of Arnsdorf.

In 1755, Kant was at last able to take a post at the university as a *Privatdozent,* or lecturer. In spite of offers of good posts at other universities, he remained in Königsberg all his life, becoming professor of logic and metaphysics in 1770 and holding the chair for 27 years. He died in 1804. But the work for which he will always be remembered by cosmologists was completed while he was merely a private tutor and was published in the year that he first took an official university post.

Wright's *An Original Theory* never enjoyed wide circulation and soon became quite rare. Kant himself, as far as we know, never saw the book itself but learned of Wright's ideas through a lengthy review of the book, which appeared in a Hamburg journal in 1751. Happily, the review Kant read, which included quotes from Wright, was not only accurate but in some ways clearer than Wright's own book, since it contained only the central kernel of Wright's ideas, including the idea of the Milky Way as a collection of stars "all moving in the same way and not much deviating from the same Plane." Kant elaborated the theme in his own book and made much stronger statements than Wright about the likely nature of the faint patches of light, the nebulae, that could be seen with telescopes but clearly were not individual stars. In his book *The Realm of the Nebulae*, Edwin Hubble, one of the twentieth-century pioneers of cosmology, provides a good translation of a key passage from *Theory of the Heavens:*

> I come now to another part of my system, and because it suggests a lofty idea of the plan of creation, it appears to me as the most seductive. The sequence of ideas that led us to it is very simple and natural. They are as follows: let us imagine a system of stars gathered together in a common plane, like those of the Milky Way, but situated so far away from us that even with the telescope we cannot distinguish the stars composing it . . . such a stellar world will appear to the observer, who contemplates it at so enormous a distance, only as a little spot feebly illumined and subtending a very small angle; its shape will be circular, if its plane is perpendicular to the line of sight, elliptical, if it is seen obliquely. The faintness of the light, its form, and its appreciable diameter will obviously distinguish such a phenomenon from the isolated stars around it.
>
> We do not need to seek far in the observations of

> astronomers to meet with such phenomena. They
> have been seen by various astronomers, who have
> wondered at their strange appearance.[*]

Hubble was particularly pleased with Kant's reasoning because it is based on what is now known as the principle of uniformity, or, slightly more tongue in cheek, the principle of terrestrial mediocrity. This says that we live in a typical, ordinary part of the Universe and that any other typical, ordinary part of the Universe would look much the same as our neck of the woods. We live in an *ordinary* galaxy, says Kant by implication, and the faint nebulae seen by the astronomers are no new phenomena but other *ordinary* galaxies like our own. Anyone living on a planet circling a star in one of those galaxies could see our Milky Way as no more than a faint patch of light barely visible through their telescopes. And as if credit for presenting the idea itself clearly for the first time were not enough, Kant is also generally credited with inventing the term "island universes" to describe the way galaxies are scattered across the immense void of space.

Kant and Wright (whose work remained for two hundred years best known through the references in Kant's writing) got the kudos, but this was clearly an idea whose time had come. Johann Lambert, a Swiss-German polymath who among other things provided the first rigorous mathematical proof that *pi,* the ratio of the circumference of a circle to its diameter, is an irrational number, independently came up with a similar scheme of the Universe and published it in 1761. Indeed, according to a letter he wrote to Kant (and we have no reason to doubt his word), Lambert first began to speculate along these lines in 1749. It was only after his own paper had been prepared that he learned of the work of Wright and Kant. From the 1760s onward, however, the island universe idea became commonly known among astronomers, although not yet generally accepted. The armchair scientists had taken their thoughts as far as they could reasonably go with the limited observations of the heavens available to them, and it was time for the observers, once again, to come to the

---

[*]*The Realm of the Nebulae,* pages 23 and 24. Full details of books mentioned in the text are given in the Bibliography.

center of the astronomical stage. Not until the twentieth century would the observations be adequate to provide the final test of the hypothesis that nebulae are galaxies in their own right, and then to provide, in an increasing flood, new waves of information for the theorists in their armchairs to digest and try to make sense of.

OBSERVING THE UNIVERSE

Few eighteenth-century observers were much interested in the nebulae in their own right, but many astronomers were interested in comets. The discovery of a comet, apart from its scientific importance, brought instant fame to any astronomer, and a "new" comet was (and still is) tradition- ally named after its discoverer. Edmond Halley, whose name is forever linked with comets, had died only in 1742, leaving untested his claim that cometary sightings in 1456, 1531, 1607, and 1682 all represented visits of the same comet to the inner part of the Solar System, and his prediction that the comet would return again in 1758. When it duly appeared on schedule, Halley's place in history was assured, as was the eagerness with which astronomers of the second half of the eighteenth century would seek out other comets. But one of the irritating things about comets is that when they are first identifiable they appear as faint little patches of light in the field of view of a telescope, just like the nebulae that Kant found so fascinating. Many an astronomer thought he had hit the jackpot, only to have his hopes of fame dashed when observations on succeeding nights showed that the patch of light he had discovered showed no signs of growing bigger and brighter as it approached the Sun but stayed always the same. What astronomers needed was a catalog of all the known, permanent nebulae so they wouldn't be fooled into mistaking them for new comets. And the first decent catalog of this kind was provided by Charles Mes- sier, a French astronomer, who made his painstaking com- pilations between 1760 and 1784. The brightest nebulae, together with clusters of stars, were pinpointed and identi-

fied not because Messier regarded them as particularly
important but because they were an annoyance that had
to be signposted "Keep off, this is not a comet." The
catalog served its purpose well; Messier himself discovered at least fifteen comets (some reports claim as many
as twenty-one). And when an astronomer came along who
was interested in nebulae in their own right, Messier's
catalog gave him an invaluable starting point for his own
observations. That astronomer was William Herschel.

Herschel was born in Hanover in 1738. Like his father, he was a musician in the band of the Hanoverian
Guards, and he visited England with the band in 1756. A
year later, a little trouble with the French led to the occu-
pation of Hanover, and Herschel left to take up permanent
residence in England, where he worked as a music teacher,
performer, and composer until in 1766 he was appointed
organist at the Octagon Chapel in Bath. Gradually his
interest in astronomy, originally no more than amateur
dabblings, became a passion, and he determined not just
to make observations of the Sun, Moon, and planets, like
most astronomers of the time, but also to study the faintest
and most distant objects he could. This passion forced him
to become an expert telescope maker, polishing his own
large mirrors to manufacture instruments capable of showing him astronomical objects fainter than anyone had ever
seen and of showing new details in known objects. His
sister Caroline, who had joined him in Bath in 1772,
shared this passion for astronomy and worked as his assistant, both in making the telescopes and in carrying out the
observations. Together they studied the skies systemati-
cally, surveying in all directions. And in one of the sweeps
of their heavens, in 1781, Herschel hit the jackpot. What
he thought at first must be a comet turned out to be a
planet that nobody had seen before, the first to be identified since ancient times. Not one to miss an opportunity,
Herschel suggested naming the new planet "George's Star,"
after King George III; in the end, the name Uranus was
adopted, but the king was suitably flattered and in 1782
Herschel was appointed court astronomer (not the same
thing as Astronomer Royal, a post held at the time by the
Reverend Nevil Maskelyne). Herschel became a Fellow of
the Royal Society in the same year, moved from Bath to

Windsor and then to Slough, and became a professional astronomer, patronized by the king, at age forty-three.

From now on, Herschel had little difficulty raising money for bigger and better telescopes with which to probe the night skies. He had been given an early list of Messier's nebulae and set out, with Caroline, to make his own compilation of nebulae. Their searches resulted in a catalog listing more than two thousand nebulae in 1802, and an even more extensive catalog published in 1820, by which time Herschel was in his eighties. He was knighted in 1816. Along the way, Herschel did much to promote the idea of island universes. He may well have gotten the idea directly from Wright's book, since the copy he owned still exists and carries a note in his own hand, made sometime after 1781. By about 1785, Herschel was convinced that all nebulae were composed of stars, much as Kant had speculated, and William and Caroline had been able to resolve many of these clouds into their component stars using their new telescopes.

In an attempt to explain why stars should be gathered together in this way, William developed a theory of the evolution of the Universe that involved the idea of widely scattered stars gathering slowly into clumps under the attraction of gravity. This was one of the first attempts to describe the Universe in terms of change, and although his specific idea does not stand up to modern scrutiny, Herschel deserves credit for having the imaginative boldness to conceive of the Universe itself as changing and evolving as time passes.

Unfortunately, a lot of Herschel's good work on behalf of the island universe hypothesis was undone later in his life, when he found that some of the clouds in space, some of the nebulae, could not be resolved into stars even with his best telescopes. This lent weight to the rival theory, which held that the nebulae really were just clouds of material glowing with their own light. He found that some of these clouds were associated with individual stars, a central star being surrounded by a glowing nebula, and this reinforced the idea that nebulae might be planetary systems in the making, stars and planets condensing out of a collapsing cloud of gas. Because of

Herschel's enormous prestige, this idea gained great currency in the early nineteenth century; and because this theory was regarded as a rival to the concept of nebulae as island universes of stars, that theory suffered a decline in standing. It took another hundred years for astronomers to appreciate fully that there are two different kinds of nebulae, one kind glowing clouds within our own Milky Way system, and the other kind island universes, other galaxies, far beyond the Milky Way.

Bigger telescopes and new astronomical techniques began to make the true situation clear in the second half of the nineteenth century. William Parsons, the third Earl of Rosse, was an Irish politician, engineer, and astronomer, born in 1800, who had an ambition to carry on observations of nebulae where Herschel had left off. Since Herschel had left no notes on how he had built his telescopes, Rosse had to reinvent most of the techniques of polishing and preparing large mirrors for himself, but his efforts culminated in the construction of a telescope weighing four tons, with a principal mirror seventy-two inches across housed in a tube more than fifty feet long, supported between two masonry piers by a system of chains and pulleys. With this magnificent instrument, dubbed "the Leviathan of Corkstown," Rosse and his assistants had resolved fifty nebulae into stars by 1848 and noted that some of them had a characteristic spiral shape, like a whirlpool viewed from above. These discoveries strongly revived the idea of island universes. A few years later came the first hard evidence that nebulae come in two varieties.

William Huggins, a British astronomer born in 1824, pioneered the use of spectroscopy in astronomy. A spectroscope is an instrument that splits light up into its component colors, like a rainbow, spreading out the light with different wavelengths for examination. As well as the different colors of the rainbow, such a spectrum characteristically shows a pattern of bright or dark lines, very sharply defined at specific wavelengths in the spectrum. These spectral lines are caused by the presence of particular elements in the material that the light is coming from—some yellow streetlights, for example, produce a very bright pair of lines associated with the element sodium. No other

element produces an identical pair of lines in exactly the
same place in the spectrum. Spectroscopy provided a way
to identify the elements present in the Sun and stars by
identifying the lines in the spectra obtained from different
celestial objects. Huggins turned to this line of research in
the 1860s following the work of Gustav Kirchhoff and
Robert Bunsen, who made spectroscopic studies of the
Sun in the late 1850s. Together with a chemist friend,
W. A. Miller, Huggins showed that starlight contained the
same spectral lines as sunlight. In other words, stars contain, by and large, the same mixture of chemical elements
as the Sun does.

When Huggins turned his attention to the nebulae,
however, he found a different pattern. Some nebulae, like
the one in the constellation Orion, or the one known, from
its shape, as the Crab Nebula, glowed with a light that did
not have this by now expected pattern of lines. Instead,
the light from these nebulae appeared in the spectroscope
just like the light from a glowing cloud of hot gas. Only
later did similar studies show that other nebulae, including the spirals, did indeed produce light with spectral lines
like those seen in starlight.

The pieces of the puzzle were beginning to pile up on
the table, but they were not yet falling into place. Kant's
ideas, now more than a century old, were, after all, no
more than the musings of an armchair scientist. The gaseous nebulae were clearly part of the Milky Way, and even
if the other nebulae were made of stars, they might well
be part of the Milky Way, too—small star systems, or stars
in the process of formation, not whole galaxies as big as
our Milky Way. And, anyway, how big *was* the Milky
Way? At the end of the nineteenth century, the scale of
the Milky Way system itself was known only in the most
approximate terms, partly from estimates of how far away
the stars must be to appear as faint as they do. The
balance of opinion held that the Milky Way *was* the Universe, although it did seem to be a flattened, disc-shaped
structure of the kind Kant had proposed. The Sun and
Solar System were placed, in the astronomers' minds, somewhere near the center of this disc, and the spiral and
elliptical nebulae were considered, by those who bothered
much about them at all, to be part of the Milky Way

system. For a little over a hundred years, astronomers had indeed been observing the Universe at large, even though they could not be sure of this. The nebulae, we now know, are the building blocks of the Universe. But in order to find out their true nature, a step beyond simple observation had to be taken. The astronomers now had to measure the Universe, to get a handle on the scale of distances in the Milky Way and beyond, before they could truly grasp the significance of what they were observing.

CHAPTER TWO

HOW FAR IS UP?

Edmond Halley was the first astronomer on record as realizing that the stars move. Because the stars move relative to one another, they cannot be objects with different brightnesses all attached firmly to the inner surface of some great sphere surrounding the Earth. Evidence that stars move is also evidence that stars are at different distances from us, spread out in three dimensions of space. In the early eighteenth century, when Halley made this discovery, it was the first direct, observational evidence that the image of stars as such lights attached to a sphere little bigger than the orbit of Saturn (Uranus had not then been discovered) must be incorrect. The discovery paved the way for later eighteenth-century thinkers such as Wright and Kant to make their speculations about the nature of the Milky Way; it also led, along a direct but slow path, to an understanding of the scale of the Universe.

HALLEY'S UNIVERSE

By the time he made this discovery, Halley was already a respected senior astronomer with a fruitful career behind him. He was born in 1656 and went to Oxford University, where he wrote and published a book on the laws discovered by Johannes Kepler that describe the orbits of the planets about the Sun. Kepler's laws gave Isaac Newton crucial clues about the nature of gravity; Halley's book was impressive enough (not least coming from an undergraduate) to bring its author to the attention of John Flamsteed, who was the Astronomer Royal (the first one, and actually called "Astronomical Observator") at the time. This was just as well, for when Halley left Oxford without finishing his degree, Flamsteed's interest helped him to get a job in astronomy, sent to the island of St. Helena, in the South Atlantic, to spend two years mapping the stars of the southern hemisphere sky. He returned to England in 1678 and was promptly elected to the Royal Society at age twenty-two. But Halley did not follow an exclusively academic career.

His adventures over the next thirty years included travels in Europe to meet other scientists and astronomers; a couple of years as deputy controller of the Mint at Chester; a spell in command of a Royal Navy warship, the *Paramour;* and some diplomatic missions to Vienna on behalf of the government. Along the way, he made major contributions to the understanding of magnetism, winds, and tides and was a key influence in persuading Newton to publish his *Principia* in its entirety—Halley even financed publication of the book. In 1703 he became professor of geometry at Oxford (not bad for an undergraduate dropout) and in 1720 was appointed Astronomer Royal in succession to Flamsteed and held the post until he died in 1742 at eighty-five. It was in the two decades at the start of the eighteenth century that Halley made his contribution to our understanding of the stars.

Halley had always had an interest in the astronomical writings of the ancients and had translated some works from the Greek. In 1710 he began a study of Ptolemy's writings that date from the second century A.D., and as a former cataloger of stars himself he paid particular attention to Ptolemy's catalog of star positions. In fact, "Ptolemy's" catalog, even older than Ptolemy himself, goes back to the work of Hipparchus in the third century B.C. This was the first important star map, containing the positions of more than eight hundred stars; Ptolemy preserved it for posterity, and he added more positions to bring the number of stars logged to over a thousand. Most of the star positions in the catalog agreed well with observations made by Halley and his contemporaries. But in 1718 Halley realized that three stars—Sirius, Procyon, and Arcturus—were not in the places that Hipparchus and Ptolemy saw them. The differences in positions were much too great to be explained as mistakes by the ancient Greeks; besides, why should they make just three mistakes among hundreds of accurate observations? Arcturus, for example, appeared in 1718 to be twice the width of the full Moon away from the position recorded in Ptolemy's writings—a full degree of arc out of position. Halley inferred that Arcturus, and the other stars, had moved over the centuries since the Greeks recorded their positions. The motion was far too slow to be noticed in a human lifetime with unaided eyes but big enough to show up over several generations.

The first three stars to have these proper motions (as they are now called) identified are among the eight brightest stars in the sky. The natural interpretation of this "coincidence" is that the stars look bright because they are much closer to us than most stars, and that we can see their movement over a few centuries for the same reason. Just as an airliner high in the sky appears to be crawling slowly along, while a child on a bicycle a few feet away rushes past in a flash, so the nearer stars ought to show a larger apparent motion across the sky than those farther away, if they all move at more or less the same speed through space. The vast majority of stars are so far away that even over a couple of thousand years they show no apparent motion from Earth; just a few are close enough to be identified as moving across this background of seemingly "fixed" stars.

It's probably worth pausing for a while to try to grasp the size of the movements astronomers now measure as routine. The angle the Moon covers on the sky is roughly half a degree, or thirty minutes of arc.* Just as each degree is divided into 60 minutes, so each minute of arc is

---

*It's 31 minutes, to be more precise.

divided into 60 seconds. The planet Jupiter cannot be distinguished as a perceptible disc with the naked eye. Telescopic observations show that when it is at its closest to the Earth, and therefore looks biggest, it covers only 50 seconds of arc. The star that has the largest measured proper motion of all is called Barnard's Star, after the American astronomer Edward Barnard, who discovered it in 1916. Barnard's Star is faint because it really is a dim little star, which is why it wasn't noticed before. But it is also close to us—so close that it hurtles across the sky at a record-breaking speed of 10.3 seconds of arc per year (that is, in five years it moves a distance equivalent to the angular width of Jupiter at its biggest). Measured proper motions usually are less than one second of arc per year. To translate these tiny proper motions into speeds through space, astronomers had to find a way to estimate the distances to the stars; but first they had to get an accurate measure of the scale of the Solar System.

FROM THE EARTH TO THE SUN

The first step toward measuring the scale of the Universe uses exactly the technique used by mapmakers on Earth to measure positions and distances—triangulation. Astronomers usually use the name parallax for the technique, but you can see how it works simply by looking at your finger.

Hold a finger up at arm's length and close one eye. Notice the position of your finger against the background of the wall of your room. Now close the eye that was open and open the one that was closed. The finger seems to move across the background, jumping to a slightly different position. The reason is that your two eyes view the finger from slightly different directions. Now try the same thing with your finger held just in front of your nose. The change in position—the parallax—is much more pronounced. The closer an object is, the bigger the parallax effect, so by measuring the parallax it is possible to work out the distance to the object. If you observe a distant object from two widely separated points you can use this effect to determine its distance. The technique works as well for a mountain or for the Moon or for the planets in the Solar System—provided that in each case you can get a wide enough separation between the two places where you make observations from, a long enough base for your triangle. To find the distance to the Moon, for example, all that is necessary is that astronomers in two widely separated observatories each note the position of the Moon against the background of distant stars at the same time. As long as they know the distance between the two ob-

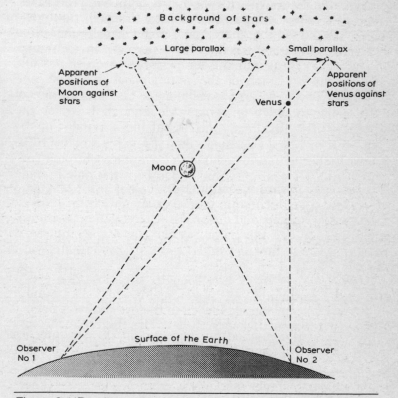

*Figure 2.1/*Parallax—the *apparent* movement of a distant object caused by a shift in the position the object is observed from—can be used to measure distances within the Solar System.

servatories (and take account of the curvature of the Earth, of course), they can use these observations to construct an imaginary triangle with the Moon at its top. Simple geometry then tells them how tall the triangle is—how far the Moon is from the Earth.

The technique works well for the Moon, because it is so close to us, about 400,000 kilometers away. The parallax effect is quite noticeable,* and although the triangle involved is rather tall and thin, the angles are easily measured. Things get a little trickier when astronomers try to find out the distances to the planets using the same techniques. The parallax effect is very small, even for two observatories on opposite sides of the Earth, and the imaginary triangle drawn with the Earth at its base and Mars, say, at its apex is incredibly skinny. But still, under the right conditions the appropriate angles can be measured and the distances worked out.

Parallax measurements for the planets were impossible before the invention of the astronomical telescope, and even then they required expeditions to far-flung corners of the globe in order to get a wide enough base for the triangle. The first really successful measurement of the parallax of Mars was made by a French team in 1671. Jean Richer led an expedition to Cayenne in French Guiana, while Giovanni Cassini, Italian-born but now French, made observations in Paris. Each noted the position of Mars on the sky at the same predetermined time. When Richer's expedition returned home, they compared notes and deduced the distance to Mars. And, armed with *that* information, they could use Kepler's laws to calculate the distance from Mars to the Sun and from the Earth to the Sun. They came up with a figure for the Earth–Sun distance of 140 million kilometers, only 10 million kilometers less than the figure obtained by modern techniques. But how could the method be improved in the seventeenth and eighteenth centuries?

---

*If one observer views the Moon directly overhead and another sees it low on the horizon at the same time, the parallax shift between their two lines of sight is 57 minutes of arc, nearly twice the Moon's angular diameter. The base line for the triangulation is then equal to the radius of the Earth, and this gives the distance to the Moon.

During his lonely vigil on St. Helena, Halley had plenty of time to think, as well as to catalog stars. He observed and timed a transit of Mercury across the Sun—a fairly rare event, when the planet appears as a tiny black disc passing slowly across the bright face of the Sun. And he realized that such transits could also provide a way to triangulate the Solar System. Because of the parallax effect, the exact instant when Mercury first seems to touch the Sun's disc depends on where on Earth you are observing the transit. The astronomers of Halley's day knew that there would be a transit of Venus across the Sun—even rarer than a transit of Mercury—in 1761. Halley prepared detailed notes on just how to make best use of observations of this transit in different parts of the world to work out the distances to Venus and to the Sun, and he published the notes in 1716. Although he had been dead for nineteen years when the transit occurred, his influence was a factor in the concerted effort to measure the parallax of Venus. Sixty-two observing stations monitored the transit of 1761, and a similar effort was made for a second transit, in 1769. When all the data had been analyzed, the calculated distance from the Earth to the Sun was 153 million kilometers, compared with the modern measurement of 149.6 million kilometers. In succeeding centuries, the measurement was refined down to its present value; but as far as the broad picture is concerned, we can say that by the end of the eighteenth century, astronomers knew the scale of the Solar System. They had measured the distance to the Sun. And this provided them with a great new opportunity. Once they knew the distance from the Earth to the Sun, they had a new base line they could use for triangulation and parallax. The measurement is so important to astronomy, indeed, that the distance from the Earth to the Sun is called the astronomical unit, or AU. With a base line 150 million kilometers long, it might be possible to triangulate the distances to the stars themselves.

FROM THE SUN TO
THE STARS

It was three quarters of a century after the transit of Venus
in 1761 that astronomers at last managed to measure the
parallax of a few nearby stars. The principle involved was
simple enough. Since the radius of the Earth's orbit is 150
million kilometers, observations made six months apart,
from opposite sides of the Sun, are at the ends of a base
line 300 million kilometers (2 AU) long (and it doesn't
matter, from the point of view of getting a first estimate of
the distances to the stars, whether the base line is 290
million kilometers or 310 million kilometers; the answers
we get will still be about right). It is a matter of simple
geometry to calculate how far away a star would have to
be to show a certain parallax displacement across such a
base line. In fact, astronomers choose to define a new
length scale in these terms. One parallax second of arc
(parsec for short) is the distance to a star that would show
a displacement of 1 second of arc from opposite ends of a
base line equal to the distance from the Earth to the Sun.
In other words, over the 300-million-kilometer base line of
the Earth's orbit, a star 1 parsec (1 pc) away will show a
parallax of 2 seconds of arc.

A parsec is a little more than 30,000 billion* kilometers;
it takes light, traveling at a speed of nearly 300 million
meters a second, 3.26 years to cover a distance of 1 parsec.
To put it another way, 1 parsec is just under 206,265
times the distance from the Earth to the Sun, the astronomical unit. No star is close enough to show this much
parallax displacement, and that is why it took until the
1830s for the first stellar parallaxes to be measured.

If you are trying to measure a change of less than one
second of arc in the position of a star, obviously you need
catalogs that give the positions of the stars to comparable
accuracy. The best catalog of the early eighteenth century,
compiled by Flamsteed and published posthumously in

---

*A billion is a thousand million, 10^9.

1725, gave positions to an accuracy of about 10 seconds of arc—a tremendous achievement at the time but not yet good enough for this purpose. The third Astronomer Royal, Halley's successor James Bradley (born in 1693), devoted a massive effort to the problem, attempting to measure the parallax of a star called Gamma Draconis. He failed, but along the way he improved observing techniques, developed better instruments, and also improved astronomers' theoretical understanding of the nature of their observations. Bradley found that Gamma Draconis did seem to shift its position in the sky over the year, but not in the way predicted by parallax. He found that the same effect occurs for all stars, and eventually he realized that the effect was due to the speed of the Earth's motion around the Sun. Light rays coming from a distant star seem to be tilted because of the Earth's motion, in exactly the same way that rain falling straight down from the sky seems to be blowing in your face when you walk forward. The effect is different at different points in the Earth's orbit

Figure 2.2/ Rain falling straight down from the sky seems to be blowing in your face when you walk forward. Light "rays" from distant stars are "tilted" in a similar fashion by the Earth's motion through space. The effect is called aberration.

(different times of year) because our planet is moving in different directions at different times. Because the speed of light is so great, the effect is small—but still noticeable at the kind of accuracy of measurement involved in parallax studies.

Bradley called the effect "aberration"; it produces a shift in the apparent positions of the stars of 20 ½ arc seconds over a year. The discovery confirmed (although it was not really news in the late eighteenth century) that light has a finite speed, and it gave an estimate for that speed close to the present-day estimate; it also confirmed that the Earth moves through space. But still there were more disturbances for Bradley to take into account when measuring star positions, including a wobble of the Earth, which he named nutation, due to the Earth's slightly nonspherical shape. The fruits of all these efforts appeared in the form of a major new catalog, of unprecedented accuracy, of about three thousand star positions—but this was published in two parts, in 1798 and 1805, more than thirty years after Bradley died.

Many astronomers took up Bradley's techniques, notable among them Friedrich Bessel, a German born in 1784, who cataloged the positions of thirty thousand stars and was one of three astronomers who each independently cracked the parallax problem at about the same time, in the late 1830s. William Herschel had been one of those who tried and failed to measure parallax in stars—sidereal parallax. He tried a trick that would have done away with the need for absolute precision in the catalogs, looking at pairs of stars very close together in the sky, in the hope that one might be very far away along the line of sight while the other might be close enough to show a parallactic displacement. If such a pair could be found, the displacement would only have to be measured relative to the more distant star, not to any absolute standard. But instead Herschel found that many of the double stars he looked at really were doubles, genuinely close to each other in space, orbiting each other like the Moon and the Earth. That was an important discovery but not what Herschel had been looking for.

The breakthrough came when the observations were good enough to measure the tiny displacements of the

stars involved and when theories were good enough to
eliminate all of the other factors, such as aberration and
nutation, that also made the positions of the stars change
with the seasons. Success came when the time was ripe,
not before; but when the time *was* ripe, success came in a
rush. The three-pronged attack of the 1830s came from
Bessel, who chose the star 61 Cygni to study because it
has a large proper motion, 5.2 seconds of arc a year, and
therefore must be very close; from Thomas Henderson, a
Scot born in 1798, who was working in South Africa and
chose to study Alpha Centauri, the third brightest star in
the night sky, on the grounds that it must be close to look
so bright; and from Friedrich von Struve, born in 1793, a
German working in Russia, who chose to study Vega (also
known as Alpha Lyrae), the fourth brightest star in the
night sky, for the same reason. Bessel was the first to
announce a successful conclusion to his work, late in
1838; Henderson actually completed his crucial set of
observations first, but announced his findings only when
he returned to Britain in January 1839; von Struve's measurements, the icing on the cake, appeared in 1840. The
three parallaxes they had discovered were indeed small—
0.3136 second of arc for 61 Cygni, 0.2613 second of arc
for Alpha Lyrae, and 1 second of arc (later refined to 0.76
second of arc) for Alpha Centauri. The Alpha Centauri
parallax is the largest known; the star (actually three stars
orbiting one another) is the closest companion to our Solar
System, 1.3 parsecs (4.3 light-years) away from us. Alpha
Lyrae, Vega, is 8.3 parsecs (27 light-years) away, and 61
Cygni, which is now known to be a double star, is at a
distance of 3.4 pc, some 11 light-years. For the first time,
astronomers had a true grasp of just how isolated the Solar
System is in the dark emptiness of space. The nearest star
is seven thousand times farther from the Sun than its
most distant planet known today, Pluto. And once they
knew the distances to even a few stars, astronomers could
work out their true brightnesses and thereby get a rough
idea of the distances to faint stars too remote to show any
measurable parallax displacement. With this and other
techniques, astronomers in the second half of the nineteenth century at last began to comprehend, in numerical
terms, the size and shape of our own Milky Way Galaxy.

But it was only in the twentieth century that they were
first able to expand the parallax technique to encompass a
large number of stars and then to move on to the realm of
the nebulae.

| | Distance | |
Star	Light-years	Parsecs
Alpha Centauri	4.29	1.32
Barnard's star	5.97	1.84
Wolf 359	7.74	2.38
Sirius	8.7	2.67
61 Cygni	11.1	3.42
Procyon	11.3	3.48

*Table 2.1/*Distances to some of the nearby stars.

STEPPING-STONES TO OUR GALAXY

It took another sixty years for even the parallax method
to make much progress, because it was only then that the
use of photographic plates on the end of a telescope,
instead of human eyes, became standard astronomical practice. A photograph has two key advantages over the eye.
First, of course, it provides a direct, permanent record of
star positions, which can then be studied at leisure and
measured accurately, even using a microscope to gauge
precisely the positions of the star images relative to one
another. Second, unlike the human eye, a photographic
plate, or film, can "see" very faint objects. The longer you
leave the plate exposed, the more light falls on it, and the
stronger each faint image becomes; with the human eye,
no matter how long you stare into space, you won't see
anything fainter than you could see when you started to
look. So astronomical photography provided many more
stars to study and made it possible to measure the positions of each of them more accurately. In 1900, when the

technique was introduced, parallaxes had been measured for just sixty stars. Half a century later, in 1950, the number of known stellar distances was close to ten thousand; but not all of these distances were direct parallax measurements.

Three techniques in particular gave astronomers stepping-stones from the tiny volume of space around the Sun in which parallax measurements provide a reliable guide to distances—only out to about 30 parsecs, or 100 light-years—into the Galaxy at large. Although it quickly became clear that not all stars have exactly the same brightness, spectroscopic studies of the stars following Huggins's pioneering work showed that there are family resemblances. A star that has a particular pattern of lines in its spectrum might be identified and its distance measured by parallax so that its true brightness was known. Then, when another, more distant star was found to have the same spectral type, it was a reasonable guess that it had the same intrinsic brightness. This more distant star appeared fainter, of course, and by precisely measuring its brightness (or faintness) compared with the star whose distance was known, the distance to the more remote star could be estimated.

The other two techniques depended on geometrical tricks but also on spectroscopy. The crucial spectroscopic element, which we shall find of even greater importance to the story of galaxies, is the shift in the position of those characteristic sharp lines in the spectrum when the source of light producing the spectrum moves toward or away from us. Think first of an object moving away from us. Any waves it emits—whether they are light waves in the case of a star, or sound waves in the case of an object on Earth, such as a police car—are stretched out by the motion. Stretching a wave makes its wavelength longer; in the case of sound, it makes the note deeper; for light, it shifts the wavelength of visible light toward the red end of the spectrum.* When the source of the wave is moving toward us, the waves are squashed, bunched up together to make a more high-pitched noise, or to shift the light toward the blue end of the spectrum.

---

*The colors are red, orange, yellow, green, blue, indigo, and violet, in order of decreasing wavelength.

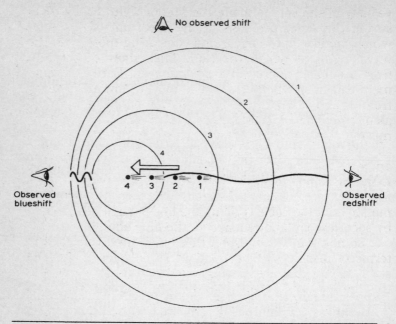

Figure 2.3/ The Doppler effect compresses light waves from an object approaching the observer and stretches light from a receding object. The circles represent light emitted from this particular object at the points labelled. Although light travels out at the same speed in all directions, the circles are bunched together in the direction of motion.

The discovery that the observed frequency of a sound wave depends on the velocity of the source relative to the observer was made in 1842 by the Austrian physicist Christian Doppler; it is called the Doppler effect in his honor. Doppler himself realized that similar changes would affect light from a moving source, and in 1848 the French physicist Armand Fizeau gave the first clear description of this redshift or blueshift effect.

The important thing is that the amount of the shift depends on the speed with which a star is approaching or receding from us. Because the whole spectrum is bodily squeezed or stretched, the wavelengths at which those characteristic lines, like the sodium lines, appear are shifted to the red or to the blue by an amount that depends on the

velocity of the source along the line of sight. So by measuring the exact positions in the spectrum of a star at
which familiar lines appear and comparing these with the
wavelengths at which the same lines show up in light
from a suitable source in a laboratory on Earth, astronomers can infer whether a star is moving toward or away
from us and at what rate. This tells you *only* about motion
along the line of sight, of course. A star may well be
moving across the line of sight, with a transverse velocity,
as well. Its actual motion through space will be at some
angle to the line of sight, and this actual motion can be
found by adding together, geometrically, the two velocities
found by observations—the transverse velocity, or proper
motion, and the velocity along the line of sight determined
by spectroscopy, the red shift or the blue shift.

So how can we interpret these measured velocities in
terms of distances? One trick works only for clusters of
stars, groups that are moving together through space and
that are not too far away from the Sun. A group of stars all
moving in the same direction are, in effect, running along
parallel lines, like a railroad track. And just as the lines of
a railroad track seem to converge at a point in the distance, so the motions of stars in such a group, measured
proper motions determined over years of observations, will
seem to converge at a point in the sky, provided the
cluster is relatively close by. This has the great advantage
of telling astronomers in which direction through space—at
what angle to the line of sight—the cluster is moving. So
when they measure the Doppler shift for the stars in this
cluster, they not only get a measure of the velocity along
the line of sight, they also know, from the angle the stars'
true motion makes to that line of sight, what proportion of
their overall velocity this represents. The proportion left
over must be the stars' true velocity, in kilometers per
second, *across* the line of sight. And since we already
know the proper motion in terms of motion across the sky
in seconds of arc, bingo! We can construct one of those
imaginary skinny triangles to deduce just how far away
that particular cluster must be for *that* speed in kilometers
per hour to produce *this* shift in seconds of arc per year. It
is a lovely trick, and although it still works only for clusters of stars that are within a few tens of parsecs of the

Sun, it did enable astronomers to work out the distance to one such cluster in particular, the Hyades cluster, which turned out to contain a lot of different types of star, all at a distance of about 40 pc. This enabled them to calibrate the brightnesses of those different spectral types and thereby to use the brightness technique on whole families of stars too remote to show measurable motion across the sky.

The other important geometrical technique sounds almost too naïve to work, but it does. Take a whole lot of stars, just close enough to us for their proper motions to be measured. They might be in the same general direction in space, as viewed from Earth, or they could be scattered all over the sky, chosen, perhaps, on the basis that they all have the same color, or the same kind of spectrum. Some will be moving this way, some that; some will be moving faster than others, some relatively slowly. But the Galaxy as a whole—certainly the region around the Sun—doesn't seem to be either collapsing in upon itself or exploding outward. The stars, by and large, are orderly. So it must be that on average all of these random motions cancel out. *On average,* we guess, there is as much chance of a star going one way as another. So if we add up the velocities of all of the stars in our group along the line of sight and take the average Doppler velocity, we would expect the average velocity of the same group of stars in any other direction, and in particular the velocity *across* the line of sight, to be much the same. Assuming this is so, it is possible to assign an "average distance" to all the stars in the chosen group by comparing the presumed actual velocities across the line of sight with the measured angular proper motions.

The technique, called "statistical parallax," is pretty hopeless if applied to an individual star, but the more stars you have to play with, the more reliable the average becomes, so it isn't too bad as an indicator of the distances to some stars—crucially, it proved possible, using this trick, to get a rough idea of the "average distance" to a group of stars that includes a couple of one particular type, the Cepheid variables. Those distances provided a yardstick for the whole Milky Way system, and out into the Universe beyond. Our scale of the Universe, as I am about to explain, depends on knowing the distance to one or two Cepheids. There are now other techniques (which I won't go into in detail) that have improved those first estimates of the Cepheid yardstick. They depend on the colors of stars and their apparent brightnesses. It turns out that if you take a group of stars that really are physically associated in a cluster, the colors of individual stars can be plotted on a graph called a color-magnitude diagram. The position of the line made by such a plot depends on the brightness of the cluster as seen from Earth, and this position can be adjusted so that all such clusters fit on to a standard line, provided that allowance is made for the distance to each cluster. In other words, assuming the stars in each cluster operate on the same physical principles (and if that isn't true we can forget about trying to do astronomy at all), we can fit each cluster in place on the color-magnitude diagram by assigning it a unique distance from us. But still we have to know the distance to at least *one* cluster, from one of the parallax techniques, to calibrate the distance scale on the color-magnitude diagram in the first place.

Of course, astronomers could see and investigate objects much farther away than they could measure by parallax. But they could only *guess* just how far away those more distant objects might be, and they could only estimate the true extent of the Milky Way Galaxy. No wonder that the idea of other galaxies, far beyond the Milky Way system, seemed to many astronomers faintly ridiculous—until, that is, a new yardstick of measurement turned up, a yardstick that could stretch across space to give a direct measurement of the distances to some of those extragalactic nebulae.

THE CEPHEID YARDSTICK

Just as the first steps out from the Solar System into the Milky Way depended on finding distances to the nearest stars, so the first steps out from the Milky Way Galaxy into the Universe at large depended on finding distances to our nearest neighbors in extragalactic space, two nebulae called the Magellanic Clouds, which are visible in the southern hemisphere skies. They were named after the explorer Magellan, having been described by the official chronicler on his circumnavigation of the globe in 1521. This was the first that European civilization knew of the clouds, one large and one small, which look like pieces of the Milky Way that have been broken off. In the sixteenth century, nobody knew what the clouds—or the Milky Way itself, for that matter—might be. Indeed, they were largely ignored by astronomers until John Herschel, the son of William, carried out his survey of southern hemisphere stars and nebulae in the 1830s. By the beginning of the twentieth century, there was no doubt that these clouds, like the Milky Way, were collections of stars. But the idea of nebulae as island galaxies had gone out of fashion, and astronomers generally felt that the Magellanic Clouds were part of the Milky Way system, or perhaps very small semi-independent systems just outside the Milky Way Galaxy, minor satellites tied to it by gravitational apron strings. The truth about the Magellanic Clouds—and about the scale of the Universe—emerged not through some blinding flash of inspiration, or the observation of some new phenomenon, but as one product of a painstaking and meticulous cataloging and analysis of thousands upon thousands of stars begun by Edward Pickering at the Harvard College Observatory in the last quarter of the nineteenth century.

Pickering was born in Boston, Massachusetts, in 1846. He taught physics at the new Massachusetts Institute of Technology in the 1860s and 1870s and was appointed professor of astronomy and Director of the observatory at Harvard in 1876. Over the next four decades he was responsible for several new catalogs of the heavens, each bigger and better than its predecessor, and he was also the inspiration for a whole generation of astronomers. In keeping with the spirit of the times, the tedious job of cataloging the positions and brightnesses of stars by filling out long rows of figures meticulously neatly written in black ink went to underpaid women; less characteristically of the period, Pickering allowed, and then encouraged, a few of those women to move on to higher things, thereby gaining a toehold in the almost exclusively masculine academic world of the time. One of these women was Henrietta Swan Leavitt, who was given the task of identifying variable stars from photographic plates of the southern sky, obtained by Pickering's brother William at an observing station in Peru.

Henrietta Leavitt was born in 1868 and studied at the Society for the Collegiate Instruction of Women, which later became Radcliffe College. She joined Pickering's program at the Harvard College Observatory in 1895 as a volunteer research assistant, received a permanent post in 1902, and soon became head of a department there. Pickering was, no doubt, delighted to have on his team someone with the skill, patience, and ability needed to make some sense out of the stacks of photographic plates from Peru, even though neither of them could have had any inkling in 1895 of what was to come out of Leavitt's research over the next seventeen years.

Variable stars—stars that vary in brightness—are obviously of interest to astronomers. Most stars seem to stay the same, at least over a human lifetime, and anything out of the ordinary is invariably a focus of attention. Some variables are really two stars orbiting around one another so that each in turn eclipses its companion and conceals the light from it. Others, we now know, are stars that pulsate, swelling up and then shrinking in upon themselves, repeating the process over a regular cycle during which their light waxes and wanes. The Cepheids are like this. And some—a few—stars are violently variable, exploding outward in a brief surge of energy after a lifetime of quiet normality, before they collapse and fade away into stellar cinders. One of the great advantages of astronomical photography is that by comparing photographs taken days, months, or years apart, it is possible to identify all these different kinds of activity. You can even investigate phenomena that weren't known to be important when the photographs were taken. In the course of her work, Leavitt identified twenty-four hundred variable stars (half of the total known to astronomy at the time of her death in 1921), as well as four of the exploding stars, called novae. And it was her study of one particular kind of variable star that gave her the key to the Universe.

The family of variable stars called Cepheids gets its name from Delta Cephei, which was identified as a vari-

able by the young English astronomer John Goodricke in
1784. He died just two years later, at the age of twenty-
one. Cepheids show a characteristically regular pattern of
variation in brightness, but different Cepheids have different periods for this variation, some less than two days,
others more than a hundred days. The average is about five
days. They can be identified as members of the same
family, however, both by the typical way in which they
brighten and dim, and because they show a family resemblance in their spectra. One of the interesting questions
about Cepheids, of course, is why there should be such a
range of different periods, when each individual star shows
a constant periodicity. As Leavitt continued her painstaking work, identifying the Cepheids (and other variables)
on the photographic plates and noting down the length of
each one's cycle and its average apparent brightness, she
began to see a pattern emerging. The brighter a Cepheid
was, the more slowly it went through its cycle of variation.

In 1908, Leavitt said as much when she published a
preliminary report on the progress of her work. It took
another four years for this impression to be pinned down
in numbers in black and white. But when it was pinned
down, in 1912, it provided real hope of establishing an
accurate distance scale for the Galaxy, and it was all
thanks to the Magellanic Clouds.

At that time, Leavitt had identified twenty-five Cepheids
in the smaller of the two Magellanic Clouds (sometimes
called the SMC, for obvious reasons). These very clearly
showed the relationship between brightness and period,
which hardly shows up at all for variables in the Milky
Way itself. The reason is easy to see. Stars in the Milky
Way are scattered at many different distances from us.
Some are nearby; others are ten, or a hundred, or even
more times farther away. A star twice as bright and twice
as far away as another star actually looks the fainter of the
two—apparent brightness depends on the actual luminosity divided by the square of the distance. So the period-
luminosity relation, as it is known, was masked by distance
effects within our Galaxy.

But things are different for the stars in the Small
Magellanic Cloud. The cloud is so far away from us that
all the stars in it can be regarded as being roughly the

same distance from Earth. One may be a little closer than another, but not one of them is even as much as twice as far away as any of the others. The scale of the differences in distance is much less than the average distance to the cloud, in the same way that to me, writing this book in a small village in England, everybody in New York can be thought of as the same distance away. The nearest town to me is a little over a mile away, and the far side of the town is more than twice as far away as the nearest side. A difference of a mile is important when I am planning a journey into one part of town or another. For all practical purposes, however, I am equally distant from Times Square and from the Statue of Liberty. A couple of miles counts for little compared with the width of the North Atlantic Ocean.

So it was that Leavitt was able to work out the relationship between luminosity and period for Cepheids using her twenty-five variables in the SMC. She found that, for example, if one Cepheid has a period of three days and another one of thirty days, then the star with the longer period is six times brighter than the star with the shorter period. Assuming the rule she found for Cepheids in the Magellanic Clouds holds for all Cepheids, this immediately meant that Cepheids in the Milky Way could be used to give an indication of the *relative* distances to stars and clusters of stars across the Milky Way. But nobody knew the actual intrinsic brightness of even one Cepheid, so the distance scale was uncalibrated. Astronomers had a measuring stick for the Galaxy, but they didn't know the length of the stick; they could tell that one star, or cluster of stars, was twice as far away as another, but they didn't know if they were measuring, to mix the analogy, in miles or kilometers. So they still didn't know if the Magellanic Clouds were small systems within the Milky Way, or much more distant objects, galaxies in their own right.

It took only a year for the truth to emerge. Ejnar Hertzprung, a Danish astronomer and physicist (who was born in 1873 and remained active in research until just before his death in 1967), made the first estimate of the distances to some of the nearer Cepheids, using a variation on the statistical parallax technique. With all its imperfections, that technique gave him an indication of the actual distances to one or two Cepheids. By comparing their apparent brightnesses with the distances, he could easily calculate the actual brightness in each case. From that it was a simple step to calculate the actual distance to any other Cepheid, using its period to indicate how much brighter or dimmer it must be in reality compared to the few whose distances and absolute luminosities had been measured. Hertzprung concluded that the SMC was 30,000 light-years (in round terms, 10,000 parsecs) away, which was much farther than anyone had suspected. But this measurement did not immediately open the eyes of astronomers to the true size of the cosmos, for two reasons. First, because he had not allowed for the fact that dust in space blocks out some of the light from distant stars and makes them look dimmer than they really are, Hertzprung's calibration was a little off—the best modern calculations give an even more impressive distance of 170,000 light-years, or 52,000 parsecs, to the Large Magellanic Cloud, and 63,000 parsecs (63 kiloparsecs, kpc) to the SMC. And second, astronomers were far too busy using their wonderful new yardstick to measure the size of the Milky Way to worry much, for the next few years, about what lay beyond the Milky Way. To go beyond the Magellanic Clouds and into the real Universe required a new leap of the imagination and a new generation of telescopes. Before we make those two leaps, however, it is only right to acknowledge the great achievements of the astronomers who did map out our own Galaxy, using techniques that form the foundations of later investigations deeper into space.

THE SCALE OF THE GALAXY

The two men who together were largely responsible for the next step toward an understanding of the scale of the Universe came from very different backgrounds. George Ellery Hale, the greatest telescope builder of the twentieth century—perhaps of all time, even allowing for the advance of technology since the time of Galileo, Herschel, or Rosse—was a wealthy man, the son of an elevator manufacturer. He was born in 1868 in Chicago, and his education progressed smoothly through conventional channels to MIT and an appointment in 1892 as professor of astronomy at the University of Chicago. Hale's enthusiasm for astronomy had been fired in childhood when he learned that light from the Sun could be analyzed by spectroscopy to reveal the composition of our nearest star. By the age of twenty he was designing new kinds of spectroscopic instruments with which to dissect the Sun's light more efficiently; it was a lifelong dream of this astronomer, born ten years after the publication of Darwin's *Origin of Species,* that science might one day be able to explain the origin and evolution of stars and the origin and evolution of life in one grand package. Today it is possible to argue that that dream is all but fulfilled—that is the justification for writing this book. And it is in no small measure due to Hale's enthusiasm and skill as a telescope builder, fund raiser, and observatory director that we are so close to fulfilling his dream.

Hale's career as the moving force behind the construction of a new generation of telescopes and observatories began by chance, when he heard that the University of Southern California had ordered the lenses to make a 40-inch refracting telescope but had been unable to pay for them. Telescopes are measured in terms of the diameter of their main magnifying lens or mirror, and at that time, in the 1890s, the largest refracting telescope (that is, one using a main lens rather than a mirror) was the 36-inch at the Lick Observatory, on Mount Hamilton near San Jose, California. This is close to the practical limit for constructing accurate astronomical lenses, because bigger ones are bent out of shape by their own weight. The biggest telescopes of today are all reflectors, using big parabolic mirrors, not lenses, to focus the light they gather from the stars. A mirror has the great advantage over a lens that, because no light is passing through, the back can be supported by a framework to hold the mirror in shape. By the 1890s, it was beginning to be clear that the next step forward in telescope design would involve large mirrors; but Hale was intrigued by the possibility of obtaining these ready-made lenses, which were in store at the Paris workshop where they had been manufactured, and using them to build an even bigger telescope than the one at Lick. As the son of a wealthy man, he had the right connections to seek the money needed for the project, and he duly made the rounds of other wealthy Chicago families, eventually obtaining a promise of the required funds from Charles Yerkes, a trolley-car magnate. The sum required was $349,000, which Yerkes only grudgingly coughed up, in dribs and drabs, over the next few years, as Hale kept up his campaign. But the money did come, and the telescope was built, forming the centerpiece of the Yerkes Observatory of the University of Chicago, with Hale appointed as its first director, in 1897, at age twenty-nine. The 40-inch (roughly 1-meter) Yerkes telescope is still the largest refractor in the world.

Hale now had the bit between his teeth. The big refractor, in its observatory at Williams Bay, Wisconsin, was all very well, but he wanted something bigger and better, located at an even more desirable site. The best place to see the stars from Earth is on the top of a high mountain, clear of all the dust and clouds in the lower atmosphere of our planet and far away from city lights. Soon Hale was off to Mount Wilson in California, camping out in an abandoned shack while testing the view of the heavens using a small telescope. Back on the stump again, he drummed up support from the Carnegie Institution of Washington, for a new observatory to be built on Mount Wilson, equipped initially with a reflecting telescope with a main mirror 60 inches (1.5 meters) across and with Hale as its director. The mirror itself was a gift from Hale's father; the telescope came into use in 1908 and was the main tool used by the man who established the true scale of the Milky Way, our Galaxy.

Harlow Shapley was born in Missouri in 1885 and came from a farming background. He received little formal education as a child, and at the age of sixteen he was working as a crime reporter on a Kansas newspaper. But Shapley figured that a formal education would help his career, and after two years at the Carthage Presbyterian Collegiate Institute, he set off to the University of Missouri to enroll in the journalism course. On arrival in 1907, he found that the course would not open for another year and, feeling that he had wasted enough time already trying to catch up on his education, he decided to study something else—anything else—rather than hang around. Late in life (Shapley died only in 1972.) he always said that he picked astronomy because it began with the letter "A" and so caught his eye near the top of the list of courses available. After four years, Shapley emerged with a B.A. and an M.A. in his randomly chosen speciality, and he went on to Princeton, where Henry Norris Russell set him the task of studying binary stars. Most of Shapley's work over the next three years concerned eclipsing binaries; he also established once and for all that the Cepheid variables are not binaries but pulsating stars. And in 1914, seven years after finding that the University of Missouri had no journalism course to offer him, Shapley emerged from Princeton with a Ph.D. and a reputation as one of the brightest of the new generation of astronomers. His reward was a job at the new observatory on Mount Wilson, with a salary of $135 a month and, much more important, access to the biggest telescope in the world, the new 60-inch.

This was one year after Hertzprung had made the first attempt to use Cepheids as distance indicators, and Cepheids had formed a part, albeit the lesser part, of Shapley's own Ph.D. work. With the best telescope in the world at his disposal, Shapley set out to map the Milky Way using Cepheids. The approach he used picked out another feature of our Galaxy, something quite different from anything we have encountered so far. These are the globular clusters, spherical groups of stars that each contain anything from a few tens of thousands up to a few tens of millions of separate stars packed together, and that shine like beautiful jewels in the field of view of even a modest telescope.* These globular clusters lie mainly in one part of the sky, and they seem to be arranged in a sphere themselves. But was it a small sphere close by, or a large sphere far away? Fortunately, globular clusters often contain regular variables—several may be found in just

---

*The stars in such a cluster appear packed together when viewed through a telescope, and they are close to one another compared with stars that are not in clusters, but there is still plenty of space between them. In the dense heart of a globular cluster, stars are separated from one another by, on average, about one tenth the separation between stars in the neighborhood of the Sun.

one cluster. So Shapley was able to use the new yardstick and the new telescope to find out the true distances to some of the clusters. As he did this, he found that the brightest stars in each cluster always seemed to be about the same intrinsic brightness as the brightest stars in any other cluster. With the aid of the Cepheid yardstick, he had found a new measure of the Milky Way—the distances to even those globular clusters where no Cepheids could be seen could be estimated by assuming their brightest stars were the same brightness as those in other clusters, and calculating distance from the apparent brightness (or dimness) of those giant stars.

The outcome of all this was a new map of our Galaxy. The globular clusters were seen to fill a vast sphere very far from us, centered on a point in the direction of the constellation Sagittarius at the heart of the Milky Way. The only plausible conclusion was that the center of this spherical system is indeed the center of the Milky Way Galaxy and that the Sun and Solar System are located well out in the stellar suburbs, about two thirds of the way to the edge of the spiral system of stars. Shapley's results were published in a series of papers over a period of several months in 1918 and 1919. The actual size he came up with for the whole Milky Way system was nearly three times too big, because he had not allowed for the effects of obscuring dust on the light from distant globular clusters

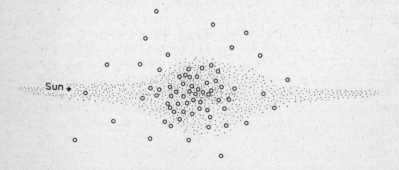

Figure 2.4/ Harlow Shapley found that the distribution of globular clusters, represented here by circles, shows that the Sun and our Solar System lie far from the center of the Milky Way system.

(a cluster whose light is dimmed by dust looks fainter; Shapley estimated it as being farther away than it really is). But his main conclusions were correct. We now calculate that the Milky Way Galaxy is a flattened disc, just as Wright and Kant imagined, about 100,000 light-years (30 kiloparsecs) across. The distance from the center of the disc to the edge is about 50,000 light-years, and the Sun is about 30,000 light-years (10 kpc) out from the center. We live very much in the backwoods of our own Galaxy. But how significant is our Galaxy in the cosmic scheme of things? Leavitt, Hertzsprung, and Shapley had together pushed astronomy's best estimates of how far "up" we can see into the sky out into the hundreds of thousands of light-years range. How much farther might "up" extend?

ACROSS THE UNIVERSE

At this point Shapley faltered and took a wrong turn. It wasn't entirely his fault—his attempt to provide a mental picture, an imaginary model, of the whole Universe depended on observations and interpretations made by others. But the mistake was to set his whole career on a different path, so that although he achieved considerable eminence and respect among his peers, he always looked back on the years from 1914 to 1920, on Mount Wilson, as the pinnacle of his career.

Shapley's inflated estimates of the size of the Milky Way made it look as if the Magellanic Clouds were just part of our own Galaxy, not separate galaxies in their own right. And if the clouds were not real galaxies, the obvious conclusion, for Shapley, seemed to be that other nebulae, such as the great spiral in the constellation Andromeda, must also be, at best, minor satellites of our own Galaxy. According to this picture, the Milky Way *was*, essentially, the Universe; the limit of "up" had already been seen. But there were other astronomers who thought that the nebulae must also be galaxies in their own right and that Shapley's estimate of the size of the Milky Way must be too big, even if they didn't know why it was too big. This alternate view was expressed most vociferously by Heber Curtis, an astronomer at the Lick Observatory.*

Curtis was another researcher who came to astromony by a strange route. Born in 1872 in Muskegon, Michigan, he studied classics and became professor of Latin at Napa College, California, at age twenty-two. There he became interested in astronomy, and when the college merged with the University of the Pacific in 1897, he became professor of astronomy and mathematics—a somewhat startling turnaround to anyone used to the career structure in universities today! After several short periods of research at various observatories, Curtis settled at Lick in 1902 where he stayed, apart from a spell observing the southern skies from Chile, until 1920. It was after he returned from Chile, in 1909, that he concentrated on determining the nature of what were then still known as the spiral nebulae. Increasingly better photographs of these nebulae were becoming available in those years, and these pictures convinced Curtis that the nebulae were galaxies like our own, sometimes seen edge on; sometimes viewed in plan, with the full glory of the disc and spiral structure visible; and sometimes seen at intermediate orientations. If so, these external galaxies, beyond the Milky Way, must lie at truly vast distances in order to appear only as little clouds of light in our telescopes. But how could the distances to the nebulae be measured? That question was open to two answers in the years up to 1920, and one of the interpretations was based on an unfortunate misunderstanding of an event that was seen on Earth in 1885. Unfortunately for Shapley, he backed the wrong horse.

On August 20, 1885, Ernst Hartwig noticed a new star, or nova, shining in the Andromeda Nebula. The star soon faded, but not before its peak intensity had been noted. This was the first time an individual star had been seen associated with the nebula, and one interpretation of the event was that Hartwig and his contemporaries had witnessed the birth of a new star out of a swirling cloud of

---

*Hardly surprisingly, there was for many years an intense, sometimes bitter, rivalry between the two great observatories in California, Lick associated with the University of California, and Mount Wilson associated with the Carnegie Institution and later with CalTech. The hatchet has, however, long since been buried.

gas and dust within the Milky Way system. Whatever the star was, it had briefly shone as bright as all the rest of the Andromeda Nebula put together. A chance to calibrate just how bright that might be came, it seemed, in 1901, when another star exploded, in the direction of the constellation Perseus. This nova was so close that its distance could be estimated, by parallax, as about 100 light-years from the Sun. With no better estimate of distances available, astronomers of the time guessed that the nova in Andromeda might have been the same absolute brightness as the nova in Perseus, and that would have placed it, judging by its apparent brightness, sixteen times farther away, just 1,600 light-years from us. That meant that the Andromeda Nebula must be quite large but still placed it within the Milky Way system.

This was, essentially, the reasoning adopted by Shapley in support of his claim that the Milky Way dominated the Universe and that the spiral nebulae were mere incidentals. Curtis, convinced that the nebulae were galaxies in their own right, sought evidence to back his case. Suppose that the new star seen in Andromeda in 1885 really had been much brighter than the nova in Perseus in 1901. If the Andromeda Nebula were a whole galaxy like the Milky Way, it would, indeed, have had to be as bright, briefly, as a thousand million ordinary stars, something that struck Shapley as absurd. Who can blame him? But we now know that very occasional "supernovae" do indeed shine that brightly. And one reason we know that is because Curtis set out to find other novae in Andromeda and to compare their brightness with the event of 1885 and the brightness of Nova Persei in 1901.

The fact that Curtis actually found several novae in Andromeda (more than a hundred have now been recorded) proved that it must be a collection of very many stars, since novae are not all that common. And the fact that all of those novae were much dimmer than the event seen in 1885 suggested that these were the right phenomena to compare with Nova Persei. That revision increased the distance scale to Andromeda more than a hundredfold, placing it hundreds of thousands of light-years away, far beyond the edge of the Milky Way. So who was right, Curtis or Shapley? There was so much interest in the issue that the National Academy of Sciences organized a debate between the two astronomers in Washington, D.C., in 1920. The debate, attended by, among others, Albert Einstein, was widely publicized. The general feeling was that Shapley lost—Curtis's interpretation of the scale of the Universe was correct.* It was in the wake of this defeat that Shapley quit Mount Wilson, heading off to Harvard, where he took up the directorship of Harvard College Observatory, which he had first been offered in 1919, when Pickering died. It was a decision he must have regretted, in spite of his many other contributions to astronomy, as he saw a new man at Mount Wilson, Edwin Hubble, pick up where he had left off. Hubble built on Shapley's technique of estimating distances using Cepheids and globular clusters; and he also had a new telescope to play with, even bigger and better than the 60-inch.

Hubble was the greatest single beneficiary of Hale's industrious activity. Not content with just the 60-inch telescope for his Mount Wilson Observatory, Hale had cajoled a Los Angeles businessman, John D. Hooker, into funding a telescope with a main mirror 100 inches (2.5 meters) across. This Hooker telescope was completed in 1918 and was for three decades the biggest telescope in the world. Hale himself, worn out by his efforts, resigned as director of the Mount Wilson Observatory on medical advice in 1923, when he was fifty-five. His idea of a quiet retirement, at his home near Pasadena, involved building a small observatory and inventing a new kind of spectroscope to study the Sun. He then tried to raise money to build an observatory in the southern hemisphere and failed, suffering his second nervous breakdown. But soon he was back in circulation again with another scheme, for yet another giant telescope, this one to have a mirror 200 inches (5 meters) across. The Rockefeller Foundation came up with $6 million for the project, to be carried out under the auspices of the California Institute of Technology, in

---

*Ironically, Curtis, while right about the distance to the Andromeda galaxy, was wrong on almost every point of his view about our own Galaxy. He thought the Sun was at the center of the Milky Way and made an estimate for the size of the whole system that was much too small. To get the best picture of the Universe in 1920, you needed half of Shapley's picture and half of Curtis's.

1929. Hale was chairman of the group planning the construction of his masterpiece, which was to be built on Mount Palomar in California. The project took twenty years to complete, delayed by, among other things, World War II, and Hale died in 1938 before seeing his masterwork finished.* It came into operation, as the Hale telescope, in 1948; in 1969 the twin observatories on Mount Wilson and Mount Palomar were, fittingly, renamed the Hale Observatories in tribute to the man who placed American astronomy at the forefront in the twentieth century. By then, Ed Hubble had long since opened the eyes of all astronomers to the true scale of the Universe.

Hubble, like Shapley, was born (in 1889) in Missouri. Hubble came from the town of Marshfield, the fifth of seven sons of a local lawyer, and attended both high school and college in Chicago, overlapping at the University of Chicago with Hale's time there as a professor. Hubble was a superb natural athlete and was offered a chance to turn professional as a boxer to fight the great Jack Johnson. Instead, he took up the offer of a Rhodes scholarship to travel to Oxford University in England, where he studied law, represented the university as an athlete, and fought the French boxer and champion Georges Carpentier as an amateur in an exhibition bout. On his return to the United States in 1913 Hubble joined the Kentucky bar, but practiced as a lawyer for only a few months before deciding this was not the career he wanted. Reverting to an interest in astronomy that had been partly stimulated by Hale during his University of Chicago days, Hubble returned to that university, studying astronomy and working as a research assistant at the Yerkes Observatory. He finished this research in 1917 and was awarded a Ph.D.; Hale offered him a post at Mount Wilson, but first Hubble enlisted in the infantry and went off to fight in France,

---

*Along the way, the spin-off from the project had a major impact on American, and world, astronomy. The Corning Glass Company of New York, commissioned to create the 200-inch mirror, decided to learn the tricks of the trade by casting a series of smaller mirrors first. These test castings were not wasted—two 61-inch mirrors went to Shapley at Harvard; a 76-inch mirror went to Toronto; an 82-inch to the McDonald Observatory in Texas; a 98-inch to the observatory at the University of Michigan; and a 120-inch to Lick.

where he was wounded by shell fragments in his right arm. So it was in 1919 that he arrived at Mount Wilson just as the new hundred-inch telescope was coming into full use and just before Shapley departed for Harvard. Hubble's timing couldn't have been better. It had only been as recently as 1917 that a nova had been identified for the first time on a photographic plate (by George Ritchey, at Mount Wilson), stimulating Curtis to search back through the photographic records at Lick and find the evidence that gave him the first direct measure of the distances to extragalactic nebulae. For hundreds of years, the nature of those nebulae had been open to debate; by 1924, the debate was over, and the combination of the hundred-inch telescope and Edwin Hubble had given mankind a new picture of the Universe, with more startling discoveries still to come.

HUBBLE'S UNIVERSE

Hubble believed that the spiral nebulae were galaxies far beyond the Milky Way, but he wasn't going to be rushed into any overhasty attempt to prove the point. First he tackled the problem of the other nebulae, the ones that didn't show the characteristic spiral structure and that were almost certainly part of the Milky Way system. Using a variety of telescopes, often the 60-inch and occasionally, at first, being allowed time on the 100-inch, by 1922 Hubble had completed a major study that showed that these gaseous nebulae (they also contain dust) shine not with their own light like stars but either because they reflect the light from stars within or close to the nebula, or because the energy the nebula absorbs from nearby stars is enough to make the hot gas glow. The association between gaseous nebulae and stars in our Galaxy was confirmation that the nebulae themselves were indeed part of the Milky Way system. But what of the spiral nebulae? His "apprenticeship" served, Hubble now turned his attention to the problem closest to his heart.

Even in the early 1920s, and even with the aid of the

100-inch telescope, it still had not proved possible to obtain pictures of any spiral nebulae that clearly showed them resolved into separate stars, like the Magellanic Clouds. The best photographs Hubble could obtain seemed, under a magnifying glass (if the light was right and Hubble's mood was optimistic), to show a hint that the wash of light might be broken up into the granular structure that would reveal the nebula in question to be a collection of individual stars. But it wasn't the sort of evidence that as cautious a man as Hubble would stake his reputation on. If the spirals couldn't be resolved into separate stars, Hubble determined to investigate a star cloud that *could* be resolved, even if it was only a faint, irregular patch on the sky, less significant than the Magellanic Clouds. He settled on a group of stars called NGC (for "New Galactic Catalog") 6822 and spent two years obtaining the best series of photographs of the cloud that he could. On a good night it might be possible to get one useful photograph of the cloud; on other occasions it took two separate nights of observing to get a single decent photograph, hour upon hour of patient observing while Hubble kept the cloud locked in the sights of the hundred-inch. And, of course, there were other demands on the telescope's time. So it was that it took most of 1923 and 1924 for Hubble to get a set of fifty good plates of NGC 6822. The result was the identification of just over a dozen Cepheids in this cloud, and using Shapley's techniques Hubble was able to set the distance to this little, irregular galaxy as seven times the distance to the Small Magellanic Cloud. This was in 1924.

In the middle of the observation program on NGC 6822, another extragalactic Cepheid was identified, in the Andromeda Nebula, also known as M31 (number 31 in Messier's catalog). The discovery was made in the autumn of 1923, during a survey aimed at finding novae in the Andromeda Nebula, novae that might be used to test Curtis's ideas concerning the nature of the nebula. "The first good plate in the program," recalled Hubble on page 93 in his book *The Realm of the Nebulae*, "made with the 100-inch reflector, led to the discovery of two ordinary novae and a faint object which was at first presumed to be another nova. Reference to the long series of plates pre-

viously assembled by observers at Mount Wilson in their
search for novae, established the faint object as a variable
star and readily indicated the nature of the variation. It
was a typical Cepheid with a period of about a month . . .
the required distance was of the order of 900,000 light-
years." For various reasons, that distance estimate has
now been revised upward, to more than 2 million light-
years (670 kpc). But that is a minor detail compared with
the breakthrough of this discovery. With no new assumptions at all (unlike Curtis, who could only *guess* that novae
in Andromeda were the same intrinsically as novae in the
Milky Way) but using the same yardstick that had been
used by Shapley to map the Milky Way, Hubble could now
measure the distances to the nearer external galaxies.

That, perhaps, is the most important point to take in
just now. The breathtaking leap out to a distance of 2
million light-years represented simply the first step out
into the cosmos, to one of the *nearest* of the other galaxies
like our Milky Way. The whole Galaxy in which we live
was suddenly shrunken, in the astronomical imagination,
into a tiny mote floating in a vast, dark sea of emptiness.

It took a little while for the actual insignificance of the
Milky Way Galaxy to sink in. At first it seemed that our
Galaxy was larger and more impressive than the others. It
was only in 1952, with a revision of the Cepheid distance
scale, that it became clear that other galaxies are just as
big as our own, and even farther away than Hubble had
estimated. With improved photographic emulsions, Hubble succeeded in 1923 in resolving the outer part of the
Andromeda Nebula into dense swarms of stars, and he
identified more Cepheids in both M31 and another spiral
about the same distance away, M33, over the next few
months and years. Sufficient evidence to settle the issue of
the nature of the spiral nebulae was in by the end of 1924
and presented by Hubble to a meeting of the American
Astronomical Society; over the next five years Hubble
accumulated more evidence, and he produced the definitive summing up of that evidence in the last year of that
decade. By then, he had also begun to establish techniques for estimating the distances to nebulae—galaxies—
far beyond the range where individual stars could be
resolved and the Cepheid yardstick applied.

Cepheids themselves can be identified in only about thirty of the closest galaxies, even using the 200-inch telescope. If all goes well, the planned orbiting Space Telescope should improve on this, but other techniques for measuring distances to more remote galaxies will always be needed. The first step Hubble used, again borrowing from Shapley, was to use supergiant stars as distance indicators, just as they are used to indicate the distances to globular clusters in our own Galaxy. That took Hubble out to four times the distance over which Cepheids could be seen, a distance he estimated as about 10 million light-years. Globular clusters themselves can be and have been used as a rough yardstick of the Universe, on the assumption that the brightest clusters in each galaxy are the same intrinsic brightness as the brightest in our own Galaxy, but by now astronomers are beginning to scrape the bottom of the barrel in their search for ways to measure the distance "up" to more and more remote galaxies. To go further Hubble had to make a bold and only roughly accurate assumption. When he looked at a large cluster of galaxies in the direction of the constellation Virgo, he found that they all appeared roughly as bright as each other—at least, the brightest of these galaxies outshone the dimmest by a factor of ten only. By assuming that all galaxies were equally bright and had an absolute luminosity three times that of the dimmest galaxy, or one third of that of the brightest, Hubble could estimate distances and be reasonably sure that the estimates would be within a factor of three of the right answers—perhaps three times too big, or three times too small, but no worse than that. This kind of technique was later improved by using only the brightest galaxy in a cluster as the standard. (It turns out that brightest galaxies do seem to be much of a muchness, like the brightest supergiant stars.) Approximate though it was, the technique took Hubble out to about 500 *million* light-years.* That distance encompasses a volume of space that contains about 100 million galaxies. But each of these distance measurements depends on the initial calibration of the Cepheid yardstick using statistical paral-

---

*These are Hubble's figures, now revised upward considerably, but they give you a flavor of the advances he was making.

lax techniques (and, now, the color-magnitude diagram) within our own Galaxy—indeed, within the immediate proximity of the Sun. The seeming wealth of information we now have about distances across the Universe is like an inverted pyramid expanding upward and outward from that one Cepheid calibration at the point on which the pyramid is balanced. Without measuring the distances to those 30-odd galaxies in which Cepheids have been identified, there is no way to calibrate the other, more rough-and-ready, yardsticks at all. If that Cepheid yardstick has been incorrectly calibrated and is later revised, we have to change the whole scale of the Universe. That, as we shall see, has happened several times over the decades, most importantly in the early 1950s. But none of these revisions alters the basic picture of the Universe established by Hubble.

Hubble's universe—our Universe—extends for hundreds and thousands of millions of light-years. Some of the galaxies whose images are viewed today by giant telescopes like the 100-inch and 200-inch are so remote that the light we see them by set out on its journey to us even before the Earth itself was formed. There really is no way in which the human mind can comprehend the size of the Universe. All we can do is gaze at the numbers, which tell us that even our nearer neighbors M33 and M31 are so far away that light takes 2 million years or more to cross the gap from them to our Galaxy, and admit that we are bemused by it all. Even the greatest of cosmologists, an Albert Einstein or a Stephen Hawking, must have some sympathy, in his heart of hearts, with Carlyle's remark: "I don't pretend to understand the Universe—it's a great deal bigger than I am."

But still, astronomers attempt to understand the Universe, or as much of it as they can be aware of. Hubble laid the groundwork for modern cosmology. He not only established the scale of the Universe, he also described and classified the main types of galaxies—75 percent of those that can be seen are spirals; most of the rest are cigar, or American football-shaped ellipticals; and only a few irregulars are seen (probably because most of them are too small and faint to be visible at such distances). In addition, he analyzed the distribution of galaxies through space and found that the distribution is, by and large, uniform. Although galaxies come in clusters, the clusters themselves are distributed at random over the sky, and there is just as much chance of seeing a galaxy, or cluster of galaxies, in one part of the sky as in any other, once allowance has been made for the obscuring effects of dust in the Milky Way. This was a major discovery in its own right, suggesting that the ultimate structural pattern of the Universe might have been discovered; its importance is only slightly diminished by very recent evidence that there may be one more layer of structure, involving clusters of clusters of galaxies. It is still fundamentally important that the Universe is the same in all directions, that there is no special place anywhere in the Universe. But even this fundamentally important observation paled into insignificance compared with the bombshell Hubble dropped in 1929. He found that all of these millions upon millions of galaxies are moving apart from one another, rushing away from each other with speeds of up to a sizable fraction of the speed of light. The whole Universe was found to be expanding; and that discovery pointed clearly toward the fact that the whole Universe must have had a definite beginning in time. There seemed to be no limit to how far up astronomers could look into the dark night sky; but the implication of that universal expansion was that there was a limit to how far back in time the history of the Universe extended. It was the discovery of the universal expansion that, only as recently as 1929, set astronomers firmly on the trail of the Big Bang.

CHAPTER THREE

THE EXPANDING UNIVERSE

Science doesn't always progress in an orderly fashion. A discovery made today may have to wait years, or decades, for its significance to be appreciated and slotted into place, while another observation, made tomorrow, may be of obvious and immediate importance. Different lines of research can proceed seemingly independently for a generation or more, until some linking factor shows them to be simply two facets of a greater whole. The two great lines of research in which Edwin Hubble was closely involved weren't quite like that. It was obvious from the moment that the large velocities of galaxies were discovered that these velocities were telling us something significant about the nature of the Universe, just as were Hubble's surveys of the number and distribution of faint and distant galaxies. But progress on both fronts took place in fits and starts, and any historical account of the landmarks in the research has to follow one track for a time, then backtrack to pick up the other main theme.

The work that showed the Universe to be filled with a homogeneous distribution of galaxy clusters, the same in all directions for as far as the telescope can see, continued throughout the 1930s and beyond; it continues, indeed, to the present day. One of Hubble's original ambitions, his colleagues have told many times, was to take a photograph of part of the night sky, using the 100-inch telescope, in which there would be as many galaxies visible on the final print as there were foreground stars from our Milky Way. That ambition was achieved on March 8, 1934, confirming that the galaxies are as numerous in terms of the Universe as stars are in terms of the Milky Way. The date provides a convenient landmark for us, the moment when the extent of the Universe and the nature of galaxies as its fundamental visible building blocks were established beyond reasonable doubt. From his counts of the number of galaxies photographed on plates like this, Hubble calculated that one hundred million galaxies were in principle photographable; with the 200-inch and other large telescopes now available, astronomers calculate that a billion (10^9) galaxies could now be photographed if we had the time and inclination to survey the whole sky in detail. This is, indeed, in round terms the same as the number of stars in our Milky Way Galaxy. But it was five years earlier, half a decade before he obtained that landmark photograph in 1934, that Hubble had reported the discovery that all these galaxies, except our nearest neighbors, are not only moving away from us as the Universe expands but also doing so in accordance with a simple physical law. And it was seventeen years before that, in 1912, that the first measurements of the velocities of what were then still called "the nebulae" were made.

RED SHIFTS AND BLUE SHIFTS

The story of the red shifts of distant galaxies actually begins with the fascination the red planet, Mars, held for Percival Lowell, the wealthy scion of a prominent Boston family of the nineteenth century. Lowell was born in 1855 and studied mathematics at Harvard University, from which he graduated in 1876. This was a year before the Italian

astronomer Giovanni Schiaparelli reported his first detailed
observations of *canali* on Mars. The correct translation of
canali is "channels"; during his long study of Mars,
Schiaparelli made it quite clear that he used this term, and
the equivalent terms for "seas" and "continents," in a
purely descriptive sense to identify features on Mars, and
not with the intention of making any claim that these
features corresponded to the seas, continents, and channels (let alone canals) of Earth. But partly through a
mistranslation of *canali* as "canals," and partly through
wishful thinking, Schiaparelli's reports created a wave of
interest in France, Britain, and North America that lasted
for decades, with many serious astronomers, not to mention huge numbers of ordinary folk, convinced that there
was intelligent life on Mars, with Martians busily constructing canals to carry water from the polar caps to the
equator. The culmination of this misrepresentation of
Schiaparelli's observations must, I suppose, have been the
famous radio broadcast of Orson Welles's version of H. G.
Wells's *War of the Worlds,* which was itself written in the
1890s, at the height of the interest in Mars roused by
Schiaparelli. In 1938, this radio play, presented in the
form of a factual news account, described an attack on
New Jersey by invaders from Mars, and panicked thousands of listeners who didn't realize they were tuning in
to a work of fiction.

But all that was half a century in the future, when
Schiaparelli's discoveries, in their garbled and mistranslated
form, reached the United States in the late 1870s and
caught the attention of young Percival Lowell. The seed
that was planted then was a long time coming to fruition.
Lowell spent a year traveling after graduating, then six
years in his father's cotton business before quitting to
spend the best part of ten years in Japan and the Far East.
It was only on his return to the United States, in 1893,
that he decided to take up astronomy, and especially the
study of the planets, seriously. A man of means, he was
able to finance the construction of his own observatory at
Flagstaff, Arizona, in the clear air more than 2,000 meters
above sea level and far from any major city. For 15 years
he studied Mars using a 24-inch refracting telescope, reporting not only canals but also oases and clear signs of

vegetation to an eager world. The discoveries owed much
to his imagination, but other astronomers made similar
mistakes—even the best telescopes on Earth give only a
poor image of Mars, because details are blurred by the
Earth's atmosphere. A bigger telescope simply magnifies
the blurring. Lowell was wrong about life on Mars, but he
certainly excited the interest of a generation of Americans
in astronomy. And he also predicted that there must be a
ninth planet, outside the orbit of Neptune, revealed by its
disturbing influence on the orbits of the other outer planets. Pluto was discovered, exactly where Lowell had predicted, in 1930, fourteen years after he died. This may
have been a fluke; astronomers today think that Pluto is
too small to account for the effects on the orbits of the
outer planets and that there may be a tenth planet that is
really responsible for these wobbles. Even so, Lowell's
achievements were real and many and were recognized by
the scientific community as much more than the work of a
rich dilettante with an interest in astronomy. In 1902,
indeed, Lowell was appointed nonresident professor of astronomy at MIT, a post he held for the rest of his life and
that involved several series of lectures at the institute. But
perhaps Lowell's greatest contribution to astronomy was to
hire a young observer called Vesto Slipher and to set
him the task of taking spectra of spiral nebulae and looking for Doppler shifts in their light. Lowell's motivation
was his interest in planets—he thought, like many astronomers of the time, that the nebulae might be planetary
systems in the process of formation. But the motive for the
survey doesn't matter; the results do.

Slipher was in many ways the antithesis of Lowell.
Where Lowell was a flamboyant extrovert eager to jump to
conclusions, Slipher was quiet and methodical, painstaking, and never willing to announce his discoveries until he
had dotted the i's and crossed the t's. The difference in
their characters was so marked that it has been suggested
that Lowell, aware of his own strengths and weaknesses,
deliberately picked Slipher to join the team at the Lowell
Observatory to provide the necessary ballast to Lowell's
own impulsiveness.

Slipher was born in 1875, in Mulberry, Indiana. He
attended Indiana University, graduated in 1901, and was

promptly invited to join the Lowell Observatory by Lowell himself. Slipher stayed there for the rest of his career, during which he gained an M.A. in 1903 and Ph.D. in 1909, both from Indiana University, became acting director of the Lowell Observatory in 1916 following Lowell's death and then director in 1926. It was Slipher who initiated the search that led to the discovery of Pluto in 1930, and although he retired in 1952 he lived until 1969, spanning the time from the days when astronomers still thought that the Milky Way was the entire Universe through to the discovery of radio galaxies, quasars, and the microwave background radiation that is thought to be the echo of the Big Bang itself. The theory that predicted the existence of that background radiation drew in large measure on the line of research begun by Slipher with his measurement, in 1912, of the Doppler shift in the light from the Andromeda Nebula, which we now know to be the nearest large galaxy to the Milky Way.

The Doppler shift, remember, is a displacement of the bright or dark lines seen in the spectrum of light from a moving object. If the object is moving toward us, the shift is toward the blue end of the optical spectrum and is called a blue shift. If the object is moving away from us there is a corresponding red shift. And the size of the shift, compared with the position in the spectrum of the equivalent lines in light from a stationary object, gives a direct measurement of the speed with which the object is moving toward or away from us, its Doppler velocity.

It's worth pointing out the technical achievement involved in these first measurements of Doppler velocities for nebulae. The 24-inch telescope was a fine instrument, one of the best of its day. But that day just preceded the great leap forward in telescope technology initiated by Hale. Using the best technology available—the best spectroscopes and the best photographic plates—Slipher still had to expose one photograph for twenty, thirty, or even forty hours (spread over several nights, of course) to obtain one spectrum from which the Doppler shift could be measured. All of this, remember, while working in an unheated telescope dome, because warm air would produce convection currents that would blur the image in the telescope, or in the slit of the spectrograph; working in the cold air at altitude; and keeping, literally, a close eye on the image in the telescope to make sure that the nebula being photographed stayed precisely in position at the center of the field of view. When he had the photographs, Slipher's problems were far from over. The light from a star is concentrated in a point in the image formed by a telescope, and even when this point of light is spread out by the spectroscope, the spread-out image is still bright enough for the lines to be identified, and for their displacements, if any, to be measured with relative ease. The faint image of a nebula—a galaxy—on the other hand, is spread out to start with, and the spectroscopic spreading out of the already faint image makes it fainter still, with the lines in the spectrum difficult to pick out and identify. If the spread-out image is too big, the lines are too faint to be seen; if the image is bright enough for the lines to show up, the chances are it is too small for the shift in the lines to be measured. The success of the Doppler measurement technique depends crucially on the efficiency, or speed, of the photographic emulsions used to record the images.* In spite of all these difficulties, in 1912 Slipher obtained four spectrograms of the Andromeda Nebula, M31, which all showed the same clear evidence of a Doppler shift corresponding to a velocity of 300 kilometers per second. This blue shift in the light from Andromeda showed not only that the nebula is approaching us, but also that it is doing so at a speed greater than the velocity of any other astronomical object—star, planet, or whatever—that had been measured at that time.

Once the breakthrough was achieved, other Doppler velocities for several nebulae were soon measured, although not exactly in a headlong rush. Painstakingly, pushing his equipment to the limit, Slipher extended the list of measured Doppler shifts for nebulae up to thirteen by 1914. Now a pattern began to emerge. Only two of these thirteen measurements showed a blue shift; the other eleven

---

*This is a continuing story, with new breakthroughs in the 1980s giving astrophotographers the best views yet of astronomical objects and the best spectra from them. David Malin and Paul Murdin describe many of these techniques, and present some breathtaking photographs produced by them, in their book *Colours of the Stars*, published by Cambridge University Press in 1984.

were all red shifts, indicating that the nebulae being studied were all rushing *away* from us, with velocities of
hundreds of kilometers a second. It could still have been a
coincidence that a preponderance of red shifts showed up
in the first spectra measured by Slipher. After all, although you expect a perfectly balanced coin to come up
heads or tails in roughly equal numbers when tossed repeatedly, it wouldn't be too astonishing to get a run of
thirteen tosses that included only two heads. But as more
and more red shifts were measured, the pattern stayed the
same. By 1925, Slipher had measured forty-one nebular
Doppler shifts, and other astronomers had added four more
to the list (some indication of Slipher's achievement—he
had measured ten times as many as everyone else put
together); now it was forty-three out of forty-five that
showed a red shift, and the record recession velocity measured was above 1,000 kilometers per second. It began to
look like much more than a coincidence, even though at
that time astronomers still had no final proof that the
nebulae were external galaxies in their own right, far
beyond the Milky Way. But they had their suspicions.
Arthur Eddington, a great British astronomer who was
also a great popularizer of science, wrote in 1923:

> One of the most perplexing problems of cosmology is
> the great speed of the spiral nebulae. Their radial
> velocities average about 600 kilometres per second
> and there is a great preponderance of velocities of
> recession from the solar system. It is usually sup-
> posed that these are the most remote objects known
> (though this view is opposed by some authorities), so
> that here if anywhere we might look for effects due to
> general properties of the world.

By "world," of course, Eddington meant what we now call
the Universe. He went on:

> The great preponderance of positive (receding) veloc-
> ities is very striking; but the lack of observations of
> southern nebulae is unfortunate, and forbids a final
> conclusion.*

---

*Quoted, with no source given, by Dennis Sciama in *Modern Cosmology*,
page 43.

Over the next couple of years an important correction to the Doppler measurements was made when it was confirmed that the Milky Way as a whole is rotating, and a variety of techniques made it possible to estimate the speed of the Sun in its orbit around the center of the Milky Way. This showed that the Solar System is moving at about 250 kilometers per second in, it happens, more or less the direction of the Andromeda Nebula. That impressive blue shift of 300 kilometers per second is actually mainly due to our motion around the Milky Way; only about 50 kilometers per second is genuinely due to the motion of the Andromeda Nebula toward the Milky Way as a whole. While measured red shifts were setting ever higher speed records, even the couple of known blue shifts were being relegated to much more modest proportions than first impressions had indicated. The stage was set for the work by Hubble and his colleague Milton Humason that gave us the first version of the modern picture of the universe.

RED SHIFTS RULE THE ROOST

In the mid-1920s, there was a suspicion among some astronomers, most notably the German Carl Wirtz, that the largest velocities of recession that Slipher had measured belonged to the most distant of the nebulae being investigated. But this was no more than a suspicion, because nobody, before Hubble, had much idea of the distances to the nebulae. So, naturally enough, it fell to Hubble to put the two pieces of evidence—red shifts and distances—alongside one another and to come up with a red-shift–distance relation. After the Sun's velocity around the Milky Way was determined, partly thanks to Wirtz's work, in 1927 the pattern could be discerned even among the forty-odd galaxies whose red shifts had been measured, and that provided the impetus for a major new project to determine red shifts of ever fainter and more distant galaxies, a project largely carried out by Milton Humason.

Wirtz had shown in 1924 that the apparent diameters of nebulae as viewed from Earth seemed to be correlated with their recession velocities. He had data for forty-two galaxies and found that the smaller a galaxy looked, the bigger its red shift was likely to be. Assuming all galaxies are really more or less the same size, this immediately suggested that the smaller nebulae only *look* small, because they are more distant, and that therefore greater distance from us and greater recession velocity went hand in hand. But this was only a rule of thumb, since at that time there was no direct measure of the absolute distances to the nebulae. The matter rested until 1929. Slipher had turned his attention to other problems, and only forty-six red shifts of galaxies beyond the Milky Way were known even then. But by then it was clear that these objects *were* galaxies in their own right, and Hubble's development of the pioneering work of Leavitt and Shapley had given him a good idea of their relative distances. Even though we now know that Hubble's base-line calibration was wrong, he could still say, with complete accuracy, that one galaxy was twice as far from us as another, or 1½ times as far, or whatever the rate might be. And that was all the information he needed. Even so, it is astonishing that Hubble drew the (correct) far-reaching conclusion from a very small number of data.

Hubble had forty-six red shifts, largely inherited from Slipher, but out of those forty-six objects he had distances for only eighteen isolated galaxies and the Virgo cluster. One obvious way to compare the red shifts and distances of these nineteen objects was to plot a graph of velocity (red shift) against distance. Each object has a unique velocity and a unique distance, so it corresponds to a point on such a graph. When all nineteen points were plotted, Hubble concluded that they lay on a straight line, which meant that velocity must be directly proportional to distance—a galaxy twice as far from us as another galaxy is seen to be receding twice as fast as the nearer galaxy. In truth, this seems a sweeping generalization to make on the basis of the few scattered points Hubble had plotted on his graph (see page 65). You need a lot of faith and not a little imagination to draw a straight line through those points and say that the points fall on the line. But astronomers are used to making hazards of this kind, and, as we shall see, it may well be that Hubble already had an inkling of the kind of relationship he was looking for. Shaky though the foundations of the relationship may seem today, further research soon established its basic truth beyond all doubt, and today it is known as Hubble's Law: Red shift is proportional to distance. If the law really is universal, and assuming the constant of proportionality has been correctly calibrated, it gives astronomers the ultimate yardstick of the Universe. All they have to do is measure red shift and they know distance. The significance of the discovery goes far beyond that, however, but before we look at the implications we should pay tribute to the man who picked up red-shift studies where Slipher left off and who did more than even Hubble himself to establish the validity of "Hubble's Law."

Milton Humason was born at Dodge Center, Minnesota,

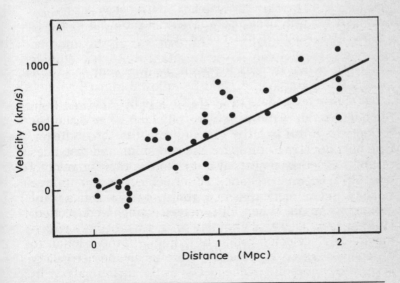

Figure 3.1/ A. One of Edwin Hubble's earliest redshift-distance plots, with just 33 data points and a rather optimistic straight line drawn through them in 1929.

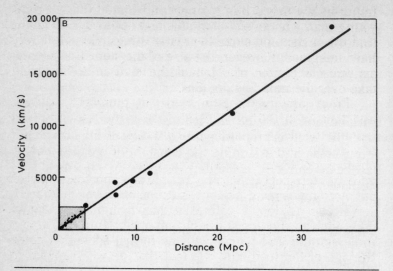

Figure 3.1/B. By 1931 the accuracy of Hubble's bold mixture of guesswork and science had been confirmed. Hubble and Milton Humason had pushed their redshift studies much further, so that the data of 3.1A all lie within the box on the bottom left-hand corner of this plot, made just two years later. But the straight line is still there, and looks much more believable.

in 1891. When he was fourteen, he was sent to summer camp on Mount Wilson, and he enjoyed himself so much that within a few days of going back to high school he had persuaded his parents to let him take a year off from school to go back to the mountain. He never returned to formal education, but by a circuitous route became one of the foremost observational astronomers of his generation. As an academic dropout he became for a time a mule driver, guiding packtrains up the trail to the mountaintop while the Mount Wilson Observatory was being constructed. He was fascinated by both the mountain and the observatory work, but also found time to fall in love and marry the daughter of the observatory's engineer in 1911. With his new responsibility as a married man, Humason gave up mule skinning and tried to settle down on a ranch owned by a relative in La Verne. But in 1917, when a janitor's job at the Mount Wilson Observatory fell vacant, Humason's father-in-law urged him to apply and hinted that a bright young man who loved mountains and observatories might find this a stepping-stone to greater things. He can hardly have imagined, however, the size of the steps the twenty-six-year-old janitor who joined the staff in 1917 would take over the next few decades.

From janitor Humason soon was promoted to night assistant, with the job of looking after the telescope and helping the observational astronomers go about their tasks; any night assistant worth his salt soon wangled some observing of his own, and Humason showed so much skill with the telescopes that in 1919 he was appointed Assistant Astronomer and became a junior member of the observatory's academic staff. Hale had to fight off a lot of opposition to the appointment—after all, Humason was a mule skinner and janitor with no formal education since the age of fourteen, and the fact that he was married to the engineer's daughter also counted against him in the eyes of those who suspected foul play concerning his promotion. But Hale knew his man and stuck to his guns. Humason stayed Assistant Astronomer until 1954, when he became a full Astronomer at the Mount Wilson and Palomar observatories; since 1947 he had been Secretary of the Observatories, responsible for public relations and various administrative duties. He received honorary degrees, but never one of the more common kind, and lived to within a few weeks of his eighty-first birthday in 1972. His meticulous handling of delicate instruments and skill with the large telescopes enabled him to provide the baseline data with which cosmologists were able to build their first detailed imaginative models of the Universe and to cast their ideas back to the Big Bang itself. And this all began in 1928, when Hubble first steered Humason toward the task of measuring the red shifts of faint and distant galaxies.

These observations required new instruments, new photographic techniques, and the almost unique combination of patience and skill that enabled Humason to spend hours at the telescope, spread over several nights, guiding it precisely so that he could obtain the spectrum of a far distant galaxy on a tiny photographic plate just half an

inch wide. By 1935 he had added 150 red shifts to Slipher's
list and was clocking up red shifts corresponding to recession velocities in excess of 40,000 kilometers per second—
more than one eighth the speed of light. With the advent
of the 200-inch telescope, he extended the search still
deeper into space, and by the late 1950s the speed record
was more than 100,000 kilometers per second, one third
the speed of light, corresponding to a distance of several
billion light-years. From the end of the 1920s onward, it
became increasingly clear that the Universe is a very big
place indeed, that galaxies, or clusters of galaxies, are its
building blocks, and that red shifts rule the roost. The
Universe is expanding like crazy.

So what does it all mean? It was the turn of the
theorists to step in to the limelight for a while, with the
somewhat sheepish admission that they could have told
you the Universe was like that, if only they had had
sufficient faith in what their theories had been telling
them for the past decade. It is a story that will become
familiar as we follow the search for the Big Bang. Contrary
to what often is believed, theorists—certainly cosmological
theorists—don't seem to have much faith in their own
ideas. They don't go out to bat for them in a big way, but
tuck them away in the scientific journals, where often
they lie unremarked on for years.* From the 1930s to the
1980s, theorists were repeatedly being surprised by new
observational discoveries that, it turned out, were exactly
in line with what someone had predicted, halfheartedly, or
ignored altogether, ten or twenty years before. And who
was the first of these halfhearted theoretical cosmologists,
who didn't believe what his own theory was telling him?
None other than Albert Einstein.

---

*There are good reasons for this, of course, and the caricature I sketch here
doesn't really do justice to the theorists. They were right to feel tentative
about the early, simple cosmological models, which hardly looked sophisticated enough to account for the complexity of the observed Universe. It was
only gradually, over decades, that reasons began to appear for these almost
childish models to be recognized as reasonable indications of the nature of
the Universe. The reasons for believing in those simple models have now
become highly sophisticated; but it remains a great and fundamental truth
that the Universe seems to run according to rules that are so simple that the
theorists initially felt they *must* be inadequate descriptions of reality.

EINSTEIN

Einstein has become an almost mythical figure, part of the folklore of our times. He is the archetypal genius, the white-haired, slightly eccentric, but amiable old man who pierced to the heart of complex problems by applying an almost childlike naïveté and asking questions so obvious that nobody else had thought to ask them. Much of this is true, just as it is true that he was not thought to be particularly bright at school, made no pronounced impact on the academic world as a student, and had to work as a technical expert in a patent office in the early years of this century while he developed three major new ideas in physics in his spare time. But in one respect the stereotypical image doesn't tell us the truth about the man who made these revolutionary contributions to science. In the early 1900s, Einstein was *not* a white-haired, genial patriarch who dressed for comfort rather than elegance and sometimes didn't bother to wear socks. As pictures from that period show, he was a dark-haired, handsome young man who dressed with conventional smartness. This is important, for Einstein's greatest ideas were *youthful* ideas. They provided new insights, overturned established wisdoms, and were truly revolutionary. The burst of activity that brought Einstein to the wide attention of the scientific community was completed in 1905, when he was twenty-six; his greatest achievement, the General Theory of Relativity, was published just ten years later. And although he lived until 1955, becoming the genial old professor of folklore, his greatest works were all behind him before the end of the First World War. Science, especially the mathematical side of science, is like that. Only young minds can stretch to discover and embrace new concepts— and if the new concepts are as dramatically different from old concepts as those Einstein developed, it can take the rest of your life, or several lifetimes, to work out the implications.

Einstein graduated, with no great distinction, from the Swiss Federal Polytechnic in 1900. He had by then already had a checkered academic career—he didn't talk until he was three, and although he got some good school reports and some bad, he ended up being expelled from high school (the Munich Gymnasium) at the age of fifteen as a "disruptive influence." The expulsion may have been engineered by Einstein—his parents, following a business failure, had already left Germany to live in Italy, and young Albert had such a deep loathing of the militaristic nature of German society that he renounced his citizenship at about this time, becoming stateless rather than be a German. After a happy year of freedom with his family in Milan, in 1895 Einstein applied for admission to the Zurich Polytechnic—and failed the entrance examination. But a year's cramming at a Swiss school in Aarau saw him safely past this hurdle at the second attempt, and he entered the Poly in the fall of 1896, aged 17½.

It was during this year at Aarau that Einstein began to puzzle over a question that would lead him, ten years later, to the Special Theory of Relativity. Albert puzzled over how a light wave would look if you could run fast enough to catch up with it. Here, indeed, is the prime example of the naïve, childlike approach to the Universe that was to be his hallmark. It is a ridiculous question, isn't it? Like the three-year-old who asks you, "Why is grass green?" But hold on to it for a while, for there is more to this question than meets the eye.

It was more through boredom than lack of ability that Einstein only scraped through his examinations at the Poly—he didn't bother to study things he wasn't interested in. His arrogance as a student upset his teachers, one of whom, Heinrich Weber, is reported to have burst out, "You're a clever fellow! But you have one fault. You won't let anyone tell you a thing. You won't let anyone tell you a thing."* And it was as much through this alienation of people in a position to help him as his indifference to his studies that Einstein found himself unable to get an academic post, scraping a living as a tutor until he got the famous job at the patent office in Berne in 1902 and

*See, for example, *Albert Einstein* by Banesh Hoffman, page 32.

became a Swiss citizen. It was a steady job, which he found easy and which gave him both security and plenty of time to think about such puzzles as the nature of a speeding light wave. But nobody could have anticipated the burst of ideas that would come out of this modest hothouse within three years.

EINSTEIN'S THEORIES

Volume 17 of the German journal *Annalen der Physik* was published in 1905 and is now a collector's item marveled over by scientists. In that one volume of the journal, young Einstein, the unknown patent office clerk (he didn't even have a Ph.D. at the time), published three papers giving key new insights into the nature of the world. One of these helped to establish the reality of atoms; another hinted that light might not be simply a wave but could also behave like a series of particles. Both those papers were to prove important in the development of quantum physics, and it was for the second of them, on the photoelectric effect, that Einstein received the Nobel Prize seventeen years later.* But it is the third paper that has become the most famous. It fills thirty pages and carries the unimpressive title "On the Electrodynamics of Moving Bodies." That is the paper that tells us that neither space nor time is absolute but can be squeezed or stretched depending on your point of view; that moving bodies get heavier; that $E = mc^2$; and that points the way to atomic bombs and nuclear power plants, as well as an understanding of what keeps the Sun and other stars hot inside. If that sounds impressive, remember that in 1905 what was to prove by far Einstein's greatest work still lay ten years in the future.

The 1905 paper, the foundation stone of the Special Theory of Relativity, is important enough in today's world,

---

*See my book *In Search of Schrödinger's Cat* for the story of the roots of quantum physics. I deal in more detail with some of the noncosmological implications of relativity theory in my books *Spacewarps* and *Timewarps*.

but it is a minor sideshow on the road to the Big Bang. Einstein's puzzling over the nature of light had its roots in the work of the great nineteenth-century Scottish physicist James Clerk Maxwell, who had set up the equations that describe light as electromagnetic waves moving at a certain speed, commonly denoted by c. The question of what these waves would look like if you could run alongside them at speed c actually provided an important insight into a contradiction between the behavior of light and the "common sense" rules we learn from experience in the everyday world. If you ran as Einstein imagined, then the electromagnetic wave would still, presumably, be waving, but as far as you were concerned it wouldn't be moving, in contradiction with Maxwell's equations. Something must be wrong with this view of the world. Maxwell's equations didn't square up with preconceptions based on everyday common sense, and something had to give. Einstein's genius lay in accepting Maxwell's equations but throwing out those preconceptions to come up with a new and better description of reality.

By the early 1900s, experiments had shown that every measurement of the speed of light always gave the same answer, c. Historians of science still argue about whether or not Einstein was aware of these experiments at the time, but that doesn't matter. By subtle arrangements of light beams and mirrors, it is possible to measure the speed of a beam of light moving in the same direction as the Earth through space, or in the opposite direction. Common sense tells you that the answers ought to be different. If I see a bus moving off at 10 miles per hour and run after it at 9 miles an hour in a vain bid to catch it, the speed of the bus relative to me is just 1 mile per hour; if I ride in a bus traveling at 30 miles per hour and another bus on the opposite side of the highway passes in the opposite direction at 30 miles per hour, relative to me the second bus is moving at 60 miles per hour. But light isn't like that. The Earth moves through space at some velocity, which we might as well call v. A light beam overtaking us at velocity c does *not* have a speed $c - v$, nor does a beam of light approaching us from the opposite direction have a speed $c + v$. Whatever our velocity and whichever direction the beam of light is coming from, when we measure its speed we always get the answer c.*

So, Einstein said, we have to reject our everyday preconceptions. When we are dealing wth velocities, 1 plus 1 doesn't have to equal 2. He worked out a mathematical framework within which the speed of light could always be the same for any observer who measured it from a reference frame moving in a straight line at a steady speed. All of these reference frames can be moving relative to one another (that's where the "relativity" comes in), but they mustn't be rotating or accelerating (hence the "special," to show that the theory deals only with certain problems in physics). Everybody in such a reference frame finds the same laws of physics and is entitled to regard the frame they live in as "at rest." And everybody measures the speed of light as c. There is no special reference frame in the Universe.†

Without going into details, the results of Einstein's calculations can be summed up simply. The improved law for adding up two velocities v_1 and v_2 is not $V = (v_1 + v_2)$ but rather $V = (v_1 + v_2)$ *divided by* $(1 + v_1 v_2/c^2)$, where c is the speed of light. Because c is so big, 300,000 kilometers a second, for everyday velocities like 10 miles per hour and 30 miles per hour the number you divide by is indistinguishable from 1: The $v_1 v_2/c^2$ bit is virtually 0. But if you make one of the velocities, v_1 or v_2 (or even both of them), equal to c, strange things start to happen. You can

---

*And light from the Andromeda galaxy, which has a blue shift corresponding to a large velocity of that galaxy toward us, still has only a velocity c relative to us.

†Even if there are intelligent beings living on a planet in one of those galaxies receding from us at one third the speed of light, when they measure the speed of the light leaving their galaxy it is c, and when we measure it as it arrives here it is still c, not $\frac{2}{3}c$. The moral of all this is still relevant to scientific research today. As Bill McCrea pointed out when commenting on this chapter, Newton's ideas must have seemed exotic and counter to "common sense" to people who had never met mathematical physics before. Newton invented mathematical physics, which was a revolutionary innovation at the time. Einstein elaborated on the basic ideas Newton put forward but used the same techniques Newton had invented. So Newton was, perhaps, the greater innovator. And the moral? It is not to regard *anything* as "common sense" or "obvious" but to approach everything with an open mind and without preconceptions—that is what Einstein did, and that is the genius behind Einstein's work.

never add up two velocities that are less than the speed of light and get an answer that is bigger than the speed of light.

Similar equations fall out of the mathematics to tell us that a moving object gets heavier as its velocity, in our chosen frame of reference, approaches the speed of light, and that at the same time the moving object contracts in the direction of its motion. A moving clock runs slowly compared with one that is stationary in our frame of reference. And, the icing on the cake, the notion of two events occurring simultaneously has meaning only in one frame of reference—an observer moving past you at constant velocity will have a different view of which events precede others or occur at the same time as each other. And all of this is part of engineering today. Machines that accelerate particles such as protons and electrons to close to the speed of light are built in accordance with Einstein's equations. They wouldn't work if the equations were not a good description of the way the world works, and as they work they provide physicists with direct measurements of the mass increase, the time dilation, and other effects predicted by Einstein. Special Relativity works perfectly as a description of the everyday world, marrying the older mechanics of Newton (still perfectly adequate if you don't deal with things moving at close to the speed of light) and the equations of electromagnetism developed by Maxwell. But still it was only the "Special" Theory of Relativity. It didn't deal properly with gravity, and gravity is the force that dominates the Universe at large. So it couldn't provide a complete description of the Universe at large. To do that, Einstein needed a more general theory.

The Special Theory was a child of its time. There was an obvious need to reconcile Newton's and Maxwell's ideas, and if Einstein hadn't come up with Special Relativity in 1905, someone else would have, probably within a year or two. But the General Theory was something else again. Nobody except Einstein bothered much about the limitations of the special theory. Probably nobody of his generation except Einstein *could have* come up with a general theory of relativity. But after ten years' more work (not single-minded work on this one puzzle; Einstein made other significant contributions to quantum theory in those same ten years) he produced a theory that was far more complete than the current *observations* of the Universe. When the observers still hadn't established the distance scale to the nebulae and didn't know for sure that the nebulae were other galaxies, let alone that those galaxies were almost all rapidly receding from us, Einstein produced a theory that naturally and almost of its own accord described a universe that was a large, empty place that ought to be expanding. Einstein had not set out to describe *the* Universe with his equations. He was primarily interested in getting a model of the Universe—a mathematical model—so he could check that General Relativity could indeed deal with complete universes, and did not run into problems with the conditions at infinity, or at the "edge" of the universe—the so-called boundary conditions. That was a far deeper mathematical truth. So he was not greatly bothered that his simplest complete and self-consistent theory, which needed no special boundary conditions, did not seem to describe the actual Universe. He was far more interested in the fact that the model was indeed complete and needed no special boundary conditions. In a sense, he didn't accept what the theory was trying to tell him. And for once in his life he did not follow the rule about casting aside all preconceptions. To make his model fit more closely to his preconceived idea of the Universe as a static place, he adjusted the equations a little, making them slightly more complicated, to produce a slightly different complete model with no special boundary conditions.

General Relativity is, above all else, a theory of gravity. Almost exactly halfway between the arrival of the Special Theory and the full publication of the General Theory, Einstein published another paper in the *Annalen der Physik*, in 1911, which shows how his mind was working toward a theory of gravity. It was titled "The Influence of Gravitation upon the Propagation of Light," and although it contains a mixture of half truths and conjecture rather than any blinding new insight, it points the way forward and brings out another of those naïve questions that reveal deep truths about the Universe. Einstein was struck by the way in which the force of gravity is canceled out for a falling object—not just for one falling object, but for all of them, in exactly the same way. Galileo had pointed out that all objects fall at the same rate, regardless of how much they weigh; Newton had made use of this insight in formulating his own laws of motion. The effect of a force on an object is to produce an acceleration proportional to its mass—one of Newton's famous three laws. And the size of the force of gravity on an object is also proportional to its mass. So mass cancels out, and all objects fall at the same rate.

Einstein, when he wasn't thinking about the man running after a light ray, seems to have spent a lot of time thinking about another man (or perhaps it was the same one?) trapped inside a falling elevator whose cable had snapped. This was Einstein's way of marveling at the way things behave when they are falling freely under the influence of gravity. Inside the falling elevator, everything falls at the same rate, and there is no relative motion. The man inside the elevator will float, completely weightless, able to push himself from wall to wall or floor to ceiling with effortless ease. Of course, we have all seen pictures of astronauts doing exactly this inside spacecraft; they can do it for the same reason, they are in "free fall" under the influence of gravity. Even an orbit around the Earth is a special kind of controlled falling. But Einstein had to *imagine* all the things we have seen for ourselves on TV: a pencil left weightless in midair in the falling elevator; liquids that refuse to pour but form round globules; and so on. The objects inside the falling elevator (or a spaceship) obey the Newtonian laws of motion we learned in school— they move in straight lines at constant velocity unless they are acted upon by some force. In the world outside the falling elevator, things are different because of the force of gravity. Einstein's genius saw the important point missed by everybody else. If the acceleration of the falling elevator can *precisely* cancel out the force of gravity, as it does, that must mean that force and acceleration are exactly equivalent to one another.

Why is this such an important insight? Suppose that the elevator is now replaced in the imagination by a large physics lab, with no windows in it. The lab sits on the surface of the Earth, and a physicist inside can measure how things fall, and work out the force of gravity. Now imagine the lab floating in space. The physicist has no trouble working out that he is in free fall. But what happens if the lab is pushed by a steady force, exactly as strong as the force of gravity on the Earth's surface, but in an "upward" direction, in terms of the arrangement of the floor and ceiling of the lab? Everything in the lab falls to the floor, just as airplane passengers are pressed back in their seats when the plane accelerates on takeoff. That pressure soon eases off as the plane levels off at a steady speed. But in our imaginary lab the downward force persists as long as the lab is being accelerated upward. The physicist can repeat all his experiments and get exactly the same results he did when the lab was stationary on the ground. There is *no way* to tell whether the lab is stationary in a gravitational field, or being accelerated upward. Gravity and acceleration are equivalent.

What has this to do with light? Go back to the lab being pushed through space by a constant force.* The physicist inside might decide to do some experiments involving light. He sets up a light beam so that it starts out on one side of the lab and crosses to the other side. It takes a definite amount of time for the light to cross the lab, and during that time the lab has kept on accelerating upward, so the wall will have moved up a bit before the light beam reaches it.† The physicist can, in principle, measure how far down the wall the spot of light falls and deduce that his lab is being accelerated. He can even measure the acceleration by measuring how much the beam of light has bent. It looks as if there is, after all, a way to distinguish gravity from acceleration. Not a bit of it, says Einstein. We must keep the idea that gravity and acceleration are equivalent until (and unless) they are

---

*It doesn't even have to be a *constant* force; but let's keep it simple for now.
†It is important to distinguish the effects of velocity and of acceleration here. If the mythical space lab is floating with a steady velocity, then anything crossing the lab from one side to the other has the same velocity, and although both the lab and the object move forward, they move by the same amount. It is acceleration, a changing velocity, that makes the lab move an extra amount forward while the light beam is traveling across it. In the falling elevator, the light beam is also under the influence of gravity and is accelerated, so the appropriate thought experiment really is a lab in space being pushed by some outside force, like its rockets, not one falling under the influence of gravity.

proved not to be. If the light beam is bent in an accelerating frame of reference, then if the theory is correct it must also be bent by gravity, and by the exactly equivalent amount.

This principle of equivalence is the heart of the correct insight in the 1911 paper.* Unfortunately, the calculation of the size of the bending effect was wrong, but no matter. Over the next four years Einstein developed these ideas into his complete General Theory of Relativity, and the complete theory also predicted that light can be deflected by gravity—indeed, by more than the amount of deflection calculated in 1911. The best way to understand how this light bending occurs is to cast aside our preconceived ideas about force and space and to take on board the ideas presented by Einstein, initially in 1915 and in a complete form in 1916. These ideas envisage what we think of in everyday terms as empty space as something almost tangible, a continuum in four dimensions (three of space and one of time) that can be bent and distorted by the presence of material objects. It is those bends and distortions that provide the "force" of gravity.

Forget about the four dimensions of space-time for a moment and think of a two-dimension elastic surface. Imagine a rubber sheet stretched tightly across a frame to make a flat surface. That is a "model" of Einstein's version of empty space. Now imagine dumping a heavy bowling ball in the middle of the sheet. It bends. That is Einstein's "model" of the way space distorts near a large lump of matter. When you roll marbles across the flat rubber sheet, they travel in straight lines. But when the sheet is distorted by the bowling ball, any marble you roll near the ball follows a curved trajectory around the depression in the rubber sheet. That, said Einstein in effect, is where the "force" of gravity comes from. There really isn't any force. Objects are simply following a path of least resistance, the equivalent of a straight line, through a curved

*McCrea says he doubts whether Einstein actually derived his ideas *starting* from the principle of equivalence. He suggests that this is simply a useful device Einstein used in expounding his ideas after he had developed them. But McCrea also says that most of his colleagues would disagree with this interpretation of the evidence, so I have stuck by the traditional version of the story here.

portion of space, or space-time. The object can be a marble, a planet, or a beam of light. The effect is the same. When it moves near a large mass—through a gravitational field of force, on the old picture—it gets bent. General Relativity predicted exactly how much a beam of light should get bent when it passes near the Sun. The mathematics may be esoteric and the concepts, such as bent space, bizarre. But Einstein's General Theory made a clear-cut and testable prediction. It appeared in 1916, when Einstein was working in Germany. The British astronomer Arthur Eddington learned of the new theory, and its prediction, from a colleague in neutral Holland. And this German prediction was confirmed by a British observation made in 1919, when the two countries were still technically at war, having signed an armistice but not yet a peace treaty. Partly for these reasons, it caught the popular imagination like no other discovery in the physical sciences, causing a stir comparable only to the stir caused by the publication of Darwin's ideas on evolution in the previous century.

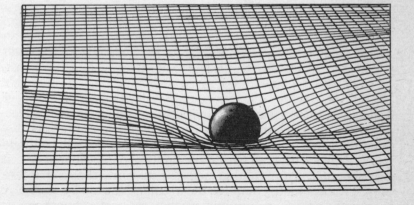

Figure 3.2 / The way in which the mass of a body distorts space-time in its vicinity can be represented by the distortions produced in a smooth rubber sheet by the weight of a heavy ball.

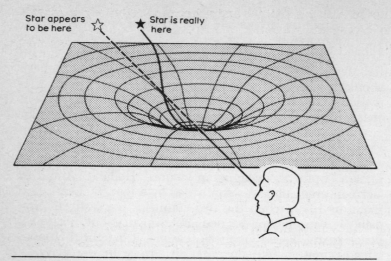

Star appears to be here

Star is really here

Figure 3.3 / Light traveling through space-time follows the distortions produced by massive objects. Using the image of the ball resting on a rubber sheet, we can represent the distortion of space-time produced by the Sun, and the effect this has on the light from a distant star.

THE PROOF

A scientific theory can never, strictly speaking, be *proved* correct. The best any theorist can hope for is that his or her theory will make a prediction that can be tested and found to be accurate to within the limits of observational or experimental error. In that sense, Einstein's theory has proved to be a more complete theory than Newton's theory of gravity, producing predictions that more closely agree with observations. This is the special, restricted sense in which Einstein's theory was "proved" right in 1919. And the man chiefly responsible for obtaining the proof was the British astronomer Arthur Eddington.

Eddington was three years younger than Einstein, having been born in 1882 in Kendal, Cumbria, England. But his father died in 1884, and the young Eddington moved with his mother and sister to Weston-Super-Mare, in Somerset, England, where he was brought up and attended the local school. He was a Quaker throughout his life—something that was to be important to the confirmation of the Einsteinian prediction of light bending, in a roundabout sort of way—and an outstanding scholar who went first to Owens College in Manchester (the college that became the University of Manchester) and then, on graduating in 1902, to Cambridge. Three years later he graduated from the University of Cambridge, and after a short spell teaching in 1907 he became a Fellow of Trinity College and also took up a post at the Royal Greenwich Observatory as Chief Assistant. In 1912, at age thirty, he became Plumian Professor of Astronomy and Experimental Philosophy (my favorite academic title) at the University of Cambridge and in 1914 became Director of the Cambridge Observatories.

If all that makes him sound like a formidable man, the impression would be only half correct. Eddington was also a brilliant communicator who became one of the leading popularizers of science in the 1920s and 1930s, and he had a well-developed sense of humor and of the bizarre. In later life he told how one of his schoolboy games was to make up phrases that obeyed all the rules of English grammar but made no sense—one example was "to stand by the hedge and sound like a turnip." And in his writings on theories such as quantum physics and relativity he was prone to slip in a bit of Lewis Carroll to help get a point across. There certainly has to be something out of the ordinary run of academics about a man who can begin a chapter of a book titled *Philosophy of Physical Science* with this sentence:

> I believe there are 15 747 724 136 275 002 577 605 653 961 181 555 468 044 717 914 527 116 709 366 231 425 076 185 631 031 296 protons in the universe, and the same number of electrons.

Perhaps even more remarkably, the reasons why Eddington came up with this large number still interest cosmologists, as we shall see.

Eddington will be remembered for two great achievements. As much as anyone else, he invented the subject of astrophysics, the study of how physical laws deduced here on Earth, together with observations of the light from stars, can explain the processes going on inside stars that keep them hot, and how the stars must change as they age. And he was also the definitive popularizer of Einstein's theories of relativity in the English language, not just in the sense of communicating these ideas to laypersons, but also as the scientific interpreter who made them clear to his colleagues, and wrote textbooks on the subject that helped to spread its message. Fascinating though all of Eddington's life and work were, the one thing I can pick out here is his response to the prediction that light must be bent when it passes near the Sun.

Einstein's first announcements of the General Theory were communicated to the Berlin Academy of Sciences during the latter half of 1915 and published in more detailed form the following year.* Copies of Einstein's papers went, naturally enough, to his friends in the neutral Netherlands, and one of those friends, Willem de Sitter, sent copies of Einstein's papers to Eddington. In 1916 and 1917, de Sitter also sent three of his own papers to the Royal Astronomical Society for publication. These were partly reviews of Einstein's work, explaining its significance, but in the last of the three de Sitter also presented for the first time a description of the Universe, based on General Relativity, which required expansion. More of this in its place. Eddington was Secretary of the Royal Astronomical Society at the time, and we know that he read the papers carefully and reported on them to the society's meetings prior to their publication. The one person who had the intellectual ability and background to appreciate fully the significance of Einstein's new work was in exactly the right place, at the right time, to get the news. Fate had several more twists to add to the story before Einstein's new theory was proved correct.

The way to test the light bending, Einstein pointed out, was to look at stars near the Sun during an eclipse. Normally, of course, the bright light of the Sun makes it

---

*It appeared in, of course, *Annalen der Physik* (Volume 49, page 769). The paper is called "The foundation of the General Theory of Relativity" and is widely accepted as the greatest paper Einstein ever wrote.

impossible to see stars in that part of the sky, but with
the Sun's light temporarily blotted out by the Moon it
would be possible to photograph the positions of stars that
lie far beyond the Sun but in the same direction on the
sky. By comparing such photographs with photographs of
the same part of the sky made six months earlier or later,
when the Sun was on the other side of the Earth, it would
be possible to see any shift in the apparent positions of the
stars produced by the light-bending effect. What the astronomers needed was an eclipse of the Sun. Ideally, if
they could have chosen the eclipse they wanted, they
would have asked for one on May 29, in any year, because
just then the Sun is seen passing in front of an exception-
ally rich field of bright stars in the direction of the Hyades.
Quite frequently eclipses are visible from some part of the
Earth, but an eclipse on May 29 (or any other particular
day of the year) is something that happens only very
rarely. As Eddington himself commented, "It might have
been necessary to wait some thousands of years for a total
eclipse of the Sun to happen on the lucky date." But by a
remarkable stroke of good fortune there was an eclipse
due in 1919—on May 29. It was too good an opportunity to
miss, provided the war was over in time to organize an
expedition to observe the eclipse, which would be visible
from Brazil and from the island of Príncipe off the western
coast of Africa.

In 1917, the plot began to thicken. The Astronomer
Royal, Sir Frank Dyson, was enthusiastically in favor of
organizing two expeditions to observe the 1919 eclipse,
and contingency plans were made. Meanwhile, conscrip-
tion was introduced in Britain, with all able-bodied men
eligible for the draft. Eddington was thirty-four and able-
bodied; he was also a devout Quaker and a conscientious
objector. This was a difficult thing to be in 1917, and his
position was further complicated by the recognition of the
scientific community that Eddington was a scientist of the
first rank. The physics community still felt deeply the loss
of Henry Moseley, a pioneering X-ray crystallographer killed
in action at Gallipoli in 1915, and questioned the wisdom
of the government in sending the best scientists of the day
to die, perhaps, in the trenches. A group of eminent scientists pressed the Home Office to give Eddington an ex-

emption, on the grounds that Britain's long-term interests
would be best served by keeping him at his proper work.
The Home Office eventually agreed and wrote to Eddington, sending a letter for him to sign and return. But
Eddington added a footnote to the letter to the effect that
if he were not deferred on the stated grounds he would
claim deferment on the grounds of conscience anyway. It
was an honest and principled stand, which left the Home
Office with a problem, and the scientists who had pleaded
on Eddington's behalf more than a little upset. The law of
the time said that a conscientious objector must be sent to
do not very congenial work in agriculture or industry;
Eddington was quite prepared to go and join his Quaker
friends. The upshot of a further round of debate, involving
Dyson as the Astronomer Royal, was that Eddington's
draft was deferred, but with the "condition" that if the war
ended by May 1919 he *must* lead an expedition to test the
light-bending prediction of Einstein's theory!*

Eddington had led an expedition to Brazil to study the
1912 eclipse of the Sun. And he needed all his experience
to ensure the success of his part of the twin 1919 expeditions, which were planned throughout 1918. The idea was
that Eddington and a Cambridge team would go to Príncipe,
while Dyson would organize a team from the Royal Observatory at Greenwich to observe the eclipse from Brazil. But
no work could be done by the instrumentmakers until the
armistice was signed. They were too busy building weapons of war. But the expeditions had to sail in February
1919. The armistice was signed, of course, on November
11, 1918. In a few hectic weeks, everything was made
ready and the expeditions set off. The Brazil expedition
had perfect weather for the occasion and obtained a series
of excellent photographic plates of the star field around
the Sun at the time of the eclipse. But for logistical reasons these plates were not processed and studied immediately. On Príncipe, Eddington waited anxiously as the
appointed day dawned rainy, with a cloud-covered sky.

---

*There are several versions of this story that give slightly different emphases
but report the same series of events. I have followed the account given by S.
Chandrasekhar in his book *Eddington*, which is also the source of the direct
quotes from and about Eddington given here.

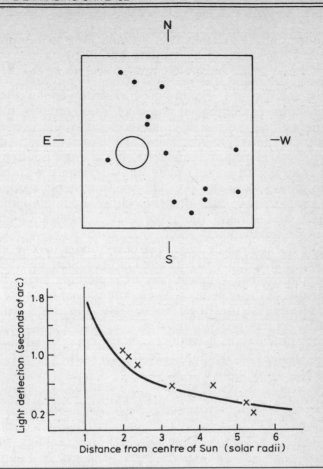

Figure 3.4/ During the eclipse of 1919, Arthur Eddington was able to measure the positions of several stars, shown in the top diagram, which lay in nearly the same direction on the sky as the Sun (circle) at the time of the eclipse. The stars are, of course, much further away from us than the Sun is, but this juxtaposition means that light from the distant stars passes through the region of space affected by the Sun's gravity, as in Figure 3.3.

When these positions were compared with the measured positions of the same stars when the Sun was on the opposite side of the sky, Eddington found that they were apparently deflected, each by an amount which depended on the angular separation of the star from the Sun at the eclipse. Light had been "bent" as it passed by the Sun. And these "deflections" (crosses in lower figure) fell exactly on the curve predicted by Einstein's theory.

More in hope than expectation, all the arrangements to photograph the eclipse were made, and just near the time of totality, the Sun showed dimly and the plates were exposed. The result was just two plates showing the stars needed for the test. Eddington had arranged for these plates to be examined on the spot, "not entirely from impatience," as he put it, "but as a precaution against mishap on the way home." One of the successful plates was duly developed and analyzed on Príncipe, Eddington comparing it with another plate he had brought with him of the same part of the sky. The measurements required were simple. Three days after the eclipse, Eddington knew he held in his hand the proof that Einstein's General Theory of Relativity was right.

The full analysis of the eclipse observations took several months, and definite news that his prediction had been confirmed reached Einstein only in September 1919. The full results of the expeditions were announced to a packed joint meeting of the Royal Society and the Royal Astronomical Society on November 6, 1919, and produced a wave of publicity in a world eager for news of anything except war. The headlines read "Light Does Not Go Straight," "Revolution in Science," "Newtonian Ideas Overthrown," and "Space 'Warped.'" Einstein was established in the public eye as the greatest scientist of the twentieth century, perhaps of all time. And the General Theory of Relativity was accepted as the greatest scientific theory of all time—more than a little incorrectly, since the quantum theory must rank as of at least equal importance. There were other tests of Einstein's theory. It had already explained a tiny variation in the orbit of Mercury around the Sun that is not predicted by Newton's theory of gravity, and so in a sense the eclipse results merely confirmed to astronomers what they already knew, that Einstein's theory worked better than Newton's. Other eclipse expeditions followed,* and the tests have been repeated many

---

*Following the two expeditions of 1919, the next eclipse study was in 1922, when a Lick Observatory expedition to Wallal, in Western Australia, provided the third measurement of the Einsteinian light-bending effect and again showed the results predicted by the General Theory of Relativity. The news was announced to the April 1923 meeting of the Royal Astronomical Society, where Eddington, characteristically, quoted Lewis Carroll: "I think

times, often far more accurately than Eddington's first analysis of his plates on Príncipe. Totally different tests of General Relativity, involving red shifts caused by gravity in the light from stars, and subtle changes in the radiation from pulsars (undreamed of in 1919), all point to the same conclusion. But whatever its successful explanations prior to 1919, and whatever tests have been carried out since, May 29, 1919, stands as the day when science made the observations that proved Einstein correct, and November 6, 1919, stands as the day the public was made aware of the fact. Meanwhile, though, the astronomers had a puzzle. If Einstein's theory was such a good description of space and time, why did it say such peculiar things about the Universe?

EINSTEIN'S UNIVERSE

General Relativity is about the geometry of the Universe—the geometry of space-time. For the past fifty years or more, one of the cosmologists who has made himself most familiar with the equations and meaning of General Relativity is Bill McCrea, still active as Professor Emeritus Sir William McCrea, at the University of Sussex. McCrea was born in 1904 and graduated from Trinity College, Cambridge, in 1926. He was just of the generation that was the first to receive Einstein's ideas fresh, at the start of their academic careers. Early in a long and distinguished career, McCrea was responsible, with Edward Arthur Milne, for showing how even the rules of Newton's theory of gravity, subject to certain simplifying assumptions, make the same kind of predictions about the evolution of the Universe, especially its expansion, that come out of General Relativity. He has also investigated galaxy formation, studied the significance of those large numbers that so fascinated Eddington, and made important contributions to quantum physics and stellar astronomy. There is no-

---

that it was Bellman in 'The Hunting of the Snark' who laid down the rule 'When I say it three times, it is right.' The stars have now said it three times to three separate expeditions; and I am convinced their answer is right."

body better around today to turn to for a lucid explanation of what General Relativity is all about, and I learned my own cosmology as a student of McCrea's in the late 1960s*. So without stumbling through all of the historical processes that led up to the modern understanding of General Relativity, and with suitable apologies to Einstein and Eddington, I shall give you my own interpretation of General Relativity.

Special Relativity combines space and time into one physical identity with a specific mathematical description, space-time. This space-time is geometrically "flat"—mathematically speaking, it has the same kind of geometry as the flat surface of a floor, or of a billiard table. So it is a special case among a family of more general possibilities, a family of curved surfaces. To a mathematician, a "curved" surface means anything not flat—the undulations of mountains and valleys over the surface of the Earth, as well as the way the surface of the Earth is wrapped around to make a more or less spherical globe. A perfectly spherical surface is as much a special case as a perfectly flat floor, and even curved surfaces can have ripples, like the mountains and valleys on the surface of the Earth.

In a similar way, space-time can be thought of as curved, and this is the generalization that makes "General Relativity." When they look at the Universe and try to describe (or predict) its behavior mathematically, cosmologists are selecting one or two families of curved surfaces from the array of possibilities to see which ones fit best. The chosen examples are called models, but they have no physical reality like a Plasticine model; they exist only in the minds of the cosmologists and in their equations. In such models, only the broad features are interpreted, and the lesser ripples, comparable with the mountains and valleys on Earth, are on too fine a scale (if they exist at all) to enter into the calculations. But the distortion in space-time produced by the Sun that causes the bending of

---

*McCrea gives a very good, readable account of General Relativity in his contribution to the volume *Cosmology Today*, which I edited. I would not have ventured to describe General Relativity here without checking this chapter with McCrea, who says that my account is "quite defensible." I *think* that means it is okay, if not quite the way he would have told the story himself!

starlight as it passes nearby is just such a ripple in the fabric of the Universe.

General Relativity goes farther than Special Relativity in another way. As I have explained, it describes matter as well as space and time. Special Relativity gave us space-time; General Relativity in effect gives us matter-space-time, although I have never seen the term used as such. It is the matter that bends, or distorts, the fabric of space-time, and General Relativity gives a well-defined physical meaning to a completely specified geometry of matter, space and time—a universe, where the lower case means that we are referring to just one of the many possible mathematical models, not necessarily to the actual Universe we live in. Strictly speaking, General Relativity deals *only* with complete universes. When Einstein's equations are used to describe the way light bends as it passes the

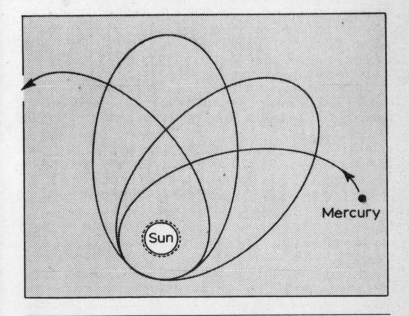

Figure 3.5 / The planet Mercury follows an elliptical orbit around the Sun, but the whole orbit also moves around, tracing out a pattern like the petals of a daisy. This movement of the orbit is unexplained by Newton's theory of gravity, but is predicted by General Relativity.

Sun, or how the orbit of Mercury shifts slightly each time the planet moves around the Sun, they are being used in an approximate sense. In practice, these approximations can be made as accurate as you like. There are what are called "boundary conditions" that join on the equations describing a little local object like the Sun to the rest of the Universe. But the important point is that Einstein did not have to expand his theory, in some sense, to make it capable of dealing with the whole Universe. General Relativity, from its birth, dealt with whole universes quite happily; the subtlety is focusing it down to deal with such a minor and insignificant part of space-time as our Solar System.

In 1917, the received wisdom was that our Milky Way Galaxy was the entire Universe, a stable collection of stars. Individual stars might wander within the cloud, but taking the Milky Way as a whole, the preeminent feature of the Universe seemed to be stability. The Milky Way wasn't getting any bigger or any smaller and had been there, for all anyone knew, throughout eternity. Some stars might be born and others die, but the overall appearance of the Milky Way stayed much the same, in a steady state. So when Einstein took the wonderful new tool he had invented and applied it to make a description of the Universe, he expected it at least to allow for the possibility of a universe existing in such a steady state. In another paper to the Berlin Academy of Sciences, he described in 1917 his own surprise at what the equations told him and how he managed to force them to fit into the box of his preconceptions. The paper was called "Cosmological Considerations on the General Theory of Relativity"; McCrea quotes Einstein (in translation) as saying in the paper, "I shall conduct the reader over the road that I have travelled, rather a rough and winding road, because otherwise I cannot hope that he will take much interest in the result at the end of the journey." And McCrea describes the whole paper as "tentative . . . out of character for Einstein."* Truly, the great man was baffled by the fruits of his own labors—because, we now know, the *observations* of the Universe were misleading.

---

*Quotes from McCrea, op. cit.

Einstein tried to describe the simplest possible model universe that bore any relation to reality, one that contained matter spread out uniformly through space. The universe was closed, like the surface of a sphere, wrapped around on itself so there could be no edge.* But it wouldn't stay still. When Einstein put the equations describing such a static universe through the appropriate manipulations of General Relativity, they said that the universe must be either expanding or contracting but that it could not stand still. The only way he could hold the model universe still, to mimic the appearance of the Milky Way, was to add an extra term to the equations of General Relativity, a term called the "cosmical constant" and often represented by the Greek letter lambda. Then and only then would the equations provide a description of a universe that neither expanded nor contracted. The last sentence of Einstein's 1917 paper reads, "That term is necessary only for the purpose of making possible a quasi-static distribution of matter, as required by the fact of the small velocities of the stars." A dozen years later, Hubble had shown that the Milky Way was not the entire Universe and had discovered the very *large* velocities, all of recession, of the distant galaxies. The reason for the existence of the lambda term had gone, and the existence of the expanding Universe remains the greatest prediction Einstein never made. What Einstein's own equations had been trying to tell him, that we live in a dynamic, expanding Universe, not a static universe, was plain for all astronomers to see. Einstein later described the introduction of the lambda term as "the biggest blunder of my life"; but it is hard to see how anyone studying the nature of the Universe in 1917 could have failed to make such a blunder. Theory had run ahead of the observations, and it was only when Hubble and Humason showed that we do live in an expanding Universe—Einstein's universe—that General Relativity at last took its rightful place as a description of the origin and evolution of the entire Universe.

---

*The "Newtonian cosmology" invented by Milne and McCrea cannot really cope with the problem of edges because it doesn't allow for bent space-time, so it doesn't really provide a valid description of the Universe—or any universe. So it cannot be said in any real sense to be a rival to relativistic cosmology. But it does have its uses.

But before we look in detail at that description of the Universe—the Big Bang model itself—it is perhaps worth pausing to marvel at the way very powerful deductions about the nature of the Universe can be drawn from simple observations. Whatever the appearance of the Milky Way, you don't really need observations of distant galaxies to tell you that the Universe must be in a state of change, and Einstein might perhaps never have gotten embroiled with the lambda term if he had been more familiar with some of the ideas of the philosophers of previous generations. On the other hand, part of his interest in the role of matter in the Universe came from another, semiphilosophical line of thought, one that went back to Newton and could, even in 1917, have been used to predict some of Hubble's discoveries about the distribution of matter across the Universe. Together, those two lines of philosophical thinking could have been used to predict that the Universe is full of galaxies that are rushing apart from one another—but the prediction was never made.

THE PHILOSOPHERS' UNIVERSE

For an observer falling freely from the roof of a house there exists no gravitational field.

Albert Einstein

Einstein gave us the mathematical tool—General Relativity—with which it was possible to construct detailed models of the Universe in which we live. Those mathematical models led cosmologists, almost against their will, to the idea that the Universe was created out of a superdense state, the Big Bang. General Relativity took cosmology out of the realm of the philosophers and metaphysicians and made it a part of science. But, before we look in detail at the implications of the scientific investigation of cosmology, it is interesting to consider, with the benefit of hindsight, just how far the philosophers might have gone down that same path, if they had only had the courage of their convictions.

At the time he was developing the General Theory of Relativity, Einstein was fascinated by an idea he learned from the Austrian physicist Ernst Mach and that he gave the name "Mach's Principle," although in fact the idea goes back much farther than Mach. The idea relates the very large—the Universe as a whole—with the very small—

things in the laboratory, or everyday life, here on Earth. General Relativity was intended to incorporate Mach's Principle, linking the Universe at large with our everyday world, but it did not seem to do so satisfactorily, and late in his life Einstein rejected the whole notion, just as, ironically, Mach himself, as an old man, had rejected General Relativity shortly before he died in 1916. Perhaps they both acted too hastily, for in one of the unsung byways of research in the 1980s and over recent decades, a handful of mathematicians have been reworking some of Einstein's equations and establishing that there really is a link between the large and the small and that the equations of General Relativity really do provide the framework for an understanding of that link. What is more, there may be applications of the new work to exotic objects, spinning pulsars, and X-ray–spitting black holes that were not even dreamed of in 1916. Such exotica have only marginal relevance to the search for the Big Bang. But Mach's Principle, as it was expressed and known by the 1920s, could, with a little thought, have led philosophers to predict the existence of other galaxies in the Universe purely on the basis of the known structure of our own Milky Way Galaxy. Nobody, however, not even Einstein, took Mach's Principle seriously enough to apply it in this way. Philosophers are astonished when it turns out that their metaphysical musings really can tell us new things about the Universe we live in; cosmologists, those most philosophical of all scientists, seem to have inherited this attitude of uncertainty about their own work. So let's just pause for thought and look, not too seriously, at some of the might-have-beens of the early 1920s.

THE PUZZLE OF INERTIA

When you stir cream into your coffee and idly watch the pretty patterns it makes, do you ever stop to ponder how the liquid knows it is in motion? The question is deeper than it looks. The obvious answer is that the liquid "knows" it is rotating because it is moving past the side of the cup.

But not at all. The change in the shape of the surface of the liquid, from flat to concave, is trying to tell us something very deep about the nature of the Universe and of inertia.

Galileo, in fact, seems to have been the first person to realize that it is not the velocity with which an object moves but its acceleration that reveals that forces are acting upon it. On Earth, there are always external forces— friction—that slow down a moving object unless we keep pushing it, and the nearest we can come to truly undisturbed motion is a hockey puck skimming across smooth ice. That really does seem to keep moving in the same direction at the same speed (with constant velocity) until it is acted upon by an external force. Newton quantified the relationship—force equals mass times acceleration— and extended it to explain the motion of the planets in their orbits around the Sun. A frame of reference in which things move with constant velocity unless acted upon by forces is called an inertial frame, and Newton had the idea that there must be some fundamental inertial frame, an absolute standard of rest defined, in some sense, by empty space. Things moved at constant velocity *through empty space*, he argued, unless accelerated by external forces.

It's a little tricky to pin down empty space. You can't hammer a nail into it and measure your velocity relative to the nail to find out if you are in an inertial frame or not. Whatever the practical value of Newton's laws, their philosophical basis looks a little unsound. But Newton reckoned he could establish the fundamental frame of reference by a simple experiment, not on bodies moving in straight lines but using rotating objects—specifically, a bucket of water.

Who better to describe the experiment than Newton himself, writing in his *Principia* in 1686:

> The effects which distinguish absolute motion from relative motion are, the forces of receding from the axis of circular motion . . . if a vessel, hung by a long cord, is so often turned about that the cord is strongly twisted, then filled with water, and held at rest together with the water; thereupon, by the sudden action of another force, it is whirled about the contrary way, and while the cord is untwisting itself . . .

the surface of the water will at first be plain, as
before the vessel began to move; but after that, the
vessel, by gradually communicating its motion to the
water, will make it begin sensibly to revolve, and
recede by little and little from the middle, and ascend
to the sides of the vessel, forming itself into a concave figure (as I have experienced), and the swifter
the motion becomes, the higher the water will rise.

The coffee in your cup does the same thing when you
stir it. And the important point is that it is not the relative
motion of the liquid and the container that matters, but
the absolute rotation of the liquid. You could stand your
bucket, or coffee cup, carefully in the dead center of a
turntable and rotate the whole thing. The pronounced dip
in the surface of the liquid occurs even when the liquid is
stationary compared with the cup. The liquid "knows" it is
rotating and responds accordingly. Newton said it was
rotating relative to fixed space. Those philosophers who
still objected to the idea of absolute space, on the grounds
that something completely unobservable cannot be real,
had to find some other way to explain the effect of rotation
on a bucket of water. It took them thirty years, but then
George Berkeley, an Irishman born in 1685 who grew up
to become a philosopher, economist, mathematician, physicist, and bishop (not necessarily in that order), came up
with an answer.

Berkeley argued that all motion is relative and must be
measured against something. Since "absolute space" cannot be perceived, that will not do as a reference point.
Suppose, he said, everything in the Universe were annihilated except for one globe. Then it would be impossible to
imagine any motion of that globe—the notion would be
meaningless. Even if there were two perfectly smooth
globes in orbit around one another, there would be no way
to measure that motion. But "suppose that the heaven of
fixed stars was suddenly created and we shall be in a
position to imagine the motions of the globes by their
relative position to the different parts of the Universe."* It

---

*Quotes from Berkeley, and the translation of the passage from the *Prin-
cipia,* are taken from Dennis Sciama's book *The Unity of the Universe*
(London: Faber & Faber, 1959).

is because the coffee in your cup knows that it is rotating *relative to the distant stars,* argued Berkeley in effect, that it rises up the sides of the cup in protest.

He was 150 years ahead of his time. Although his ideas gained some currency in the eighteenth century, they were regarded as a little strange and largely ignored. How could the mere existence of the distant stars affect the motion of tangible objects on Earth? What magic influence reached out across the emptiness of space to keep a hold on the water in a bucket? The idea was not taken seriously by Berkeley's contemporaries. But the spark was there, ready to be fanned into flame in the second half of the nineteenth century by Ernst Mach, whose name is immortalized in the number used to measure the speed of aircraft relative to the speed of sound.

Mach was born in 1838 in a part of Austria-Hungary that is now in Czechoslovakia. He studied at the University of Vienna and was awarded his Ph.D. in 1860 for work on electricity. After lecturing in Vienna and at Graz, in 1867 he became professor of experimental physics at the University of Prague, where he stayed for twenty-eight years before returning to Vienna as Professor of History and Theory of Inductive Sciences. In spite of a stroke in 1897 that affected his right side, on his retirement from the university in 1901 he served for twelve years in the upper chamber of the Austrian Parliament and remained mentally active until his death in 1916, the day after his seventy-eighth birthday. His interests ranged widely across experimental and theoretical physics and the philosophy of science. His influence on Einstein came through the book *Die Mechanik,* published in 1883 (and translated as *The Science of Mechanics* in a 1919 edition from Open Court publishers, Chicago). Among other things, this set out Mach's thoughts on inertia. Perhaps we ought to remind ourselves of the kind of inertial forces that worried Mach, and had worried Bishop Berkeley, before we see how Einstein attempted to explain them away.

THE CENTRIFUGAL MYTH

The centrifugal force that physicists invoke to explain the motion of bodies in a rotating frame of reference doesn't really exist. It is one of several fictitious forces that are useful in understanding the movement of objects in such a frame, all of which owe their origin to the reluctance of moving objects to deviate from a straight line—their inertia. The trick is to imagine the rotation brought to a halt, and then to apply the appropriate imaginary force to ensure that objects move with respect to the now stationary frame of reference just as they do when it is rotating and there are no fictitious forces at work.

Perhaps the simplest example of this kind is the Coriolis "force." It explains, among other things, why Britain's weather comes from the west, off the Atlantic.

Because the Earth is rotating, air at the equator has angular momentum. It is moving from west to east, circling once around the Earth's 40,035-kilometer circumference in twenty-four hours. In other words, it has a speed of 1,668 kilometers per hour. Air at the poles is not rotating at all and has no angular momentum. At intermediate latitudes there are the appropriate intermediate states. The circulation of the atmosphere is driven by the heat of the Sun, which warms the tropics and sets air in motion by convection. Hot air rises and moves north or south to higher latitudes, displaced by cool air moving in to the equator at sea level. When the warm air cools and sinks, it reaches the surface of the Earth at some latitude between the equator and a pole. There the appropriate angular momentum for each packet of air is less than at the equator, but the air from the tropics still carries its own momentum, a memory of its origin, until friction gets to work and slows it down. It tries to continue to move in the same direction and at the same speed it was moving before. So it tends to move from west to east, overtaking the rotation of the Earth at its new latitude.

Similarly, air returning to the equator at sea level blows not just due south (in the northern hemisphere) but also to the west, lagging behind the rotation of the spinning Earth at lower latitudes. So the trade winds blow from the northeast to the southwest.

From the point of view of anyone who lives on the Earth and wants to regard the Earth's surface as a stable frame of reference, it is as if a force were pushing the winds to one side. This is the Coriolis force. It has to be invoked to calculate accurately the flight of an artillery shell, for example, and to "explain" why railway tracks that run from north to south get worn down more on one side.

You can think of centrifugal force another way. When you stand on solid ground, gravity (a real force) pulls you down. If there were no ground in the way to stop you, you would fall freely toward the center of the Earth. The ground stops you by applying a force that cancels out the acceleration due to gravity. The ground pushes up, your weight pushes down, and the two forces are equal and opposite, so you stay put.

Now imagine yourself in a rapidly rotating cylinder that is in free fall (perhaps in orbit around the Earth). If you are in contact with the rotating wall of the cylinder, your natural state of motion, in line with Newton's insight, would be to continue in a straight line, at a tangent to the rotating cylinder. But you can't do this, because the floor of the cylinder presses against your feet, and keeps pushing you sideways, off your straight-line trajectory. The result of all this sideways pushing is that you move in a circle, effectively glued to the inside of the spinning cylinder. (The same thing happens in the rotating drum at the fair.) The real force is the inward push of the floor (or wall) of the cylinder on your feet, or on your back. The net effect is that you stay where you are as far as the wall of the rotating cylinder is concerned, but follow a circular path from the point of view of an observer outside the cylinder. A change in the direction of motion is just as much an acceleration as a change in speed is, and if the cylinder rotates at the appropriate speed you will feel exactly the same accelerating force as you do on the surface of the Earth—stand on a weighing machine on the wall of the rotating cylinder, and it will register the weight you expect it to show in your own bathroom. It *feels* the same as when you are standing on a solid floor on the surface of the Earth, and the human brain can easily be fooled in such circumstances into thinking that the cylinder is still and that gravity is holding things "down" on the floor of the cylinder. But try pouring liquids, or bouncing a ball, in such an environment, and the truth soon becomes obvious as Coriolis forces come into play.

Apart from a cup of coffee, the most familiar example of all this is the great Foucault pendulum in the science museum. Set swinging ponderously to and fro in one plane of space, the pendulum (and all other massive, perfectly suspended pendulums) keeps swinging in the same plane, even while the Earth rotates underneath it. To us, standing on the rotating Earth, it is the line of the pendulum's swing that seems to rotate, at a rate that depends on the latitude where the pendulum is set up. Like the coffee in your cup, the pendulum "knows" where all of the matter in the Universe is and holds itself steady compared with all the distant galaxies.

Neither Coriolis force nor centrifugal force exist in the absence of rotation relative to the distant galaxies. They are sometimes referred to as "fictitious forces," with the implication that they are less real than, say, the force of gravity. But that kind of description reveals our inner preconceptions once again; how can we say that any force is more or less "real" than another? What matters is whether we can obtain a good description of how objects move by allowing for the effects of the forces, and provided that both are included, the motion of objects in a rotating system can be calculated correctly using Newton's laws and ignoring the motion. That is a powerful incentive to use them for practical engineering and physics. But *why* is inertia different in a rotating frame of reference? Where do the Coriolis and centrifugal forces come from? Berkeley and Mach simply said, in effect, "from the fixed stars." Einstein tried to put that on a mathematical footing.

THE PHILOSOPHY BEHIND RELATIVITY

Einstein knew Mach's book from his student days and later wrote enthusiastically to Mach of his admiration for it. Mach, in the first decade of the twentieth century, was equally enthusiastic about Einstein's work on Special Relativity. In Special Relativity inertial frames have essentially the same status as in Newtonian mechanics. For Newton, inertia was intrinsic to a body; for Mach, inertia was caused by the "fixed stars." It made no difference, to his way of thinking, whether we thought of the Earth as rotating relative to the distant stars, or of the stars rotating around the stationary Earth. Either way, if the stars were removed, inertia would disappear with them, and the effects of rotation, such as the bulging outward of the Earth at the equator, would disappear with them as well.

Mach scarcely contributed anything more than Berkeley to the argument, but by the accident of his birth date he was saying the same things about motion, space, and the fixed stars in the 1880s, just at a time when a profound rethinking of the nature of space, time, and the Universe was about to appear. Like Berkeley, Mach said that the outward forces—centrifugal forces—are produced when a body rotates relative to the fixed stars, but he went a little farther than Berkeley in suggesting that "it does not matter if we think of the Earth as turning round on its axis, or at rest while the fixed stars revolve around it." It is the *relative* motion that is responsible for the outward forces, which in this case make the Earth bulge out at the equator. Einstein learned of the idea through Mach's work, and it was Einstein who dubbed the concept "Mach's Principle." It removed the Newtonian concept of absolute space and insisted that all motion is relative—influential ideas in the development of both the Special and the General theories of relativity. But it remained controversial and was denounced by, among others, Lenin and Bertrand Russell.

One of the foundation stones of Einstein's General

Theory is the principle of equivalence. In Newton's Second Law, force equals mass times acceleration. The mass involved represents the amount of a body's resistance to changes in motion, its inertial mass. The gravitational force between two objects also depends on mass. This mass reaches out across space to influence other objects. It is the gravitational mass. Gravity is also proportional to mass, and there is no way to distinguish between the gravitational mass and the inertial mass of an object. Why should these two masses be identical? After all, one represents the ability of a body to reach out and pull on other bodies, while the other represents the resistance of a body to being pushed by other bodies. Logically they could be quite different from one another. Einstein argued that the similarity between gravitational and inertial mass arises because inertial forces themselves are really gravitational in origin.

You can make a good hand-waving argument in these terms. The distant stars reach out with their gravitational fingers to keep a hold on everything here on Earth. When we try to move something, accelerating it in a straight line or rotating it, it is accelerating through that gravitational web, and some sort of back reaction produces the familiar gut-wrenching forces we experience on a roller coaster or a merry-go-round. But *what* sort of back reaction? The "obvious" possibility is that disturbing the motion of a body causes some sort of gravitational ripple to spread out through the Universe to the distant stars, or galaxies, which then send back a reflection of some kind, trying to maintain the status quo. But if signals can travel no faster than the speed of light, as Einstein's equations require, then how is it that when I poke at a pencil on my desk it instantaneously knows just how much it should resist my push—how much inertia it should have? The answer comes from understanding the way matter, space, and time are inextricably linked into one whole. According to this Machian interpretation of Einstein's work, the structure of space-time here and now, where I am standing, depends on the average distribution of all the matter in the Universe. And the inertia of an object here and now—its resistance to an applied force—depends on the structure of space-time. The principle—the philosophy, if you like—

seems clear enough. The trouble came when Einstein tried to build that philosophy into the equations of General Relativity.

When Einstein set out to develop his General Theory of Relativity, he intended to include Mach's Principle in it—or, rather, he intended that Mach's Principle should be a natural consequence of his theory. He thought he had succeeded. The equations of General Relativity are supposed to include the effects of distant masses (today we talk about distant galaxies rather than the fixed stars) against which accelerations, inertial forces, and rotations are measured. One of the oddities of this, however, is that Einstein's equations only produce the right Machian influences in one particular kind of universe, one in which there is enough matter to bend space gravitationally back upon itself, so that the universe is closed. If this is correct, it means that we live in a vast black hole and has important implications for the present debate about the origin and ultimate fate of the Universe, which is discussed in Part Three. Mach, who never liked the General Theory, died in 1916 while planning a book that would rebut this claim, and there has been intermittent debate ever since about whether or not relativity really does include Mach's Principle in a mathematically satisfactory way. The relevant equations are horribly complicated (one reason why Mach rejected the theory), and the debate remained one for mathematicians and philosophers alone until very recently. But now it seems that a solution to those equations has been found, vindicating Einstein, and it may be possible to design a practicable experiment that would test the accuracy of the version of Mach's Principle incorporated in Einstein's theory.

If the local reference frame, the standard of rest, really is determined by some averaged-out effect of all the matter in the Universe, there ought to be some way to arrange a local concentration of matter to produce a measurable change in the standard of rest. Imagine an object placed within a large spherical shell of material, with the shell itself made to rotate compared with the distant galaxies. If Mach's Principle is correct, there ought to be a small dragging effect from the rotating shell, trying to tug the body inside around with it. And any theory, such as General Relativity, that is alleged to incorporate Mach's Principle should first of all predict such a dragging of the inertial frame inside the shell, and second tell us how big the effect ought to be. As early as 1918, H. Thirring solved the relevant relativistic equations, but only using what is called the "weak field approximation," which applies only to relatively modest gravitational fields. The results showed that Einstein's equations did indeed require a Machian dragging of inertial frames inside a rotating shell of matter, or close to a rotating mass like the Earth, but the predicted size of the effect was far too small to be measured.

In the 1950s, the debate was revived by Robert Dicke of Princeton University, who pointed out that nobody had yet solved the corresponding equations for the strong field case, which would apply to a very massive shell that, according to Mach, ought to *dominate* the inertial system in its interior. Over the past twenty years, Jeffrey Cohen of Yale University, and a series of colleagues, have tackled the strong-field case step by step. They have now shown that there are solutions to the relevant relativistic equations and that they do indeed make "Machian" predictions about the behavior of rotating objects locked inside very massive rotating shells of matter. And while all this abstruse mathematical theorizing has been going on, new discoveries about the Universe have opened up practical possibilities for testing the numbers that are now beginning to come out of the equations.

The details are, unfortunately, complex. They involve ten nonlinear simultaneous differential equations, which are as nasty as they sound. Einstein set the equations up but couldn't solve them. And he knew that if no solutions to these equations existed, then General Relativity could not explain the swing of a pendulum or the swirl of liquid in a bucket and would have to be scrapped. Interestingly, though, the mathematics that has now been used to solve the problem Einstein gave up on was already in existence in Einstein's day. It uses a method devised by the French mathematician Elie Cartan, who lived from 1869 to 1951 but whose work became widely known only toward the end of his life. His work on calculus and differential geometry, now regarded as some of the most original mathematical work of the twentieth century, provided Cohen and his colleagues with the mathematical tool they needed, and Cohen proudly points out, in this computer-dominated age, that all of the computations themselves were carried out using nothing more sophisticated than pencil and paper—quite a lot of paper. Cohen's solutions, assuming they stand up to scrutiny by other mathematicians, therefore fill in an embarrassing gap in General Relativity. They also provide a way for mathematical physicists to tackle the puzzle of what goes on in very dense rotating objects, such as the neutron stars that power pulsars. And they provide the framework for an understanding of how the coffee in your cup knows where it is, and how it is moving, compared with the average distribution of all of the matter in the Universe. Ponder that the next time you reach for the cream.

Rotation involving strong gravitational fields also crops up at the site of a spinning neutron star—a pulsar—or a black hole. Just possibly, the numbers now coming out of the equations set up, but not solved, by Einstein almost seventy years ago will make a prediction about the observable properties of such objects that will provide a test of the theory. Alternatively, even the weak-field solution may yet come up with a test, thanks to the improvements in technology since Thirring's day. A team at Stanford University has been planning, since the 1960s, an experiment involving a weightless gyroscope in orbit around the Earth. Such an instrument would be influenced by the rotation of the Earth itself, dragging the local inertial frame around with it. In the weightless conditions of orbit, even these subtle influences might be detectable, because there would be no friction forces to confuse the issue. It is touch and go whether the Stanford weightless gyro experiment could measure the effects predicted by Thirring, even if it does ever get off the ground. But even the possibility indicates the enormous strides made over the past few decades.

Maybe, though, we don't really need any of these subtleties. What of the cosmological implications of Mach's Principle that I alluded to earlier? Mach, like Berkeley, talked of the "fixed stars" because nobody then knew that our Milky Way is just one galaxy among millions scattered through space. But even before Hubble's survey of the nebulae showed that our Milky Way Galaxy is just one of the islands in the Universe, observations had shown that the Milky Way is a flattened, disc-shaped system. Thomas Wright knew that—Herschel and others had put the idea on a respectable footing before Mach was born. Our Galaxy is a flattened, disc-shaped system, its shape determined by rotation and centrifugal force. Suppose Mach, or some other nineteenth-century astronomer, had taken the evidence for the shape of the Milky Way and considered that evidence in the light of Mach's Principle. The argument might have gone like this. Centrifugal forces caused by motion relative to the fixed stars make water go up the side of a bucket. The hypothesis is that these forces arise because the water is rotating compared with the fixed stars. But now we see that the "fixed stars" are themselves part of a system that is rotating and is distorted by centrifugal forces. Either Newton was right, and the system of the fixed stars is rotating, as a whole, relative to absolute space; or, if Mach is correct, there must be, far beyond the Milky Way, some distribution of matter that establishes a frame of reference against which the rotation of our Galaxy is measured.

The existence of vast numbers of far-distant galaxies could have been *predicted* in the nineteenth century on the basis of known facts about the Milky Way and Mach's Principle. If the prediction had ever been made, Edwin Hubble's pioneering work in the 1920s, which established the scale of the Universe, might have come as less of a surprise and been seen as confirming the accuracy of both Mach's Principle and General Relativity.

All very well, you may say, but nobody ever did make such a prediction. That's true. And I wonder just how seriously any such prediction would have been taken, in the light—or perhaps I should say darkness—of what happened to another philosophical speculation, which was made in the nineteenth century and earlier and that ought, with hindsight, to have led to the prediction that the Universe would be found to be evolving.

THE DARK NIGHT SKY

The Universe we live in is not only dark and empty, it is also cold. This is another way of saying it is dark, since hot things, like the Sun, radiate energy in the form of light. It is one of the fundamental laws of nature—the Second Law of Thermodynamics—that energy moves from a hotter object to a cooler one, so that over a long enough period of time differences in temperature tend to get smoothed out. In view of this, it is startling to find that the cold, dark Universe is dotted with very bright, hot objects, the stars. At least it *ought* to be startling, but we are so used to the appearance of the dark night sky that we take this arrangement for granted and never stop to think that the Universe is in a very unusual state, one that cannot last forever, or even for very long on the cosmic time scale, according to the most basic physical laws. The darkness of the night sky is a puzzle that needs explaining, and the explanation of the puzzle tells us fundamental things about the Universe we live in.

The puzzle is often referred to as "Olbers' Paradox," a name popularized in the 1950s by cosmologist Hermann Bondi in honor of Heinrich Olbers, the German astronomer who lived from 1758 to 1840 and wrote a landmark paper discussing the puzzle in 1823. But the name is an unfortunate misnomer. Just as Mach was not the first person to discuss "Mach's Principle," so Olbers was not the first person to puzzle over "Olbers' Paradox"; worse, for those who like meticulous accuracy in such matters, the puzzle is not really a paradox at all, just a puzzle, albeit a particularly interesting and informative one. Nevertheless, the name has stuck. So what *is* Olbers' Paradox?

The puzzle rests upon three assumptions: that the Universe is infinitely big, that it is filled with stars more or less like the Sun and the stars of the Milky Way, and that it is eternal and unchanging. In that case, when we look out into the Universe, we ought to see stars in every direction. So why do we see dark spaces between the stars? If you imagine drawing a straight line out into the universe in any direction—a "line of sight"—then in an infinite universe uniformly filled with stars that line must come to a star somewhere. Since light travels in straight lines, light from that star ought to travel along the line of sight to us. Everywhere we look we should see a star; the whole sky should be a blaze of light.

This is just a simple argument, the kind astronomers refer to, for obvious reasons, as "hand waving." But the "paradox" can be put on a secure mathematical footing with the aid of a little elementary geometry. Imagine the Earth at the center of a large sphere encompassing many stars. There will be stars dotted around the boundary of that sphere, and we can, for the sake of argument, imagine a thin shell around the sphere, like the skin on an orange, that contains a certain number of stars. If the numbers we are playing with are big enough (easy to arrange in an infinite universe), we can say, in round terms, that each star contributes the same average brightness to the appearance of the night sky from Earth. The brightness of each star depends on its real, absolute brightness, of course, and is inversely proportional to the square of its distance from us. So the whole shell of stars—the whole skin—contributes a brightness equal to the number of stars in the shell, multiplied by the standard brightness, divided by the square of the distance. And the distance to each of the stars in the spherical shell is just the radius of the sphere.

Individual stars that are all the same intrinsic brightness look fainter if they are farther away. So you might think that shells of this kind, dotted with stars, will appear fainter if they have a larger radius. But the geometry doesn't work like that. A bigger shell is more distant from us, but it also contains more stars, because it is bigger. If the stars are distributed uniformly through infinite space, it is straightforward to calculate how many stars each shell contains. And because the surface area of a sphere goes as the square of its radius, it turns out that the number of stars in each shell also goes as the square of its radius. The brightness of each star is *reduced* as the square of the radius, but the number of stars in each shell is *increased*

by exactly the proportion that cancels this decrease out.*
The result is that every spherical shell contributes the
same brightness to the night sky!

This is far worse than the hand-waving argument
suggested, because in an infinite universe there must be
an infinite number of such shells, so their combined effect
would be an infinitely bright sky. Of course, the nearer
stars will block out the light from more distant ones, and
that removes the infinities—it merely leaves the prediction
that the entire sky should be as bright as the surface of a
typical star, as bright as the surface of the Sun. The
puzzle becomes not why the sky is dark at *night*, but why
it is so dark even in the daytime.

There is a technique of argument called *reductio ad
absurdum*, which depends on starting out from some basic
assumption and reaching a clearly ridiculous conclusion.
That establishes beyond doubt that the initial assumption
was wrong. Olbers' Paradox is that simple assumptions
lead inevitably to the conclusion that the sky should be
bright, but in fact the sky is dark. So at least one of the
basic assumptions must be wrong. You can't get around it
by acknowledging that the Milky Way Galaxy is just an
island in space, so that we run out of stars to count at the
edge of our Galaxy. The same line of argument holds up if
we replace the word "stars" by the word "galaxies" throughout. What Olbers' Paradox is telling us is that the Universe is not in thermodynamic equilibrium. Most of it is
cold, in spite of the efforts of all the stars in all the galaxies
pouring out energy to warm it up.

Just how surprised you are by the discovery that the
sky is dark at night depends on how strongly you hold to
the initial assumptions that lead to the paradoxical conclusion—and that depends very much on culture, the hab-
its of scientific thinking you grow up with. Indeed, the
first astronomers to notice the puzzle of the dark night sky
were happily ignorant of the full force of the argument
and so expressed little surprise at it. This, perhaps, is why

---

*A little thought explains why. The brightness of each star at a certain
distance depends on the distance squared because the light from that star is
filling an expanding bubble of space that has a surface area proportional to
radius squared. The geometry is symmetrical, which is why the distances
cancel out.

they didn't get the "paradox" named after them, although Ed Harrison, an astronomer now working at the University of Massachusetts, has done his best to set the historical record straight.* And this certainly helps to bring out just what it is that the misnamed Olbers' Paradox is telling us about the Universe—which of the basic assumptions must be wrong.

THE ROOTS OF THE RIDDLE

The first basic assumption is that the Universe is infinite in extent, and that is a relatively recent concept. The ancients were happy with such ideas as a flat Earth riding on the back of a giant turtle and never contemplated the possibility of an infinite universe. More recently, the accepted picture was of the Earth surrounded by a series of celestial spheres carrying the planets, with the visible stars fixed to an outermost sphere around the Earth, like tiny lights in the dome of some large but very definitely finite cathedral. It took the Englishman Thomas Digges, writing in 1576, to take this Ptolemaic idea and disperse the single crystal sphere of the fixed stars into an endless infinity of space stretching out across the Universe. Digges takes the credit for introducing the concept of infinity to the modern picture of the Universe (although, to be fair, the Greek thinker Democritus also considered infinite space). And Digges also acknowledged the need to explain why, in an infinite universe, the sky should be dark at night. As Harrison reports, Digges believed that the sky was dark because the more distant stars were simply too faint to be seen. That was a perfectly acceptable "explanation" in the late sixteenth century. It doesn't hold water, we know now, because of the way the light from the more distant spherical shells adds up. But Digges introduced the idea of

*Several times, in fact, most recently in Science, Volume 226, pages 941–45. This review includes references to all the major sources of information about Olbers' Paradox.

an infinite universe filled with stars, and he noticed the need to explain why we see dark gaps between the stars. He set astronomers on the path that would lead them to Olbers' Paradox.

In 1610 Johannes Kepler took up the puzzle, and Harrison's search of the historical records suggests that Kepler was the first person to realize that the darkness of the night sky directly conflicts with the idea of an infinite universe filled with bright stars. It might have been "Kepler's Paradox"—but Kepler never set the puzzle up in those terms, because he believed that there must be an edge to the Universe, and so he saw the darkness of the night sky simply as confirmation that the Universe is finite in extent. In effect, Kepler said that when we look through the gaps between the stars we see a dark wall that surrounds the universe. But when Edmond Halley, of comet fame, took up the puzzle in his turn in 1721, he went back to the idea that more distant stars are simply too faint to be seen. And so the stage was set for the man who first presented the puzzle in more or less the form outlined here—not Olbers, but the Swiss astronomer Jean-Philippe Loÿs de Chéseaux, born in 1718.

De Chéseaux was a child prodigy who was taught by his grandfather, himself a distinguished scholar, and was responsible, at the age of eighteen, for the construction of the first observatory in Switzerland. He made his name in the early 1740s with the discovery of two comets and wrote a book about these observations. It was in an appendix to that book that he put forward his version of the dark night sky puzzle. De Chéseaux didn't go in for hand-waving arguments. He calculated the distances to the stars, as best he could by comparing their brightnesses with those of the Sun and the planets, and he calculated how much of the sky a star like the Sun would cover at the appropriate distance from us. Step by step, he moved on to the conclusion that if stars are spaced through the Universe at about the distances they are spaced near us, then in a sphere as large as (in modern terms) 10^{15} light-years (a million billion light-years), there would be a star visible in every direction that we look into space. So either the stars are not distributed uniformly through infinite space, or something stops us from seeing the light from distant stars.* Unlike Halley and Digges, de Chéseaux realized that the geometry of the situation ensures that the faintness of distant stars is exactly canceled out by their large numbers and that we cannot simply say that the distant stars are too faint to be seen. He suggested instead that empty space must absorb the energy in the light from the stars, so that it gets fainter and fainter as it travels through space. And that was the idea that was taken up by Heinrich Olbers in 1823 in *his* discussion of the puzzle.

Olbers was born near Bremen in 1758 and studied medicine at Göttingen University, where he also attended lectures in physics and astronomy. Throughout his career as a doctor, astronomy remained a consuming interest; Olbers turned the second floor of his house into an observatory, and he discovered both comets and asteroids using his own telescopes. But it was in the year he retired from medical practice, at the age of sixty-four, that he published his discussion of the puzzle of the dark night sky. Olbers thought that the resolution of the puzzle could be found in the form of cold material between the stars—a thin gruel of gas and dust spread through space. Clouds of such material would absorb radiation from distant stars, blocking out their light and heat from us. The argument made sense as far as it went, but it didn't go far enough. What happens to all the energy the clouds absorb? It makes the clouds hotter, of course, and eventually they become so hot that they radiate energy in their turn. In an infinite and unchanging universe, there has been ample time—literally forever—for the clouds to heat up in this way, to the point where they are in perfect equilibrium with the radiation reaching them from the stars. In such a state, the energy they absorb would be exactly balanced by the energy they radiate, and we would be back with the puzzle of why the sky is dark at night. Olbers simply had not thought through the full implications of the assumption that the Universe is unchanging. That assumption was so deeply ingrained by his cultural conditioning that it probably never occurred to him to question it. But as soon

---

*And once again, of course, you can make the equivalent argument translating "stars" into "galaxies."

as those implications are spelled out, it begins to look as if *that* is the assumption that has to be discarded to avoid the absurdity of Olbers' Paradox.

SOLVING THE PUZZLE

With telescopes that probe far into the depths of space, Hubble and his successors have shown that the Universe we live in is at the very least so big that it can be treated as infinite for the purposes of the puzzle of the dark night sky. And they have shown that it is remarkably uniform, with galaxies and clusters of galaxies spread through the Universe in all directions as far as we can see. That leaves only the assumption of constancy to be challenged, and, of course, Hubble also showed that the Universe is not constant. The Universe is expanding, with galaxies moving farther apart from one another as time passes. Light from distant galaxies is red-shifted—it is stretched to longer wavelengths, which correspond to less energy. Could *that* explain where the energy from all those distant stars and galaxies has gone, and why the sky is dark at night? Maybe, but even that is only part of the answer. The other part concerns a more abrupt change, something that the seventeenth- and eighteenth-century philosophers and astronomers ought, ironically, to have been better conditioned to accept than ourselves, in some ways. Suppose the Universe had a definite beginning—that there is an "edge" to the Universe, not in space but in *time*.

Because light travels at a finite speed, when we look at distant stars and galaxies, we see them as they were long ago. Light from a star 5 light-years away from us takes 5 years to reach us, insofar as we can measure its journey in terms of clocks here on Earth. Similarly, light from a galaxy 50,000 light-years away takes 50,000 years to reach us. The "paradox" is only a puzzle provided there have been stars and galaxies around in the Universe long enough for enough light to reach us to make the night sky blaze. If there was a definite moment of creation, and if it was recent enough, then there is no paradox. This is the whole crux of the matter.

With hindsight, it is astonishing that Isaac Newton and his contemporaries didn't hit on this explanation of the puzzle. The finite speed of light had been determined by the Danish astronomer Ole Roemer in 1676, from studies of the eclipses of the moons of Jupiter, and was well known to Newton, who mentioned it in his *Opticks*, published in 1704. When Halley presented his two papers on the puzzle of the dark night sky to the Royal Society in 1721, Newton was in the chair. Yet neither he nor anyone else for two centuries pointed out that the puzzle could be solved by assuming that no stars existed until relatively recently.

This is even more baffling in view of the accepted teaching of the Church in those days, that the Creation took place in 4004 B.C. Any astronomer of Newton's day who really believed that could have said immediately that no stars farther away than 4,004 plus 1,721 light-years could be visible yet on Earth, and a sphere of space less than 5,000 light-years in diameter is far too small to hold enough stars to make the night sky bright. Perhaps the philosophers' failure to point this out indicates how little faith they had in the "official" date for the Creation, rather than their ignorance of the implications! But Edgar Allan Poe pointed out in 1848 that by looking out into space and back in time we may see the darkness that existed before the stars were born, and the theme was taken up and elaborated by the British scientist Fournier d'Albe in 1907.*

So there are two solutions to Olbers' Paradox, or at least two variations on the theme of change. The first is that the energy of the light from distant galaxies has been so weakened by the red shift of the expanding Universe that it cannot light the night sky; the second is that the Universe came into existence only a short time ago and has not yet had time to settle into thermodynamic equilibrium—there has been no time for the radiation from all the stars to fill up the cold, dark spaces in between. The debate, which now goes back four hundred years to the time of Digges, still isn't over, for there are still discussions today about which of these effects is the more important.

---

*Details are given by Harrison.

One line of attack is expressed strongly by Hermann Bondi, the man responsible for reviving interest in Olbers' Paradox in the 1950s. In those days, Bondi was cofounder of the idea of the Steady State universe. This intriguing idea said that even though the Universe is expanding and clusters of galaxies are moving apart from one another, it might still be essentially unchanging, because new matter could be created, out of nothing at all, to fill in the gaps by creating new stars and galaxies as the old ones moved apart. The idea gained some supporters in the 1950s but lost ground in the 1960s when evidence came in that there really was a moment of creation, that the Universe was born out of a Big Bang some 15 billion years ago. But, obviously, in a genuine steady state universe, infinite in both time and space, Olbers' Paradox is a real problem, and the only solution to the problem is that the energy of starlight gets dissipated by the red shift.

These days, Bondi prefers, as I do, to discuss the puzzle in terms of thermodynamic equilibrium.* The temperature at the surface of a star is about 5,000 K, but the temperature of interstellar space is only a few K, a few degrees above the absolute zero of temperature, which is -273°C. And a star, or a galaxy of stars, cannot last forever. Its heat and light come from thermonuclear reactions that convert hydrogen into heavier elements. There is a limit to how much energy is available, and the life of a star is only a few thousand million years. There simply is not enough energy available to heat the whole Universe up to the point where the night sky blazes with light. Indeed, the trend is actually all the other way. The stars are inexorably burning out, and when thermodynamic equilibrium is reached—if it ever is—it won't be at a temperature of 5,000K but at a temperature a few degrees above absolute zero, a few K. The puzzle has now been turned on its head—not "Why are the gaps between stars so dark?" but "Why are there any bright stars at all?" And the answer, once again, is that the Universe has been created in a state very different from thermodynamic equilibrium and that it was created in such a state not more than a few stellar lifetimes ago.

---

*See his contribution to *Science Update,* edited by H. Messel (Oxford: Pergamon Press, 1983).

Ed Harrison puts it poetically: "Through the gaps between stars we look back to the beginning of the Universe." And what do we see in those gaps? A faint hiss of radiation, with a very uniform energy equivalent to a temperature of about 3 K. That radiation is the echo of creation, the very highly red-shifted remains of the energy of a fireball more intense than any star. The expanding Universe *has* been responsible for the darkness of the night sky, after all.

The philosophers of centuries gone by could not have anticipated the existence of this background radiation, nor could they have specified the nature of the moment of creation. But from the evidence of the dark night sky they could, and should, have realized that there was indeed a beginning to the Universe, and not so very long ago compared with the ages of the stars. Having missed the opportunity of applying Mach's Principle to deduce that the Universe is much bigger than they had imagined, they also missed the opportunity of using Olbers' Paradox to deduce that the Universe is much younger than they had imagined. The philosophers' track record in interpreting the Universe is far from impressive; and this is a recurrent feature of scientists' thinking about the Universe, even in the twentieth century. There seems to have been a pervasive attitude, the cultural conditioning of our times, that while these abstract theories were intriguing to play with, they couldn't *really* be telling us about the actual creation and evolution of the Universe we live in. That smacked of metaphysics, and consciously or unconsciously the early cosmologists, from the 1920s to the 1960s, failed to grasp the genuine metaphysical import of their work. So perhaps we shouldn't be too hard on the philosophers of old for their failures to make the most of the evidence they had available. The remarkable thing is that a few simple observations and some careful thought *are* enough to reveal deep truths about the Universe we live in. But the time has come to leave the metaphysics to one side once again and get back to the work of astronomers in the 1920s and 1930s, who combined Einstein's General Theory of Relativity and Hubble's observations of the expanding Universe to bring about the birth of modern cosmology and begin to probe the mystery of the Big Bang itself.

PART TWO

THE BIG BANG

I am always surprised when a young man tells me he wants to work at cosmology; I think of cosmology as something that happens to one, not something one can choose.

William McCrea

CHAPTER FOUR

THE COSMIC EGG

Modern cosmology began with Einstein's General Theory of Relativity, and his first cosmological paper, in 1917, in which he struggled to make the equations of relativity fit the mistaken belief of the time that the Universe was static and eternal. But these ideas did not spring out of nothing at all. The seeds, in the form of ideas about curved space and non-Euclidean geometry, were planted by the middle of the nineteenth century. And even the idea that these concepts might have some bearing on the real Universe was voiced before the end of that century by the Englishman William Clifford, who unfortunately died in 1879 (the year Einstein was born) at the age of thirty-four, before he had time to develop his thoughts into what might have become the first modern cosmological model.

The pioneers of the mathematical study of non-Euclidean geometry included Karl Friedrich Gauss, the brilliant German theorist who lived from 1777 to 1855; although his investigation of geometries in which parallel lines do not behave in the common-sense way of the everyday world and of Euclid's geometry was fairly limited, he deserves pride of place for coining the phrase that translates as "non-Euclidean geometry." Pride of place for working out a *comprehensive* non-Euclidean geometry, however, goes jointly to the Russian Nikolai Ivanovich Lobachevski (immortalized in an entertaining ditty by Tom Lehrer) and the Hungarian Janos Bolyai, working independently of each other in the 1820s. Lobachevski and Bolyai each came up with specific kinds of non-Euclidean geometry; in 1854 another German, Bernhard Riemann, put this branch of mathematics on a secure footing by looking at the whole basis of geometry, in a mathematical sense, and laying the groundwork for a whole range of different possible geometries, each as valid as each of the others, with Euclid's geometry included as just one example of the wealth of mathematical possibilities. And Riemann's work, by its generality, allowed for the possibility of developing geometry into the realms of more than three dimensions. The new mathematics that developed in the wake of Riemann's work became a vital tool for Einstein; it is Riemannian geometry that, among other things, allows the possibility of investigating mathematically a theoretical model of the Universe that is a four-dimensional analog of a sphere, a "hypersphere" in which each of the three dimensions of space that we experience directly is curved, with constant curvature, through a fourth dimension, doubling back upon itself in just the same way that "straight lines" drawn upon the surface of a globe double back upon themselves to make a "closed" universe.

Clifford helped to introduce these ideas to the English-speaking world. He translated Riemann's work into English, and like Riemann he was certainly aware of the possibility of a "finite but unbounded" universe, the higher-dimensional equivalent of the surface of a sphere. It was in 1870 that he read a paper before the Cambridge Philosophical Society in which he talked of "variation in the curvature of space" and made the analogy that "small portions of space *are* in fact of nature analogous to little hills on a surface which is on the average flat; namely, that the ordinary laws of geometry are not valid in them."[*]

---

[*]Quoted by North, page 73. In a posthumously published work *Common Sense of the Exact Sciences*, Clifford went even further, speculating that space may be curved evenly in all directions but that "its degree of curvature may change as a whole with time." This is a remarkable precursor of the expanding universe of relativistic cosmology. See Edward Harrison, *Cosmology*, page 155.

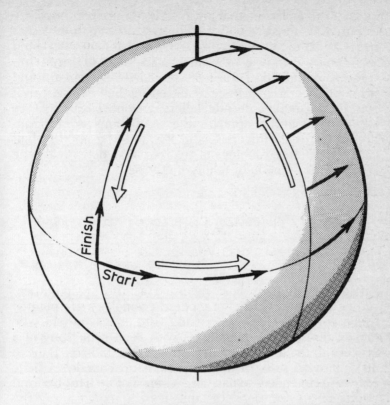

Figure 4.1 / A simple example of the oddities of non-Euclidean geometry. On the surface of a sphere, it is possible to take a little arrow (a vector) on a journey around the equator, up to the pole and back to its starting point. The direction in which the arrow points is very carefully kept the same on each stage of its journey. But when it gets back to the start, the arrow is pointing due north instead of due east!

J. D. North, in his book *The Measure of the Universe,*[*] mentions more than eighty scientific papers on the statics, dynamics, and kinematics of non-Euclidean geometry published in the half century ending in 1915. Any of those authors might, perhaps, have made the leap of imagination needed to suggest that the resulting equations could

---

*London: Oxford University Press, 1965.

be applied to the real Universe. But they did not. The required imaginative leap had to await the man who was never afraid to move into uncharted scientific territory and who built a complete new theory of gravity *and* the Universe with the aid of the tools provided by Riemann and his contemporaries. Einstein started the ball rolling. But it was to be another decade before anyone began to take seriously the idea of applying these equations as a description of the real Universe—and it was to be another half century before cosmologists realized just how "real" the resulting description of reality might be.

THE FATHERS OF COSMOLOGY

Einstein is perhaps best regarded as the "grandfather" rather than the "father" of modern cosmology. He pointed the way and set the ball rolling. But it was others who picked the ball up and ran off with it, at something of a tangent to the direction Einstein had first indicated. From 1917 onward, *all* the new mathematical models of the Universe included expansion, even before Hubble and Humason unequivocally established the expansion of the real Universe.

The first of these new models came hot on the heels of Einstein's static universe, from Willem de Sitter, the Dutchman who had passed on news of the General Theory of Relativity to Eddington in London. By 1915, when news of Einstein's new theory arrived in Leiden, de Sitter was already an experienced and senior astronomer. He had been born in 1872 and studied at the University of Groningen and at the Royal Observatory in Cape Town. He was awarded his Ph.D. in 1901, and by 1908 he was professor of theoretical astronomy at the University of Leiden. He later became in addition the director of the observatory at Leiden. He died in 1934 of pneumonia. Professor de Sitter had been one of the few astronomers to consider the implications of the Special Theory of Relativity for his craft—the theory was mostly seen as of interest to mathematicians, and of no practical relevance, in the first decade after it was published. And he was possibly the first person after Einstein to make any application of General Relativity, in part, of course, thanks to his luck in being one of the first people to hear of Einstein's new work.

When Einstein sought a description of the Universe in terms of General Relativity, that is exactly what he sought—a description, a single, unique solution to the equations. His static model, with the cosmological constant, seemed to fit the bill. But in one of the papers de Sitter sent to the Royal Astronomical Society in London in 1917, where it was read with great interest by the then Secretary of the society, Arthur Eddington, he showed that there was another solution to the equations, a solution that represented a different model universe. Obviously, both solutions could not represent the real world. We now know that neither of them represents the real world, and that is not seen as a problem. But at the time this was something of a blow to Einstein's theory, since it could be argued that if the theory offered a choice of universes, all consistent with the basic equations, it couldn't be telling us much, if anything, about the real Universe. That argument scarcely held up once the expansion of the Universe was understood, and astronomers realized that Einstein's equations had indeed been predicting this for at least ten years before Hubble's announcement of the red-shift—distance relation.

De Sitter's universe, like Einstein's, was in a mathematical sense static (and, like Einstein's, it included a cosmological constant). Unlike Einstein's, however, it contained no matter at all—it was a mathematical description of a completely empty universe. It is difficult to know what "static" means in a completely empty universe, since there is nothing that can be used as a marker against which motion can be measured. And when the theorists tried the mathematical equivalent of sprinkling a few specks of matter into de Sitter's universe they found a curious thing— these specks of matter, test particles, promptly rushed away from one another. Furthermore, when they calculated how light from one of the test particles would look as seen from one of the other test particles, the mathematicians found a red shift proportional to the distance between the particles. The de Sitter universe seemed to be static only because it was empty; in a universe containing just a little bit of matter, a few galaxies scattered here and there throughout space, astronomers would see exactly the red-shift–distance relation that Hubble and Humason were to find in the late 1920s. Much later, Eddington summed up the distinction between the first two relativistic cosmologies: Einstein's universe contains matter but no motion; de Sitter's universe contains motion but no matter.*

Eddington was one of the few people at the time to take seriously the expansion of a de Sitter universe containing a trace of matter. From the limited red-shift data that were coming in in the early 1920s, mainly from Slipher, Eddington concluded that de Sitter's variation on the relativistic theme was telling astronomers something about the real world. Eddington later developed his own variation, a model in which the universe sat for a long time (perhaps an infinitely long time) in a static state, like the Einstein universe, and then began to expand, like the de Sitter universe, as galaxies formed. But this model soon turned out to have little bearing on the nature of the real Universe. Einstein and de Sitter themselves had important second thoughts about their cosmological models once the red-shift–distance relation began to look like an important feature of the real Universe. In 1932 they put their heads together and came up with yet another model universe, the Einstein-de Sitter model (not to be confused with either of their solo efforts), in which they went back, in a sense, to the roots. The cosmological constant had originally been introduced to hold the model static, but the real Universe was seen to be expanding—so away with the constant. The earlier models had involved curved space (and in de Sitter's case, curved time as well), but there was no direct evidence that space was curved—so away with curved space (but not with curved *space-time*). The Einstein-de Sitter universe is the simplest universe that

---

*The aphorism is widely quoted and is generally attributed to Eddington. Although it is just possible that he picked it up from someone else, it has his characteristic ring about it, and it certainly appeared in a paper of his in the *Proceedings of the Physical Society* in 1932 (Volume 44, page 6).

can be constructed using the basic equations of General Relativity. It expands, as the equations require, and the space that is expanding is flat, the space of Special Relativity. And because nothing is added to the model to stop the inevitable happening when we look back in time, the model requires that there was a definite creation event, long ago, when the universe was born out of a mathematical point, a state of infinite density, called a singularity.

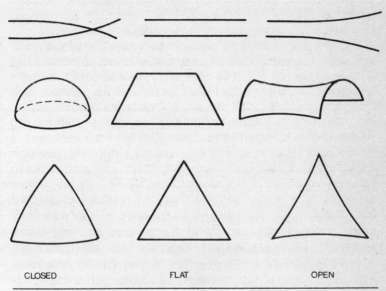

CLOSED   FLAT   OPEN

Figure 4.2 / Space may conform to one of three basic geometries. Although our space is three-dimensional, we can see the three possibilities by looking at the curvature of a two-dimensional "universe."

If it is positively curved, or closed, like the surface of a sphere, then "parallel" lines must eventually cross, and the angles of a triangle add up to more than 180 degrees.

If it is negatively curved, or open, like a saddle surface, then parallel lines diverge from one another and the angles of a triangle add up to less than 180 degrees.

Flat space corresponds to a special case, dividing the closed universes from the open universes. Only in this very special universe do parallel lines stay the same distance apart, and the angles of a triangle add up to precisely 180 degrees. Our Universe is very nearly flat. Explaining why this should be so is a fundamental cosmological problem.

As the simplest solution to the equations, the Einstein-de Sitter model is a very useful case study. It has pride of place in many courses on cosmology today, on the reasonable grounds that students ought to start with the simplest examples and work their way up to more complex and more interesting things. But it is far from clear just how much pride Einstein and de Sitter had in their creation. Chandrasekhar reports Eddington's comments just after the Einstein-de Sitter paper appeared in 1932:*

> Einstein came to stay with me shortly afterwards, and I took him to task about it. He replied "I did not think the paper very important myself, but de Sitter was keen on it." Just after Einstein had gone, de Sitter wrote to me announcing a visit. He added: "You will have seen the paper by Einstein and myself. I do not myself consider the result of much importance, but Einstein seemed to think that it was."

With hindsight, the key feature of the Einstein-de Sitter model, and the reason it is so widely taught, is that it includes that moment of creation, what we now call the Big Bang. But the hesitant way in which the two pioneers put forward their model perhaps indicates their own discomfort with this idea—an idea that was not theirs but that had come independently from the two other founders of modern cosmology in the 1920s and gained attention only after Hubble's publication of the red-shift–distance relation. The Big Bang was to become fully respectable only in the 1940s and it wasn't to become the *dominant* theory in cosmology until the 1960s.

Alexander Friedman never lived to see his work recognized as one of the key contributions to twentieth-century cosmology. Einstein had forced his equations to describe a static universe; de Sitter set up the equations of a static but empty universe, only for it to be found that with matter in it, that universe would expand. He found an expanding model of the Universe by accident. But Friedman was the first person to appreciate that expansion was an integral part of the relativistic description of reality and that it should be incorporated into cosmological models

---

Eddington, page 38.

from the outset. Although Friedman's life was short, it was full of incident. He was born in 1888 in what was then St. Petersburg, and studied mathematics at the city's university from 1906 to 1910. He became a member of the mathematics faculty of the university, served in the Russian air force during the First World War, lived through the revolution of 1917 to become a full professor at Perm University, and then returned to St. Petersburg in 1920 to carry out research at the Academy of Sciences. By the time he died in 1925, the city had become Leningrad.

Friedman's research interests originally centered on the Earth sciences—geomagnetism, hydromechanics, and meteorology. But as an able mathematician he was keenly interested in Einstein's work and in 1922 published his solutions to the cosmological equations of General Relativity. Two key features of this work remain fundamental to modern cosmology. First, from the outset Friedman realized he was dealing with a *family* of solutions to the equations. He understood that there was no unique solution, as Einstein had hoped, but instead a set of different variations, each describing a different kind of universe. Second, Friedman incorporated expansion into his models as of right. In a way, this echoed the work of Clifford in the 1880s, the idea that space might be uniformly curved, like the spherical surface of a soap bubble, but that this curvature might be changing with time—decreasing, perhaps—as the "bubble" expands. Friedman's models offered several variations on the theme.* In some versions, the bubble expanded forever; in others, it expanded up to a certain limiting size and then collapsed back upon itself as the force of gravity overcame the expansion. There were versions with a cosmological constant, and alternatives—the preferred alternatives today—in which the cosmological constant was set to be zero.† But in all the models there was at least a period—an interval of time— during which the whole universe expanded in such a way that it would produce a recession velocity proportional to distance.

*They were published in the German journal *Zeitschrift für Physik* in two papers, in 1922 and 1924.
†The Einstein-de Sitter model is a special, very simple solution to the Friedman equations.

Friedman also appreciated a point that cannot be stressed too highly and merits repetition. The red shift in the expanding Universe (or universes) is not caused by the galaxies moving apart from one another *through* space. It is caused by space itself stretching, like a stretching rubber sheet, between the galaxies. Space—or better, space-time—expands, and carries the galaxies along with it for the ride.

It is something of a mystery why Friedman's work, which was published in a well-known and widely read journal, was ignored. It was drawn to Einstein's attention by one of Friedman's colleagues on a visit to Berlin, and he acknowledged its accuracy in a brief note to Friedman, but even Einstein failed to realize that it might be telling us about the real Universe. Mathematicians in the 1920s had little contact with astronomers; the astronomers seldom followed new developments in mathematics; and Europe and America were much more separate scientific worlds then than they are today. So new mathematical ideas in Europe were not immediately matched up with new astronomical observations being made in the United States. And could there have been an element of prejudice among the theorists against the Russian mathematician better known for his work in meteorology? Whatever the reasons, Friedman died in obscurity in 1925—and, ironically, it may well have been his interest in meteorology that caused his death. Many of the official biographies report that Friedman died of typhoid. But according to the cosmologist George Gamow, the cause of his death was pneumonia, contracted following a chill Friedman caught while flying in a meteorological balloon. Gamow, who became a key figure among the next generation of cosmologists, ought to have known, since he was one of Friedman's students, and only moved to the United States in the middle 1930s.*

---

*See Gamow's autobiography, *My World Line* (New York: Viking Press, 1970). The story is repeated by Harrison in his book *Cosmology*, on page 297. Gamow also gives a curious insight into Einstein's initial response to Friedman's work. He says that Friedman wrote to Einstein about this before the work was published, but received no reply until a colleague from Russia who was visiting Berlin approached Einstein about it and obtained a "grumpy letter" acknowledging that the work was correct. Only after this grudging

. So it was left to the next person to solve Einstein's equations in the same way as Friedman (but quite independently, and with no knowledge of Friedman's work) to make the breakthrough into seeing these solutions accepted as a worthwhile tool for cosmologists probing the nature of the Universe. The breakthrough was made by Georges Lemaître, a Belgian cosmologist. His original publication, in an obscure Belgian journal in 1927, attracted little notice. But following the announcement of the redshift–distance relation, the ubiquitous Eddington learned of Lemaître's paper and arranged for an English translation, which appeared in the *Monthly Notices of the Royal Astronomical Society* in 1931.* If anyone deserves the title "father of the Big Bang" it is Lemaître—which has led to some awful puns over the years, since as well as being a cosmologist and mathematician, Lemaître was a priest.

He had been born in 1894 and trained as a civil engineer. During the First World War he served as an artillery officer with the Belgian army. After the war he studied at the University of Louvain, graduating in 1920 before joining a seminary and being ordained as a Roman Catholic priest in 1923. He then spent a year in Cambridge, where he worked with Eddington, and a year in the United States, divided between Harvard and MIT, before returning to Louvain, where he became professor of astronomy in 1927 and stayed for the rest of his career. Throughout his long career—he died in 1966—Lemaître continued to develop his cosmological ideas, and he lived to see many of them incorporated into mainstream cosmology. The most important of these was the idea of the Big Bang itself,

---

nod from the great man did Friedman go ahead with publication of his 1922 paper. Einstein's grumpiness may have had something to do with the fact that Friedman pointed out a simple mistake in Einstein's 1917 paper. Einstein had divided both sides of an equation, in effect, by the cosmological constant, forgetting that the constant could be set to zero and that division by zero is not allowed. Gamow, whose own arithmetic was notoriously unreliable, took great delight in this story.

*Lemaître's original paper appeared in the *Annals* of the Scientific Society of Brussels (Volume 47A, page 49). Eddington's enthusiastic espousal of the work led first to a review of this paper by Eddington himself, which appeared in an article in the *Monthly Notices* in 1930 (Volume 90, page 668) and then to the English translation of the original, which appeared in 1931 (Volume 91, page 483).

although he did not give it that name. Lemaître's equations were essentially the same solutions as those found by Friedman, although Lemaître preferred throughout his life to retain the cosmological constant that even Einstein had abandoned in the 1930s. But unlike Friedman—or, indeed, anyone else before him—Lemaître tackled the question of what those equations were telling about the origin of the Universe.

Unlike Friedman, Lemaître clearly knew something of the observations of galaxy red shifts being made at the time. In his 1927 paper he recognized that galaxies might provide the "test particles" by which universal expansion could be measured, and he gave, without any reference, a value for the constant of proportionality in the red-shift–distance relation (what later became known as Hubble's constant) so close to the value Hubble published a little later that, as one modern cosmologist has put it, "there must have been communication of some sort between the two."* Lemaître saw what both the observations and General Relativity were saying. If galaxies are far apart today and getting farther apart, that must mean that they were closer together in the past. If we look back far enough into the past, there can have been no empty space between the galaxies. Earlier still, there must have been a time when there was no empty space between the stars, and even earlier a time when there was no space between the atoms, or between the nuclei that lie at the hearts of atoms. That was as far back as even Lemaître's bold imagination took him. He envisaged a time when the entire content of the Universe was packed into a sphere only about thirty times bigger than our Sun, what he called a "primeval atom." This atom then exploded outward, breaking up into fragments that became the atoms, stars, and galaxies that we know, with the galaxies separating from one another because of the expansion of the Universe. The process has been likened to the way in which an unstable, radioactive atomic nucleus may spontaneously split into pieces that go their separate ways—nuclear fission, the power source of

---

*P. J. E. Peebles, *Modern Cosmology* (Princeton, N.J.: Princeton University Press, 1971), page 8.

the atomic bomb. This simple idea has been developed and modified considerably since the 1930s. But modern cosmology retains at its heart the idea, first propounded by Lemaître, that our Universe was born out of a superdense state that gave birth to everything we can see in the expanding Universe. With the observations by Hubble and Humason that showed our Universe to be expanding, and with Lemaître's idea of the primeval atom in print in English in the early 1930s, modern cosmology was off and running.

Of course, there were other pioneers, even in the 1920s, who made important contributions to the development of relativistic cosmology. The American Howard Robertson, a mathematician who extended de Sitter's work and made a major contribution to the mathematical basis of cosmology, certainly deserves a mention. Together with his English colleague Arthur Walker he developed, in 1935, a mathematical description of homogeneous and isotropic space-times called the Robertson-Walker metric, which describes universes with uniformly curved space but a cosmic time that is the same for all observers that move with the expansion of the universe. Such idealized universes, the Robertson-Walker models, are widely discussed today. But the key theoretical developments came from four people, exactly during the ten years or so that Slipher, Hubble, and Humason were gathering the evidence that would show the Universe to be expanding. These "fathers of cosmology" were Einstein, de Sitter, Friedman, and Lemaître—with Eddington, perhaps, as the benevolent godfather who helped the infant along the first faltering steps on the road to maturity. By the early 1930s, theory and observation had come together in a remarkable fashion to point firmly in the direction of the Big Bang. It was another decade before George Gamow, Friedman's former student, developed a fully worked-out version of the new cosmology. Meanwhile, the various alternative models had been developed more fully. Leaving aside some bizarre variations that were espoused at various times by individual cosmologists, the solutions to the equations—solutions unveiled by Friedman and Lemaître in the 1920s—fall into three main categories, and all have a finite age.

THE AGE OF THE UNIVERSE

One reason why the new cosmological models failed to take the scientific world completely by storm in the 1930s was the problem of the time scale implied by the best interpretation then available of the red-shift data gathered by Hubble and Humason. The red shifts give a measure of how quickly galaxies a certain distance apart from one another are separating.* If we make the simplest possible assumption, that the universe has been expanding at the same rate ever since it emerged from the Big Bang, it is very easy to calculate the time that has elapsed since the Big Bang—the "age of the Universe," if you like. When astronomers did this in the 1930s, they hit a snag. The recession velocity is equal to Hubble's constant, H, multiplied by the distance between two galaxies. If the expansion has continued always at the same rate, the time since the beginning of the expansion—the time since the two galaxies were touching—is just $1/H$. Using the value of the Hubble constant deduced by Hubble himself, they found that the implied age of the Universe was only about 2 billion years (2×10^9 years).

---

*It is better to think in terms of the separation of any two distant galaxies, rather than in terms of the recession of distant galaxies "from us." Our measurements of red shift have to be made from here on Earth and do show up as a recession of distant galaxies from us, but this is misleading. We are not at some special place, the center of repulsion in the Universe. It is simply that the entire fabric of space-time is expanding, so that *all* observers, living anywhere in the Universe, see the same effect. Think of a perfectly smooth bubble marked with tiny spots of paint. As the bubble expands, *every* spot gets farther away from every other spot, and the "view" from one spot—any spot—will be of all the other spots receding from it. In his 1917 paper on cosmology, Einstein proposed a fundamental postulate, that there is no average property of the Universe that defines either a special place in the Universe or a special direction in the Universe. This is known as the Cosmological Principle, and in effect it says that we live in a typical, ordinary region of the Universe and that the view we get is just the same, on average, as the view anyone else would get anywhere else in the Universe. Of course, it may be that Einstein started out from this fundamental assumption for no more subtle reason than that it provided the simplest model he could think

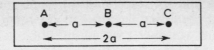

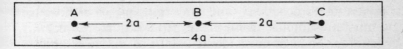

Figure 4.3 / Expanding space-time is like stretching a piece of rubber. The "galaxies" A, B, and C do not move through the space between them. But when the space expands to double the distance between A and B, it also doubles the distance between every other pair of galaxies, including A and C. From the viewpoint of every galaxy in this universe, every other galaxy is receding at a rate which is proportional to its distance. Because C is twice as far away from A as B is, for example, when all distances are doubled (when the scale factor doubles) it seems that C has "moved away" from A twice as fast as B has.

of, and he wanted to try his equations out on simple models, at least to start with. It is the growing realization that our Universe seems to fit this simplest possible description that has elevated the Cosmological Principle to its present exalted status.

Uniform expansion of space-time (or uniform contraction, which is its mirror image mathematically) is the only kind of dynamic distortion of the Universe that conforms to the Cosmological Principle—an impressive indication that Einstein's postulate (or guess) is telling us something fundamental about our Universe, especially bearing in mind that when he laid down the principle he did not know the Universe was expanding. Had his thoughts turned in that direction, he could have predicted, from the Cosmological Principle alone, that if astronomers were to discover large-scale motion in the Universe, they would discover either uniform expansion, or uniform contraction, and nothing else. Indeed, the equations *did* make this prediction—until Einstein stopped them by putting in his cosmological constant.

The Cosmological Principle is a close philosophical relation to Mach's Principle. Subsequent observations of the distribution and large-scale motion of matter in the Universe provide strong circumstantial evidence in its favor, but it is one of those things that can never actually be *proved* correct. However, if the Universe were constructed in such a way that it looked very different to different observers, there would not be much point in doing cosmology at all, since we would not be able to deduce anything about the Universe at large from observations we make in our little corner of it. Without the Cosmological Principle, in a very real sense there would be no cosmology.

This was embarrassing, because there was already good evidence that the Earth and the stars (including our Sun) are older than that. Over the next twenty years or so the conflict got worse as a variety of different techniques clearly indicated that most of the things we can see in the Universe are older than this simple estimate for the "age of the Universe" itself. Geological evidence, and measurements of radioactivity and the remains of radioactive atoms in samples from the Earth (and more recently the Moon) and from meteorites point to an age of at least 4 billion years, and probably close to 4.6 billion years, for the Solar System; as an understanding of nuclear physics developed in the 1930s, astronomers (with Eddington prominent among them) began to work out what kept the Sun and stars hot for such a long time, and inferred that many of the stars and galaxies we can see had been around not for just 4 billion years but for 10 billion years or more.

One way around the difficulty was to make the cosmological models more complicated, providing a breathing space in which everything could age. After all, nothing in the equations said that the Universe *must* have been expanding at the same steady rate ever since the Big Bang. Lemaître favored a variation on the theme that started out from the primeval atom but that included a cosmological constant slightly bigger than the one in Einstein's static model. Such a universe expands fairly quickly at first, then slows down and moves over into an almost static state, where it hovers for a time until the expansion picks up again. By choosing the exact value of the constant appropriately, the Lemaître model could be made to stay for as long as you liked in the quasistatic state, a hesitation giving ample time for the stars and galaxies to form and evolve.

Eddington had another solution. He found the idea of the primeval atom and the Big Bang "unaesthetically abrupt" and pointed out that the Universe could have existed in a static state from the beginning of time (whatever that meant) until some disturbance caused it to start to expand a few billion years ago. Such ideas gained few adherents, apart from their own proponents.* They were considered by most astronomers to be artificially forced into an unnatural mold, just as Einstein had originally forced his cosmological equations to fit the static picture of the Universe.† And, once again, it turned out that it was the picture of the Universe that astronomers had that was wrong, not the simpler versions of the cosmological equations.

If the Universe really has to be 10 billion years, or more, old and the simple interpretation of the expansion was correct, then it must mean that the accepted value of Hubble's constant was too large. Because the age of the Universe goes as $1/H$, halving the constant, for example, would double the calculated age of the Universe. And in the early 1950s there was just such a dramatic revision of the cosmological time scale.

Hubble's constant is deduced from measurements of red shifts and distances to remote galaxies. There was never any doubt about the red shifts, but the distance scale of the Universe rested on very shaky ground, right

---

*The best, and philosophically most aesthetically pleasing, proposed resolution of the time-scale difficulty came in the late 1940s, from Hermann Bondi, Tommy Gold, and Fred Hoyle. They came up with the idea of an *expanding* Steady State universe in which new matter was constantly being created to fill in the gaps left between the old galaxies as time passed and the universe grew. The wonderful simplicity of this idea appealed to many mathematician cosmologists, while many observational astronomers realized that the Steady State theory at least provided them with a target to shoot at, whether or not they liked the philosophy behind it, and whether or not they cared if it was "right" or "wrong." The only definite cosmological test they could carry out was to see if any observation would invalidate the Steady State model. (It is much harder to invalidate the Big Bang idea, of course, since almost anything, including a long interval of steady state behavior, fits in with one of the Big Bang models!) So the steady state idea stimulated research over two decades. It gave the observers predictions that could be tested, and it suggested observations that would decide between the Steady State and the Big Bang models. By stimulating observers to redoubled efforts, the Steady State model undoubtedly hastened the pace of cosmological research. Unfortunately for those, like myself, who still find the philosophy behind it attractive, it fell by the wayside when increasing evidence that there really was a Big Bang came in. But though it may have been an *incorrect* hypothesis, it was certainly a *good* hypothesis—one that could be tested and that hastened the development of scientific understanding.

†There's a nice irony in the fact that Einstein rejected his cosmological constant largely as a result of Lemaître's work, while Lemaître retained the cosmological constant to get what he regarded as a satisfactory model!

back to those few measurements by direct trigonometrical methods that gave a handful of distances to a few Cepheids that were thereby calibrated as cosmic distance markers. The whole distance scale for objects beyond our Milky Way was dramatically revised upward (and with it the estimate of the age of the Universe) as a result of Hale's legacy of large telescopes, the presence of a German-born astronomer in Los Angeles in the 1940s, and the involvement of the United States in World War Two.

Walter Baade was born in Shröttinghausen, now part of West Germany, in 1893. He was the son of a schoolteacher and worked his way up through the academic system to emerge from Göttingen University with a Ph.D. in 1919. Right through the 1920s, the decade when both observation and theory began to reveal the true nature of the Universe in which we live, Baade was working in the Bergedorf Observatory, part of Hamburg University. But in 1931 the changing political climate in Germany led Baade, like so many of his contemporaries, to depart for the United States, where he worked at the Mount Wilson and Palomar Observatories for twenty-seven years, returning to Germany in 1958. He died at Göttingen in 1960. In the middle of his sojourn in California, Baade was touched by one of life's little ironies. As a German national, when the United States entered the war he was not considered a suitable person to participate in the war effort directly, and while most of his astronomical colleagues were inducted into military research, he was left in more or less splendid isolation with unlimited access to the then biggest telescope in the world, the 100-inch (2.5-meter). With Los Angeles blacked out under wartime restrictions and nobody else breathing down his neck for a turn on the instrument, in 1943 Baade was able to push the telescope to its very limits, taking photographs that resolved stars in the inner part of the Andromeda galaxy into individual points of light, where Hubble had been able to see only a fuzzy haze. The observations showed Baade that there were two very different types of star in our neighboring galaxy. The first type, which he called Population I, are young stars, many of them hot and blue, which are found in the spiral arms. The other type, found in the central part of the galaxy and in the globular clusters of the halo, are older and, by and large, cooler and redder. He called them Population II. We now know that this is a typical pattern found in all spiral galaxies, including our own. Population I stars are young; Population II stars are old. And there are other important differences between the populations.

When the lights of Los Angeles came back on and his colleagues returned from wartime service, Baade was able to continue this work, because by 1948 the 200-inch (5-meter) telescope was in operation. Its greater size more than compensated for the deterioration in viewing conditions. Soon Baade showed that each population of stars in the Andromeda galaxy had its own type of Cepheid variable. Both Population I Cepheids and Population II Cepheids had well-defined period-luminosity relations—but their two period-luminosity relations were different from one another. The period-luminosity relation used by Hubble was the right one for Population II Cepheids, like those in the halo of our Galaxy. But it had been applied to the hotter and brighter blue Population I Cepheids of the Andromeda galaxy, in ignorance of the fact that these stars had a different period-luminosity relation. The Population I Cepheids were much brighter than their Population II counterparts (which is why Hubble was able to resolve them at all), and when Baade recalculated the distance to the Andromeda galaxy using the correct period-luminosity relation, he came up with a figure of 2 million light-years instead of the 800,000 light-years Hubble had estimated. The Andromeda galaxy was both brighter and more distant than Hubble had realized.

Because the distance to the Andromeda galaxy had been a crucial step in Hubble's estimate of the scale of the Universe, at a stroke this more than doubled the distance estimated to every external galaxy and reduced Hubble's constant to less than half its previously calculated value. If they were much farther away than had been thought, the galaxies beyond the Milky Way must be that much bigger than had been calculated, in order to appear as large as they did through telescopes on Earth. Indeed, they had to be about the same size as our own Galaxy—some of them bigger still. Instead of our Galaxy seeming to be a giant in the Universe, it now appeared as very average, much the

same size as the other galaxies. Newspaper headline writ-
ers had fun with the announcement of Baade's results,
making much of the fact that the "size of the Universe"
had "doubled." But it was of far more importance to cosmologists that the calculated *age* of the Universe had also
more than doubled, from 2 billion to 5 billion years. At
least the Universe now seemed, as of the early 1950s, to be
older than the Earth and the Solar System.

Over the following thirty years, estimates of the distance
scale and age of the Universe were almost continually
being refined as more observations were made. Baade's
original estimate itself proved to be distinctly on the low
side. Continuing work with the 200-inch, notably by Allen
Sandage, an American-born astronomer who joined the
team at the Hale Observatories in 1952, suggests that the
Universe could be as much as 20 billion years old. There
is still a range of uncertainty in all these estimates—
remember the tenuous chain of distance estimates that
links our measurements in the backwoods of one ordinary
galaxy with the far reaches of the cosmos.* But few if any
astronomers today would argue with an estimate that sets
the age of the Universe—the time since the Big Bang—as
somewhere between 13 billion and 20 billion years. There
still is room for disagreements within that range. Some
evidence suggests that the oldest known stars are themselves about 20 billion years old, but some of the studies
of the dynamics of the Universe are interpreted as indicating an age of 15 billion years or less. This conflict is
important in trying to decide the ultimate fate of the
expanding Universe. But it is largely irrelevant to the
search for the Big Bang. In the 1930s, the supposed age
of the Universe flatly contradicted the simple Big Bang
models; today, such disagreement as there is amounts
to discussions over the fine tuning. By and large, the
observations and calculations of the Hubble constant agree
very well with the simplest kinds of model universes that
can be constructed using the Friedman-Lemaître equations.

---

*Since the 1950s, the Universe has been probed not just with optical tele-
scopes but by radio telescopes as well, and lately by X-ray and other instruments carried above the Earth's atmosphere. Radio observations played an
important part in determining that the Universe is evolving, but the detailed
history of radio astronomy is outside the scope of this book.

˙A CHOICE OF UNIVERSES

Our Universe is expanding and was more dense in the past than it is today. This has now been established, not only by interpreting the red shift of distant galaxies as an expansion effect, but also by counting the number of radio galaxies at very high red shift and comparing them with the numbers found in equivalent volumes of space at low red shift. Because light takes time to travel across (or through) space to us, we see distant portions of the Universe (those at high red shift) as they were long ago. If the red shift is so great that light has been 5 billion years on the journey, in effect we see the galaxies from which the light has come as they were 5 billion years ago. So there is direct evidence that the Universe is *both* expanding *and* came from a higher-density state—the simple steady state model of cosmology is ruled out. This also means that we can rule out of consideration all the simple collapsing models that are allowed for by the equations. The only models that could possibly be relevant to the real Universe are the ones that include at least a phase of expansion. That still leaves room for some rather strange models, including some in which the model universe begins life in a state of very low density, contracts for a long time, slows down, and then expands once again. But because, as we shall see in the next chapter, there is now very good evidence that the Universe as we know it started out from a very dense, very hot state, I shall ignore these exotic ideas as well. (Of course, if this particular variation on the theme contracts so much that it reaches a state of *very* high temperature and density before expanding once again, then it becomes, from the point of view of all human observations, a Big Bang model.)

The very dense, very hot state in which the Universe was born is commonly called the Big Bang. Fred Hoyle seems to have been the person who introduced the term to astronomy, in a scientific paper he published in 1950. Many astronomers don't like the term, because it is in some ways misleading. It gives the impression of an explosion occurring in the middle of empty space, like a giant firecracker or a scaled-up nuclear bomb. But when space itself is part of the expansion, and matter is just carried along by the expanding space, the bomb analogy breaks down. Even when the Universe was very dense, it was very smooth. There was no difference in pressure forcing it to expand, and there were no sound waves to make the "bang" audible. The expansion was a smooth affair, which continues to this day. But though the purists may, rightly, bemoan the fact, we are stuck with the name Big Bang now, and I shan't try to swim against the tide.

The variety of possible universes depends on the curvature of space-time. Positive curvature can give the equivalent of a closed surface, like that of a sphere, but even a surface with positive curvature may not be closed in this way; it could extend off to infinity. Perhaps this is easier to understand in terms of lines, one-dimensional objects. A line may be closed back on itself, like a circle, so that it has a definite size, the circumference of the circle. Or it may be open, like a hyperbola, which extends out to infinity on either side of the bend that gives it its distinctive shape. The Universe we live in may be closed, the equivalent of a circle (or a sphere) and with a finite extent. Or it may be open, like a hyperbola or a vast hyperbolic bowl, stretching out to infinity and containing an infinite amount of matter. What decides the amount of curvature, and thereby whether or not the Universe is open or closed, is the amount of matter in the Universe, because gravity, produced by matter, is what curves space-time. This is important in deciding the ultimate fate of the Universe but has little bearing on the search for the Big Bang, since both the open and closed variations on the theme start out in very much the same way.

Negative curvature is equivalent to a type of curved surface that can *only* be open, like a saddle surface. The amount of the curvature itself depends once again on how much matter there is in the universe (or, more accurately, on the density of matter at any time in its evolution, any "cosmic epoch"). Einstein's cosmological constant provides more room for variety, but I will mention only one of those extra possibilities.

The best way to get a handle on all this is to look at a

property the cosmologists call the "scale factor" and see how it changes as a particular model universe evolves. The scale factor can be thought of as the separation between a chosen pair of galaxies—it increases as the universe expands and is denoted by the letter R. When R doubles, the distance between every pair of galaxies doubles, and so on. Pushing the observed behavior of the real Universe—its expansion—back to the point where everything was touching everything else, R starts out from zero, equivalent to the birth of the universe in an infinitely dense state. If we plot a graph with the scale factor R against the time since the Big Bang, t, we can see how the main types of model universe differ from one another. What matters is the extent to which *space* is curved, and how the curvature of space (not space-time) changes as time passes. In all cases (assuming that the cosmological constant is zero) the expansion of the universe slows down as t increases. This can easily be understood in terms of the effect of gravity, holding back the expansion of the universe. But the rate at which the slowdown occurs depends on how much matter there is in the universe, which decides whether or not it is open or closed.

The expansion of the universe slows down as time passes, so that R increases by a smaller amount in later time intervals that are the same size. This slowdown occurs most rapidly in the closed universes. For all the universes with positive curvature, the R curve bends determinedly to the right, eventually turning over and becoming a description of a collapsing, not an expanding, universe. Such a universe contains so much matter that gravity eventually causes it to recollapse. With ever-increasing speed, such a universe then rushes back into a state of infinite density, like the Big Bang in which it was born. The space in such a closed universe is closed in the same sense that the surface of a sphere is closed; the change in curvature as time passes is equivalent to the sphere being first inflated and then deflated. In a universe with negative curvature, the expansion continues forever even though it is always slowing down, and the universe, like a saddle surface, is infinite. The space of such a universe is called hyperbolic, in the same way that the space of a closed universe is termed spherical.* There are whole families of closed universe models and whole families of open universe models; the Einstein-de Sitter universe is a special case exactly balanced between models with positive curvature and those with negative curvature.

Having been stuck with the name Big Bang for the birth of the universe, cosmologists have at least been consistent with their terminology for its possible end. A universe that recollapses ends in a "big crunch," while the ones that expand forever end, logically enough, in what T. S. Eliot told us was the opposite of a bang—"this is the way the world ends, not with a bang but a whimper." So there are two basic alternatives, the bang-crunch universes and the bang-whimper universes. Everything else is just fine tuning.†

Figure 4.4 gives an indication of how these different types of universe evolve. The figure also shows how our estimates of the age of the real universe in terms of Hubble's parameter, H must be only an approximation. By setting the age of the Universe as $1/H$, we assume that the expansion has always continued at the same rate—in effect, we draw a tangent to the R/t curve and extrapolate it back to find when it crosses the axis, the time when R was zero. If the expansion is slowing down in a space of positive curvature, then this estimate, $1/H$, is always *more*

---

*All this talk of spherical and hyperbolic spaces may make you wonder whether there are other alternatives, comparable, perhaps, to the ellipses. The analogy doesn't really follow through at this level, and it is best at this stage to concentrate on the distinction between hyperbolic (open) models and spherical (closed) models. But cosmologists do sometimes dabble with the equations of a space with a slightly different topology, which they call elliptical space. This has several interesting properties. It has only half the volume of the equivalent spherical space with the same "radius." This is because although in spherical space every point has its equivalent antipodeal point (like the North and South poles of the Earth), in elliptical space when you travel to the farthest "point" from a chosen point you could be anywhere in a region of space, in the same way that all points on the equator are at the same distance from the North Pole. But even if the space-time we live in is elliptical in this sense (and there is no evidence that it is), that doesn't affect the puzzle of why it is expanding and how it was born in a Big Bang.

†Just what these differences, and the fine tuning, mean for the fate of our Universe is an important topic that is outside the scope of this book. But it is perhaps worth mentioning here that a universe that is closed by gravity is precisely the equivalent of a black hole. Indeed, it *is* a black hole—or, putting it another way, the black holes that caught the public imagination so much in the 1970s and 1980s are pocket universes, described completely by Einstein's equations for a region of space-time closed by gravity.

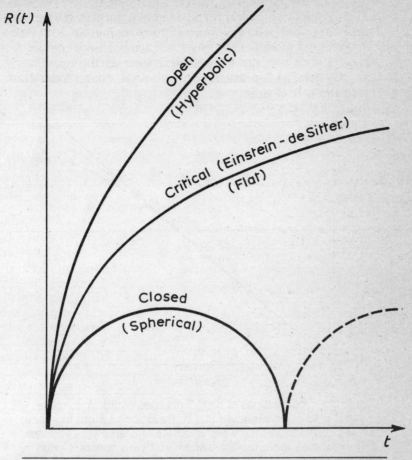

Figure 4.4 / The three geometries of space described in Figure 4.2 (page 125) correspond to three types of Universe which all start from a compact state and expand, at least initially, as time passes. *R* is the scale factor of the universe; *t* represents time. Both the open and the flat universes expand forever; the closed universes collapse eventually, and may then undergo further cycles of expansion and collapse.

than the true age of the Universe. This made the contradiction between the Hubble age for the Universe and the estimated age of the Earth and stars even more embarrassing in the 1940s—you need a reasonable amount of leeway in the Hubble age to be sure that the Universe is old enough for stars and planets to have formed. It's hardly surprising that when George Gamow came up with the first detailed model of the Big Bang itself, in the middle of the 1940s, it was not immediately seen as the answer to the cosmologists' prayers. Nevertheless, that model has stood the test of time.

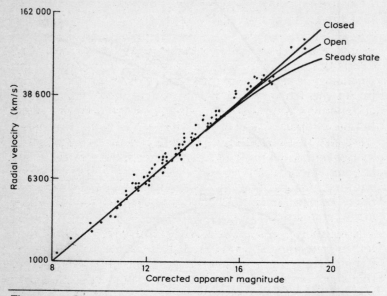

*Figure 4.5/*Observations of distant galaxies could, in principle, tell us what kind of universe we live in. By looking far out to space, we see galaxies as they were when the Universe was younger and expanding more rapidly—when "Hubble's constant" was different. So the straight line in Hubble's diagram should be bent slightly, by an amount which indicates how quickly the expansion of the Universe is slowing down. Unfortunately, the range of our telescopes scarcely begins to provide enough evidence to decide which of the models of Figure 4.4 is the best bet. Although it does look as if the Steady State model is ruled out, there is no way in which the available observations (collected over the years by Allen Sandage) can distinguish whether our Universe is open or closed. From this evidence, our Universe is seen to be very close to the special, in between case—a flat spacetime. In this diagram, magnitude effectively corresponds to distance, and radial velocity to redshift; it is the modern, vastly extended, version of Hubble's diagram in Figure 3.1.

THE LARGE AND
THE SMALL

Lemaître's model of the Universe brought together, for the first time, the best available ideas about the world of the very small and the world of the very large in one description of reality. This was a bold step at the time, but in the 1980s the combination of ideas from particle physics and cosmology is seen as the only route toward an understanding of the Universe we live in. In the late 1920s, when astronomers were just beginning to understand the distribution of matter across the visible Universe, physicists were also just beginning to understand the distribution of matter *within* atoms. The discovery of radioactivity, in the late nineteenth century, gave physicists a tool to probe within the atom. They used so-called alpha particles, produced by naturally radioactive atoms, as tiny bullets to shoot at the atoms in a crystal, or in a thin foil of metal. Using this technique, researchers at the University of Manchester in England, working in the department headed by Ernest Rutherford, a New Zealand-born physicist, found that most often alpha particles went right through a thin metal foil target but that occasionally a particle would be bounced back almost the way it came. Rutherford came up with an explanation of this behavior in 1911 and gave us the basic model of the atom that we learn about in school today.*

Rutherford realized that most of the material of an atom must be concentrated in a tiny inner core, which he called the nucleus, surrounded by a cloud of electrons. Alpha particles, which come from radioactive atoms, are actually fragments of atomic nucleus. When such a particle hits the electron cloud of an atom, it brushes its way through almost unaffected. But electrons carry negative charge, while atoms as a whole are electrically neutral. So the

---

*A fuller account of all of this pioneering work in particle physics is provided in my book *In Search of Schrödinger's Cat*. The sketch given here is scarcely more than a caricature, but one that I hope shows how physics and cosmology developed alongside one another.

positive charge of an atom must be concentrated, like its mass, in the nucleus. Alpha particles, too, are positively charged. And when an alpha particle hits an atomic nucleus head-on, the repulsion between like charges halts it in its tracks and then pushes it back from where it came. Later experiments confirmed the broad accuracy of Rutherford's picture of the atom. Most of the mass and all the positive charge is concentrated in a nucleus about one hundred-thousandth the size of the atom. The rest of the space is occupied by a tenuous cloud of very light electrons that carry negative charge. In round numbers, a nucleus is about 10^{-13} centimeters across, while an atom is about 10^{-8} centimeters across. Very roughly, the proportion is like a grain of sand at the center of Carnegie Hall. The empty hall is the "atom"; the grain of sand is the "nucleus."

The particle that carries the positive charge in the nucleus is called the proton. It has a charge exactly the same size as the charge of the electron, but with opposite sign. Each proton is about 2,000 times as massive as each electron. In the simplest version of Rutherford's model of the atom, there was nothing but electrons and protons, in equal numbers but with the protons confined to the nucleus, in spite of them all having the same charge, which ought to make them repel one another (like charges behave in the same way as like magnetic poles do in this respect). There must be another force, which operates only at very short ranges, that overcomes the electric force and glues the nucleus together; more of this in Part Three. But over the twenty years following Rutherford's proposal of this model of the atom, a suspicion grew up among physicists that there ought to be another particle, a counterpart of the proton with much the same mass but electrically neutral. Among other things, the presence of such particles in the nucleus would provide something for the positively charged protons to hold on to without being electrically repulsed. And the presence of neutrons, as they were soon called, could explain why some atoms could have identical chemical properties to one another but slightly different mass. Chemical properties depend on the electron cloud of an atom, the visible "face" it shows to other atoms. Atoms with identical chemistry must have identical numbers of electrons and therefore identical numbers of protons. But they could have different numbers of neutrons and therefore different masses. Such close atomic cousins are now called isotopes.*

The great variety of elements in the world are all built on this simple scheme. Hydrogen, with a nucleus consisting of one proton, and with one electron outside it, is the simplest; the most common form of carbon, an atom that is the very basis of living things, including ourselves, has six protons and six neutrons in the nucleus of each atom, with six electrons in a cloud surrounding the nucleus. But there are nuclei that contain many more particles (more nucleons) than this. Iron has 26 protons in its nucleus and, in the most common isotope, 30 neutrons, making 56 nucleons in all, while uranium is one of the most massive naturally occurring elements, with 92 protons and no less than 143 neutrons in each nucleus of uranium-235, the radioactive isotope used as a source of nuclear energy. Energy can be obtained from the fission of very heavy nuclei because the most stable state an atomic nucleus could possibly be in, with the least energy, is iron-56. In terms of energy, iron-56 lies at the bottom of a valley, with lighter nuclei, including those of oxygen, carbon, helium, and hydrogen up one side, and heavier nuclei, including cobalt, nickel, uranium, and plutonium, up the other side. Just as a ball that lies on the valley's sloping side can more easily be kicked down into the bottom of the valley than higher up the slope, so if heavy nuclei can be persuaded to split, they can, under the right circumstances, form more stable nuclei "lower down the slope," with energy being released; equally, if light nuclei can be persuaded to fuse together, then they, too, form a more stable configuration, with energy being released.† The fission process, which

---

*A fuller account of how chemistry "works" at the atomic level can be found in my book *In Search of the Double Helix*.

†And just as you *can* kick the ball higher up the slope, if you put enough energy into the kick, so it is *possible* to make very heavy elements by pushing energy into the fusion process. Equally, just as the ball will sit happily halfway up the slope if left alone, so many nuclei are quite stable, even though they are, strictly speaking, in a more energetic state than the iron-56 minimum. All this is important to an understanding of how the elements formed in the first place, a main theme of the next chapter.

Lemaître tried to extend to the primeval atom, is what powers an atomic bomb; the fusion process, which Gamow applied in his model of the Big Bang, is what provides the energy from a hydrogen, or fusion, bomb, in which hydrogen nuclei are converted into helium nuclei. But all that still lay in the future in the 1920s. Although there was circumstantial evidence for the existence of neutrons in that decade, it was only in 1932 that James Chadwick, a former student of Rutherford and who was by then working at the Cavendish Laboratory in Cambridge (where Rutherford was the director), carried out experiments that proved that neutrons really exist.

So when Lemaître first proposed his "primeval atom" model of the origin of the Universe, nobody actually knew what a real atom was like. The term "primeval atom" is itself a misnomer, and "primeval nucleus" would be much better. When we talk of atoms "splitting" or undergoing radioactive decay, what we really mean is that their *nuclei* break up into two or more parts, or that one nucleus ejects a particle, such as an alpha particle, and changes into the nucleus of a lighter element. Lemaître envisaged this as the process that, by repeated fission, produced all the matter in the Universe from one "nucleus." But this could not explain (quite apart from more technical problems, which I won't go into) why well over half the matter in stars and galaxies is in the form of hydrogen, the lightest and simplest element, while most of the rest is helium, the next lightest element. Spectroscopic studies of stars and galaxies unambiguously show the Universe to be dominated by the two simplest elements, hydrogen with just one proton in its nucleus and one electron to go with it, and helium with two protons and two neutrons in its nucleus, and two electrons outside. Splitting all of the primeval nucleus into such simple components is too big a task; but Gamow hit on the idea that the Big Bang might have started out with the very simplest particles and that the Universe then built up the heavier elements by adding more protons and neutrons to the simplest nuclei. After all, if you *start* with hydrogen, then at a stroke you explain the existence of more than half of the nuclei in the Universe.

GAMOW'S UNIVERSE

George Gamow was a larger-than-life character with a boundless imagination that took him from nuclear physics to cosmology and then into the world of molecular biology. He made significant contributions in all three areas of science—*the* three key areas of twentieth-century science—and found time along the way to write books for the layman, carry out elaborate practical jokes on his colleagues, and generally to illuminate the world of science in the middle decades of the century. He achieved all this despite being indifferent about such minor details of life as spelling or dates, and being hopeless at working out simple arithmetic. Born in the Ukraine, at Odessa, in 1904, after he moved permanently to the United States in the mid-1930s he always signed his letters to his friends "Geo.," an abbreviation that he was unshakably convinced was pronounced "Joe"; so "Joe" he was, to the very large number of those friends, until his death in 1968.

Having lived through the turmoil of revolution and civil war in Russia, in 1922 Gamow enrolled at Novorossysky University but soon transferred to the University of Leningrad, where he stayed until 1928, gaining a Ph.D. and learning about Friedman's models of the Universe from Friedman himself. Once qualified, Gamow traveled to the University of Göttingen, then to the Institute of Theoretical Physics in Copenhagen, then to the Cavendish Laboratory in Cambridge, and then back to Copenhagen. The three scientific centers he visited in the years from 1928 to 1931 were at the heart of the revolution in physics then taking place, the discovery of quantum physics and the beginnings of the application of the new theory to an understanding of atoms. Gamow learned his quantum physics from the pioneers in the subject, just as he learned his cosmology from one of the pioneers. And during his visit to Göttingen he made the first of his major contributions to science, applying quantum theory to explain how an alpha particle could escape from an atomic nucleus.

Each of these alpha particles, it is now known, consists of two protons and two neutrons held together by the strong nuclear force that overcomes the electric force of repulsion between the protons. They are, indeed, identical to helium nuclei, in effect helium atoms from which the two electrons (all that the atom possesses) have been removed. When an alpha particle is inside the nucleus of a very heavy atom, it is held in by the strong nuclear force. If an alpha particle is just outside the nucleus, however, the electric repulsion force dominates, because the nuclear force has only a very short range, and so the particle is ejected. Extending the idea of a stable state as being at the bottom of a valley, in energy terms, for the alpha particle the nucleus is like the interior of an extinct volcano. Deep in the heart of the volcano, it is energetically stable; but if it were just a little bit outside the volcano it would be on the steeply sloping sides of the mountain and would rapidly roll away. Gamow showed how an alpha particle could get over the hill, as it were, from just inside

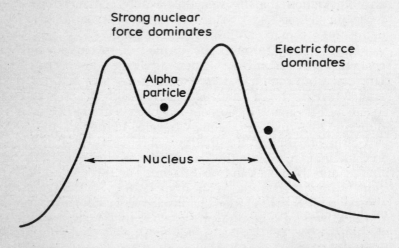

*Figure 4.6/*An alpha particle inside a nucleus is trapped by the strong nuclear force. The same particle just outside the nucleus would "roll away" as it is pushed by the electric force. But how can an alpha particle get out of the nucleus without enough energy to climb the intervening hill? George Gamow's explanation of this alpha decay process was the first successful application of quantum physics to the nucleus.

the nucleus to just outside—and his explanation of alpha decay was the first successful application of quantum theory to the nucleus.

In 1931, Gamow was called back to the USSR, where he was appointed Master of Research at the Academy of Sciences in Leningrad and Professor of Physics at Leningrad University. But his ebullient nature and independence of mind hardly suited him to a happy life under Stalin's regime in the 1930s, and when he was allowed to attend a scientific conference in Brussels in 1933 he seized the opportunity to stay away, moving to George Washington University in Washington, D.C., where he was professor of physics from 1934 to 1956, and then to the University of Colorado in Boulder, where he stayed until his death.

Gamow's interest in how things got *out* of atomic nuclei led him to wonder about the possibility of particles getting *in*, climbing the hill from outside and dropping into the region where the strong nuclear force dominates. He was involved in pioneering calculations that showed that if protons could be fired into atoms with energies of a few hundred kilovolts, they would trigger the kind of nuclear reactions that cause nuclear fission and alpha decay. John Cockroft and Ernest Walton, working at the Cavendish Lab, did just that in 1932, creating the world's first particle accelerator, using a high-voltage electric field to accelerate protons and smash them into atoms, and triggering reactions in exactly the way Gamow had predicted. This was the first step along the road that led eventually to the atomic bomb, and to the first nuclear power stations, deriving energy from the fission process. But the idea of sticking protons onto existing nuclei by, in effect, pushing them together hard enough to overcome the long-range electric repulsive forces and allow the short-range nuclear forces to dominate, also led Gamow to the Big Bang.

The neutron is the key component of Gamow's universe. As long as a neutron is inside a stable atomic nucleus, it retains its identity as a neutron. But left to their own devices, individual neutrons themselves decay, each of them breaking down into one proton and one electron. This decay occurs quite rapidly, with a half life of about 13 minutes.* So if you started out with a very dense universe full of neutrons, a kind of neutron gas, you would very quickly have a supply of protons and electrons as well, with precisely enough particles of each kind around (the same number of electrons as protons) for every stable atom that might be formed to have an equal number of protons and electrons and leave no excess electric charge left over.

Gamow's idea immediately supplied hydrogen for the universe. Each hydrogen atom consists simply of one proton with one electron held in its neighborhood by the electric force of attraction between opposite charges. Allow a neutron to decay, and there you are with a bare hydrogen nucleus and a handy electron, all ready to make an atom. But where do the rest of the atoms, those corresponding to helium and the heavier elements, come from?

During the 1940s, Gamow was joined at George Washington University by Ralph Alpher, a graduate student to whom he assigned the task of working out the details of how more complex nuclei might have been built up from hydrogen (a process known as nucleosynthesis) in the Big Bang. The model they developed depended on collisions between the particles in the cosmic soup of dense material in the first few minutes of the life of the universe.† The calculations showed that it would be relatively easy for a proton (hydrogen nucleus) and a neutron to collide strongly enough to overcome electrostatic repulsion and stick to-

*The half life is the time it takes for half of the particles in a sample to decay. If you start with 100 neutrons, after 13 minutes there will be 50 left, after 26 minutes there will be 25 left, after 39 minutes a dozen, and so on. This kind of statistical behavior, in which the fate of an individual particle cannot be predicted (there is no way to tell *which* of the original neutrons will decay in the first 13 minutes, or in any subsequent period) but in which the overall behavior of a large group (it should really, of course, be far more than 100) is completely predictable, is one of the most striking aspects of quantum physics. It applies to all radioactive decays and to other processes, not just to the decay of the neutron.

†Where did the dense soup come from? In the 1940s (and, indeed, in the 1950s, 1960s, and 1970s) that question was unanswerable. Gamow got around the problem by invoking one of the Friedman models that starts out very thin, collapses down into the cosmic soup stage, and then expands again. But there are now other resolutions of this dilemma, the subject of Part Three of this book.

gether, to form a nucleus of deuterium, also known as heavy hydrogen. Another collision with a neutron would produce a nucleus of tritium, containing one proton and two neutrons. But tritium is unstable, so that one of its neutrons soon spits out an electron and becomes a proton. The nucleus has now evolved into one that corresponds to an isotope of helium, containing two protons and one neutron, and called, for obvious reasons, helium-3. All it needs now is for another neutron to stick to the growing nucleus to make an alpha particle, the nucleus of a helium-4 atom. So far, so good. There was no need to worry about the electrons, since once the nuclei were manufactured they could easily pick up the electrons they needed from the swarm of particles in the primeval soup. But at that point the model ran into a snag.

The helium-4 nucleus, the alpha particle, is particularly stable. It is very disinclined either to break up into smaller components, or to accept additional components and grow into something more complex. Worse, there is no naturally occurring element that has a nucleus containing five particles, and when such a nucleus is made artificially in the lab by bombarding helium-4 with neutrons, it immediately breaks down to helium-4 again. To get around this difficulty, Gamow and Alpher had to speculate that a single helium-4 nucleus might occasionally be struck *simultaneously* by two particles and capture them both to form a nucleus containing six particles. Even if this happens, the same problem arises for the nucleus containing eight particles, which very rapidly breaks down into two alpha particles.* And with the universe rapidly thinning out as it expands away from the superdense state of the Big Bang, by the time you have made the helium, the chance of a double collision of this kind is small and rapidly getting smaller. In the 1940s, although the prospect of getting over these gaps by the capture of two particles at once seemed unlikely, there was just enough ignorance about

*The image of a smoothly sloping valley with iron-56 at the bottom is, of course, an oversimplification. The helium-4 nucleus, to extend the analogy, sits in its own hole in the ground on the side of the valley, from which it cannot easily be dislodged; the nucleus with eight particles might be thought of as balanced on top of a molehill on the valley side (a very sharply pointed molehill!), from which it topples at the slightest provocation.

conditions in the early Universe, and about the rates at which such nuclear reactions might occur, to allow Gamow and Alpher to get away with the idea as a working hypothesis. After all, as Gamow used to tell anyone who was interested, the theory explained where all of the hydrogen and all of the helium in the Universe came from, and that accounted for more than 99 percent of the matter visible in stars and galaxies. Even if the theory didn't properly explain the synthesis of the heavy elements (to an astronomer, anything except hydrogen and helium is a "heavy" element), they represented less than 1 percent of the problem.

The detailed calculations of how nuclei can capture neutrons or protons (the numbers that come out of the calculations are called capture cross sections) formed the basis of Alpher's Ph.D. thesis, submitted in 1948. It clearly deserved a wider audience, however, and Alpher and Gamow wrote a paper for submission to the *Physical Review*. At this point, Gamow's sense of fun overcame him, and he perpetrated his most famous scientific joke. "It seemed unfair to the Greek alphabet," he wrote later,* "to have the article signed by Alpher and Gamow only, and so the name of Dr. Hans A. Bethe (*in absentia*) was inserted in preparing the manuscript for print. Dr. Bethe, who received a copy of the manuscript, did not object." So the classic paper in which the modern version of the Big Bang model first saw the light of day appeared, on April 1, 1948 (a coincidence that delighted Gamow), under the names Alpher, Bethe, and Gamow. To this day, it is known as the "alpha, beta, gamma" paper, a suitable reflection of the fact that it deals with the beginning of things, and also of the importance of particle physics to cosmology (alpha particles we have already met; beta particle is another name for electron; and gamma ray is the name for an intense pulse of electromagnetic radiation, an energetic photon).

This early version of the Big Bang appeared in the same year, 1948, that Fred Hoyle, Tommy Gold, and Hermann Bondi came up with their idea of an expanding Steady State universe. Right through the 1950s and into the 1960s

*The Creation of the Universe, page 65.

the two rival ideas stirred debate among the experts, with Hoyle as the leading Steady Stater and Gamow as the leading Big Banger in friendly rivalry. Ironically, it was to be Hoyle who would show how to resolve the greatest difficulty with Gamow's universe, finding a way to make the heavy elements inside stars, once the initial job of cooking up helium in the Big Bang had been carried out. But there is an even greater irony in the story, involving one of the most significant missed opportunities in the history of science and emphasizing the way even cosmologists failed to take their equations seriously at that time.

TWO QUESTIONS

In those days, cosmology was very much a game. Rival models were developed and tested against one another almost as a kind of abstract mathematical duel, with little thought that one of these models might, in fact, be a correct mathematical description of our own Universe. Even Gamow, who loved his theory of the universe as if it were his own son, fell into this trap.

The conditions needed to make even helium in the Big Bang (never mind the heavy elements for now) include both very high density *and* very high temperature. Although you might imagine a cold soup of neutrons expanding away from a state of very high density, quite simple calculations show that such a cold neutron soup is very rapidly converted almost entirely into helium. It is only in a hot Big Bang that most of the matter stays as hydrogen, and (curiously but just one of those things) it doesn't make much difference what the exact density of the model universe is a few seconds after the moment of creation. Provided the universe is hot, you always end up with about a third of the matter being turned into helium, with the rest staying as hydrogen until it is reprocessed in stars as the universe evolves.

Most of the hydrogen is prevented from being cooked into helium while the universe is very dense by the presence of a great deal of energetic radiation. This electromagnetic radiation can be thought of in terms of particles called photons. Alpher and another young researcher, Robert Herman, used the fact that about a third of the Universe is helium and the rest hydrogen to calculate how many photons there must be in the Universe; it comes out at a staggering billion photons for every nuclear particle (that is, for every proton or neutron). Radiation—photons—is a form of energy, and the density of the radiation (the amount of energy in a certain volume of space) can be expressed in terms of temperature. Winding back the Friedman equations to the early seconds of the Universe, Alpher and Herman showed that there must have been a time when the energy density of the radiation was greater than the energy density of the matter, given in terms of Einstein's famous equation $E = mc^2$. The Gamow universe was born out of a fireball of radiation, quickly cooling as it expanded, and becoming dominated by matter only after it had expanded, and cooled, by a critical amount. But the radiation would still be there, filling the entire universe but getting thinner, cooler, and weaker as time went by. In 1948, Alpher and Herman published a paper in which they calculated that the temperature of this leftover radiation today must be about five degrees Absolute, 5 K.*

In his popular book *The Creation of the Universe,* published in 1952, Gamow gives a slightly different estimate for the temperature of the Universe today (and also bemoans Herman's stubborn refusal to change his name to Delter). Gamow derives an equation that says that the temperature is equal to 1.5×10^{10} divided by the square root of the age of the Universe in seconds. This gave him an estimate of about 50 K. At other times in the early 1950s, Gamow and his colleagues came up with other figures in the range from 5 K to 50 K, depending on what assumptions they made about the state of the early Universe and its age. Today particle physicists calculate that a more accurate version of Gamow's equation simply sets the temperature now as 10^{10} divided by the square root of the

---

*The zero of the Kelvin scale of temperature is $-273°C$, to the nearest whole number. It is the absolute zero of temperature at which all particles are in their lowest energy levels, called zero-point states; there can be nothing colder.

universe's age in seconds, and in addition the estimates for the age have increased, all of which reduces the top estimate for the temperature of the Universe at present. This equation is only an approximate relation, and there are better ways to calculate the temperature of the Universe at any epoch. But it is a useful rule of thumb, which tells us, for instance, that one second after the moment of creation the temperature was 10 billion degrees, that after 100 seconds it had already cooled to 1 billion degrees, and that after an hour it was down to 170 million degrees. For comparison, the temperature at the heart of our Sun is calculated to be about 15 million degrees.

Here was a clear prediction made by the hot Big Bang theory. It said that the Universe ought to be filled with a sea of radiation with an energy equivalent to a temperature of a few K. Such radiation would be detectable at radio wavelengths, and radio astronomy was just getting started in the early 1950s. But no radio astronomer picked up the idea and went out to test it, while Gamow and his team went their own ways into other areas of research (Gamow himself becoming fascinated by the problem of cracking the genetic code of DNA) and never went out on the campaign trail to drum up interest in the idea and encourage, or force, the radio astronomers into appropriate action. What went wrong? The best explanation is the one put forward by physicist Steven Weinberg in his book *The First Three Minutes*. "It was," he said, "extraordinarily difficult for physicists to take seriously *any* theory of the early universe" in those days. "Our mistake is not that we take our theories too seriously, but that we do not take them seriously enough. It is always hard to realize that these numbers and equations that we play with at our desks have something to do with the real world."*

By 1956, when Gamow went on his way to Colorado and the team disbanded, the early version of the hot Big Bang model had posed two questions, the answers to which were to provide the basis for further developments. One of those questions was widely recognized, and great strides toward answering it were made in the late 1950s and early 1960s. It was the question of where the heavy elements

---

*André Deutsch edition, pages 131 and 132.

come from if they are not manufactured in the Big Bang. The other question was unnoticed and remained buried in the scientific literature until it was answered by accident in 1964. It was the question of the background temperature of the universe today. The combination of these two answers—each of which led to the award of a Nobel Prize— with Gamow's universe initiated the modern era in cosmology.

CHAPTER FIVE

TWO KEYS TO THE UNIVERSE

In the 1930s, astrophysicists were much more interested in the workings of the Sun and stars than in the origin of the Universe. The mystery of creation still seemed more a topic for the metaphysicians to muse over than something that fell within the scope of scientific investigation; and the puzzle of how the stars shone was both a fascinating one and something that was just being understood in terms of the revolutionary new understanding of physics that had broken through in the 1920s. But as it turned out, the investigation of how stars stay hot led directly to a better understanding of the Universe at large and of the Big Bang itself.

Our Sun is the nearest star and the one we know most about. If astronomers were to have any hope of understanding the workings of stars in general, they had to understand at least the outlines of the workings of our own Sun. But at first even the new physics, quantum physics, seemed inadequate for the task.

All the evidence that the Earth had been around for 4 billion or 5 billion years clearly implied a similar age for the Sun, and even in the nineteenth century, physicists appreciated that no ordinary chemical process of combustion could have kept the Sun hot for that long. A solid ball of coal, for example, the size of the Sun and burning in an atmosphere of pure oxygen to generate the same amount of heat every second that the Sun is putting out today, would have burned to a cinder in about 1,500 years. The first attempts to explain how stars could stay hot for a very long time, by invoking astrophysical processes, processes that operate in the stars but not here on Earth, came in the second half of the nineteenth century from the German physicist Hermann Helmholtz and the British physicist William Thomson (later Lord Kelvin, in whose honor the absolute scale of temperature is named).

Helmholtz and Thomson were both major figures in the scientific world of the time, with wide-ranging interests. Their paths crossed through a common interest in the age of the Earth, and therefore the age of the Sun. In 1854, Helmholtz came up with an age of 25 million years; a little later, Thomson came up with a slightly longer estimate, giving 100 million years as the most likely figure. Even Thomson, we now know, was more than ten times too modest in his assessment of the age of the Solar System. But these estimates were a significant step away from the idea of a creation only a few thousand years ago, an idea still accepted by some Church authorities at that time (Darwin's *Origin of Species* was published in 1859; the estimates of the age of the Earth made by Helmholtz and Thomson were very far from being esoteric scientific data and were directly relevant to the greatest scientific and philosophical debate of the time). But where could the energy come from to keep the Sun hot for even 100 million years?

The answer seemed to be "gravity." If the Sun had started out as a thin cloud of gas in space, falling together into a more compact ball under the tug of its own gravity, then it would have warmed up as it collapsed. If you stretch a spring, you have to do work (put in energy) to overcome the elastic forces in the spring; when you let go of the spring, the energy is released. The same sort of thing happens if you lift a weight up from the ground. You are putting energy—in this case, in the form of gravitational potential energy—into the weight. When you drop

the weight, that energy is turned into kinetic energy as
the weight falls, and then the kinetic energy is turned into
heat energy when the ground stops the weight's fall. All
the particles that make up the Sun would "like" to fall to
its center, to the center of mass of the system they are part
of. If they could do so, they would give up gravitational
potential energy, ultimately in the form of heat, in the
same way that a falling weight gives up energy as heat. A
more compact star is at a lower energy state than a more
diffuse star, because its component particles are closer to
the center of mass.* So if you start out with a star like the
Sun but slightly bigger, and leave it to contract slowly
under the tug of its own gravity, then you would expect
heat to be generated.

THE AGE OF THE SUN

Astronomers are well able to calculate the distance to the
Sun (the astronomical unit of distance) and its mass from
the orbital motions of bodies in the Solar System, the
strength of tides on Earth, and so on. They know how
much energy it radiates each second, because they know
how bright it must actually be to look as bright as it does
in our sky. The energy released is, in fact, about 4×10^{33}
ergs per second, some 10^{41} ergs per year. When Helmholtz and Thomson calculated how much energy a star
like the Sun would release if it contracted slightly, they
found that the collapse from a diffuse gas cloud into the
star would provide enough energy to keep the star radiating this strongly for 10 million or 100 million years, before
the interior of the star must cool sufficiently to trigger
another major collapse. Somewhat unfairly on Helmholtz,
both alphabetically and in chronological order of making

---

*One way to visualize this is to extend the spring analogy. If you wanted to
spread the Sun back out into a thin cloud, you would have to do work,
against the pull of gravity, on every particle in it to move it farther away from
the center of mass. The particles in the diffuse state store up that energy as
gravitational potential energy. And that is the energy liberated as heat when
such a cloud contracts.

the calculations, this time scale is known today as the Kelvin-Helmholtz time scale. It is undoubtedly important in the early stages of the life of a star, and the gravitational heating effect is the process that makes stars hot in the first place and causes them to begin to shine. But by the 1920s it was clear that the Earth and the Sun (and therefore presumably the stars) must be much older than Kelvin and Helmholtz had thought—billions of years old, not tens of millions of years old. So where had the energy come from to maintain those 4×10^{33} ergs per second for all that time, and to keep the Sun shining today?*

Kelvin's estimate for the age of the Earth was based on measurements of the temperature at the surface of the Earth compared with the temperature down deep mine shafts. Heat is leaking out from the interior, and by estimating how rapidly heat is escaping, and working backward in time, he concluded that the whole of our planet must have been molten a few tens of millions of years ago. Kelvin, and the astronomers, found the agreement between this age for the Earth and the Kelvin-Helmholtz age for the Sun persuasive. But even in the late nineteenth century, geologists had clear evidence that the Earth must be much more than 100 million years old, or there would not have been time for the great thicknesses of folded rocks in structures like the Alps to have formed, while evolutionary biologists also preferred a longer time scale of Earth history during which evolution could have been at work to produce the complexity of life on Earth today. Kelvin's estimate for the age of the Earth was wrong, and the reason became clear at the turn of the century with the discovery of radioactivity. Radioactive elements occur naturally in common rocks all over the world, and the whole basis for their radioactivity is that their nuclei are moving to a lower energy state by splitting into two or more parts, ejecting alpha particles or whatever. The change in energy of the radioactive nucleus when it decays ap-

---

*One implication of the Kelvin-Helmholtz effect is that it would take about 10 million years for the Sun to adjust to any drastic change in the heating processes in its interior. If those processes, *whatever* they may be, were suddenly switched off, we here on Earth wouldn't notice for several million years, because gradual gravitational collapse would keep the Sun hot. A comforting thought, perhaps, in these uncertain times.

pears as heat, and in round terms about 90 percent of the heat flow through the rocks of the Earth's crust is due to radioactivity. So Kelvin's age for the Earth has to be multiplied by something between 10 and 100 to give a more accurate, but still rough, guide to how long the Sun and planets have been in existence.

During the 1920s several developments led to the beginning of a better understanding of how the Sun and the other stars work. First, the spectroscopists were able to show that our Sun is composed of about 70 percent hydrogen, 28 percent helium, and just 2 percent of heavy elements. Then Arthur Eddington, inventing the science of astrophysics almost single-handedly, discovered, from studies of binary stars, that the brightness of a star is directly related to its mass. This discovery, announced in 1924, was a key step toward an understanding of how stars work, and in 1926 Eddington published a landmark book, *The Internal Constitution of the Stars*, which showed how this and other properties of stars could be explained in terms of the basic laws of physics describing the behavior of a large, hot ball of gas. At the same time, continued probing of the atom and investigation of radioactivity, following on from Rutherford's pioneering work, had begun to make physicists familiar (or, at least, less unfamiliar) with one of the more startling predictions of Einstein's Special Theory of Relativity, which had been published back in 1905.

This was the prediction that energy and mass are equivalent and interchangeable, that $E = mc^2$. As physicists became able to measure the masses of atoms (and therefore of their nuclei) more accurately, and as their understanding of the forces that hold nuclei together slowly developed, it became clear that when a heavy nucleus splits into two lighter components, the energy liberated is exactly compensated for by a loss in mass of the components. When nucleus A splits into B and C, the mass of B and C added together is *less* than the mass of A by just the amount needed to provide the energy released by the fission, from the rule $E = mc^2$. In the 1920s and then increasingly in the 1930s, physicists, armed with the new quantum theory as well as relativity, began to come to grips with the implications of Einstein's theory for the world of nuclei.

The same rule, balancing energy gained and mass lost, applies to nuclei on the other side of the valley of stability. But in that case, of course, it is the *addition* of two lighter components to make a heavier nucleus that produces a loss of mass and a corresponding release of energy. A nucleus of helium-4, for instance, consists of two protons and two neutrons. Physicists measure the masses of atoms and nuclei in terms of the mass of an atom of carbon-12, which contains six protons and six neutrons (plus six electrons in a cloud outside the nucleus). This mass is defined as 12 atomic mass units. On this scale, the mass of a proton is 1.007275, and the mass of a neutron is 1.008664. Take two protons and two neutrons and you "ought" to get a total mass of 4.031878. But the mass of an alpha particle, a helium nucleus, is 4.00140 atomic mass units. A little more than 0.03 atomic mass units have been "lost," and appear as heat energy every time the four constituent particles combine together to make a helium nucleus. The amount of mass converted into energy is about 0.75 percent of the total you started with, and since this mass has to be multiplied by the square of the speed of light, and the speed of light is 3×10^{10} centimeters per second, that becomes very significant as soon as you have a means to manufacture helium nuclei inside stars.*

In the late 1920s and early 1930s, Eddington and his colleagues did not have a detailed theory of just how four hydrogen nuclei could be converted into one helium nucleus. But they knew that mass would be lost in the process, converted into energy, and they knew how much energy the Sun was radiating every second. Using Ein-

---

*Inside a star like the Sun, the raw material is all hydrogen nuclei, protons. Half of these have to be turned into neutrons along the way, which involves ejecting a positron to carry off the "spare" electric charge. Positrons are the positively charged counterparts to electrons, and when a positron meets an electron, the pair annihilate and all their mass is converted into energy. The result is that the numbers that go into the calculation are slightly different, and the calculations are that little bit more complicated, but you still end up with the "answer" that just over 0.7 percent of the original mass is turned into energy every time a helium nucleus is manufactured.

stein's equation, it is simple to calculate that the present brightness of the Sun can be maintained by converting just over 4 million tons of matter into energy every second. That is the amount of matter converted into energy when a little over 600 million tons of hydrogen (protons) is converted into helium (alpha particles). It sounds like a lot, but it is a tiny fraction of the Sun's mass. In round numbers, the mass of the Sun is 2×10^{33} grams, or 2×10^{27} tons. Converting 600 million (6×10^8) tons of hydrogen into helium each second, the Sun "burns" just under 2×10^{16} tons of fuel each year. In 1,000 years, it burns 2×10^{19} tons of hydrogen; in 1 million years, 2×10^{22} tons. And even after 10 billion years of hydrogen burning at this rate it has used only 2×10^{26} tons, just over 10 percent of the star's total mass. About 7 percent of this fuel, more than 14×10^{24} tons of matter, is converted totally into energy in the process. So it would take, in round terms, 10 billion years of "burning" hydrogen into helium at this rate to change the composition of the Sun to the point where its visible appearance would alter significantly. Here, immediately, is the reconciliation between the age of the Earth and the age of the Sun. If the Earth is 4 billion or 5 billion years old, and if a star like the Sun can burn hydrogen steadily for about 10 billion years, then we are scarcely halfway through the lifetime of the Sun in the form that we know it.

Although the broad outlines of the theory looked very good indeed, when Eddington proposed that fusion of hydrogen into helium must be the power source of the Sun and stars, many of his physicist contemporaries dismissed the idea. Their reason for doing so made sense at the time. Eddington's application of the basic laws of physics to the structure of the Sun and stars included a calculation of the temperature that must be maintained at the center of the Sun to provide its visible surface luminosity and to produce a pressure strong enough to hold the star up against the inward pull of gravity. This temperature is about 15 million degrees on the Kelvin scale. Temperature is simply a measure of the kinetic energy shared among a lot of particles—in the case of the air in my study, the temperature is an indicator of how fast, on average, a typical molecule in the air is moving. At the heart of the

to achieve the agreement between the superpowers banning atmospheric testing of nuclear weapons, and he continued to advise on nuclear disarmament issues after the signing of the treaty that came out of those negotiations. He received many honors during his career. But his major contribution to science came with the work carried out in 1938, and published in 1939, that showed how to generate energy by making helium inside a star. It was largely for this work that he received the Nobel Prize.*

The first mechanism Bethe came up with for energy generation inside stars involved the presence of heavier nuclei, particularly carbon, as well as hydrogen. He calculated that under the right conditions the collision of a proton with a nucleus of carbon-12 could produce a nucleus of nitrogen-13, which would then emit a positron and become a nucleus of carbon-13. In the same way, further collisions between the nucleus and other protons (hydrogen nuclei) at the heart of the star would produce first a nucleus of nitrogen-14, then one of oxygen-15, which decays by emission of a positron to nitrogen-15. At that point, when another proton comes along, the most likely result of the collision is not to produce a nucleus of oxygen-16, but for four nucleons to split off as an alpha particle, forming a helium nucleus and leaving behind a nucleus of carbon-12, exactly what you started with. Only about once in a thousand collisions would a nucleus of oxygen-16 form, and even that, after a couple of more protons had been taken on board, would emit an alpha particle and decay into nitrogen-14, rejoining the cycle. The net effect is that four protons have been converted into one helium nucleus, with the appropriate release of energy. And since the carbon-12 is put back where it came from to act as a catalyst for further fusion cycles, only a little carbon is needed to ensure a lot of nuclear fusion and the production of a lot of energy.

---

*At the same time, in 1938, another German physicist, Carl von Weizsäcker, proposed the same basic mechanism for keeping the Sun hot. Like Bethe, von Weizsäcker also worked on the problem of making an atomic bomb during the 1940s—but he was working in Germany at the time, and this may explain why he did not share the Nobel award with Bethe in 1967, even though it has been suggested that von Weizsäcker did everything in his power to ensure that the work of his team did not, in fact, provide the Nazis with nuclear weapons.

The process involves carbon, nitrogen, and oxygen nuclei as well as those of hydrogen and helium, and it goes in a circle, starting and ending with carbon-12 and converting four protons into one helium nucleus along the way. Naturally, it is called the carbon nitrogen oxygen cycle, or CNO cycle.* Bethe and a colleague, Charles Critchfield, then came up with an alternative route for hydrogen fusion inside stars. This is the step-by-step process starting with hydrogen nuclei and building first deuterium, then helium-3 and helium-4, either directly or by collisions between helium nuclei that produce nuclei containing seven nucleons each, ready to be converted into two alpha particles by the addition of just one more proton. This process—the one we met in the previous chapter, that halts at element number four, helium—starts with two protons colliding to make deuterium; it is called the proton-proton (or pp) chain.

Table 5.1

The CNO-cycle

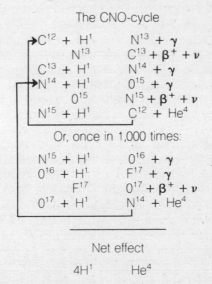

Or, once in 1,000 times:

Net effect

$$4H^1 \qquad He^4$$

---

*To be strictly accurate, only the CN part of the cycle was proposed in 1938–39; the minor role played by oxygen, and the change of name to CNO cycle, came later. There are really two cycles, involving CN and NO, respectively. Some astronomers, with a shameless addiction to puns, therefore refer to the CNO "bi-cycle."

Table 5.2

The pp-Chain

$$H^1 + H^1 \qquad D^2 + \beta^+ + \nu$$
$$D^2 + H^1 \qquad He^3 + \gamma$$
$$He^3 + He^3 \qquad He^4 + 2H^1$$

---

or

$$He^3 + He^4 \qquad Be^7 + \gamma$$
$$Be^7 + e^- \qquad Li^7 + \nu + \gamma$$
$$Li^7 + H^1 \qquad 2He^4$$

---

or

$$Be^7 + H^1 \qquad B^8 + \gamma$$
$$B^8 \qquad Be^8 + \beta^+ + \nu$$
$$Be^8 \qquad 2He^4$$

Net effect

$$4H^1 \qquad He^4$$

Bethe's calculations showed that such reactions could proceed under the conditions of temperature and pressure that Eddington had showed must exist inside stars. In fact, for our Sun the dominant process of energy production is thought to be the pp chain, which operates at the required efficiency at a temperature of about 15 million K; the CNO cycle works better at higher temperatures, above 20 million K, and so it is more important in more massive stars, which have to be hotter inside to be held up against the possibility of gravitational collapse. But these interesting details are not directly relevant to the story of the search for the Big Bang.

COOKING THE ELEMENTS

Bethe's work did not explain how carbon came to be inside stars in the first place, but it did explain how a star like our Sun could make use of the energy that ought to be available from the conversion of hydrogen into helium. The calculations were based on measurements of the way particles interacted with one another—their cross sections— under laboratory conditions, and these cross sections then had to be extrapolated to the conditions that the laws of physics said must exist inside stars. This is a huge step, scientifically speaking—not so much because it turns out that the behavior of particles measured in the lab *can* be extrapolated to tell us how stars work, but because of the way this discovery changes the whole conceptual approach of astrophysicists. Thanks to Eddington and Bethe, astrophysics became an *experimental* science; it was now possible to plan to carry out experiments here on Earth, with colliding beams of particles, that would unlock the secrets of nuclear fusion in the hearts of stars. When Bethe's first paper on the CN cycle (as it then was) appeared in *Physical Review* in 1939,* it made just this impact on a group of nuclear physicists working at the Kellogg Radiation Laboratory, part of the California Institute of Technology.

There, the senior physicist Charles Lauritsen and two younger men, his son Thomas and Willy Fowler, were involved in measurements of the cross sections for interactions involving carbon and nitrogen nuclei bombarded with a beam of protons. Bethe's paper showed them that they were studying, in the laboratory, processes that occur in the Sun and stars. Forty-four years later, in his Nobel address, Fowler said "it made a lasting impression on us."† So strong was the impact, indeed, that when the laboratory got back to basic nuclear research in 1946, the senior Lauritsen decided to concentrate on the study of just those nuclear reactions that were thought to take

*Volume 55, page 434.
†The address is reprinted in *Science*, Volume 226, page 922.

place inside stars. Fowler took up the challenge and became the leader of the CalTech investigation of how stars work.

Fowler is an ebullient, extroverted character who is still very much active in research today. "I intend to remain active," he told reporters when the award of his Nobel Prize was announced, "until they carry me out." He was born in 1911 in Pittsburgh and studied physics at Ohio State University, graduating in 1933, before he moved to California and gained his Ph.D. at CalTech in 1936. His main base has remained there ever since, although he often spends a few months at other research centers around the world. Fowler and the Kellogg lab played a key role in developing our understanding of stellar nucleosynthesis, and also in the modern calculations of precisely how much helium could have been produced in the Big Bang. But, as Fowler also acknowledged in his Nobel address, the "grand concept" of nucleosynthesis in stars came from Fred (now Sir Fred) Hoyle in two papers published in 1946 and 1954.

The dates are important, especially to Hoyle. When Fowler's Nobel award was announced, many of the popular accounts of the work for which it was given mentioned Hoyle's contribution, and some of them were quick to point out that the need to find a way to synthesize the elements inside stars was an obvious requirement for one of the inventors of the Steady State theory. After all, if there was no Big Bang, then the Steady Staters *had* to make their elements inside stars! Since the steady state theory is now discredited, these reports suggested that Hoyle had hit on the right idea for the wrong reason—and hinted that, perhaps, this was why he hadn't shared the award with Fowler. But the Steady State theory did not "come along," as Hoyle pointed out to me at the time of Fowler's award, until 1948, whereas his first paper on nucleosynthesis was written in 1945 and published in 1946.* And besides, the Big Bangers can't make anything heavier than helium in the Big Bang, in any case.

Hoyle gives the outward appearance of being a prickly character. His reluctance to suffer fools gladly has not endeared him to the establishment and led to his prema-

---

Monthly Notices of the Royal Astronomical Society, Volume 106, page 343.

ture retirement from his posts at the University of Cambridge in 1973, at the age of fifty-eight. In fact, he is basically a shy introvert who lives for his work and has clearly developed a more forceful persona as a means of communicating the importance of his ideas to others. He was born in Bingley, Yorkshire, in 1915 and sometimes gives his opponents the impression that his "Yorkshire blunt speaking" is carefully cultivated—sometimes what might otherwise be regarded as downright rudeness seems to be forgivable as the traditional frankness of a Northerner. But he has clearly been deeply wounded by the failure of the British scientific establishment, in particular, to recognize fully the merits of his own work and ideas about how science ought to be run. If he were really as thick-skinned and insensitive as the image implies, he would surely have soldiered on longer in Cambridge.

His early career, though, followed conventional lines, through the local grammar school to Emmanuel College in Cambridge, and then a Fellowship at St. John's College in 1945. In 1958 he became Plumian Professor, and he was the inspiration behind and first Director of the Institute of Theoretical Astronomy, founded in Cambridge in 1967. But this was the peak of his establishment career; although Hoyle served on many high-level committees (while finding enough spare time to write popular books of science fact and science fiction), was elected a Fellow of the Royal Society, and was honored with a knighthood, he fell out with the authorities in Cambridge concerning the role and development of astronomical research within the university, he disagreed violently with the administrators of British science about how science as a whole should be funded and carried out, and in the 1970s and 1980s he alienated many of his scientific colleagues by espousing ideas about the origin of life in the Universe that many regarded as unsound. But none of that, nor any opinions other astronomers may hold about the Steady State model or any other of Hoyle's wide-ranging views about the nature of the Universe, should be allowed to detract from the key role he played in the discovery of how elements are cooked inside stars.

The problem began to be a pressing one for astronomers not because of any interest in the Big Bang or Steady

State models of the Universe but because their improving observations of stellar spectra increasingly showed, in the 1940s and 1950s, that different stars contained different amounts of the different elements. You might speculate that the material from which stars formed came from a Big Bang, or you might speculate that the material to make new stars is being created continuously in the spaces between the galaxies. But when you find that there are systematic differences in the composition of the stars, with some stars richer in heavier elements than others, you begin to suspect that some of those elements are being manufactured out of the primordial material (whatever that may have been) inside the stars themselves.

Hoyle's 1946 paper presented, for the first time, a clear exposition of the basic ideas of nucleosynthesis within the accepted framework of stellar structure and evolution and using the best information about nuclear reaction rates, cross sections, and so on. As Gamow's team struggled to find a way to make elements heavier than helium in the Big Bang, Hoyle struggled to find ways to make them inside stars, visiting CalTech for the first time in 1953 and soon joining forces with Fowler. The key problem was how to get past the instability of the boron-8 nucleus. The only way to do this was to invoke a triple collision, with three alpha particles colliding almost simultaneously to form a nucleus of carbon-12. Gamow couldn't make this work in the Big Bang, because even a few minutes after the moment of creation, matter in the Universe was spread too thin, and the temperature was too low, for such collisions to happen often enough to produce the amount of heavy elements we see in the Universe today. Inside stars, however, it is both hot and dense, and the inside of a star stays hot and dense for many millions of years, giving a much better opportunity for even relatively rare triple collisions to occur often enough to produce a significant amount of carbon.

The idea looked good, but it ran into problems rather like the problems Eddington encountered when the physicists told him the Sun was not hot enough for hydrogen fusion to occur. When Ed Salpeter, a physicist visiting the Kellogg lab in 1951, made the appropriate calculations, he found that the cross sections still weren't big enough. You could make *some* carbon-12 inside stars, but nowhere near enough. Now Hoyle made a dramatic contribution. He came to CalTech in 1953 convinced that all the heavy elements are made in stars. He had tackled the calculation from the other end, using the observed measurements (from spectroscopy) of the abundances of heavy elements in stars to deduce how fast the triple-collision reaction *must* proceed, and he found that it had to go much faster than Salpeter had calculated. So he predicted that the carbon-12 nucleus must be capable of existing in what is called an excited state, a state that has more energy than the minimum value appropriate for that nucleus. If such an excited state existed, with precisely the right amount of energy, then and only then could the collision of three alpha particles together be encouraged to form carbon-12 nuclei sufficiently often to make all the carbon observed in the spectra of stars. The reaction is encouraged by a process called resonance between the energy state of the three alpha particles and the energy state of the carbon-12 nucleus, and the resonance occurs only if the carbon-12 energy level is just right, which is how Hoyle was able to predict what the excited energy state of carbon-12 must be.

Hoyle badgered the physicists at CalTech until a group of them went away to look for an excited state of carbon-12, using a reaction involving deuterium particles colliding with nitrogen-14 nuclei to make carbon-12 plus an alpha particle. And they found it, almost exactly where Hoyle had predicted.

This was still one step short of proving that the excited state of carbon-12 could be produced by the interaction of three alpha particles, but now Fowler, working with the two Lauritsens and Charles Cook, manufactured "excited" carbon-12 from the decay of boron-12. They found that although some of the excited carbon-12 then fell back into its minimum energy state (the ground state) and stayed as carbon-12, some of it broke up into three alpha particles. Other things being equal (and in this case they are), these kinds of nuclear reaction are reversible. Since excited carbon-12 can decay into three alpha particles, there is no doubt that three alpha particles can combine to form excited carbon-12. Here was the proof that as well as burning hydrogen to make helium, stars could burn helium to make carbon. The helium-burning process explained how large stars, called red giants, are kept hot, and it also got astrophysicists over the hurdle of nucleosynthesis at element number eight. And, of course, it provided the carbon needed for the CNO cycle to operate. By looking at information from stellar spectroscopy, Hoyle had correctly predicted what physicists would find in experiments in the lab here on Earth. That gave them the confidence to continue their measurements of interaction rates in the lab, and use the information to calculate the whole chain of reactions needed to build up all of the naturally occurring elements, in all their varieties of isotopes, in the stars.

In a brief survey of how stellar nucleosynthesis became understood, it is inevitable that the rest, after the production of carbon-12, may seem almost an anticlimax, just the icing on the cake that Hoyle, together with Fowler and his colleagues, had already baked. In outline, it was now easy to understand how all the elements are made in stars. Alpha particles (helium nuclei) are added to the nuclei, increasing their mass four units at a time; decays that eject electrons, positrons, or neutrons then form the other elements and isotopes. For very heavy elements (heavier than iron), capture of individual neutrons, increasing the mass of the nucleus by one unit at a time, also becomes important. But there are no more yawning chasms to worry about like the one facing astrophysicists trying to build carbon-12 out of alpha particles. The rest was a question of painstaking, detailed work to measure all the necessary cross sections and reaction rates, and to fit these to the calculated conditions of temperature and pressure inside stars and to the observed abundances of the elements deduced from stellar spectroscopy.

The cross-section measurements were no small task in themselves; extrapolating these from the relatively high energy conditions of collisions in accelerators in the lab to the much lower energy conditions of collisions between particles inside the stars required great skill; and the observers were stretched to find out just what the composition of the Universe is, anyway. But everything came together in the mid-1950s. Fowler spent the academic year 1954–55 in Cambridge, working with Hoyle and with Margaret and Geoffrey Burbidge, a British husband-and-wife team of astronomers. The collaboration continued long after Fowler returned to CalTech, with now Hoyle and then the Burbidges (sometimes all three) visiting the Kellogg lab in turn. In 1956, astronomers Hans Suess and Harold Urey published the best data yet on the relative abundances of all the naturally occurring elements; that same year, the four collaborators produced a short paper in *Science* on the origin of the elements, and in 1957 they followed it with a paper in *Reviews of Modern Physics** that remains one of the classic scientific papers of all time. In alphabetical order, the paper was signed "Burbidge, Burbidge, Fowler, and Hoyle"; it is known to all astronomers simply as "B^2FH," and no further reference is needed when citing it. The paper describes how all the naturally occurring varieties of nuclei, except for hydrogen and helium, are built up inside the stars—and in the words of the Swedish Academy of Sciences' announcement of Fowler's Nobel prize, this paper "is still the basis of our knowledge in this field, and the most recent progress in nuclear physics and space research has further confirmed its correctness." On a more personal note, I still recall the thrill I got when I first came across the paper as a graduate student in 1966; the awe of knowing that the equations in the paper I held explained where all the atoms in my own body (except for the primordial hydrogen) came from, and how all those atoms had been cooked in stars. As far as any piece of scientific investigation could, this paper closed a chapter of research, with the complete answer to a major puzzle not just in science but also in philosophy, an answer it had taken Hoyle and his collaborators just ten

---

*Volume 29, page 547. Alastair Cameron, a Canadian-born American astrophysicist, came to similar conclusions independently and published his calculations in 1957 in *Publications of the Astronomical Society of the Pacific*, Volume 69, page 201. If it seems a little unfair that he should be relegated to a footnote, remember that it was, after all, Hoyle who came up with what Fowler calls "the grand concept of element synthesis in the stars" (Nobel address, op. cit.), and it was Fowler's team who carried through the reaction rate studies in the lab. History probably is correct to give B^2FH pride of place, though you might think the Burbidges were lucky to have been in the right place at the right time to join Fowler and Hoyle in their endeavors.

years to track down, from the time he had published his first landmark paper on the subject.

The B^2FH paper marked the end of the puzzle of stellar nucleosynthesis, except for dotting the i's and crossing the t's. But it didn't mark the end of the puzzle of all nucleosynthesis. Starting out with about 70 to 75 percent hydrogen and 25 to 30 percent helium in the first generation of stars in the Universe, the astrophysicists could show how all the heavier elements were made, and they could guess that these heavy elements are then scattered across space when some old stars explode, as novae and supernovae, to enrich the mixture of gases from which later stars are made. Our own Sun is relatively young; it contains the recycled material from older stars, long since dead, and that is where its 2 percent of heavy elements, and the material of which the Earth and ourselves are made, comes from. Sixty-five percent of your body weight is oxygen; 18 percent is carbon. It has all been through the triple alpha capture process, among other reactions, inside stars. But stellar nucleosynthesis could not explain why there was so much helium in the Universe. This "helium problem" bedeviled astrophysicists in the late 1950s and early 1960s, in spite of Gamow and Alpher's earlier success in making helium in the Big Bang. Perhaps because they had failed in their intended objective of making *all* the elements in this way, their success with helium was overlooked; whatever the reason, it was left to Fowler, with his student Robert Wagoner and, once again, Fred Hoyle,* to apply their improved knowledge of nuclear reaction rates to the conditions that were thought to have applied in the first few minutes of the creation of the Universe.

With reaction rates for almost 100 nuclear processes determined by Fowler's group included in the calculations, and using the fact that other reactions had been shown in the laboratory to be insignificant, this team established that no significant quantities of any element heavier than helium could be produced in the Big Bang,

---

*The two were, scientifically, almost inseparable. Fowler has published between two hundred and three hundred scientific papers to date; of these, no less than twenty-five (about 10 percent) carry Hoyle's name as well. It is, indeed, a shame that the Nobel Committee did not see fit to keep the two names together in 1983.

that the proportion of helium-4 coming out of the Big Bang ought to be about 25 percent, and that associated with it there should be deuterium, helium-3, and a trace of lithium-7, in proportions similar to those in which these elements are found in the Solar System.

Wagoner, Fowler, and Hoyle published their findings in 1967. It was another personal landmark for me—my first visit to Cambridge was to hear the team give a report of these findings, and I clearly recall the penetrating questions asked at the gathering by an unknown Cambridge research student, Stephen Hawking. That visit, and the excitement of the meeting, were instrumental in encouraging me to move from the University of Sussex to Cambridge, intending to do research in cosmology. I ended up working on problems in stellar structure, but I still think the trip was worthwhile! Far more importantly, though, the Wagoner, Fowler, and Hoyle collaboration had a major impact on cosmology. "It was this paper," says Sir William McCrea, "that caused many physicists to accept hot big bang cosmology as serious quantitative science."*

The science was so "serious," indeed, that it was able to address a much more subtle problem than the abundance of helium in the Universe. The helium is manufactured by the fusion of deuterons, nuclei of heavy hydrogen (deuterium). Very nearly all the deuterons are used up in the process, but a small fraction—between .01 and .001 percent—of all the hydrogen in the Universe today seems to be in the form of deuterium, judging by spectroscopic

---

*Physics Bulletin, Volume 35, page 17. McCrea surely knows what he is talking about. Like Hoyle, he was one of the pioneers in developing the Steady State model, and as a good scientist who thinks deeply about the nature of the scientific endeavor, he still cautions that the Big Bang model is not "proved" correct. Simple Big Bang and simple Steady State models represent two extremes in a vast range of possibilities, and there are many shades of gray in between. The important thing, he says, is to discuss all the possibilities with an open mind—and then, although one model may seem a better description than any other of the world we live in today, it is unlikely that any scientist will be able to say, with absolute conviction, "this is right." But the hot Big Bang model *is* accepted as by far the best model of the Universe by the great majority of astronomers today. The irony that Hoyle, chief proponent of the Steady State model, should be coauthor of a landmark paper that persuaded people of the validity of the Big Bang model gives a wry twist to the tale.

studies of stars and galaxies. Although the proportion of helium that emerges from the Big Bang is not very sensitive to such factors as the overall density of the matter emerging from the Big Bang, it turns out that the deuterium abundance *is* a very sensitive indicator of density. If the model used in the calculations is more dense, then the reactions proceed faster and the deuterons are used up more quickly. And the kind of calculation carried out by Wagoner, Fowler, and Hoyle indicates that the density of everyday matter in the Universe is less than the critical amount needed to make the Universe closed and ensure that it will one day collapse back into a fireball. This is the strongest piece of evidence in favor of the possibility that our Universe is open and will expand forever. But it is not the last word on the subject. The latest ideas in cosmology, discussed in Part Three of this book, include the possibility that there may be a great deal of other matter in the Universe, in forms that did not take part in the nuclear reactions described by Wagoner, Fowler, and Hoyle and their successors, and that might "close" the Universe gravitationally regardless of what the deuterium is telling us about the amount of ordinary matter (by which I mean atoms and atomic nuclei) that came out of the Big Bang. But that is getting ahead of the story as it stood in the late 1960s.

The investigation of nucleosynthesis had by then provided a beautifully dovetailing pair of pieces of evidence in favor of the hot Big Bang. All the investigations, from Gamow onward, had shown that no elements heavier than helium could be made in the Big Bang. They had to be made somewhere else. The equations of stellar nucleosynthesis showed that everything heavier than helium could indeed be made in stars but that the observed amount of helium in the Universe could not; it must have been made somewhere else. Big Bang theory needed stellar nucleosynthesis; stellar nucleosynthesis needed the Big Bang. Together, the combination of a hot Big Bang and nucleosynthesis inside the stars provided a beautiful, complete picture of where *everything* came from.

And there was another piece of "quantitative science" in that 1967 paper that helped to make the physicists sit up and take notice of the Big Bang theory. Wagoner,

Fowler, and Hoyle included in their work the first quantitative application of a new discovery, the cosmic microwave background radiation, in establishing the parameters of their model. This cosmic background is the radiation that was half predicted by Gamow and his colleagues in the 1950s and then forgotten. It is the second piece of powerful evidence that the Universe did indeed emerge from a hot fireball—the second key to the Universe.

THE LOST YEARS

The idea of taking the temperature of the Universe and using the measurement to find out more about the Big Bang in which the Universe was born may have been too farfetched for physicists and astronomers to take seriously in the 1950s. But that doesn't mean the idea was totally ignored, and more than one astronomer has looked back ruefully to that decade and metaphorically kicked himself for failing to follow the idea through to its logical conclusion. Indeed, Gamow, Alpher, and Herman must have shared these feelings—not least since some astronomical observations that clearly implied a background temperature of the Universe of about 3 K had already been carried out in the 1930s and were certainly known to Gamow and his colleagues in the 1950s.

These observations, like so much of our information from space, depend on spectroscopy. In the 1930s, astronomers began to identify, for the first time, spectral features corresponding to the presence of molecules in interstellar space. Starlight carries with it the spectral signature of the atoms (or more accurately ions, atoms with some electrons stripped off) present in the atmosphere of the star. The characteristic lines stand out as either bright emission lines (radiating energy) or dark absorption lines (absorbing energy from the star below) in the electromagnetic spectrum. The strength of these lines and the extent of the ionization they reveal enable astronomers to deduce the temperature of a distant star as well as to determine its composition. But there are also lines in some spectra that correspond to compounds that could not possibly be stable at the temperature at the surface of a star. One of the earliest of these to be identified is cyanogen, CN, a stable pairing of one carbon atom and one nitrogen atom to produce what is known as a radical. Such compounds occur not in the stars themselves, where the heat would soon break them into their component atoms, but in cool clouds of gas and dust between the stars. Their presence is revealed by the dark lines they impose on the light from distant stars shining through the cool clouds.

Just as observations of stellar spectra reveal the temperatures of the stars, so observations of these absorption spectra can reveal the temperatures of the clouds of interstellar material. In 1940, W. S. Adams, at Mount Wilson, observed interstellar spectral lines corresponding to an energetic state of cyanogen, and Andrew McKellar, of the Dominion Astrophysical Observatory in Canada, interpreted those observations as indicating a temperature for the interstellar clouds of about 2.3 K. By 1950, the result was enshrined in a standard textbook on spectroscopy* and was very well known to astronomers, including Gamow. But nobody thought of interpreting the temperature of the coldest clouds of material found in space as "the temperature of the Universe." One of the nearest misses came in 1956, when Fred Hoyle and George Gamow were cruising around La Jolla, in Southern California, in a brand-new white Cadillac convertible.

Hoyle recounted the tale in an article in *New Scientist* published in 1981.† He was visiting Willy Fowler and his colleagues at CalTech that summer, and Gamow called them from La Jolla to invite Fowler, Hoyle, and the Burbidges down for a visit. Gamow was in La Jolla because he was spending two months as a consultant with General Dynamics, a job that was very lucrative (the two months' consultation fee paid for the white Cadillac convertible) and apparently required little real work, but for which Gamow was obliged to stay in La Jolla somewhere

---

*G. Herzberg, *Spectra of Diatomic Molecules,* second edition (Princeton, N.J.: Van Nostrand, 1950).

†And since reprinted in the collection *Observing the Universe,* edited by Nigel Henbest (Oxford: Blackwell, 1984). The quote is taken from page 9 of that volume.

(even on the beach) to be on call immediately if his services were required. So the B^2FH team made their way,
not too reluctantly, south to La Jolla. At that time, Gamow's
estimates for the temperature of the Universe today were
in the range of about 5 K to a few tens of K; Hoyle, as a
steady stater, thought there should be no background radiation at all. So they both missed the truth that lay under
their noses. Hoyle takes up the story:

> There were times when George and I would go off for
> a discussion by ourselves. I recall George driving me
> around in the white Cadillac, explaining his convic-
> tion that the Universe must have a microwave back-
> ground, and I recall my telling George that it was
> impossible for the Universe to have a microwave back-
> ground with a temperature as high as he was claim-
> ing, because observations of the CH and CN radicals
> by Andrew McKellar had set an upper limit of 3 K for
> any such background. Whether it was the too-great
> comfort of the Cadillac, or because George wanted a
> temperature higher than 3 K whereas I wanted a
> temperature of zero K, we missed the chance . . . For
> my sins, I missed it again in exactly the same way in
> a discussion with Bob Dicke at the twentieth Varenna
> summer school on relativity in 1961. In respect of the
> microwave background, I was evidently not "discov-
> ery prone. . . ."

The Bob Dicke that Hoyle discussed the problem with
in Varenna in 1961 deserves a special place in the hall of
missed opportunities, for, quite apart from that conversation, he missed the chance to go down in history as "the
man who took the temperature of the Universe" not once
but *twice*—and on the second occasion he had forgotten
about his own earlier work on the problem! Just a year
younger than Hoyle, Dicke was born in St. Louis, Missouri, in 1916. He graduated from Princeton in the late
1930s, completed a Ph.D. at Rochester University in 1941,
and worked on radar at MIT during World War Two before joining the faculty at Princeton in 1946. He has
stayed there ever since, to become chairman of the department of physics and Albert Einstein Professor of Science.
Dicke is nobody's fool. But he, too, could not see in the
1940s what now seems obvious with hindsight.

During his time at MIT, Dicke developed an instrument for measuring very short wavelength radio radiation in the microwave part of the electromagnetic spectrum. The instrument is called a Dicke radiometer; its principles are incorporated in modern instruments designed to do the same job. With three of his colleagues, Dicke pointed one of these instruments at the sky, looking to see if there were any background of microwave radiation from the external galaxies. One way of interpreting the strength of such radiation is in terms of temperature; Dicke and his colleagues concluded that there was a background radiation with a temperature below 20 K, the limit that could be set by their instrument, and they wrote a paper reporting this result. It was published in *Physical Review*, in the same volume in which Gamow's 1946 paper on nucleosynthesis appeared. The paper by Dicke's team appeared first (Volume 70, page 340); Gamow's came along a little later (Volume 70, page 572). There is nothing to link the two papers, but they appear in the same bound volume of the journal, and every student, or more senior researcher, in the 1950s who went to look up Gamow's paper, perhaps following the story back from the alpha, beta, gamma paper, or from the work by Alpher and Herman, literally held in his (or her) hands the evidence that the cosmic fireball really had existed. Anyone—Hoyle, Gamow, or some unknown student—looking up Gamow's paper might have come across the Dicke team's paper and put two and two together; but it didn't turn out that way. Sometimes scientific discoveries seem to have a will of their own, waiting until the time is ripe for them to happen.

By the early 1960s, Dicke himself had forgotten all about this measurement. But his thoughts were turning to cosmology, and in surprising, but seemingly complete, ignorance of the pioneering efforts of Gamow, Alpher, and Herman, he independently investigated the implications of a model universe that collapses down from a very great size into a fireball, then bounces away from the very high density state and expands. Dicke was intrigued by the idea that the Universe might be in the expansion phase of an oscillation that could continue forever, with each cycle of expansion followed by one of collapse, each collapse followed by a bounce and a new phase of expansion. And he needed the collapse to continue down to a state of very high temperature and density before the "bounce" occurred, so that all the material in the collapsing universe would be broken back down into neutrons and protons before a new phase of expansion began—there must be no "information," as it were, carried over from one cycle of the universe to the next, and to anyone living in the expanding universe it would be just as if the universe had been created in a Big Bang.

All this was still very much in the spirit of cosmology as a game, an intellectual exercise. But Dicke's experience (albeit half-forgotten experience) as an observer set him and his colleagues on the right trail at last. He gave a young researcher at Princeton, P. J. E. Peebles, the task of working out the way the temperature of such a model universe would change as it evolved; repeating, unknowingly, the calculations Alpher and Herman had carried through more than fifteen years before, Peebles found that if the Universe we live in had started out in a hot Big Bang, then it should be filled with a background sea of radiation with a temperature of about 10 K. In 1964, in the light of Peebles's calculations, Dicke encouraged two other members of the Princeton research staff to carry out a search for this radiation. P. G. Roll and D. T. Wilkinson set up a detector (a version of the Dicke radiometer), and they began to construct a small antenna on the roof of the physics lab at Princeton to detect any cosmic background radiation with a temperature of a few K. Then, on the point of making an epochal discovery, the rug was pulled from under the Princeton team. Dicke received a phone call from a young man at the Bell Research Laboratories, just 30 miles away from Princeton, at Holmdel, New Jersey. The caller, Arno Penzias, and a colleague, Robert Wilson, had been getting some funny results from their radio telescope, a 20-foot horn antenna used in some of the early experiments with communications satellites. Someone had suggested Dicke might be able to explain this puzzling cosmic background radiation; perhaps they could all get together to discuss it . . .

THE ECHO OF CREATION

Arno Penzias comes from a Jewish family in Munich. He was born in 1933, on the same day (April 26) that the Gestapo was formed. The family was one of the last to get out of Nazi Germany to England in 1939—Arno and his brother were sent in the spring and were later followed by his father and, finally, mother. Reunited, the family left England in December 1939, sailing for New York, where they landed in January 1940 and stayed. Education provided the opportunity for this son of an impoverished immigrant family to make his way in the world, and in 1954 Penzias graduated from the City College of New York with a degree in physics. After two years in the Army Signal Corps, he attended Columbia University as a graduate student, working for his Ph.D., which was awarded in 1962.

Penzias worked at Columbia with Charles Townes, a physicist who played a key role in the development of masers and lasers* and who was to receive a Nobel Prize for his efforts in 1964. A maser can be used as the basis of an amplifying system to detect weak radio emissions, and Penzias built a maser receiver designed to operate at 21-centimeter wavelength. This is the natural wavelength at which hydrogen gas radiates, and Penzias hoped to detect the 21-centimeter "line" of intergalactic hydrogen. But he failed, largely because there isn't any intergalactic hydrogen to be observed, and he was only able to set an upper limit on how much hydrogen there might be between the galaxies. This kind of "failure" is not at all uncommon for a doctoral student, or even for other research projects, and clearly the examiners at Columbia were happy that Penzias had carried out his work effectively, even if it came up with a negative result. But he took a harsher view of his

---

*Maser is an acronym for microwave amplification by stimulated emission of radiation; the important words in the present context are "microwave" (which means it operates at wavelengths of a few centimeters) and "amplification" (which means it makes a weak radio input stronger). A laser is the same kind of thing but operates with light instead of microwaves.

own work. As he told Jeremy Bernstein, author of the book *Three Degrees Above Zero,* "I just got through Columbia by the skin of my teeth ... it was a dreadful thesis." Dreadful or not, though, the association with Townes and his first attempt at radio astronomy profoundly influenced the rest of Penzias's career.

Townes had come to Columbia University from Bell Labs in 1948. Bell Labs was originally a research division of the Bell Telephone Company, later swallowed up by AT&T, and more recently involved in antitrust legislation to break up the conglomerate, which has meant some uncertainty about the continuing role of Bell Labs as an independent research institution. Whatever their fate, though, Bell Labs has a proud history of research, including the first discovery of radio noise from space by Karl Jansky, a Bell researcher and the founder of radio astronomy, in the 1930s. Through Townes's continuing contacts with Bell Labs, Penzias joined their Radio Research Laboratory at Crawford Hill near Holmdel in 1961, shortly before the award of his Ph.D. Although fundamentally devoted to practical research to benefit the parent company, Bell Labs has always maintained a tradition of academic research as well, which helps to ensure that first-rate scientists are always eager to join the team and which keeps Bell Labs' practical side in touch with new developments coming out of the universities and other academic institutions. Penzias worked at first on problems associated with the systems that were used for the first satellite communications links, using the Echo and Telstar satellites. Then he was allowed to turn to radio astronomy again, making only a little headway before he was joined at Crawford Hill by another would-be radio astronomer, Robert Wilson. One radio astronomy post was the ration allowed, so Penzias and Wilson split it between them, each devoting half their time to radio astronomy and half to other projects.

Wilson comes from a very different background than Penzias's. Born in Houston, Texas, in 1936, he is the son of a chemical engineer, and both his parents went to college. With straight A's in all his science courses at Rice University in Houston, when Wilson graduated in 1957 he was offered places in the graduate schools at both MIT and CalTech, the two premier scientific research institutes in the United States; he chose CalTech, but with no clear idea of just what line of research he would like to take up. There he was influenced by two British astronomers—Fred Hoyle, who taught the cosmology course during a spell as visiting professor at CalTech and whose presentation left Wilson with a fondness for the Steady State theory; and David Dewhirst, who suggested that Wilson might like to work with John Bolton, an Australian radio astronomer then at CalTech. So Wilson worked with Bolton on a radio survey of the Milky Way, mapping out the clouds of hydrogen gas in our own Galaxy. The result wasn't exactly world-shatteringly important; the map was made, and it confirmed the accuracy of a similar map made by a group in Australia. Wilson remains as deprecating as Penzias about the quality of his first research project: "Frankly, I don't think much scientifically ever came out of the thesis, although it was a good learning experience, and I did get a chance to meet most of the world's radio astronomers, who came through CalTech to visit."* Whereas Penzias left Columbia just before completing his Ph.D., Wilson stayed on at CalTech for a year after completing his, in 1962. So it was in 1963 that, hearing about Bell Labs' interest in radio astronomy and the availability of the still relatively new horn antenna at Crawford Hill, he decided to take the plunge, and joined Penzias in New Jersey.

The antenna had been put up to work with the Echo series of satellites. These were simply large metaled balloons that inflated in orbit and were used to bounce radio signals around the world. They had no amplifiers of their own but acted like mirrors in the sky, so the signals were pretty weak by the time they got back to the ground stations, and needed to be caught by a good antenna system and amplified considerably if they were to be of any use. With the advent of active communications satellites—Telstar and its successors, which amplify the signals they receive from the ground before they rebroadcast them to other ground stations—the designed role of the Crawford Hill antenna was at an end, so Penzias and Wilson were allowed to take the communications receiver

*Bernstein, op. cit.

out and turn the antenna into a radio telescope. This took several months. They wanted the new receiver to be as sensitive as possible so it could detect very weak astronomical radio noise. So they had to eliminate, as far as they could, all the sources of noise in the electrical systems used to amplify the radio waves from space. This noise is a bit like the static you get on an AM radio; some of the hiss of background noise is from stray radio waves (including radio waves from space), but some is due to the inefficiency of the radio receiver itself. The static, or background noise, can be measured in terms of temperature, and the engineers working with the Crawford Hill antenna on tests with the Echo satellites had noticed that there was a little more static than they could explain in their system. In effect, the antenna was too hot; in an article that appeared in the *Bell Systems Technical Journal* in 1961, one of the engineers, E. A. Ohm, reported an excess noise, after subtracting everything that could be explained away, equivalent to radiation with a temperature of about 3 K. This wasn't enough to disrupt the Echo communications system, so the engineers weren't too worried about it. But it was just the sort of thing that Penzias and Wilson had to track down and eliminate, or at least identify, before they could begin their planned program of radio astronomy research.

While Penzias and Wilson were trying to track down this infuriating source of noise in their system—even going so far as to clean out pigeon droppings from the horn itself, with no effect—the Princeton team was calmly proceeding with the plans to construct an instrument to detect the cosmic background radiation. At the same time, in 1964, over in England, Fred Hoyle (that man again!) and Roger Tayler were beginning to move along the same lines, with calculations of the background temperature of a Big Bang universe today. And in the Soviet Union there was a veritable flurry of activity. Ya. B. Zel'dovich had also carried out the calculation that showed that in order to explain the observed abundances of hydrogen, helium, and deuterium in the Universe, it must have started in a hot Big Bang and have a temperature of a few K today; he even knew of Ohm's article in the *Bell Systems Technical Journal* but misunderstood Ohm's terminology and thought that his measurements implied that the background temperature of the Universe was less than 1 K. Another Soviet researcher, Yu. N. Smirnov, calculated a background, or relict, radiation temperature in the range of 1 to 30 K and, jumping off from Smirnov's calculations, A. G. Doroshkevich and I. D. Novikov wrote a paper discussing the implications of various existing radio astronomy measurements in terms of the microwave background. They concluded that the best antenna then existing in the world for a search for this radiation was the Bell Labs antenna at Crawford Hill, and they suggested in their paper that the antenna be used for this purpose. All of this work was being carried out, and most of it published, in 1964. The idea of the cosmic microwave background had clearly decided the time was ripe for it to come out into the open. But with all the interest in at least four research centers spread across two continents, Penzias and Wilson themselves remained blissfully ignorant of the solution to their puzzle of where the excess noise in their system was coming from.

The accounts of how that ignorance was broken differ slightly, but the essentials are the same. According to one version, Penzias had been to an astronomical gathering in Montreal and was returning, in December 1964, in an airplane where he sat next to Bernard Burke, who was based at MIT. During the flight, Penzias mentioned the problems he and Wilson were having eliminating the background noise from their system, and as a result Burke telephoned Penzias a few days later to put him on the trail of the Princeton group. The other version of the story has it that Penzias just happened to mention the background noise in a phone call to Burke that he initiated, to discuss other matters. Either way, there is no doubt that it was during a telephone conversation in January 1965 that Burke, at MIT, told Penzias, at Crawford Hill, that yet another astronomer, Ken Turner, of the Carnegie Institution in Washington, D.C., had heard a talk by P. J. E. Peebles, the Princeton theorist, in which he predicted a background noise of electromagnetic radiation filling the Universe, with a temperature equivalent of about 10 K. Burke suggested that Penzias get in touch with the Princeton group; Penzias phoned Dicke, and very soon all four members of the Princeton team made the half-hour drive to Crawford Hill to find out what was going on. At last the theory and the observations had been put together; two plus two really *did* make four.

The Princeton team was much more excited about the discovery than Penzias and Wilson were. To the Princeton researchers, the observation was in line with a prediction made by theory (what they thought was their theory), a good example of the scientific method at work. To Penzias and Wilson, although it was a relief to have some explanation of the radio noise they were measuring, it still seemed that other explanations might come along. Besides, Wilson was reluctant to accept that the Steady State hypothesis was dead until more evidence came in. In particular, the measurements had been made only at one wavelength, just over 7 centimeters; they would have to be made at many other wavelengths, using different receivers, before the true nature of the background radiation could be reliably understood.

So the news, although it spread rapidly throughout the scientific community, appeared in print in an extremely modest way. Penzias and Wilson agreed with the Princeton team that each group should submit a paper to the *Astrophysical Journal,* to be published alongside each other. The Princeton paper was much the more exciting and interesting of the two and appeared first (Volume 142, page 414); Penzias and Wilson's paper followed it, under the inauspicious title "A Measurement of Excess Antenna Temperature at 4,080 Mc/s" (Volume 142, page 419). News of the discovery for which they were to receive a Nobel Prize in 1978 was put in context only by the sentence "a possible explanation for the observed excess noise temperature is the one given by Dicke, Peebles, Roll, and Wilkinson in a companion letter in this issue." But perhaps the most remarkable feature of that issue of the *Astrophysical Journal* is that *neither* paper makes any reference to the work of Gamow, Alpher, and Herman. The omission was soon corrected, and later publications invariably gave credit to those pioneers, but not before they had all been deeply upset at the way their work had been ignored.

Later measurements at different wavelengths established beyond doubt that the "excess noise" referred to by Penzias and Wilson is indeed a cosmic background of electromagnetic radiation, exactly the kind of "black body" radiation, with a temperature close to 2.7 K, required by the Big Bang model of the origin of our Universe.* It really is the echo of creation, a leftover piece of the Big Bang that we are able to reach out and touch with our instruments. The discovery ranks with the most important scientific discoveries ever made, and it changed the face of cosmology by making the participants realize that they were not playing some intellectual game but were dealing with equations that really could describe the origin of our Universe and everything in it. The question "Where do we come from?" moved from the realm of philosophy into the realm of science with the recognition of the relict radiation for what it was. And this is why Gamow and his colleagues were ahead of their time—because they were almost alone, in the 1940s and 1950s, in *believing* the equations. Steven Weinberg, one of the physicists who turned to cosmology once the realization that cosmology was indeed a science spread with news of the background radiation, has summed the situation up appositely:

> Gamow, Alpher, and Herman deserve tremendous credit above all for being willing to take the early universe seriously, for working out what known physical laws have to say about the first three minutes. Yet even they did not take the final step, to convince radio astronomers that they ought to look for a microwave radiation background. The most important thing accomplished by the ultimate discovery of the 3 K radiation background in 1965 was to force us all to take seriously the idea that there *was* an early universe.†

---

*But it is *possible* to provide alternative explanations for the background radiation. David Layzer of Harvard University has recently argued vociferously that it may be produced by radiation from a generation of massive stars that formed *before* galaxies formed, in an initially cold universe. Such possibilities are certainly worthy of discussion and serve as reminders that the accepted "best buy" model of the Universe does not necessarily represent the last word. Layzer makes the case for his version of cosmology in his book *Constructing the Universe;* unfortunately (if understandably), he fails to provide a balanced view, and presents his version as the "best buy" while dismissing the standard model almost out of hand.

†*The First Three Minutes,* Deutsch edition, page 132.

Lemaître heard the news shortly before he died in 1966. Gamow outlived him by only a couple of years. Had they lived a little longer, or had the discovery of the background radiation been made a little sooner, they might well have shared a Nobel Prize for developing the concept of the Big Bang, a concept made real by that discovery. But Nobel Prizes are never awarded posthumously, and when the Nobel Committee decided, in 1978, that the time had come to take note of the reality of the early Universe, they were faced with what must have seemed a ticklish problem—who to give the award to. There was no shortage of candidates. On the one hand, there was a pair of young radio astronomers who had found something funny but had no idea what it was until somebody else told them, and who even then didn't really believe it at first. On the other, there was a team that had between them predicted the existence of a background, built an instrument to detect it, and, only a little after the fateful meeting at Crawford Hill, had found it just as predicted using their own instrument. Leaving aside all the near misses from the Soviets, Hoyle and Tayler, and so on, there was and still is a third "hand" to be considered, Alpher and Herman, the surviving members of the Gamow team, who said it all first, even though they were ignored.

The award went to Penzias and Wilson. Under the circumstances, it could hardly have gone anywhere else without being spread so thin as to be ridiculous. Or could it? I wonder if the committee entertained, even for one moment, what would have been an inspired decision. Why, after all, could the award not have gone to the person who first reported the detection of the 3 K background—E. A. Ohm? He may not have known what he had found, but then, neither did Penzias and Wilson, and Ohm *did* find it first.

Such speculation is idle, however. What is done is done and cannot be undone. The same seems to be true of the Universe. It did start in a Big Bang and has evolved steadily ever since. With that one measurement, the temperature of the Universe today, available to calibrate the Big Bang, cosmologists were able to refine their calculations and come up with what is now the standard model of creation, the story of the Universe from a fraction of a second after the moment of creation up to date. And when they had done that, they were able to tackle the task of probing back into that first split second of creation itself, the strange world of the Universe before the Big Bang.

CHAPTER SIX

THE STANDARD MODEL

We live in an expanding Universe that is uniformly filled with a sea of very weak electromagnetic radiation and that contains matter in clumps dotted uniformly (on the large scale) throughout its volume. To find out what conditions were like long ago, we have to imagine winding the clock back so that the resulting model of the Universe contracts. The effect of contraction is to increase the density of the model universe. The density of matter increases because the same amount of matter is being squeezed into a smaller volume as time goes by, and the density of radiation increases as well. The increase in radiation density shows up as blue shift, a shortening of the wavelength of the radiation, and can also be expressed in terms of temperature, starting out from the present-day 3 K and getting hotter the farther back in time we go.

From now on I shall be describing the standard model of the Universe, the current "best buy" among cosmologies, as if it were a description of the real Universe. This is necessary license; it would break up the flow of the story too much to keep putting in cautions about how this is the best description of the Universe that we have but that new developments may supersede it. If a model is properly worked out and expressed in equations, we can say what *must* happen in the model as it evolves. The main features of what *must* happen in the standard model look very much like what we see going on in the Universe around us, so the standard model is a good one. We hope that some of the things that must happen in the standard model but that we cannot see directly in our Universe, also tell us what the real Universe is like, in places where or at times when we cannot observe it directly. But the model can never tell us what *must* happen in the real Universe. I will tell the story as if it were the history of our Universe; that is the only way to tell it coherently. But keep at the back of your mind the understanding that this story is really all about a mathematical model universe, one that bears such striking similarities to our Universe today that we think we can use it to get an understanding of what happened long ago when the Universe was young.

Looking back in time corresponds to compression of the model universe, as its present expansion is time-reversed. If this compression of the model universe continued for long enough, then, the laws of physics tell us, we would reach a point when the density of both matter and radiation became infinite. Clearly, the laws of physics that we know from experiments here on Earth, and from observations of the Universe as we see it today, are inadequate to describe infinite densities of matter and energy and must break down at some stage in this imaginary journey back to the moment of creation. But if we leave aside, for the moment, the puzzle of exactly what happened in the first split second of creation itself, our observations of the expanding Universe are entirely adequate to tell us that the creation must have occurred between 10 billion and 20 billion years ago. For the sake of argument, we can pick the middle of the range of age estimates and say that there was a time $t = 0$, 15 billion years ago, when the Universe came into existence in a state of extremely high density and very high temperature, and we can describe the evolution of the Universe up to the present day in terms of the time that has elapsed since $t = 0$. We do so by winding the clock back, in our imagination, from the present to as near as we can get to the state of infinite energy density, and then imagining letting the clock run forward again as the Universe evolves. So, to start, we need to check what we know about the present-day Universe.*

First, we know that it expands. Second, we know that something like 25 percent of the material in the stars is helium and that most of the rest is hydrogen. Third, we know that the Universe is filled with radiation at a temperature of 3 K. In terms of photons, the particles that represent electromagnetic radiation, that means there are about 1,000 photons in every cubic centimeter of the Universe, and this is about a billion times more than the total number of protons and neutrons in the Universe, assuming that, as observations suggest, the density of everyday matter is roughly that required for a flat universe, somewhere near to the boundary between the open and closed states. The energy of this radiation is about one four-thousandth of the energy of the visible matter in the Universe, given by $E = mc^2$. Matter dominates the Universe today—but that was not always the case.

When we wind the clock back, we can calculate, from the simple laws of physics, how the temperature of the radiation increases as the universe contracts. The amount of energy locked in each proton or neutron stays the same, but the amount of energy locked in each photon increases as the radiation is squeezed and blue-shifted. When the temperature was about 4,000 K, the energy in each photon was one billionth of the energy in each proton or neutron, and since there are a billion times more photons in the Universe, the total energy in the radiation matched the total energy in the matter. For all higher temperatures, corresponding to earlier epochs and greater densities, the Universe was *dominated* by radiation, and matter played a secondary role. So we have our formula for reconstructing

---

*Mathematicians will tell you that we cannot literally start our clock at $t = 0$ because there is no way of getting out of the singularity, and there is no "instant" $t = 0$. The concept of time has no meaning at the singularity itself. My answer to the mathematicians is that we can set $t = 0$ as close as we like to the singularity. For the present discussion, the difference is not important. It *is* important when we bring in the effects of quantum physics and try to deal with the moment of creation itself, and the results of this kind of investigation are described in Part Three.

the conditions in the Big Bang—we know the present-day temperature of the Universe, the number of photons present for every proton or neutron, and the laws that tell us how conditions change as we wind the clock back. The simplest version of those laws, the simple Friedman-Lemaître cosmology, plus the known facts about the background radiation today, turn out to be precisely the recipe needed to cook 25 percent of the original matter into helium in the first few minutes of the evolution of the Universe.

THE COSMIC FIREBALL

How far back—how close to $t = 0$—can we push the laws of physics to provide a working description of the Universe? The greatest density of matter occurring naturally in the world today is in the nucleus of an atom, where protons and neutrons are packed alongside each other, cheek by jowl. Nuclear reactions—reactions involving protons and neutrons—are responsible for the existence of the variety of chemical elements we see about us, and similar reactions shortly after the birth of the Universe established the proportions of hydrogen and helium that went as fuel into the first generation of stars. The standard model of the Big Bang derives from the work by Wagoner, Fowler, and Hoyle that calculated how much helium could have been produced in the Big Bang, and it effectively tells the story of the evolution of the Universe from the time when the density of matter was about the same as the density of matter in an atomic nucleus today, or perhaps a little lower. The temperature at which this occurred was about 10^{12} K (1,000 billion K), the density was the density of nuclear matter (10^{14} grams per cubic centimeter), and the time was .0001 (10^{-4}) second after $t = 0$.

These conditions are so extreme that before we can look in detail at how the Universe developed from that state—from the Big Bang itself—we need to remind ourselves of the relevant laws of physics that describe such extreme conditions. One crucial point is that radiation plays a far more important role in the Big Bang than it does in the Universe today, and the reason is easy to see. If you picture the model of a universe being wound back in time and contracting, nothing very much happens to the individual atoms, let alone their nuclei, for a very long time. Because galaxies are so far apart from one another, it takes billions of years of contraction to bring them into contact. And even then, the contraction still has a long way to go before individual stars are squeezed together into one amorphous lump. But the background radiation, although only a weak hiss with a temperature of 3 K, fills the Universe entirely today, and it always has filled the Universe entirely. As soon as the imaginary contraction begins, the radiation is affected, and its temperature begins to rise. By the time stars are at last squeezed closely enough together for individual atomic nuclei to begin to feel the effects, the density of radiation at every point in space has increased to the point where it carries far more energy than the energy stored up in particles. It is no longer "background" radiation but very much at the forefront of physical processes going on in the hot, dense universe.

The energy equivalent of a particle of mass m is, of course, mc^2; and the mass equivalent of radiation with energy E is simply E/c^2. The relation $E = mc^2$ tells us that a sufficiently energetic packet of radiation (a photon) can convert into matter with the appropriate mass, and vice versa (there are also other rules that have to be followed, quantum rules, which we shall meet shortly). At the high energies and densities of the Big Bang, it does indeed make sense to think of radiation in terms of particles; in fact, as we shall shortly see, in the strange world of quantum physics all particles can also be thought of as waves, and all waves can be thought of as particles. Energy and mass are equivalent and interchangeable, and so are the concepts of particle and wave. But a photon, a packet of energy, cannot just disappear and be replaced by a single particle. Particles come in pairs, each with a counterpart, called an antiparticle, that is in a sense a "mirror image" of the particle. The mirror image of an electron is a particle called a positron, which carries a positive charge instead of the electron's negative charge, hence its name. If an electron meets a positron, the pair annihilate in a burst of high-energy radiation, gamma radiation. And a sufficiently energetic burst of gamma radiation can produce a *pair* of particles, a positron and an electron.

At the time we are talking about now, in the Big Bang between 10^{-4} and 0.1 (10^{-1}) second after $t = 0$, the Universe was dominated by radiation. You can think of this dominance in two ways. First, the density of the radiation (the amount of energy it contained in each small volume) was so great that there was an energy equivalent to a positron-electron pair (roughly speaking) in each volume of space corresponding to the size of a positron-electron pair. So the energy could happily switch from electromagnetic energy into electrons and positrons and back again. Or think of it in terms of particles of electromagnetic energy, photons. For every nuclear particle (every proton and every neutron) there were a billion photons, and each of those photons could, and did, change into a electron-positron pair, while positrons and electrons, meeting up in this primeval maelstrom, would annihilate and produce more gamma photons to replace the ones that were turning into electron-positron pairs. The fireball was dominated by photons, electrons, and positrons, and by massless particles called neutrinos. Perhaps, however, "fireball" is not the best term for the Universe at that time. At 0.01 second after $t = 0$, the energy density of the Universe, in terms of $E = mc^2$, was equivalent to nearly four billion times the density of water here on Earth. Some fireball!

The protons and neutrons (collectively dubbed nucleons, since they are the nuclear particles) were relatively stable even under those extreme conditions. Left on its own, a neutron will decay spontaneously in a few minutes, turning into a proton, an electron, and a neutrino. But the time scale of the fireball involves fractions of a second, so a particle that is stable for several minutes is effectively eternal. The proton and the neutron have similar mass to one another, and this is a bit less than two thousand times the mass of the electron. So to make proton-antiproton pairs, or neutron-antineutron pairs, you need correspondingly greater energy density of radiation (more energetic photons). The required energy was available even earlier in the life of the Universe, before $t = 10^{-4}$ seconds, but the standard Big Bang, as developed in the late 1960s, deals only with events after the density of the Universe fell below the density of nuclear matter, and protons and neutrons condensed out of the radiation.

The final point that needs to be emphasized before we look at what happened as the universe cooled still further concerns the time scale on which all these changes were happening. Today the Universe as a whole doesn't change noticeably in 0.0001 second, or even in 10 million years. Cosmologists say that the age of the Universe is between 10 billion and 20 billion years, and they are supremely untroubled about the range of possible values, which covers a factor of 2 ($2 \times$). But conditions changed more rapidly when the Universe was young, and fractions of a second become important in interpreting events in the Big Bang. A characteristic time scale, at any stage of the evolution of the Universe, can be thought of as the time it takes for any chosen region of the Universe to double in size (today that would be equivalent to the time it takes for the distance between any two galaxy clusters to double). Gravity is continually slowing down the expansion of the Universe, so this significant time scale is itself increasing as the aeons pass. It takes longer and longer for anything significant to happen to the appearance of the Universe at large. The corollary to that is that the closer you get to $t = 0$, the less time it took for significant changes to occur. The characteristic time is roughly proportional to the reciprocal of the square root of the density of the Universe at any epoch (the bigger the density, the shorter the characteristic time), and at the start of the era dominated by photons, electrons and positrons, and neutrinos, this time scale was a mere 0.02 second.

You can get a rough feel for how the important time scale changed as the Universe aged by thinking in terms of powers of 10 and working backward in time. The age of the Universe is about 15 billion years, or in round powers of 10, 10^{10} years. Astronomers are happy with their estimates for the age of the Universe, because those estimates all agree to the same power of 10—there are no estimates as small as 10^9 years and none as large as 10^{11} years. If we look back into the cosmic past, the first significant landmark might be at about 10^9 years, when the Universe was one tenth as old as it is today and would have looked noticeably different. The next landmark would be when it was a tenth younger still, at 10^8 years (100 million years), 1 percent of its present age, and so on. In those terms, everything that happened in the interval from the first tenth of a second (0.1 second) to the end of the first second is about as interesting, and significant, as everything that happened in the interval from the first hundredth of a second (0.01 second) to the end of the first 0.1 second, and so on. The analogy is not precise, but it gives a flavor for the importance of the fast-changing world of the early Universe. And there is still another way to put this in perspective. The age of the Universe, in seconds, is a few times 10^{17} seconds. One second is 10^0. The interval from the present to the first second covers a span of seventeen powers of 10. If we travel back in time the same distance the other side of 1 second, we arrive at 10^{-17} second. In a very real sense, the interval from 10^{-17} second to 1 second is equivalent to the interval from 1 second to the present; and physicists now talk in terms of events that occurred back to within 10^{-40} second of $t = 0$, which in the same terminology lies 2½ times farther back toward the moment of creation than we are from the time $t = 1$ second. In those terms, the events from 10^{-4} second to about 4 minutes seem almost mundane—but those events shaped our Universe.

THE FIRST FOUR MINUTES

The best-known description of the cosmic fireball from the era dominated by radiation, electron-positron pairs, and neutrinos onward is Steven Weinberg's book *The First Three Minutes*. As Weinberg acknowledges in that book, the title is really a bit of author's license. His account of the Big Bang actually starts at $t = 10^{-2}$ second, one hundredth of a second after the moment of creation, and the main action he describes occupies the next 3 minutes, 46 seconds of the life of the Universe. He was writing in

1976, and at that time physicists had only the haziest of ideas about what happened during the first hundredth of a second, so his starting point is reasonable enough. And the book still provides a very clear guide to what happened during those crucial three and three-quarter minutes.* So I shall follow Weinberg's now classic summary of how conditions changed during the 4 minutes in which the Universe was transformed from a uniform, very dense soup of radiation and matter into a mixture of about 75 percent hydrogen and 25 percent helium, with the radiation decoupled from the matter and left to fade away into the weak background we know today.

The story begins with the Universe at a temperature of 100 billion K (10^{11} K) at time $t = 10^{-2}$ second. It is dominated by radiation, by the electron-positron pairs that are both produced by the radiation and that annihilate to produce radiation, and by the massless neutrinos and their antineutrino counterparts. The protons and neutrons that are so important to the material world today and make up all the stars and planets, the clouds of gas and dust in space and the atoms in our own bodies, are at this time simply an insignificant component of the soup, their numbers a mere one billionth of the total number of photons. The nucleons are being constantly bombarded by the electrons, positrons, and neutrinos, and this bombardment causes them to change their spots continually. An antineutrino colliding with a proton produces a positron and a neutron, while a neutrino colliding with a neutron produces an electron and a proton, and both of these reactions can run in either direction. *Individual* nucleons are constantly bombarded, and they change repeatedly from neutron to proton and back again. But on average, as long as the energy of the fireball is great enough for all these reactions to proceed easily, there will be just about the same number of protons as there are neutrons in any specified volume of the Universe. Things begin to change, however, when the temperature drops to about 30 billion K.

---

*I. D. Novikov's book *Evolution of the Universe*, written in 1978, gives a slightly more detailed and technical, but still very readable, account of the first instants. If you read this and Weinberg's book together, you will get a very clear picture of the understanding of the Universe cosmologists had at the end of the 1970s.

Particle physicists often measure energy and mass (which is the same thing, if you allow for the factor c^2) in units of electron volts. One eV is the energy an electron would gain when accelerated across a potential difference of 1 volt. This is a pretty small unit. A typical photon of visible light carries an energy of about 2.5 eV, and the mass of an electron is 510,000 eV, just over 0.5 MeV.* The mass of a proton is 935 MeV, and the mass of a neutron is almost, but not quite, the same as the mass of a proton. That "not quite" is the key to the next stage in the evolution of the Universe.

When the temperature of the Universe was as high as 10^{11} K, the typical energy carried by each electron, photon, or other particle was about 10 MeV, 10 million electron volts. Some had more energy, some less, but this was a good average value. This is a lot less than the masses of the nucleons, which is why the nucleons were able to retain their identity at that time. And it is a lot more than the mass of an electron-positron pair, which is why such pairs could be created so easily at that time. But it is also a lot more than the *difference* in mass between a proton and a neutron, which is just under 1.3 MeV. To an electron or a neutrino carrying 10 MeV of energy, it made very little difference whether it reacted with a proton or a neutron, and the two key reactions for converting protons into neutrons and neutrons into protons went equally happily in each direction. But as the temperature of the Universe fell, the energy carried by each particle declined in proportion. With less energy available to drive the reactions, the mass difference between protons and neutrons began to be important, and it became relatively more difficult to trigger the reactions that converted the lighter protons into the heavier neutrons. The "uphill" reaction could still occur if a sufficiently energetic electron collided with a proton, but sufficiently energetic electrons became scarcer and scarcer and were, from now on, significantly less abundant than the particles with slightly lower energy needed to convert neutrons into protons.

Just over one tenth of a second after $t = 0$, the

---

*So you need a photon with an energy of more than 1 MeV to create an electron-positron pair.

temperature of the Universe was 3×10^{10} K, the energy density had fallen to 30 million times the energy density of water, the expansion rate had slowed so much that the characteristic time scale of the Universe was now 0.2 second, and although the proportion of nucleons to photons was still a modest 1 in 1 billion, the proportion of neutrons to protons was no longer 50:50, but 38 percent neutrons to 62 percent protons.

About a third of a second after $t = 0$, a major change occurs in the Universe. At the high temperatures of the early fireball, the particles were happily involved in many interactions, including an interchange among electrons, positrons, and neutrinos by which an electron-positron pair could annihilate to produce a neutrino-antineutrino pair, and vice versa, as well as the nucleon reactions already mentioned. But neutrinos are very reluctant to interact with other matter under any conditions that we would regard as normal. They pass right through the Earth without being affected—indeed, neutrinos produced in nuclear reactions at the heart of the Sun stream out through the Sun itself without being significantly affected on the way. To neutrinos, ordinary matter is transparent. And "ordinary matter" to neutrinos means anything less extreme than the conditions that existed a third of a second after the moment of creation. Then, or soon after, the neutrinos ceased to interact with electrons, positrons, or anything else but remained as a background sea (rather like the cosmic microwave background radiation, but far less easy to detect), filling the Universe but playing only a minor part in its evolution.*

So by the time the temperature had cooled to 10^{10} K (10 billion K), at $t = 1.1$ seconds the density was down to a mere 380,000 times the density of water, neutrinos had ceased to interact with matter (they had decoupled), and

---

*Except through gravity. The energy stored by the neutrino sea itself contributes to the gravity of the whole Universe, and there have been speculations that neutrinos may not be completely massless, but that each might carry a mass of a few eV. If so, because there are so many of them, the total mass would be a major fraction of the total mass of the Universe, with profound implications for the ultimate fate of the Universe, perhaps ensuring that it is closed in spite of the implications of the deuterium abundance for the density of nucleonic matter.

the characteristic expansion time of the Universe had stretched to 2 seconds, while the balance between protons and neutrons had shifted still farther, with 24 percent neutrons and 76 percent protons. With the temperature continuing to fall, below 10^{10} K, photons carrying enough energy to create electron-positron pairs became increasingly rare, and during this phase of the evolution of the Universe, electrons and positrons were annihilating one another faster than new pairs were being created.

From now on, the breathless pace of evolution is slowed to something almost familiar; we deal in whole seconds, not fractions of a second, and the particles and their reactions are very similar to the particles and reactions that provide the energy of the Sun and the other stars today.

By the time the temperature has dropped to 3 billion K (3×10^9 K), 13.8 seconds after $t = 0$, no more electron-positron pairs are being produced, and the ones that remain are being annihilated. Nuclei of deuterium (one proton plus one neutron) can form temporarily but are knocked apart by collisions with other particles almost as soon as they do form. And although neutrons are still being converted into protons, with less energy available this reaction is slowing down dramatically, and still 17 percent of the nucleons are in the form of neutrons. Three minutes and 2 seconds from the moment of creation, the temperature of the Universe has cooled to 10^9 K, and at last we can compare this with something in the present-day Universe. The temperature at the heart of the Sun is about 15 million K; 3 minutes after $t = 0$, the Universe had cooled to a temperature only seventy times greater than this. The particle reactions that were so important a few minutes earlier have virtually ceased, but now the Universe is old enough for the natural decay of the neutron to become important, and in every 100 seconds from now on, 10 percent of the remaining free neutrons will decay into protons; the proportion of neutrons is already down to about 14 percent. But they are saved from extinction as the temperature falls still further, to the point where deuterium nuclei can hold together.

Now, at last, the reactions described in outline by Gamow and his colleagues, and in detail by Wagoner, Fowler, and Hoyle, can take place. Nucleosynthesis rap-

idly builds up nuclei of helium-4 but essentially stops
there because, as we have seen, there are no stable nuclei
with masses 5 or 8, and nucleosynthesis can bridge those
gaps, as Hoyle explained back in the early 1950s, only
under the conditions found inside stars—which don't yet
exist.*

Once helium production begins, all the available neutrons are quickly bound up in this way, and they are then
stable. This happens when the proportion of neutrons is
about 13 or 14 percent of the total number of nucleons,
and in nuclei of helium-4 and neutron is accompanied by one
proton. So the proportion of the total mass of nucleons
converted into helium-4 is simply twice the abundance of
neutrons when the reactions begin, about 26 to 28 percent. Nucleosynthesis begins at a temperature of 900
million K (9×10^8 K) at 3 minutes, and 46 seconds
after the moment of creation. By $t = 4$ minutes, the
standard model of the Big Bang has created the conditions
that produce just the amount of helium observed in the
Universe.

This great triumph of the standard model depends
crucially on the fact that the reactions converting protons
into neutrons and neutrons into protons "froze" just when
they did, so that a residue of 14 or 15 percent neutrons
was left at the time nucleosynthesis began. These critical
reactions, and the point at which they freeze, are very
sensitive not just to temperature but also to the rate at
which the temperature of the early Universe was falling. If
the freeze happened at an "age of the Universe" of a few
seconds, then the proportion of helium in the Universe is
indeed just under 30 percent. But if everything happened
a little bit faster, and the freeze happened at 0.1 second,
the proportion of helium produced by the Big Bang would
be almost 100 percent (because nucleosynthesis also gets
going that much quicker), while if the freeze happened at
100 seconds, in a universe evolving that much more slowly,
there would be no helium produced in the Big Bang,

*Heavier nuclei do form early on, at high densities, but are broken apart
again and never "freeze out" of the fireball. Only hydrogen, helium, a little
deuterium, and a trace of lithium, plus neutrinos and other nonnucleonic
particles, emerge from the Big Bang.

because all the neutrons would have turned into protons before nucleosynthesis could begin.

The rate of fall in temperature is specified by the standard model in its simplest form and is tied in with the temperature of the cosmic microwave background today, which gives the crucially important estimate of 10^9 photons for every nucleon in the Universe. The ratio holds today, observations of the cosmic microwave background tell us, even though the photons are spread out through the Universe while the nucleons are concentrated in material lumps. So it must have held in the fireball stage of the Universe, when the radiation dominated the matter and drove the reactions in just the right way to produce the amount of helium we see. And the standard model also sets some constraints on the possibility of other particles existing in the Universe today. Neutrinos and antineutrinos interfere with the processes that convert protons into neutrons, and neutrons into protons, so the success of the standard model also tells us something about the number and kind of neutrinos present in the Big Bang and therefore left over for us to find now, as we shall see later.

So we have a second successful prediction—or requirement—of the standard model to add to the astonishing discovery, in the 1920s, that the Universe is expanding. The requirement that there is three times as much hydrogen as there is helium in the Universe is a striking vindication of the simplest cosmological models of the Big Bang. The third leg of the tripod on which the standard model rests is the presence of the cosmic microwave background radiation; but to see exactly where that comes from, we have to move on from the moment of creation not in steps of a few seconds or even minutes, but in thousands and then billions of years.

THE NEXT TEN BILLION YEARS

A little more than half an hour after $t = 0$ (at $t = 34$ minutes and 40 seconds, to be precise), almost all of the electrons and positrons have been annihilated, and the Universe has begun to resemble the empty state we find it in today. Almost, but not quite, all of the matter has gone. In addition to the billionth part of the number of photons that is present as nucleons, when the electron-positron pairs finally annihilate, just one electron in a billion is also left over, exactly the amount required to balance the positive charge on all the protons in the Universe and to ensure that eventually the matter will settle out as stable, uncharged atoms, with every proton in every atomic nucleus matched by an electron in the cloud on the outside of the atom. Where does this tiny proportion of matter come from? Why isn't there a perfect symmetry between particles and antiparticles so that everything annihilates and only radiation is left as the Universe cools? The answers emerge from an understanding of the world of particle physics under conditions even more extreme than those during the epoch of the life of the Universe following the first hundredth of a second, and they are among the simplest but also most profound of the puzzles resolved by the discoveries described in Part Three. For now, though, let's stick with the expanding, cooling fireball half an hour after the moment of creation.

By now, the temperature of the fireball is down to 300 million K, and the energy density of the Universe is only 10 percent of the mass density of water. About 69 percent of this energy is carried by photons and 31 percent by neutrinos, and the expansion time scale appropriate at this time has stretched to 75 minutes. Although all the available neutrons have been cooked into helium nuclei, the Universe still is too hot for stable atoms to form—as soon as a positively charged proton or helium-4 nucleus latches on to a negatively charged electron, the electron is knocked out of its grip by an energetic photon. This is the "radiation era" of the Universe, with no significant particle interactions to worry about and with the remaining matter dominated by the radiation. It lasts for about 700,000 years, until the temperature drops to about 4,000 K and the nuclei and electrons are at last able to hold together against the ever-decreasing battering they receive from photons.

The time at which this occurs is not well defined. As

early as 300,000 years after the moment of creation, some hydrogen atoms are beginning to form and survive for a reasonable length of time without being ionized by the radiation; after $t = 10^6$ years, all the electrons have been bound up in atoms, so efficiently that only one electron and one proton are left out on their own for every 100,000 stable atoms, and the "decoupling" of matter from radiation is complete. From now on, radiation and matter scarcely interact at all, since although electromagnetic radiation and charged particles interact strongly, neutral particles, such as atoms, have little effect on radiation, or radiation on them. Like the sea of neutrinos that decoupled earlier on, the photons are left to fade away into a cosmic background.

The decoupling era, a little less than a million years after the Big Bang, marks the last time matter and radiation were closely involved with one another. So the cosmic background we see today is in effect a view of the Universe at that time. The fact that the cosmic background is uniform, isotropic, and homogeneous tells us that the Universe as a whole was uniform, homogeneous, and isotropic 700,000 years after $t = 0$. This is the closest direct observation of the Big Bang we have. But remember the primordial neutrinos. In principle, they might be detected, and the equations of the standard model tell us that they should form a background sea filling the Universe today with a temperature 70 percent of the temperature of the photon background, about 2 K. And they decoupled only just over a second after $t = 0$. If these neutrinos are ever detected, they would provide the most dramatic confirmation yet of the accuracy of the standard model and would give us a view, distant though it is, of the Universe when it was one second old.

Just before the decoupling of matter and radiation, the entire Universe resembled the surface of the Sun. It was hot, opaque, and filled with a yellow light. As matter and radiation decoupled, it suddenly became transparent, and at about the same time, the energy density of the radiation fell below the equivalent density of the matter in the Universe. From about $t = 10^6$ years onward, the Universe has been dominated by matter and by gravity. And in round terms you can get some sort of feel for how long ago that was in terms of the red shift. The greatest red shifts ever measured for any astronomical objects are those of a few quasars, with red shifts (z) of between 3.5 and 4.* The red shift of the decoupling epoch and of the epoch when matter began to dominate the Universe each correspond to about $z = 1,000$. The wavelength of each photon in the cosmic microwave background has been stretched by a factor of 1,000 since it last interacted with matter.

Although the radiation era seems at first sight to have been one in which nothing much happened, compared with the first four minutes, it was probably at this time that the irregularities that later grew up to become galaxies and clusters of galaxies first developed. At the end of the radiation era, when stable atoms had just formed, there were about ten million atoms in every liter of the Universe. Today there is only one atom, on average, in every thousand or so liters of space. The number density of atoms at decoupling was at least a thousand times greater than the density of even a galaxy today, so, clearly, galaxies as we know them must have formed after decoupling. But the matter that became the dominant feature of the Universe probably inherited irregularities from the radiation era. In some places, the density was already slightly greater than in other places. By the time matter

---

*The red shift z is defined in terms of the amount by which a spectrum has been stretched. If a feature in the spectrum occurs at a certain wavelength, λ, as measured by someone who is stationary compared with the source of the spectrum, then an observer who is moving in such a way that the source of the spectrum seems to be receding from him will measure the same feature at a longer wavelength. The difference between the two wavelengths is written as $\Delta \lambda$; and $z = \frac{\Delta \lambda}{\lambda}$. The yellow sodium D line, for example, occurs at a wavelength of 589 nanometers in the laboratory. If we examine the spectrum of a star, or any other object, and find that the sodium D line is at a wavelength of, say, 600 nanometers, then the red shift of that object is 11/589—that is, $z = 0.01868$. For such a small red shift, the implied velocity of recession is simply the speed of light, c, times z, which comes out to about 5,000 kilometers per second for this hypothetical example. For red shifts bigger than about 0.4, it is essential to use a slightly more complicated formula, taking account of relativistic effects. This says that for an object receding at velocity v,

$$(1 + z) = \neq (c + v) / (c - v).$$

At a red shift of 2, this formula gives the correct recession velocity of $0.8c$, 80 percent of the speed of light. But no matter how big the red shift is, v can never exceed c.

was dominating the evolution of a transparent, dark, and cooling Universe, it was already grouped into clumps that, because of the insistent pull of their own gravity, did not thin out as rapidly as the Universe at large. Within such clumps of matter with above-average density, some regions formed clouds of gas that began to break up and collapse, eventually forming the stars of our own Milky Way and other galaxies. By the time half the present age of the Universe had elapsed, our own Milky Way Galaxy was in existence in much the form we see it today; 4.5 billion years ago, our Sun and its system of planets were in existence, having formed out of interstellar material that had already been processed and reprocessed in the interiors of many stars, and contained an enrichment of heavy elements as well as its inheritance of hydrogen and helium from the Big Bang.

For most of the past 10 billion years, most of the matter in the Universe has been bound up in stars and galaxies, with the only large-scale change being the steady separation of clusters of galaxies from one another as the Universe expands, and the steady cooling of the ever more red-shifted background radiation. But the details of galaxy formation remain obscure, and there are rival theories, put forward by different groups of astronomers, to explain how the matter in the Universe got to be grouped into the patterns we see it in today. Once again, it turns out that the latest understanding of particle physics provides a clue. Indeed, the answers to most of the questions left unanswered by the standard model turn out to lie in a better understanding not of the way the Universe is today, but of the way it was in the first hundredth of a second, *before* the Big Bang as described by the standard model.

REMAINING QUESTIONS

In spite of the enormous success of the standard model in the 1960s and 1970s, it left a handful of unanswered questions. Where did the tiny proportion of matter (compared with the number of photons) come from? Why is the Universe so extraordinarily uniform and homogeneous? Why is the density of the Universe so close to making it flat? What happened in the interval from $t = 0$ to the end of the first millisecond? And, after all, how did the Universe come into being—what *did* happen at the moment of creation itself?

At last we have come down to the metaphysical nitty-gritty, the questions that used to be regarded as beyond the scope of science. But now science knows no limitations and can tackle all of these questions, even if the answers are not yet complete, or completely understood. We even have, thanks to researchers such as Stephen Hawking in Cambridge, a line of attack on the problem of the creation itself. Understanding of all of these deep mysteries depends on getting a handle on what happened in the tiny fraction of a second before the time where the standard model picks up the story—before, in that sense, the Big Bang itself. As cosmologist Ted Harrison, of the University of Massachusetts, has commented, "more of cosmic history occurs in the first thousandth of a second than has occurred in 10 billion years since."* But to understand that period of cosmic history, the laws of physics that have stood us in such good stead in interpreting the subsequent evolution of the Universe are no longer enough. We need, in addition, the laws of quantum physics—the physics of the very small, and especially the rules that apply to particles and radiation at very high energy densities. Before we probe back in time before the Big Bang, we must pause to take stock of those quantum rules and to come to terms with their strangeness.

Cosmology, page 354.

QUANTUM PHYSICS

There are more questions than answers—and the more I
find out, the less I know.

Johnny Nash

General Relativity, the best description we have of space-
time at large, is alone sufficient to tell us that the Universe
was born in a superdense state, that there was indeed a
Big Bang. But the revolution in scientific understanding
that brought us General Relativity was only one of two
great scientific revolutions in the early twentieth century.
The other breakthrough gave new insights into the
behavior of matter on very small scales (within the atom)
and at very high energies, where matter and energy, as
Einstein predicted, become interchangeable. This is quantum physics. When we try to bring questions about the
very origin of the Universe out of the realm of metaphysics
and into the realm of science, General Relativity alone is
inadequate for the task, and we need quantum physics as
well to describe very energetic events occurring in a tiny
volume of space over a split second, aeons ago. So, before

we probe back before the Big Bang described by Einstein's theory alone, we need to take on board some of the salient features of the strangest and most powerful theory of physics yet developed. Before about 1900, physicists thought of the material world as being composed of little, hard objects, atoms and molecules that interacted with one another to produce the variety of materials, living and nonliving, we see around us. They also had a very good theory of how light propagated, in the form of an electromagnetic wave, in many ways analogous to the ripples on a pond, or to the sound waves that carry information in the form of vibrations in the air. Gravity was a little more mysterious. But, by and large, the division of the world into particles and waves seemed clear-cut, and physics seemed to be on the threshold of dotting all the i's and crossing all the t's. In short, the end of theoretical physics and the solution of all the great puzzles seemed to be in sight.

Scarcely had physicists started to acknowledge this cozy possibility, however, when the house of cards they had so painstakingly constructed came tumbling down. It turned out that the behavior of light could sometimes be explained only in terms of particles—photons—while the wave explanation, or model, remained the only valid one in other circumstances. A little later, physicists realized that if waves that sometimes behave as particles were not enough to worry about, particles sometimes could behave like waves. And meanwhile, Einstein was overturning established wisdom about the nature of space, time, and gravity with his theories of relativity. When the dust began to settle at the end of the 1920s, physicists had a new picture of the world, very different from the old one. This is still the basis of the picture we have today. It tells us that there are no pure particles or waves, but only, at the fundamental level, things best described as a mixture of wave and particle, occasionally referred to as "wavicles." It tells us that it is impossible to predict with absolute certainty the outcome of any atomic experiment, or indeed of any event in the Universe, and that our world is governed by probabilities. And it tells us that it is impossible to know simultaneously both the exact position of an object and its exact momentum (where it is going).

How and why physicists came to these startling conclusions I have described at length in my book *In Search of Schrödinger's Cat*. Here, I intend only to present an outline of the new world picture without going into the historical and experimental details on which it is founded. But that foundation *is* secure; quantum physics is as solidly based and as thoroughly established by experiments and observations as Einstein's General Theory of Relativity. Together they provide the best description we have of the Universe and everything in it; and where their areas of interest overlap, as we shall see, they combine to explain how the Universe came into being in the first place.

General Relativity deals with the very large—the Universe itself. Quantum physics deals with the very small—objects the size of atoms, or smaller. The two "overlapped" when the Universe was in some sense only the size of an atomic nucleus—when it had a density greater than the density of a neutron or a proton. That is why a combination of relativity theory and quantum physics is needed to explain the birth of the Universe. And that is the theme of Part Three of this book, a theme we can be equipped to comprehend only if we understand a little about quantum physics first.

PHOTONS

The best place to pick up the story is with the work of the great Scottish physicist James Clerk Maxwell in the third quarter of the nineteenth century. Maxwell, who was born in Edinburgh in 1831, made many contributions to physics, but his greatest work was undoubtedly his theory of electromagnetism. Like many of his contemporaries and immediate predecessors, Maxwell was fascinated by the fact that an electric current flowing in a wire produces a magnetic field, which in its fundamentals is exactly the same as the magnetic field of a magnet itself. The field around a wire carrying a current will, for example, deflect a small compass magnet placed nearby. But also, a moving magnet, passing by a wire, will cause a current to flow in the wire. Moving electricity, a current, produces magnetism, and moving magnets produce electric currents. Electric forces and magnetic forces, which had once seemed to be quite separate phenomena, now seemed to be different facets of some greater whole, the electromagnetic field.

Maxwell tried to write down a set of equations that would link together all of the electric and magnetic phenomena that physicists had observed and measured. There were four equations: one to describe the magnetic field produced by an electric current; a second to describe the electric field produced by a changing magnetic field; the third giving the electric field produced by an electric charge itself; and the fourth giving a description of the magnetic field itself, including the strange fact that magnetic poles always come in pairs (north matched with south). But when Maxwell examined the equations, he found that they were flawed mathematically. To correct the math, he had to introduce another term into the first equation, a term equivalent to a description of how a magnetic field could be produced by a changing electric field without any current flowing.

At that time, nobody had observed such a phenomenon. But once Maxwell had reconstructed the equations in the most elegant mathematical form, the reason for this extra term soon became clear. Physicists knew about condensers (now called capacitors), which are flat metal plates separated by a short gap, across which an electric potential difference can be applied. One plate may be connected to the positive pole of a battery and the other plate to the negative pole. In this case, one plate builds up a charge of positive electricity, and the other a negative charge. The gap between the plates is a region with a strong electric field, but no current flows across the gap, and there is no magnetic field. Maxwell's new mathematical term described, among other things, what happens between the plates of such a capacitor just as the battery is connected to the plates. While the electric charge on the plates is building up, there is a rapidly changing electric field in the gap between the plates, and according to the equations, this produces a magnetic field. Maxwell was soon able to confirm that the equations were correct, simply by placing a little compass magnet in the gap between two metal plates and watching how it was deflected when the plates were connected to a battery. Like all the best scientific theories, the new theory of electromagnetism had successfully predicted how an experiment would turn out.

But now came the really dramatic discovery. Maxwell realized that if the changing electric field could produce a changing magnetic field, and the changing magnetic field could produce a changing electric field the two components of the single, unified electromagnetic field could get along quite nicely together without any need for electric currents or magnets at all. The equations said that a self-reinforcing electromagnetic field, with the electricity producing the magnetism and the magnetism producing the electricity, could set off quite happily through space on its own once it was given a push to start it going. The continually changing electromagnetic field predicted by the equations was in the form of a wave moving at a certain speed, 300,000 kilometers per second. This is exactly the speed of light. Maxwell's equations of electromagnetism had predicted the existence of electromagnetic waves moving at the speed of light, and it didn't take Maxwell long to realize that light must indeed be an electromagnetic wave.

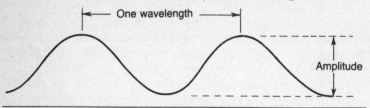

Figure 12.1/A wave.

There was already a well-established body of evidence that light was a form of wave motion, so Maxwell's discovery fitted right in to the mainstream of nineteenth-century science and was welcomed with open arms. The best evidence for the wave nature of light comes from the way it can be made to "interfere" with itself, like the interference between two sets of ripples on a pond, producing patterns of shade and light that cannot be explained in any other way. Thomas Young, a British physicist and physician who was born in Somerset in 1773, produced the crucial experimental evidence in the early 1800s when he shone a beam of pure light of one color (monochromatic light) through a pair of narrow slits in a screen to produce two sets of "ripples" and make a classic interference pattern on a second screen. This work effectively pulled the rug from under the old idea, going back to Newton, that light came in the form of tiny particles, or corpuscles.

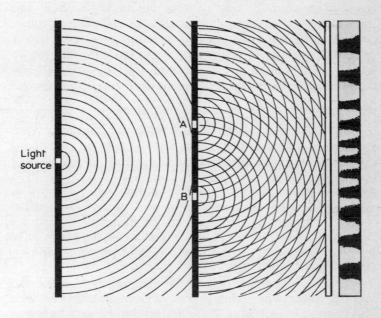

*Figure 12.2/*When two waves meet, they interfere with one another. Thomas Young used this fact to prove that light is a form of wave. Light from a source passes through two holes in a screen, A and B, to produce two sets of waves. Where the waves cancel out, they leave dark shadows on the screen to the right of the experiment; where they add together, they produce bright bands of light.

The combination of Maxwell's and Young's work provided what seemed to be a thorough understanding of light. Interference experiments made it possible to measure the wavelength of light, the distance from the crest of one wave to the next crest, which turns out to be about one ten millionth (10^{-7}) meter; the different colors of the spectrum correspond to different wavelengths, with red light having a wavelength several times longer than blue, and Maxwell deduced that there must be electromagnetic radiation with a whole range of wavelengths extending far outside the visible spectrum, some much shorter than those of visible light, and some much longer. Radio waves, with wavelengths of several meters, were produced by the German pioneer Heinrich Hertz before the end of the nineteenth century and confirmed Maxwell's prediction.

All of the electromagnetic spectrum, from radio waves to visible light and on to X-rays, obeys Maxwell's equations. Those equations, describing how electromagnetic radiation propagates as waves, are the basis of the design of such familiar everyday objects as a TV set or a radio. They are also the basis of the cosmological interpretation of the red shift, and, indeed, the notion of light as a wave is such a familiar concept that I was happy to talk about wavelengths when discussing the red-shift effect without telling you about the work of Young and Maxwell first. And yet, since the early 1900s it has been clear that Newton was right all along. Light, and all forms of electromagnetic radiation, can be described in terms of particles now called photons. In some circumstances, the behavior of light can be explained *only* in terms of photons, as Einstein pointed out in 1905.

The first hints at the corpuscular nature of light had come in 1900, when Max Planck, a German physicist who had been born in Kiel in 1858, found that he was forced to introduce the idea of discrete packets of light into the equations that describe how light, or other electromagnetic radiation, is emitted by a hot body. This had been a major puzzle for physicists in the 1890s. They guessed that light was produced by the vibration of electrically charged particles inside an object, vibrations involving the atoms themselves, with the vibrations providing the push needed to set the waves described by Maxwell's equations off and running. And they knew from observations and experiments that the kind of radiation produced by an object depends on its temperature. We know this from everyday experience—a white-hot piece of metal (such as a poker) is hotter than a red-hot piece of metal, and a piece that is too cold to emit visible light at all may still be too hot to hold in your hand. Any such object radiates electromagnetic waves over a broad range of wavelengths, but the peak intensity of the radiation always is at a wavelength characteristic of the temperature of the object and is shorter for hotter objects. The nature of the overall spectrum of radiation always is the same, and the position of the peak reveals very accurately the temperature of the radiation—for a "perfect" radiator, it is the famous "black body" spectrum, and the cosmic background radiation has a black body spectrum corresponding to a temperature of just under 3 K. But until Planck came on the scene, nobody could manipulate the electromagnetic equations in such a way that they predicted the nature of the black body spectrum.

Planck found that the only way in which the observed nature of the black body spectrum could be explained was if light (by which I now mean any form of electromagnetic radiation) can be emitted by the vibrating charges inside the atoms only in little packets of energy.* By implication, that meant that atoms could absorb light only in lumps of certain sizes, as well. Planck expressed this in terms of the frequency of the radiation, denoted by the Greek letter, nu, ν. The frequency can be thought of as the number of wave crests passing a fixed point every second; for light with a wavelength of 10^{-7} meters and a velocity of 300,000 kilometers a second, the frequency is 3×10^{15} per second, or 3×10^{15} Hertz, in honor of the radio pioneer. Planck found that the observed black body spectrum could be explained if for every frequency of light there is a characteristic amount of energy equal to the frequency multiplied by a fundamental constant, which he called h. This energy, $E = h\nu$, is the smallest amount of energy of that frequency

---

*The electron itself was discovered, by the English physicist J. J. Thomson, only in 1897, so Planck's explanation of black body radiation was necessarily a little vague on the exact nature of the charged particles within the atoms, and how they might be "vibrating" to produce electromagnetic waves. Thomson showed that electrons are parts of atoms and that although different elements are made of different atoms, the electrons in all atoms are identical to one another and carry a fundamental unit of (negative) electric charge, now dubbed e. He received a Nobel Prize for his efforts, in 1906.

that can be emitted or absorbed by any atom, and it can emit or absorb quantities that are only an exact multiple $(1, 2, 3, 4, \ldots n, \ldots)$ of this fundamental energy.

Planck did not suggest that the energy in the light only *existed* in little packets with energy $h\nu$; he thought that the restriction on the emission or absorption had something to do with the nature of the charged oscillators inside the hot objects. But he was able to calculate the value of h, which is the same for all radiation. It is now called Planck's constant, and it is tiny—6.6×10^{-34} Joule second. Even for light with a frequency of 10^{15} Hz, the fundamental unit of energy is a mere 10^{-18} Joule, and it takes 6,000 Joules to keep a typical light bulb burning for a minute. The energy being radiated by a light bulb seems to be continuous, because h is so small; in fact, the visible light is made up of billions upon billions of little packets of energy.

Planck's proposal met with a mixed reception at first. It seemed to explain the black body spectrum, but only by a kind of mathematical sleight of hand, a trick. Einstein, then an almost unknown physicist, still working at his desk in the Swiss patent office, gave that mathematical trick a respectable physical reality when he showed that another great puzzle of the time could be explained if those little packets of energy had a real existence, and that light existed *only* in pieces with energy $h\nu$. And Einstein's attack on the puzzle of the nature of light provides a much clearer physical picture of why this must be so.

The photoelectric effect occurs when light shines onto a metal surface in a vacuum. The light literally knocks electrons out of the metal, and the electrons can be detected and the energy that they carry can be measured. The effect had been discovered in 1899 by the Hungarian Phillip Lenard. It was no great surprise to find that the energy in the light could make electrons jump out of the metal, but it *was* a great surprise to find just how the energy in the light and the energy in the electrons were related. Lenard used monochromatic light, so all the waves had the same frequency. A bright light obviously carries more energy than a dim light, so you might expect that if you shine a bright light onto a metal surface the electrons that are knocked out of it would each carry more energy.

In fact, Lenard found that provided he used the same frequency of light, it made no difference to the individual electrons how bright the light was. Each electron that jumped out of the metal always had the same amount of energy.

When Lenard moved the lamp closer to the metal, so that it shone more brightly onto the surface, there were indeed *more* electrons produced by the photoelectric effect, corresponding to the extra energy available from the brighter light. But each of those electrons carried the same amount of energy, and that was also the same amount of energy that each photoelectric electron carried when the light was dimmed, although there were fewer ejected electrons then. On the other hand, if he used light with a higher frequency (corresponding to shorter wavelength), the electrons produced had more energy, even if the light was dim. They still had the same energy as each other, but this was more than the energy of electrons produced by light with a lower frequency. The reason for all this seems simple with hindsight, but the suggestion Einstein made was revolutionary at the time. He simply suggested (and provided the mathematical calculations to back up the suggestion) that a beam of light of frequency v is made up of a stream of particles, what we now call photons, each of which has energy hv. An electron is ejected from the metal when one photon strikes one atom in the right way. So each ejected electron carries the amount of energy hv provided by one photon, less the amount of energy needed to tear the electron loose. The brighter the light, the more photons there are, so the more electrons are produced. But the energy of each photon stays the same. The only way to increase the energy of an individual photoelectron is to increase the energy of the photon that knocks it out of the metal, and the only way to do that is to make v bigger.

The suggestion was far from universally acclaimed by physicists at the time. Everybody knew, and Young's double slit experiment and Maxwell's equations established beyond reasonable doubt, that light was an electromagnetic wave. Only a brash newcomer with no real understanding of physics, it seemed, would dare to revive the preposterous Newtonian idea of light corpuscles. Indeed, one experimenter, the American Robert Millikan, was so incensed by the idea that he devoted ten years to experiments aimed at proving Einstein's hypothesis wrong. He succeeded only in proving it right, obtaining a very precise measurement of the value of h along the way and helping to ensure that Planck received the Nobel Prize in Physics in 1918, that Einstein received the 1921 Prize for his explanation of the photoelectric effect, and that Millikan received the Prize in 1923. There is no doubt that all these awards were merited; the surprise is that Einstein never received a second Nobel Prize, for his General Theory of Relativity.

By the time these honors came the way of the quantum pioneers, Planck's introduction of the quantum, hv, into atomic physics had helped other physicists, led by the Dane Niels Bohr, to develop the first satisfactory model of the atom, a model based on the idea of a small, positively charged nucleus, with even smaller, negatively charged electrons orbiting around it, more or less in the way the planets orbit around the Sun. The model said that these orbits were separated by intervals corresponding to a basic quantum of energy and that an electron could jump from one orbit to another but could not exist in an in-between state. If it jumped from a higher energy orbit to a lower energy orbit, it would emit a photon with energy hv; to jump from a lower energy to a higher energy it had to absorb a photon, hv. But because there was no such thing as half a photon, it could not jump to a state halfway between two of the allowed orbits.

The model was far from complete, but it gave physicists a handle on the way electrons behaved in atoms and helped them to begin to explain the bright and dark lines of atomic spectra. Bright lines simply correspond to the emission of photons when an electron jumps down some rungs on the energy ladder; dark lines are the "gaps" left in the spectrum when electrons absorb photons with a precisely defined frequency as they jump up the rungs of the ladder. But there were many questions still open in the early 1920s. For a start, the theory of electromagnetic radiation was not one theory but two. Sometimes light and X-rays had to be described using Maxwell's wave equations; sometimes you had to use Einstein's photons; sometimes you had to use a mixture of the two ideas, as in

Planck's calculation of the black body spectrum. And, the most pressing question of all, just what *was* it that decided which energy levels inside the atom could be occupied by electrons—what accounted for the number of rungs on the energy ladder and the spacing between them? The answers came not from any rationalization of the theory of light and a return to the calm logic of the nineteenth-century "classical" physics, but from extending the revolution affecting waves to the world of particles. In particular, as Louis de Broglie suggested to a startled physics community in 1924, if light waves behave like particles, why can't electrons, which used to be thought of as particles, behave like waves?

ELECTRONS

De Broglie, who was born in 1892 and is still alive as I write these words in the spring of 1985, was the younger son of a French nobleman and later inherited the family title from his brother, to become the Duc de Broglie. His brother, Maurice, was a pioneer in the development of X-ray spectroscopy, and it was through Maurice that Louis became first aware of, and then fascinated by, the quantum revolution. The idea he developed in his doctoral thesis, submitted to the Sorbonne in 1924, was brilliantly simple but backed up by thorough mathematical analysis. I shall outline only the simple, physical picture of de Broglie's insight into the nature of matter—if you want the math, you will have to look elsewhere.

Einstein had developed the energy equation for material particles, $E = mc^2$; Planck, with a little help from Einstein, had come up with a similar equation for photons, $E = hv$. Although a photon has no mass, it does carry momentum—if it didn't, it would not be able to knock electrons out of a metal surface. For an ordinary particle, the momentum is its mass (m) times its velocity (v). A light object moving very rapidly can carry as much energy, and give you as hard a knock, as a massive object traveling slowly. Think of the impact of a bullet compared with that of a softball. But the biggest knocks, of course, come from massive objects moving quickly. The velocity of a photon is c. And if we take out the factor (mc) from Einstein's equation and replace it by the letter p to represent momentum, we have a new equation, $E = pc$, which applies equally well to both ordinary matter and to photons.

So de Broglie put this equation and Planck's equation together, $E = pc = h\nu$. Rearrange things a little and you have, for a photon, $p = h\nu /c$. But the velocity of a wave (c) divided by its frequency (ν) is just its wavelength. So de Broglie's version of the equation said that, for a photon, momentum is equal to Planck's constant divided by wavelength. This directly relates the particle nature of the photon (momentum) to its wave character (wavelength), using Planck's constant. But why, said de Broglie, stop there? Electrons have momentum, and we know the value of Planck's constant. Rearrange the equation again and we get a relation telling us that wavelength is equal to h divided by momentum. In other words, any particle, such as an electron, is also a wave, and its wavelength depends only on its momentum and on Planck's constant. For everyday particles, the mass involved, and therefore the momentum, is so big compared with h that the wave nature of matter can be ignored. For everyday objects, h divided by momentum is effectively zero. But for electrons, each with a mass of only 9×10^{-28} gram, the numbers are more nearly in balance, and the wave aspect becomes significant.

De Broglie suggested to his examiners that this strange equation had a physical reality and that experiments might be carried out to measure the wavelength of electrons. His examiners did not take this idea seriously, and they regarded this aspect of his thesis presentation as more of a clever mathematical trick than anything of practical value. Still, he was awarded the doctorate, and his thesis supervisor, Paul Langevin, sent a copy of the work to Einstein. It was Einstein who spotted at once the value of the work and its implications and who passed news of it on to other researchers. Within a few years, teams in both the United States and Britain had actually measured the wavelengths of beams of electrons by scattering them off the atoms that form regular arrays in crystals. For an electron, this is the equivalent of Young's double slit experiment, and it is just as conclusive. Only waves can interact with each other to produce interference patterns, and under the right conditions, electrons do just that. Meanwhile, the Austrian Erwin Schrödinger had developed a wave equation for the electron, equivalent to Maxwell's equations for light, which had proved to be one of the keys to developing a consistent model of the atom. De Broglie was duly awarded the 1929 Nobel Prize in Physics. By then it was clear that all "waves" have to be treated as "particles" and that all "particles" have to be treated as "waves." The confusion does not arise in everyday life, for objects big enough to see, or for waves on the ocean and ripples on the pond. But it is crucial to an understanding of atoms and subatomic phenomena. The physicists of the late 1920s were happy to have a consistent theory of the atom at last, even if the price they had to pay included some strange ideas about wave-particle duality. However, this strange aspect of atomic reality was almost the least of the strangeness of the quantum world that was then unfolding before their astonished gaze.

THE CENTRAL MYSTERY

There is one experiment that contains the essence of quantum physics and lays bare its central mystery. This is the modern version of the two-slit experiment, which Young used to prove that light is a form of wave. In practical terms, such an experiment may be carried out using light, or electrons, or other objects such as protons; it may not literally involve *two* slits but perhaps the equivalent of an array of slits, a so-called diffraction grating, or the regularly spaced atoms in a crystal, from which X-rays or electrons are bounced. But in order to describe the central mystery in its purest form, I will talk in terms of electrons and of precisely two slits. And everything I will tell you about the behavior of electrons in such circumstances has been checked and verified by experiments of this kind, involving both electrons and photons, and other "particles." None of this is just a bizarre hypothetical mathematical quirk of the equations; it is all tried and tested and true.

The idealized form of the experiment is very easy to describe. It consists of a source of electrons (an electron "gun," like the one in the tube of your TV set), a screen with two holes in it (small holes; they have to be small *compared with the wavelength of an electron,* which is why the gaps between atoms in a crystal turn out to be just right), and a detector. The detector might be a screen, like a TV screen, which flashes when an electron hits it. What matters is that we have some means of recording when and where an electron hits the detector, and of adding up the number of electrons arriving at each place on the detector screen. When waves go through such a system, each of the two holes in the first screen becomes a source of waves, spreading out in a semicircle and marching in step with the waves from the other hole. Where

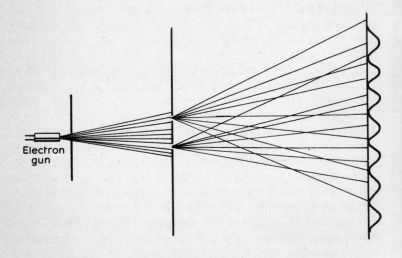

*Figure 12.3/*The equivalent of Young's two-slit experiment for light (Figure 12.2) can be carried out with electrons. It produces exactly the same result—proof that electrons are waves. But other experiments "prove," just as reliably, that both light and electrons come in the form of particles. This wave-particle duality is the central mystery of quantum mechanics.

the waves add up, they produce large vibrations; where they cancel out, there is no detectable vibration at all. This is why such an experiment with light waves produces bands of dark and light stripes on the detector screen.

If there is only one hole in the first screen, of course, then there is simply a bright spot (or band) of light on the detector, brightest at the center and fading out smoothly on either side.

The same sort of thing happens when we fire a beam of electrons through a screen with *one* hole (one slit). The detector screen records most flashes in line with the hole, and a few on either side of the region where the electron beam is most intense. With our two-slit experiment, we can test this by blocking up first one hole and then the other. In each case, one hole on its own produces on the screen a bright spot that fades away smoothly on either side. But when *both* holes are open, there is a clear diffraction pattern on the screen. The flashes that mark the arrival of individual electrons form bright stripes separated by dark regions. This is explained by the wavelike nature of electrons. The electron waves going through the two holes are interfering with one another, canceling out in some places and reinforcing in others, just like light waves.

So far, so good. It is more than a little strange that electrons can behave like waves when they are going through the experimental apparatus, then suddenly coalesce into hard little lumps to strike flashes from the detector screen, but by combining the ideas of particle and wave we can at least begin to convince ourselves that we have some idea of what is going on. After all, a water wave is actually made up of myriads of little particles (water molecules) moving about. If we are firing hundreds of thousands of electrons in a beam through the two holes, perhaps it isn't so surprising that they can be guided in some way like waves, while retaining their identity as little particles. If we fire just *one* electron at a time through the experiment, then logically we would expect that it would go through one hole or the other. The diffraction pattern we observe is simply, according to everyday logic, the result of observing many electrons at the same time.

So what happens when you do fire one electron at a

time through the experiment? Clearly, when you get one flash on the screen on the other side that doesn't tell you much about how the electron has behaved. But you can repeat the single-shot experiment time after time, observing all the flashes and noting their positions on the screen. When you do this, you find that the flashes slowly build up into the old, familiar diffraction pattern. Each individual electron, passing through the apparatus, has somehow behaved like a wave, interfering with itself and directing its own path to the appropriate bright region of the diffraction pattern. The only alternative would be that all of the electrons going through the apparatus at different times have interfered with each other, or the "memory" of each other, to produce the diffraction pattern.

It looks as if each electron goes through *both* slits. This is crazy. But we can devise an additional set of detectors that notes which slit each electron goes through, and repeat our experiment to see if that is indeed what happens. When we do this, we do not find that our detectors at the two holes each report the passage of an electron (or half an electron). Instead, sometimes the electron goes through one slit, and sometimes through the other. So what happens now when we send thousands of electrons through the apparatus, one after the other? Once again, a pattern builds up the detector screen. But it is *not* a diffraction pattern! It is simply a combination of the two bright patches we get when one or the other of the holes is open, with no evidence of interference.

This is *very* strange. Whenever we try to detect an electron, it responds like a particle. But when we are not looking at it, it behaves like a wave. When we look to see which hole it goes through, it goes through only one hole and ignores the existence of the other one. But when we don't monitor its passage, it is somehow "aware" of both holes at once and acts as if it had passed through them both.

Quantum physicists have some nice phrases to describe all this. They say that there is a wave of some sort associated with an electron. This is called the "wave function," and it is spread out, in principle, to fill the Universe. Schrödinger's equation describes these wave functions and how they interact with one another. The wave function is strongest in one region, which corresponds to the position of the electron in everyday language. It gets weaker farther away from this region but still exists even far away from the "position" of the electron. The equations are very good at predicting how particles like electrons behave under different circumstances, including how they will interfere with one another when they, or the wave functions, pass through two slits. When we look at an electron, or measure it with a particle detector, the wave function is said to "collapse." At that instant, the position of the electron is known to within the accuracy allowed by the fundamental laws. But as soon as we stop looking, the wave function spreads out again and interferes with the wave functions of other electrons—and, under the right circumstances, with itself.*

All of this is precisely quantifiable mathematically and makes it possible to calculate how electrons fit into atoms, how atoms combine to make molecules, and much more besides. The jargon "collapse of the wave function" (which has a precise mathematical significance in quantum theory) is equivalent to saying that we can know where things are only when we are actually looking at them. Blink and they are gone. And the behavior of the particles depends on whether or not we are looking. If we watch the two holes to see electrons passing by, the electrons behave differently from the way they behave when we are not looking. The observer is, in quantum physics, an integral part of the experiment, and what he or she chooses to watch plays a crucial role in deciding what happens.

The implications of all this are very deep indeed. For one thing, we can no longer say that an electron, in principle identifiable as a unique object, starts at one side of our experiment and follows a unique path, a trajectory, through to the other side. The very concept of a continuous "trajectory" is a hangover from classical Newtonian ideas and has to be abandoned. Instead, quantum physicists talk

---

*How do we know what the electron wave does when we are not looking at it? From repeated observations in many experiments of where the electrons are and which way they are moving when we do see them, physicists infer that the right mathematical description of the wave function is in line with this very simple description. But if you want the details, you will have to check them out in *In Search of Schrödinger's Cat*.

in terms of "events," which may happen in a certain order in time but which tell us nothing about what happens to the particles involved in events when they are not being observed. All we can say is that we observe an electron at the start (event 1) and that we observe an electron at the finish (event 2). We can say nothing at all about what it does in between, and indeed we cannot say that it is the same electron that is recorded at each event. Fire two electrons off together, and although two electrons arrive on the detector screen a little later, there is no way of telling which one is which.

Electrons are indistinguishable from one another in a far deeper sense than any mass-produced objects of the everyday world, such as paper clips, are indistinguishable from one another. The electrons in an atom are not physically distinct entities, each following its own well-defined orbit. Instead, all we can say is that a particular kind of atom behaves as if it had associated with it a combination of eight, or ten, or whatever the number might be, electron wave functions. If we carry out an experiment designed to prod the atom (perhaps by bombarding it with photons, as in the photoelectric experiment), one or more of the electron wave functions may be modified in such a way that there is a high probability that we will detect an electron outside the atom, as if a little particle had been ejected. But the only realities are what we observe; everything else is conjecture, hypothetical models we construct in our minds and with our equations to enable us to develop a picture of what is going on.

Which is more real, the particle or the wave? It depends on what question you ask of it. And no matter how skillful a physicist the questioner may be, there is never any absolute certainty about the answer that will come back.

CHANCE AND UNCERTAINTY

A particle is something that is well defined. It exists at a point in space, it occupies a small volume and has some kind of tangible reality in terms of our everyday experience of the world. But a wave is almost the opposite. A pure wave stretches on forever, so there is no sense in which it can be said to exist at a point. It may have a very well-defined direction—it carries momentum. But there is no way you can, even in imagination, put your finger on it and hold it still while you look at it. So how can the two aspects of the subatomic world be reconciled?

To express itself in particle terms—as a photon, or as an electron—a wave must be confined in some way. Mathematicians know all about this. The way to confine a wave is to reduce its purity. Instead of a single wave with one unique, well-defined frequency, think of a bundle of waves, with a range of frequencies, all moving together. In some places, the peaks of one wave will combine with the peaks of other waves to produce a strong wave; in other places, the peaks of one wave will coincide with the troughs of other waves, and they will cancel each other out. Using a technique called Fourier analysis, mathematicians can describe combinations of waves that cancel out almost completely everywhere except within some small, well-defined region of space. Such combinations are called wave packets. In principle, as long as you include enough different waves in the packet, you can make it as small as you like. Since mathematicians use the Greek letter delta (Δ) to denote small quantities, we can say that the length of the wave packet is Δx. By losing the purity of a single wave with a unique frequency, we can localize the wave packet until it has the dimensions of an electron.

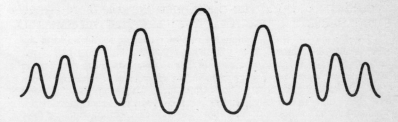

*Figure 12.4/*A wave packet is a group of waves that covers only a definite region of space.

But we have paid a price. The momentum of a wave, as de Broglie showed, is h divided by the wavelength. A pure wave has a unique wavelength and therefore has a unique momentum. But by introducing a mixture of wavelengths, or frequencies, we have introduced a mixture of momenta. The more waves we have (the smaller the wave packet) the less precise is the meaning of the term "momentum" for this wave packet. All we can say is that there is a range of momenta covering an amount Δp. Δx is the amount of uncertainty in the position of the wave packet; we know it is somewhere within a volume Δx across. Δp is the uncertainty in the momentum of the wave packet. We know roughly where the packet is going, but only to a precision of Δp. It is very simple, mathematically, to show that we can never reduce Δx or Δp to zero and that, in fact, the *product* of the two uncertainties, $\Delta x \Delta p$, always is bigger than Planck's constant, h, divided by twice the value of pi (2π). This slightly different constant is written $\hbar$ and is either referred to as "h cross" or, more sloppily, as "Planck's constant," even though it is really $h/2\pi$. The relationship between position and momentum is Heisenberg's uncertainty relation, named after the Nobel Prize–winning German physicist Werner Heisenberg, who was one of the pioneers who developed quantum mechanics in its first full form in the 1920s,* and is written:

$$\Delta x \, \Delta p > \hbar$$

It is impossible to stress too strongly that this relationship, this equation, is not just some weird mathematical trick. The empirical evidence for wave-particle duality means that it is impossible, in principle, to measure both the position of a particle and its momentum with absolute precision. Indeed, if you could measure *exactly* where an

---

*It is interesting that the dramatic new understanding of the world of the very small has its origins in breakthroughs made in the second half of the 1920s, almost exactly at the same time that observations of the world of the very large—the Universe—were revealing its extent and, by showing that it expands, hinting at its origin. I don't think there is any deep significance in this. The quantum revolution might easily have come ten years before, or ten years after, the cosmological revolution. But they were both products of their time, depending in part on the technology that made it possible to build large telescopes and to probe atomic structure with X-rays—and they both, of course, owed a lot to spectroscopy. So both were bound to happen more or less during the same scientific generation.

electron was, so that Δx is zero, then Δp would become infinite, and you would have no idea at all where in the universe the electron would pop up next. And the uncertainty is not restricted solely to our *knowledge* of the electron. It is there all the time, built into the very nature of electrons and other particles and waves. The particle itself does not "know," with absolute precision, both where it is now and where it is going next. The concept of uncertainty is intimately linked with the concept of chance in quantum physics. We cannot be certain where a particle is and we cannot be certain where it is going, so we must not be too surprised if it turns up where we don't expect it.

Position and momentum are not the only properties of a particle that are related in this way. There are other pairs of what are called "conjugate variables" that are similarly linked by the wave equations, and the most important of these are energy (E) and time (t). It turns out, from a rigorous mathematical analysis, that there is also an inherent uncertainty in the amount of energy involved in a subatomic process. If energy is transferred from one particle to another, and if the transfer takes a certain amount of time (which it must do, since nothing travels faster than light), then the uncertainty in the energy (ΔE) multiplied by the uncertainty in the time (Δt) is also bigger than h cross:

$$\Delta E\, \Delta t > \hbar$$

For a short enough time, indeed, both a particle and its immediate surroundings—or indeed the whole universe— may be uncertain about how much energy the particle has. The strange "tunnel effect," by which alpha particles get out of atomic nuclei, graphically illustrates the power of uncertainty in the subatomic world. George Gamow, of course, explained alpha emission "properly," using the full equations of quantum physics. But we can easily see in general terms what is going on.

The alpha particle, remember, sits inside the nucleus, and we can imagine it as being just inside the rim of a volcano. If the particle were just *outside* the rim, it would "roll away" and be ejected by the force of electric repulsion. The "distance" from the inside of the nucleus to the outside is Δx. An alpha particle associated with the nucleus has a very well-defined momentum, the same as the nucleus. But that means its position must be uncertain. Although it is associated with the nucleus, it is not *inside* the nucleus, in the everyday meaning of "inside." Uncertainty implies that there is a finite, and precisely calculable, chance that the particle is actually outside the nucleus. Bingo! Some particles do find themselves outside the nucleus, take note of the fact, and rush away, just as if they have "tunneled" through the intervening barrier. It is exactly as if you took some dice and rattled them in a cup until suddenly one of them appeared outside the cup, rolling across the table. And if Planck's constant were big enough, that is how dice would indeed behave in the everyday world.

Or think of it in terms of energy. The particle needs more energy to climb over the "rim" of the potential bar-

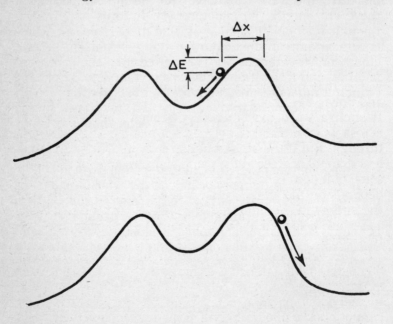

*Figure 12.5/*Quantum mechanical uncertainty explains how an alpha particle can escape from an atomic nucleus (Figure 4.6). The particle can "borrow" energy ΔE for a short time to get "over the hill"; or, from another point of view, it can tunnel through the hill because its position is uncertain to within Δx.

rier. The extra energy it needs is ΔE. For a brief enough instant of time, Δt, it might, for all the laws of physics know or care, have that extra energy. And if it does, once again it is off and running. It doesn't matter that it has to "give back" the energy it borrowed from uncertainty, after a time Δt, because by then it has escaped down the hill on the other side of the barrier.

As if all this were not mind-bending enough, the quantum theory has more tricks in store. So far we have looked mainly at the implications of a mixture of wave characteristics for particles. What happens to our understanding of waves, especially light, when we have to treat them as particles? The kind of problem the physicists encounter can be highlighted by one example. There are materials called polarizers that allow light to pass through them only if the waves are vibrating in a certain direction. Some sunglasses work like this. Since daylight contains waves vibrating in all directions, glasses that let only some of the waves through reduce glare. A "polarized" light wave is one that has been through such a filter, and so all the waves that remain are vibrating in the same plane—up and down, say, if that is the way the polarizer was set up. If such a wave meets another polarizer aligned exactly across its own plane of polarization, none of the light gets through. But if the second polarizer is aligned at an angle less than 90 degrees to the plane of polarization of the light, some of it does get through. The fraction that gets through depends on the angle; when it is 45 degrees, exactly half the energy in the light gets through the second polarizer, as a wave polarized at 45 degrees to the polarization of the first wave.

Maxwell's equations can explain all this. A polarizer at 45 degrees takes out half the energy in the wave; a polarizer at right angles takes out all the energy. But what happens to individual photons coming up to the polarizer? You cannot chop a photon in half. It is the fundamental, basic unit of energy. So in a beam of light passing through a polarizer at 45 degrees, half the photons get through and half do not. But how are they selected? By chance, at random in accordance with the statistical rules of probability. When an individual photon arrives at the polarizer there is, in this example, a precise 50:50 chance that it will get through, or that it will be stopped. The numbers change with the angle of the polarizer, but the principle does not. Individual photons are selected by the polarizer on a basis of pure chance. And this example is just a simple demonstration of what is happening throughout the quantum world. Every time subatomic particles are involved in interactions, the outcome depends on chance. The odds may be very heavily stacked in favor of one particular outcome, or they may be no better than tossing a coin on a 50:50 basis. But they are clearly and precisely laid down by the laws of quantum physics, and there is no such thing as certainty in the quantum world.

This is the point about quantum theory that made Albert Einstein reject the whole thing with his famous remark "I cannot believe that God plays dice." But all the evidence is that God *does* play dice. Every experiment confirms the accuracy of the quantum interpretation. When we carry out an experiment, which might involve measuring the position of an electron, for example, we cannot know for certain how things are going to develop later. In this simple case, we can say, perhaps, that there is a certain probability that next time we look the electron will have moved from point A to point B, a different probability that it will be at point C, and so on. The probabilities can all be calculated, in principle, and it might be far more than 99 percent probable that the electron will go from A to B. But it is never *certain*. One day, when you do the old familiar experiment in which the electron goes from A to B, it might, just by chance, turn up at point C, or D, or Z, instead.

In the everyday world, we are saved from the more bizarre possibilities by the sheer numbers of particles involved. Billions and trillions of electrons move through the circuitry to make my word processing computer work. A few mavericks somewhere in the system may indeed be blithely hopping from A to D instead of from A to B. But the vast majority do what they should, as far as I am concerned. Unless you have a taste for philosophy, you don't have to worry too much about the uncertain and chancy aspects of quantum theory in your own life. Even if, like me, you *do* have a taste for metaphysics, you can still use a computer without any *real* fear that *all* of the electrons suddenly will stop obeying orders. But the stranger aspects of quantum physics become very important when we deal with the subatomic world and with the birth of the Universe. We need just one more fundamental concept and a few bizarre tidbits from the quantum cookbook before we are, at last, ready to tackle those puzzles.

PATH INTEGRALS AND A PLURALITY OF WORLDS

The fundamental difference between quantum mechanics and classical—Newtonian—mechanics is very clearly brought out when we look closely at the way a particle such as an electron actually does get from one point (A) to another (B). In the classical view, a particle at point A has a definite speed in a definite direction. As it is acted upon by external forces, it moves along a precisely determinable path, which, for the sake of argument, passes through, or ends at, point B. The quantum-mechanical view is different. We *cannot* know, not even in principle, both the position and momentum of a particle simultaneously. There is an inherent uncertainty about where the particle is going, and if a particle starts out at point A and end is later detected at point B, we cannot know exactly how it got from A to B unless it is watched all the way along its path.

Richard Feynman, a Nobel Prize-winning physicist from the California Institute of Technology, applied this quantum-mechanical view to the history of particles as presented in the kind of space-time diagrams used by relativists. These are diagrams like graphs, with one axis representing time and the other space. Curves on the diagram—world lines—represent particle trajectories, or histories, some of which are ruled out because they would involve travel faster than light, but many of which indicate valid ways for a particle to get from A to B. Going back to the experiment with two holes, for example, you might imagine literally drawing out a map of all the possible ways in which an electron could get from the gun on one side of the screen to a particular spot on the detector screen, passing through one or another of the holes on the way. Some of these trajectories, or paths, are very straightforward and direct; others meander. Feynman's maps include time as well as space, and on them some of the trajectories represent fast passages of an electron through the experiment, and others represent slow passages. But each path, direct or circuitous, fast or slow, has associated with it a definite probability (strictly speaking, a "probability amplitude"), which can be calculated. The amplitudes are measured in terms of a quantity called action, which is energy × time and which happens to be the unit Planck's constant h, is measured in.

The probabilities of the world lines are not all "in step" with one another, and like the amplitudes of ripples on a pond they can interfere with one another to reinforce the strength of one path while canceling out the amplitudes of others. It is not unlike the way in which the waves in a wave packet cancel each other out everywhere except in a small region, Δx. Feynman's work* shows that when all of the amplitudes corresponding to possible particle trajectories are added together, the result of the interference is to wipe out all of the possible contributions except the ones that are very close to the trajectory that corresponds to the path from A to B in accordance with classical mechanics. And when the technique is applied to experiments like the two-slit experiment, the results it comes up with are exactly the same as the results you get using Schrödinger's wave equation.

Actually, the technique has been used in fully worked out detail only for some very simple, special cases. Imagine the complexity of calculating the probabilities of every path from the electron gun to *each* point on the detector screen. The number of paths involved is so enormous in most cases that it is quite impractical to apply Feynman's technique in its pure form. But the concept underlying this approach, and the fact that it can be shown mathe-

---

*Notably described in all its technically detailed glory by Feynman and A. R. Hibbs in their book *Quantum Mechanics and Path Integrals* (New York: McGraw-Hill, 1965).

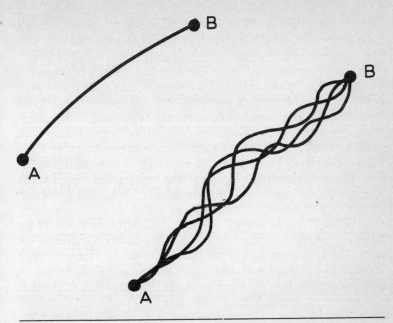

Figure 12.6/Classical—Newtonian—physics says that a particle
follows a unique trajectory from A to B. Richard Feynman's
quantum mechanical interpretation says that we must calculate
the effect of all the possible paths from A to B and add them
together. This is the "path integral," or "sum over histories,"
approach. It explains, among other things, how a single electron
can "pass through" both holes in a Young's slit experiment (Figure
12.3) and interfere with itself.

matically to make the same predictions as Schrödinger's
version of quantum physics, are fundamentally important.*
Feynman tells us that in the two-slit experiment we not
only have to think of the electron as going through both

*There are, however, ways to generalize the technique, and to calculate its
broad implications without calculating every path in detail. Feynman has
proved, for example, that the most probable path, which corresponds to the
classical trajectory, follows a line of least action, and he has established
mathematically that only paths close to the line of least action need be
included in the calculations, since the probability amplitudes from the other
paths must cancel each other out. The problem with the two-slit experiment
is that there are paths through each of the holes that each have the same
"least action," and all such paths are equally important in calculating the
fate of the electron.

holes at once, but also as taking *every possible path* through both holes at once. The conventional quantum view has it that there is *no* trajectory; from Feynman's point of view, we have to take account of *every* trajectory.

This approach to describing the trajectories of particles is called the "path integral" technique, because it involves adding up different possible paths, or sometimes, more grandiosely, the "sum over histories" approach. The alternative name echoes the idea behind an interpretation of the quantum rules that is far from being the majority view today but that I am fond of and that I discussed in *In Search of Schrödinger's Cat*. The model fits the "many worlds" description of reality developed originally by Hugh Everett of Princeton University in 1957.

What Everett found was that the equations could be interpreted, with complete validity, as implying that every time the Universe is faced with a "choice" at the quantum level it splits into two, and both options are chosen. In an experiment where an electron goes from point A to point B via an intervening screen that has two holes in it, quantum theory says that unless we watch all the time we cannot possibly tell which holes it went through—indeed, that it is meaningless to say it went either way. Its "real" trajectory is given by a sum of the two possible paths. But classical theory says there is a definite path and it must have gone through just one of the holes, even if we weren't looking. When we look to see which hole the electron goes through, of course, that particular uncertainty vanishes and we have a different experiment in which we know which path the particle took. But, says Everett (or rather, say the equations), for every observer who looks and sees the electron go through one hole, there is another observer—in another world—who looks and sees it go the other way. Both are equally real. Or, in terms of the photon passing through as piece of polarizer, every time a photon is faced with the 50:50 choice described above, the Universe divides into two. In one universe, the photon passes the filter; in the other universe, it does not. The strangest thing about this version of quantum reality is that it makes exactly the same predictions as the probabilistic interpretation for the observable outcomes of all experiments that could be carried out. This is both a strength of the model (after all, to be a good model it must agree with all those experiments done so far) and a weakness, since most theorists, with relief, say that since it makes no new, testable predictions to distinguish itself from the conventional interpretation, in that case we don't need it at all and can stick with the probabilities. Indeed, probability provides the means to retain an image of the electron as a pointlike particle if you really want to retain that image.

OUT OF THE FRYING PAN?

English physicist Paul Davies, who teaches at the University of Newcastle upon Tyne, urges this point of view in an undergraduate textbook he wrote on quantum physics.* "Resist at all costs," he says in that book, "the temptation to think of an electron as pulled asunder and smeared out in space in little ripples. The electron itself is not a wave. Rather, the way it moves about is controlled by wave-like principles. Physicists still regard the electron as a pointlike entity, but the precise location of that point may not be well-defined." And he goes on to describe the probability waves that determine where an electron is likely to turn up next by making an analogy with a crime wave. "Crime waves are not waves of undulating stuff but *probability* waves . . . crime waves, like fashions or unemployment, may move about—they have dynamics—but an individual crime still occurs, of course, at a place. It is the abstract probability which moves."

For many purposes, and especially for teaching undergraduate physics, physicists do indeed treat electrons as "real" particles, and the waves associated with them as "probability waves," which can interfere with one another, be diffracted through small holes, and do all the other tricks waves can do. "It is the probability which has the wave-like behaviour," Davies tells his students in that book, "while the particles themselves remain as little lumps,

Quantum Mechanics (London: Routledge & Kegan Paul, 1984).

albeit elusively secreted in the wave which guides their progress . . . which facet of this wave-particle duality is manifested depends on the sort of question that is asked." This is bad teaching. You might try, if only he were still alive, asking Maxwell how he felt about the suggestion that light waves are only probability waves guiding the motion of little hard lumps called photons. His response might be interesting. No matter how hard you try to hold on to the image of an electron, or a photon, or whatever, as a particle, the concept persists in slipping away.

Take spin, for example. Electrons and other subatomic particles have a property that physicists call spin. It is fundamentally important in deciding how electrons are arranged in atoms, among other things, and it is measured in the same kind of units as the spin of a top, or of the Earth rotating in space. But there the analogy stops. The spin of an electron can point in only one of two directions, "up" or "down"—never "sideways," or anywhere in between. Spin itself is quantized, like energy. The spin of a fundamental particle is measured in units of h cross. In those units, the spin of an electron is ½—either + ½ or -½, but never anything else. All the particles that we like to think of as "real" particles, like protons, neutrons, and electrons, have spin that is half integral—½, ³⁄₂, ⁵⁄₂, and so on. All such particles obey a set of statistical rules known as Fermi-Dirac statistics. The photon, which has spin one, and all particles with integer spin (1, 2, 3, and so on) obey a different set of rules called Bose-Einstein statistics; so there *is* a fundamental difference between photons and electrons.

The most important distinction is that particles like electrons (fermions) are exclusive. In terms of the "ladder" of energy levels inside an atom, this means that only two electrons can sit on each rung of the ladder—one with spin up, the other with spin down.* A third electron is excluded from that rung, because it would occupy a state

---

*I am, in fact, oversimplifying. For reasons I won't go into here, there are some sets of energy levels inside an atom where four "rungs" of the ladder, or one rung on each of four separate ladders, in effect lie side by side, so eight electrons can have states very similar to one another. The relevant point, however, is still that strictly speaking no two of these electrons are in *identical* states.

identical to that of one or the other of the two electrons already there. Photons and other integer-spin particles (collectively called bosons) are less snobbish. You can pack them in any old how, any old where. Furthermore, although fermions are conserved—overall, the number of fermions in the Universe stays the same—bosons are more ephemeral. We can make photons just by turning on a light; they vanish again when they are absorbed by atoms and give up their energy.

All of this is rather hard to reconcile with the existence of "real" little lumps being guided by probability waves. It is even harder when the physicists tell you that the spin of a fundamental particle has some other peculiar properties. If you think of an electron as rotating, for example, it has to rotate through 360 degrees not once but *twice* to get back to where it started. And although I just told you that fermions are conserved in the Universe at large, that constraint still allows you to make particles and antiparticles in equal numbers if you have the energy available to do so. An electron-positron pair, for example, counts as zero in the total number of fermions on the Universe's list. The particle and antiparticle cancel out. If you've got the energy, you can make electron-positron pairs just as they were made in the cosmic fireball. Where can you get the energy today? If you are being mundane, you might imagine getting it by smashing particles together in giant accelerators, like the one at CERN. But you can be more imaginative. The limits of the uncertainty principle allow you, if you do it quickly enough, to "borrow" enough energy from the uncertainty relation to make particles, as long as they disappear again when their allowed time is up.

Take electrons. If the mass of an electron is m, then the energy needed to make an electron-positron pair is $2mc^2$. This is about 1 MeV. The laws of quantum physics allow such a pair of particles to pop into existence out of the vacuum for a very, very tiny split second of time (Planck's constant divided by 1 MeV) and then to annihilate one another and disappear again. Such particle pairs are called "virtual" particles. Each pair can exist only for a very short time, but the vacuum is seething with such pairs, constantly being produced, disappearing, and being replaced by new pairs. At least that is what quantum physics says the vacuum is like. And the existence of virtual particles has a direct effect on the equations of particle physics. Without virtual particles, the equations do not predict correctly the interactions between charged particles. With effects due to virtual particles included, they do.

So just how "real" are any of the particles in the Universe? When Paul Davies is talking to his fellow researchers instead of to his undergraduates, he takes a rather different line. In his contribution to a book published to mark the sixtieth birthday of physicist Bryce DeWitt (one of the champions, incidentally, of the many worlds interpretation of quantum physics), Davies presented an essay provocatively titled "Particles Do Not Exist."* The nub of the argument he put forward, one that agrees with the views of many theorists, starts from the fact that we cannot see, touch, or feel fundamental particles such as electrons. All we can do is carry out experiments, make observations, and draw conclusions about what is going on based on those observations, and our experiences of everyday life. It is natural that we should try to impose concepts from our everyday world, like "wave" and "particle," on the subatomic world; but in fact all we know about the subatomic world is that if we poke it in a certain way, we get a certain response. "What I do try to discredit," says Davies at the start of this essay, "is what might be called naïve realism." And he concludes, "the concept of a particle is purely an idealized model of some utility in flat space quantum field theory." The particle concept is, he says, "nebulous" and ideally "it should be abandoned completely."

The snag is that we have nothing better, as yet, to replace it with. But it is with that cautionary word from the forefront of modern research, rather than any comforting undergraduate Linus-blanket of ideas about real little lumps being guided by probability waves, that I want to take you now into the particle world itself. Over the past fifty years, physics has revealed a wonderland of a sub-

---

*Quantum Theory of Gravity (Bristol: Adam Hilger, 1984).

atomic world populated by all kinds of strange objects. We call those objects particles, for want of a better name. What they really are, we do not know. The best theories we have explain the results of past experiments in terms of the interactions between these mythical beasts, and they predict the results of new experiments in terms of how the "particles" interact with one another. By observing the world of high energy interactions, physicists work out rules that describe those interactions, and then they use the rules to predict the outcome of the next experiment. Good theories get those predictions right; the best theories enable us to "get right" the calculation of how the Universe came into being and then exploded into its present form. But that doesn't mean that they convey ultimate truth, or that there "really are" little hard particles rattling around against each other inside the atom, or at the birth of the Big Bang. Such truth as there is in any of this work lies in the mathematics; the particle concept is simply a crutch ordinary mortals can use to help them toward an understanding of the mathematical laws. And what those mathematical laws describe are fields of force, space-time curved and recurved back upon itself in fantastic complexity, and a "reality" that fades away into a froth of virtual particles and quantum uncertainty when you try to peer closely at it.

The concepts of particles and waves are the best we have, and the most straightforward way to describe the great advances in modern physics, in our understanding of the Universe, is in terms of particles. But they are only metaphors for something that we cannot properly comprehend or understand, and I apologize in advance for the necessity of using them. I feel like a blind man trying to explain the concept of color to another blind person, having worked out a theory of color based on touch. The surprise is not that our theories are flawed but that they work at all.

PART THREE

...AND BEFORE

If we are not content with the dull accumulation of experimental facts, if we make any deductions or generalizations, if we seek for any theory to guide us, some degree of speculation cannot be avoided.

Arthur Eddington

CHAPTER SEVEN

PARTICLES AND FIELDS

At the beginning of the 1930s, apart from the mystery of exactly how you should interpret the probabilities and uncertainty built into quantum theory, it looked as if physicists had a pretty good grasp of what the world is made of. There were four particles, the electron, the proton, the neutron, and the photon, and there were two fundamental forces, gravity and electromagnetism, each of which had been known for a long time. Protons and neutrons together made up the nuclei at the hearts of atoms, and electrons occupied a more spread-out volume around the nucleus. Because protons carry positive charge, while electrons carry negative charge, each atom is electrically neutral, and the quantum physical arrangement of the electrons in different energy states, forced on them by their exclusive nature, gave each atom its unique chemical properties.

The power of the quantum theory was made impressively clear when physicists looked at the size of atoms in terms of the uncertainty principle. An atom is about one hundred-millionth (10^{-8}) centimeter across, and the mass of an electron is just over 9×10^{-28} gram. The energy that an electron possesses when it is bound up in an atom can be calculated, using Bohr's early version of quantum physics, by treating it like a particle in orbit around the nucleus—basically this is the same math that can be used to calculate the energy of the planets in their orbits around the Sun. Such naïve calculations give you a velocity for a typical electron "in its orbit" of about 10^8 centimeters per second. Together, these figures give an approximate momentum for a typical electron in an atom, about 10^{-20} gram centimeter per second, or perhaps a little less. If the electron had much more momentum (and therefore more energy) than this, it would escape from the atom, because the electric forces between the electron and the nucleus would not be strong enough to hold on to such an energetic electron. So the *uncertainty* in the momentum, p, is itself something less than 10^{-20} gram centimeter per second. Multiply this by the uncertainty in the position of the electron, a bit less than 10^{-8} centimeters, and you end up with a $\Delta p \, \Delta x$ of no more than a few times 10^{-27}, very close to the value of $h/2\pi$. Heisenberg's uncertainty relation determines the smallest size an atom can be. If the atoms were smaller, then there would be less uncertainty in the positions of the electrons, so there would be more uncertainty in their momentum, and therefore in their energy, and some would have enough energy to escape from the atom altogether, just as alpha particles "tunnel" out of the nucleus. Quantum physics can explain, or predict, the size of atoms themselves, something that had to be accepted as being the way it was "just because" it was the way it was, before quantum theory came along.

Protons and neutrons have much more mass than electrons, so they can have a larger uncertainty in momentum ($m \times v$) even though their velocities are smaller. Because their momenta are larger, they can be confined in a smaller volume (Δx) and still keep the product of uncertainties ($\Delta p \, \Delta x$) bigger than h cross. So nuclei are much smaller than the electron clouds that surround them, and their correct sizes are, once again, predicted by quantum uncertainty.

So, at the start of the 1930s, nature looked simple, and it seemed that physics had found the ultimate building blocks used by nature. Within a few years, however, the world began to seem a much more complex place, and within twenty years physicists had identified as many "elementary particles" as there are different chemical elements. It took a revolutionary new approach to bring some order to this proliferation of particles and to explain them in terms of a few units that are more basic still. Just as an atomic nucleus is imagined to be composed of protons and neutrons, so, for those who like to think in terms of particles, protons and neutrons themselves, and other particles, are now thought of as composed of quarks. But the very concept of a particle has itself undergone a dramatic change over the past fifty years. Just as photons are regarded as a manifestation of the electromagnetic field, so electrons and other particles can be thought of as manifestations of their own fields. Instead of a variety of fields and particles interacting with one another, the Universe can be thought of as made up from a variety of interacting fields alone, with the particles representing the quanta of each field, manifested in obedience to the rules of wave-particle duality and the uncertainty principle. So before we look at those new developments and how the physicists' view of our world has changed in the past fifty years, it seems appropriate to check out just what we mean by the concept of a field in physics.

FIELD THEORY

The basic idea of a field as the means by which an electric force is transmitted goes back to the pioneer Michael Faraday, who was born in Newington, England, in 1791. Faraday's career was so remarkable that it is worth a little digression to sketch out just how he came to be one of the great scientists, and great popularizers, of the Victorian era.

His father was a poor blacksmith, and Michael Faraday himself received only the basic education available to the poor in those days, leaving school at age thirteen and becoming apprenticed to a bookbinder. But Faraday had at least learned to read, and he had a voracious thirst for knowledge. So he read avidly the books he was supposed

to be binding, and at the age of fourteen became fascinated by an article on electricity in the *Encyclopaedia
Britannica*. He also read about chemistry, and carried out
his own experiments, as far as his limited resources permitted. In 1810, Faraday joined the City Philosophical
Society, attending lectures on physics and chemistry in
his spare time, and in 1812, at twenty-one, his life was
changed when he attended a series of lectures at the
Royal Institution given by Humphry Davy, a great chemist and the inventor of the safety lamp used by miners
before the availability of electricity.

Faraday was enthralled by Davy's lectures and made
extensive notes on them, which he bound up himself to
keep as a permanent record.* Faraday wanted desperately
to become a full-time scientist himself and wrote to the
President of the Royal Society asking for advice and help
but did not receive a reply. As his apprenticeship finished
in 1812, Faraday resigned himself to a life as a bookbinder. But he was rescued from this fate by an accident
in which Davy was temporarily blinded by a chemical
explosion. He asked the eager student, Faraday, to act as
his assistant until he recovered his sight. Faraday performed satisfactorily, and when Davy recovered, Faraday
sent him the bound copy of his lecture notes. Davy was
sufficiently impressed that when, a few months later in
1813, there was a vacancy at the Royal Institution for an
assistant to Davy, he offered Faraday the post. Faraday
leaped at the opportunity—even at the modest salary of a
guinea a week, less than he had been earning as a
bookbinder.

Faraday spent the rest of his career at the Royal Institution, becoming director of the laboratory in 1825 and
professor of chemistry there in 1833. He was a great
experimenter and explainer, rather than a mathematician,
and was a very successful and genuinely popular lecturer,
who founded the Royal Institution's Christmas lectures for
children that continue to this day. By the time he died in
1867, he had become a Fellow of the Royal Society and
been widely recognized as one of the scientific giants of

---

*You can still see them, in the Faraday museum at the Royal Institution in
London.

his day. But he was also modest, and along the way turned down the offer of a knighthood and *twice* refused the offer of the Presidency of the Royal Society. And, in his attempts to find a way to describe what happened when electric and magnetic forces act upon one another, he came up with the idea—what we would now call a model—of a "line of force," which Maxwell then elaborated into the first field theory.

The idea can be simply understood in terms of the forces acting between electric charges. Like charges repel each other (positive repels positive; negative repels negative), while opposite charges attract. Faraday's lines of force could be thought of as mathematical lines stretching out from each charged particle in the Universe. Every line starts on a particle with one flavor of charge and ends on a particle with the opposite charge. Like stretched rubber bands, they tend to pull opposite charges together; but like squeezed elastic, squashed up bunches of lines of force keep similar charges apart. The concept was enormously useful in getting a picture of what was going on, and the lines of force appear to have some real physical significance, because a tiny "test" particle with a small positive charge, placed between two oppositely charged, static, large objects will drift from the positive to the negative object along a line of least resistance, which (ignoring other forces such as gravity) will be along one of Faraday's lines of force.

All the lines of force filling space constitute the electric field. In the classical field theory of Faraday and Maxwell, the field is continuous—there are no "gaps" between lines of force, and no breaks in the lines themselves. So the

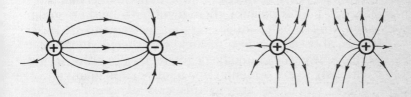

Figure 7.1 / The concept of a line of force, invented by Michael Faraday, is useful in getting a picture of how like charges repel and opposite charges attract.

analogy becomes, more appropriately, with an elastic medium filling the Universe, through which electric and magnetic forces are transmitted. This was the concept of the "ether." It seemed natural to Victorian scientists versed in the nature of mechanical objects and the triumphs of engineering, but following the development of relativity theory and then quantum theory in the twentieth century, this mechanistic view of the Universe was abandoned. The field is the field, not an elastic solid, and we cannot understand it fully in everyday terms. The most widely used "explanation" of what the field is brings the point home if you stop to think about it.

Before field theory was developed, it looked as if objects such as charged particles, or magnets, affected each other by an action that reached out across the gap between them—action at a distance. Field theory says that, rather, the action is a local phenomenon, with each charged particle interacting with the field, and the field interacting with each particle, in a way that depends on all the other interactions between the field and its particles. The often used analogy is with a spring. If you pull on either end of the spring, it stretches; if you squeeze it, it shrinks. The field, we are told, is like that. It can be stretched and compressed, and it links two particles in the way the matter in the spring joins its two ends together. The analogy seems homely and sensible enough. But what *is* the matter in the spring? It is a collection of atoms. And how do atoms interact with one another? Chiefly by electromagnetic forces. When the spring is stretched, the atoms move farther apart; when it is squeezed, they are pushed closer together. What the analogy says is that the stretching and squeezing of the electromagnetic field is like pulling atoms apart or pushing them together—in other words, it is like stretching or squeezing the electromagnetic field! Perhaps, after all, it is best to stick with the equations that describe how particles and fields interact, rather than trying too seriously to get a mental image of what is going on.

Those equations are, in this case, Maxwell's equations. Maxwell gave us the first fully worked out field theory, one that applies to both electricity and magnetism, and that says that magnetism is equivalent to moving (dynamic) electricity. It is the classical (meaning non-quantum) theory of electrodynamics. Einstein's General Theory of Relativity describes the other force familiar from everyday life and is another classical (in the same sense) field theory, this time of gravity. In the old, classical view of the world there were two basic components: material objects and the fields that linked them.

But the field is now the ultimate, fundamental concept in physics, because quantum physics tells us that particles (material objects) are themselves manifestations of fields. One of the first great surprises of quantum physics was the realization that a particle, such as an electron, had to be treated like a wave. In this first application of quantum principles, we learn to treat these matter waves as fields, with one field corresponding to each type of particle. For example, there is a general matter field filling the Universe, which is described by the wave equations of an electron.* But, as the discovery that electromagnetic waves must also be regarded in particle terms showed, a field can be directly responsible for the existence of particles. Indeed, in the quantum world a field *must* give rise to particles. Quantum physics says that the energy in the field cannot be smoothly changing from place to place, continuously, as in the classical picture. Energy comes in definite lumps called quanta, and every matter field must have its own quanta, each with a definite amount of energy, or mass. The particles are energetic bits of the field, confined to a certain region by the uncertainty principle. A photon is a quantum of the electromagnetic field; in the same way, by applying quantum principles a second time to the matter field of electrons, we find that we recover the idea of the electron as a particle, as the quantum of the electron matter field. This interpretation of particles as "field quanta" is known as second quantization. It tells us that there is nothing else in the Universe except quantum fields. So the more we know about quantum fields, the better we will understand the Universe.

Fields come in different varieties. For example, some have an inbuilt sense of direction—they are called vector fields—while others do not. A field without an inbuilt

---

*Strictly speaking, the wave function describes electron-positron pairs; more of this shortly.

sense of direction is called a scalar field. An example might be a field representing the temperature at every point in the room. Obviously, the field fills the room. If we place a thermometer at any place in the room, it will register a temperature—less by the door, where there is a draft of cold air blowing in, and more by the radiator. But the thermometer is not propelled, by its interaction with the field, either toward or away from the radiator. The field has magnitude but not direction. The electric field, on the other hand, is a vector field. I can measure the strength of the field at any place, and also its direction. A little positively charged object dropped into the field will try to move "along a line of force" away from the nearest positive pole of the field and toward a negative pole.*

There is another important distinction that applies to the quantum fields. Although I have so far talked about electrons and photons and their related fields in more or less the same way, there is a fundamental difference between them. Electrons are members of the family of fermions, all of which have a spin that is half integral, and fermions are not created or destroyed in the Universe today, except in matter-antimatter pairs. Photons, on the other hand, are bosons, and all bosons have zero or integer spin, can be created and destroyed, and are nonexclusive. So there are two fundamentally different kinds of field in nature, one fermionic and the other bosonic. This, it seems, is what leads to the distinction between what we used to think of as particles and what we used to think of as forces.

When two particles interact, they do so, on the old picture, because there is a force between them. This force can be expressed in terms of a field, and that field can in turn be expressed in terms of particles by means of the second quantization. When two electrons come close to each other, and are repelled from one another, it is because, in the new picture, one or more photons have been

---

*At a slightly more subtle level, even scalar fields can be associated with directions, because the field changes from place to place, and objects interacting with the field seek a state of minimum energy. A ball falls downward in the Earth's gravitational field for this reason. But a tiny charged object will move along a line of force even in a perfectly uniform electric field, and this is the crucial distinction.

exchanged between them. The energetic photon is a manifestation of the electric field around one or another of the electrons. It borrows energy from the uncertainty principle, pops into existence, whizzes across to the second electron and deflects it before it disappears again. The first electron recoils as the photon leaves it, and the result is that the electrons are repelled from one another.* One kind of field, corresponding to fermions, produces the material world; the other kind, corresponding to bosons, produces the interactions that hold the material world together and sometimes break bits of it apart.

The electromagnetic field around an electron can create virtual photons, provided they are short-lived and do not stray far from home. The rule of thumb, from the uncertainty principle, is that such a virtual photon can move only half its own wavelength away from the electron before it must turn back and be reabsorbed. Longer wavelength corresponds to less energy, so less energetic virtual photons stray farther from the electron. The result is a quantum picture of the electron as a charged region embedded in a sea of virtual photons, which get more energetic the closer you approach the electron itself.

Virtual photons—and, indeed, ordinary photons—can also create electrons, as virtual electron-positron pairs, provided they, too, are short-lived and exist only within the confines set by the uncertainty principle. And those electrons have their own clouds of virtual photons, and so on *ad infinitum*. The froth of activity around an electron, or involved in the repulsion, or scattering, of one electron by another is a far cry from the tranquil image most people associate with the word "vacuum." But by applying the principles of quantum theory to the electromagnetic field in this way, physicists have been able to come up with a theory of quantum electrodynamics, and a living vacuum, that describes the interactions of electrons, photons, and the electromagnetic field in quantum terms. The theory, known as QED, is one of the great triumphs of modern

---

*The analogy works so well for repulsion that I can't resist it. It is useless, though, at explaining how particles with the same kind of charge, such as two electrons, *repel* one another. Unfortunately, the quantum world cannot always be described in terms of cozy analogies.

science, so successful at accounting for the electromagnetic interaction that it is regarded as the prototype of all quantum field theories and is used as the blueprint for constructing new theories to explain other interactions. But it suffers from one crucial flaw, related to the presence of that cloud of virtual particles around each electron.

Quantum physics tells us that an electron is surrounded by a cloud of virtual photons and that any or all of these photons may be turning into electron-positron pairs, or into other pairs of virtual particles, before being reabsorbed by the electron. Extra energy is always being borrowed from the field, and from the uncertainty relation, literally without any limit to the complexity of the loops of virtual photons and virtual electron-positron pairs being produced. When the rules of quantum physics are applied with scrupulous care to calculate how much energy can be involved in these loops of virtual particles, it turns out that there is no limit—the energy of the electron plus the cloud of virtual particles around it becomes infinite, and since the electron and its cloud are inseparable, at first sight that seems to mean that electrons must have infinite mass.

The way around this difficulty seems crazy, but it works. Mathematically, the infinite mass of the cloud around the electron is compensated for by assuming that a "bare" electron (if such a thing could exist) would have infinite *negative* mass. With careful mathematical juggling, the two infinites can be made to cancel out and to leave behind a mass corresponding to the mass we measure for an electron. The trick is called renormalization. It is unsatisfactory for two reasons. First, it involves, in effect, dividing both sides of a mathematical equation by infinity, which is something we were all taught at school, quite rightly, is forbidden. Second, even then it does not predict the "correct" mass for the electron. Renormalization will give you a finite mass, but it could be *any* finite mass, and the physicists have to choose the right one and plug it in by hand. They can only solve the equations because they already know the answer they are looking for. The great thing is, though, that by putting in just one critical value by hand, the equations then give the physicists very precise, and accurate, "predictions" of the values of many other crucially important parameters—and that is why so many physicists have been happy to live with renormalization.

QED, including renormalization, works so well at explaining the behavior of charged particles and electromagnetic fields within the framework of quantum physics that most physicists choose not to think too deeply about these problems. But if they could ever come up with a theory in which the infinities canceled out by themselves, without the need for renormalization, their joy would be unconfined. Quantum electrodynamics is the best and most complete quantum field theory we have, but still it is not perfect. The search for a perfect theory that will explain all the interactions in the Universe, and the existence of the Universe itself, is now beginning to bear fruit. But before we can taste the first fruits of that success, we have to come up to date by taking stock of the veritable menagerie of new "particles" discovered in the past fifty years and of the two new "forces" needed to complete the count of quantum fields.

TWO MORE FORCES AND A PARTICLE ZOO

At the beginning of the twentieth century, scientists knew of the existence of ninety-two different chemical elements. Each element was known to consist of its own variety of atoms, and the ninety-two different kinds of atoms were regarded as the fundamental building blocks of nature—though it did seem rather profligate of nature to require so many "fundamental" building blocks. Thanks to the pioneering work of the Siberian Dmitri Mendeleev, who lived from 1834 to 1907, in the second half of the nineteenth century chemists had begun to appreciate the relationships between atoms with different weights. Mendeleev showed that when the elements were listed in order of increasing atomic weight, starting with hydrogen, then elements with similar chemical properties recurred at regular intervals throughout the resulting periodic table. This ranking of the elements by their chemical properties left some gaps in the table, and without knowing why or how the repeating pattern was produced, the simple fact of its existence enabled Mendeleev to predict that new elements would be discovered to fill the gaps and to predict what properties and atomic weights those elements would have. His predictions were subsequently confirmed, to the letter, by the discovery of "new" elements.

When physicists became able to break the atom apart and reveal its inner workings, they found that it contained three types of particles: electrons, protons, and neutrons. Quantum physics, in the hands of Niels Bohr, was able to explain the observed properties of the chemical elements, and the structure inside the atom underlying the structure in Mendeleev's periodic table. The periodic table appeared first in a paper Mendeleev published in 1869; Bohr's explanation in terms of quantum physics came in the 1920s, less than sixty years later. But just as the nature of atoms was being understood in terms of subatomic particles, so the nature of subatomic particles began to look very far from clear.

The electromagnetic force, in its quantum form, was entirely adequate to explain the behavior of negatively charged electrons as the partners, in an electrically neutral atom, to protons in the positively charged nucleus. But how could several protons, each with a positive charge, cluster together in the nucleus itself without being forced apart by electric repulsion? The New Zealander Ernest Rutherford, born in 1871, had established in 1910 that all of the positive charge in an atom is concentrated in a tiny nucleus. He and his colleagues, working at the University of Manchester in England, discovered this by firing alpha particles at the atoms in gold foil and observing how the particles were deflected. Rutherford also surmised, in the early 1920s, that there must be a neutral counterpart to the proton, a counterpart he called the neutron, having about the same mass as the proton but no electric charge.

The presence of neutrons was necessary to explain why some atoms had very similar chemical properties to one another, but different weights. Chemistry depends on the number of electrons surrounding an atom, and that is always the same as the number of protons in the nucleus.

So to change the weight of an atom without changing its chemistry you add, or subtract, electrically neutral particles, neutrons, to or from the nucleus. The atoms with the same chemistry but different atomic weights are called isotopes of the element concerned. James Chadwick, a British physicist who had been born in 1891 and was working with Rutherford (by now at the Cavendish Laboratory in Cambridge), confirmed, in a series of experiments in 1932, that neutrons exist; he received the Nobel Prize for his work, in 1935.

That brief span of three years from Chadwick's discovery of the neutron to his receipt of the Nobel Prize marks the time when subatomic physics seemed simple, and it looked as if physicists had only four types of fundamental particles to worry about. The presence of neutrons even helped to explain the stability of the nucleus, since the positively charged protons could, to some extent, hide from one another behind the neutrons. But this help was not enough to explain the stability of nuclei, and with that realization the simplicity of the particle world began to disappear.

The first blow at the foundations came from a Japanese researcher, Hideki Yukawa. Yukawa had been born in 1907 (he died only in 1981), and after attending the universities of Kyoto and Osaka, in 1935 he was working for his Ph.D. (which he obtained in 1938) and teaching at Osaka University. In 1939, he returned to Kyoto as professor of physics. Like other physicists, Yukawa was puzzled about how the atomic nucleus held together. He reasoned that there must be another force, stronger than the electromagnetic force, that kept the protons in its grip even though the electric repulsion "wanted" to separate them. But we don't see any evidence of such a strong force in the everyday world, so it must be a kind of force new to our experience, a force that operates only over a very short range, holding protons and neutrons together in the nucleus but permitting the individual particles (or, as we have seen, alpha particles) to fly free once they get beyond its range. Yukawa used an analogy with the electromagnetic force to describe his new force.

In electromagnetic field theory, the force results from the exchange of particles, virtual photons. Because photons have zero mass, the amount of energy a photon carries can be made vanishingly small by giving it a very long wavelength. So there is no limit, in principle, to the range over which electric forces can be felt—a virtual photon associated with an electron can interact, albeit very weakly and with very low energy, with another electron anywhere in the Universe—although, of course, the interaction is much stronger if the electrons are close together.

But what if the photons had mass? In that case, there would be a certain minimum amount of energy that would be required to make a virtual photon, ΔE. And the finite size of that packet of energy would set a firm time limit, Δt, on the life of such a particle, in line with Heisenberg's uncertainty relation. Since nothing can travel faster than light, this finite lifetime would mean that any such particle, in effect a "massive photon," would have only a very limited range, since it has to return to its origin, or find another particle to bury itself in before its allowed lifetime is up. So Yukawa reasoned, in 1935, that there must be another field, analogous to the electromagnetic field, associated with protons and neutrons. This field produces quanta that are, like photons, bosons, but that, unlike photons, have mass. And these bosons can be exchanged only by particles that "feel" the strong field. It just happens, said Yukawa in effect, that electrons ignore the strong force.

The beauty of Yukawa's hypothesis was that it was possible to calculate just what the mass of this new kind of boson ought to be. Its range had to be not much more than the size of an atomic nucleus, or it would prevent alpha particles from escaping, even with the aid of uncertainty, and produce other observable effects that are not, in fact, observed. And the size of a typical nucleus is only 10^{-12} centimeters, as refinements on Rutherford's team's pioneering scattering experiments show. From this single measurement and the uncertainty relation, Yukawa calculated that the carriers of the strong force must be particles with mass of about 140 MeV, more than two hundred times the mass of an electron but still only one seventh the mass of a proton.

How could Yukawa's idea be tested? At that time physicists had no way of looking inside the nucleus to find the new bosons. But while the strong force was supposed to depend on the exchange of *virtual* bosons,* there was nothing in the equations to prevent the equivalent real particles from being produced anywhere where there was enough energy to do the trick. In the cosmic fireball at the birth of the Universe, for example, such particles must have been abundant (although, don't forget, in 1935 nobody was really thinking much about the birth of the Universe; Gamow was still a quantum physicist then, and his enthusiastic promotion of the Big Bang idea still lay ten years in the future). It happens that, according to the equations, these particles ought to be unstable. The mass energy locked up in them can be converted into other, stable forms. But they can also be made by the energy available in collisions between fast-moving (that is, energetic) particles. Today, giant particle accelerators are used by physicists to smash beams of electrons and protons into one another, and into stationary targets, to manufacture showers of short-lived particles. These particles are made out of the kinetic energy of the colliding particles, in line with the equation $E = mc^2$, or if you prefer, $m = E/c^2$. This is an important point to appreciate. The "new" particles are not pieces of the particles being smashed together, broken off by the impact, but genuinely new, freshly manufactured out of pure energy. So the collisions can easily produce new particles that have a bigger rest mass than the particles involved in the collision, provided that the energy of motion involved is bigger than the required rest mass.†

---

*It is because they are virtual particles, not real ones, that the ones "inside" the nucleus can be involved in gluing the protons and neutrons together without contributing to the mass of the nucleus. In a proper quantum field theory treatment of the strong interaction, the same kind of problems with infinities arise as in QED, but they are also dealt with in the same way, by renormalization, as we shall see. But that involves a "generation" of particles one step more "fundamental" than the ones I am discussing now.

†I was initially uncomfortable about using this terminology, which takes no account of the fact that particles are "really" field quanta. But "particle" and "field" are just labels we use for convenience. When I discussed with particle physicist Frank Close how best to use these labels in my exposition, he said it doesn't matter. When he looks at "particle" experiments like those carried out at CERN and tries to understand what is going on, he thinks in terms of the flow, or transfer, of momentum through the interactions being studied. That, he says, is what really matters. Both particles and field quanta have momentum, and as long as you know where the momentum is going, the labels are of secondary importance.

In the 1930s, the only source of the necessary energetic particles was the Universe itself, which bombards the atmosphere of the Earth with the high-energy protons, electrons, and (we now know) other particles that are collectively called cosmic rays. A cosmic ray colliding with another particle high in the Earth's atmosphere can create new particles, including the bosons of the strong force. The first high-energy physicists were observers who found ways to monitor the passage of cosmic rays through their experiments—the "rays" affect photographic film, can be made to trigger sparks in apparatus rather like a grown-up version of a Geiger counter, and can be monitored in other ways. Once you've caught the fleeting passage of a cosmic ray, or a handful of cosmic rays, and photographed its trace, you can work out if it carries electric charge from the way its path bends in a magnetic field, and even deduce its momentum (and hence, eventually, its mass) from the amount by which its path is deflected by magnetic fields.

In 1936, one of the high-energy physics pioneers, the American Carl Anderson, was studying cosmic ray tracks produced in detectors on the surface of the Earth and found traces of a particle heavier than the electron but lighter than the proton. It looked as if Yukawa's carrier of the strong force had been found; the particle was dubbed the mu-meson, or muon for short. In fact, further studies soon showed that the muon was not the carrier of the strong force. It didn't have quite the right mass, and it didn't display sufficient eagerness to interact with atomic nuclei. But in 1947 another cosmic ray physicist, the Englishman Cecil Powell, found a short-lived boson with exactly the right properties, including a mass very close to the value predicted by Yukawa, and a great enthusiasm for reactions with nuclear particles. It was called the pi-meson, or pion. The muon, it turns out, is one of the things produced when a pion decays. Yukawa received the Nobel Prize in Physics in 1949, the first Japanese person to be honored in this way, and Powell was awarded the Prize in 1950. As for Anderson, he had already received the Physics Prize in 1936, the year he found the muon. But that was for a quite different discovery, one that didn't just add one member to the particle zoo, but, by implication, essentially doubled the number of inmates overnight.

Paul Dirac, a British physicist who was born in 1902, was one of the pivotal figures in the quantum revolution of the 1920s. He fused the first version of quantum mechanics, developed by Werner Heisenberg, with Einstein's Special Theory of Relativity, introducing the idea of quantum spin for the electron (an idea promptly taken over into other particles) in the process; he developed a very complete mathematical description of quantum theory, and wrote an influential textbook on the subject, still used by students and researchers today; and he played a major part in the development of QED, although to the end of his life (in 1984) he remained deeply unhappy with the business of renormalization, which he felt did no more than paper over the cracks in a flawed theory. For all that, outside of the inner circles of physicists, Dirac's best-known contribution to our understanding of the Universe is his prediction, in 1928, that the particles of the material world have their counterparts in the form of antimatter, mirror-image particles.

Ironically, for a theorist who achieved so much, so accurately, by design, Dirac's prediction of antimatter came about almost by accident, and at first he presented it to the world in an imprecise form. Dirac found that the equations he was working with, which described the behavior of electrons, actually had two sets of solutions, not one. Anyone who has come across simple quadratic equations, ones involving the *square* of an unknown quantity, can soon get a grasp of why this was so. Squares are always positive. If you multiply 2×2 you get 4, and if you multiply -2×-2 you still get four. So the "answer" to the question "What is the square root of 4?" is either 2 or -2. Both answers are correct. The equations Dirac was dealing with were a little more complicated than this, but the principle was the same. They had two sets of solutions, one corresponding to the electron (which carries negative charge) and one corresponding to an unknown, positively charged particle.

In 1928, physicists knew of only two particles, the electron and the proton, although they strongly suspected the existence of the neutron. So Dirac's first idea was that the positively charged solution to his equations must represent the proton. It is a sign of the way even so great a physicist as Dirac was groping in the dark in the 1930s that he saw no reason why the particles representing the positive and negative solutions should have the same mass. It is only now, with hindsight, that we can say "of course" the electron's counterpart must have the same mass as the electron and that the proton is too heavy to be its companion. Initially, scarcely anyone seems to have taken Dirac's proposal seriously—there was certainly no concerted hunt for the hypothetical new particle, as there would be if a similar hypothesis were made today. Physicists dismissed the idea that Dirac's calculations were telling them anything significant about the world. The existence of the other solution to the equations was ignored, just as an engineer working with quadratic equations will ignore one of the solutions to those equations and keep the one that obviously applies to the job at hand, building a bridge or whatever it might be.

But in 1932 Anderson was studying cosmic rays, using a cloud chamber, a device in which the cosmic ray particles leave trails behind them, like the condensation trails produced by high-flying aircraft. These trails are photographed, and the patterns they make can then be analyzed at leisure. One of the things Anderson did was investigate how the trails changed under the influence of a magnetic field; and he found some trails that bent by exactly the same amount as the trail of an electron, but in the opposite direction.* This could only mean that the particles responsible had the same mass as an electron but the opposite (positive) charge. The new particles—called anti-electrons or, more commonly, positrons—soon were identified with the particles predicted by Dirac's equations, and this was the work that earned Anderson his Nobel Prize. Dirac received the Prize, jointly with Erwin Schrödinger, in 1933.

---

*The trail left by an electron moving clockwise in a magnetic field is, of course, identical to the trail made by an equivalent positron moving anticlockwise. Anderson's achievement lay as much as anything in the way he determined which direction the particles making the trails were moving in, and such subtleties help to explain why his work merited the award of a Nobel Prize. It is easy enough for me to say "Anderson measured the curvature of particle trails and found positrons"; it was much harder for him to do the work.

The positron was discovered in the same year as the neutron (although, in fact, the evidence for these positively charged particles had been around in cosmic ray tracks for some time but had been mistaken for tracks of electrons moving the opposite way). Extending Dirac's calculations to all the atomic particles gave physicists six (plus the photon) to worry about—the electron and positron, the proton and a (presumed) negatively charged antiproton, and the neutron and a (presumed) antineutron.* The laws of physics require that when a particle meets its antiparticle counterpart, the two annihilate in a burst of energetic photons (gamma rays). The positron and electron cancel each other out as far as the material world is concerned. In the same way, running the equations in the other direction, if enough energy is available, electron-positron pairs, or other particle-antiparticle pairs, can be created. But you must always pair each particle with its precise mirror image in these interactions—not, for example, proton with antineutron. All of these predictions were borne out by experiments, although the antiproton and antineutron were not detected until the middle of the 1950s. And this interrelation between matter and energy, always obeying $E = mc^2$ as well as the rules of quantum physics, is, as we have seen, fundamental to the standard model of the Big Bang.

The positron and neutron were discovered in the same year, 1932. The muon was discovered in 1936, the pion in 1946. By then it was clear that matter came in two varieties: some particles that feel the strong force (protons and neutrons, and the pions that carry the force), and some that don't (the electron and, it turns out, the muon). † This led to a new way of classifying particles, both the "material" particles and the force carriers. Things that feel the strong force are called hadrons, while things that don't

---

*Even though the neutron carries no electric charge, and therefore the antineutron carries no charge, they are as distinct as the members of the other two pairs, and the implications of Dirac's calculations are as profound for them as for the others. The photon is in effect its own antiparticle, a subtlety I'll discuss later.

†Strictly speaking, I should include their antiparticles in this description. But everything that applies to protons, say, also applies to antiprotons, and so on.

feel the strong force are called leptons. All leptons are
fermions and have half-integer spin. The only leptons we
have met so far are the electron and the muon, which is
identical to the electron except for its much greater mass.
The hadrons that are also fermions ("matter") are called
baryons. Protons and neutrons are baryons. The bosons
that carry the forces between particles are now known
specifically as mesons. The pion is a meson and comes in
three varieties. There is a neutral pion, which has no
charge. When a proton and a neutron exchange a neutral
pion, they are held together but remain unchanged. Protons also exchange neutral pions with each other, and so
do neutrons. And there are two charged pions, positive
and negative, which are the antiparticles of each other.* If
a proton gives a positively charged pion to a neutron, the
proton becomes a neutron, and the neutron becomes a
proton. This is exactly the same as if the neutron gave a
negative pion to the proton. Every variation on the exchange also helps to hold the proton and neutron together.

Already the number of particles needed to describe even
the atom is growing. But there is still one more particle,
and one more field, to add to the list.

Back at the end of the nineteenth century, Rutherford, working first in Cambridge and then in Canada, had
discovered that uranium emits two kinds of radiation, and
he investigated their properties.† One of these "rays,"
alpha radiation, was later discovered to be made up of
helium nuclei, two protons and two neutrons bound together in a stable state. The other, which he called beta
radiation, was later shown to be identical to electrons. So
atoms can eject electrons. These electrons do not come
from the cloud surrounding an atomic nucleus. Rutherford and his colleague Frederick Soddy were able to show,
early in the twentieth century, that when a radioactive
atom emits an electron it becomes an atom of a different

*The antiparticle equivalent of the neutral pion turns out to be indistinguish-
able from the original; as far as any observable interaction is concerned, the
neutral pion is its own antiparticle. The same is true of the photon; although
in principle you can set up equations that describe antiphotons, in practice
the photon and the antiphoton are the same.
†He also discovered a third form of radiation, gamma rays, later identified
with energetic photons.

element. Later studies showed that a neutron in the nucleus is converted into a proton, while the electron is ejected, producing a new nucleus corresponding to an atom of a different element. In fact, this process happens only in a few, unstable nuclei. Most neutrons, in most atoms, are quite happy as they are. But a neutron that is isolated, away from an atomic nucleus, will decay, as it is called, into an electron and a proton in just a few minutes. The process is called beta decay, and it must involve both another force and another particle in addition to the ones mentioned so far.

Historically, it was the extra particle that physicists—or, rather, one physicist—came up with first. Beta decay was a main topic of research among physicists in the first decades of the twentieth century, and among their more surprising discoveries the physicists found that the electrons produced in the decay could emerge with various amounts of energy. The proton and electron produced when a neutron decays, together have a total mass about 1.5 electron masses less than the mass of the neutron.* So this much energy ought to be available, shared between the proton and the electron, as kinetic energy. When the proton is left in an atomic nucleus, of course, it doesn't move much, so it seemed that almost all the extra energy must go to the electron, giving it kinetic energy in addition to its rest mass, and that every electron produced in this way by a radioactive atom ought to run off with a large and predictable amount of kinetic energy. But experiments showed that the actual energy of a beta decay electron is always less than the energy available, and sometimes a lot less. Where has the extra energy gone?

Wolfgang Pauli, a Swiss physicist who had been born in Austria in 1900, came up with the answer in 1930.

---

*It is worth pointing out that there is no way in which an electron can be thought of as existing "inside" a neutron—that a neutron might, in that picture, be a composite of an electron and a proton, held together by electromagnetic forces. The uncertainty principle doesn't permit an electron to be confined within the diameter of even an atomic nucleus, let alone within a single neutron. To turn a neutron into a proton and an electron you *must* invoke, among other things, the mass-energy equation of relativity, which allows mass to be converted into energy and thence into another form of mass. Each electron produced by a beta decay is a newly created particle.

There must be *another* particle produced, as well as the electron and proton, and this extra particle was running off, unseen, with the "missing" energy. The particle required to do the job must have zero mass and no electric charge, or it would have been noticed by the experimenters.

Such a bizarre possibility did not meet with instant acclaim among physicists. It seemed too easy, and it held out the threat of invoking a new, undetectable particle to explain every puzzling phenomenon in experimental physics. But Pauli persisted in promoting the idea, and won support, in 1933, from an Italian-born physicist a year his junior, Enrico Fermi. Fermi took up Pauli's idea and put it on a respectable footing by introducing a new force into the calculations, the "weak" nuclear force.

Field theory required a new force to account for beta decay, anyway. It couldn't be the strong force that was responsible (electrons don't "notice" the strong force), and it certainly wasn't electromagnetism or gravity. Fermi modeled his theory as closely as he could on QED, and he came up with the idea that when a neutron changes into a proton it emits a particle that is the carrier of the new field, a charged boson usually written as $W-$. The boson (now called an intermediate vector boson) carries off the electric charge and excess energy, while the neutron changes into a proton and recoils. But this boson is very massive (just how massive the early, incomplete version of the weak-force theory could not say).* It doesn't only carry the energy needed to make the electron; it also has an enormous content of virtual energy borrowed from the vacuum, so it is very unstable and doesn't live very long at all. Indeed, it doesn't live long enough to interact with any other particles but quickly gives back its borrowed energy to the vacuum, allowing the rest to form into an electron and the new particle, in the same way that an energetic photon can disintegrate into an electron and a positron. The electron is a lepton, so, strictly speaking, in order to conserve the total number of leptons in the Universe, the

---

*In fact, Fermi's original version of the model had all the interactions occurring at a point, in effect giving the W particle zero range and infinite mass. The idea of using a particle with finite mass to describe the weak force dates from 1938, when it was introduced by the Swedish physicist Oscar Klein.

extra particle that is produced must be an *anti*lepton. (Since we start with one baryon, a neutron, and end with one baryon, a proton, baryon "number," as it is called, is also conserved.) Fermi called the extra particle a neutrino, meaning "little neutral one"; today we would call it an electron anti-neutrino.

In 1933, the English journal *Nature* rejected a paper from Fermi setting out these ideas, saying it was "too speculative." But his work was soon published in Italian, and not long after in English. Evidence for the existence of the neutrino came in 1953, from experiments making use of the flood of such particles produced by a nuclear reactor. It has all the properties (or lack of properties) expected from the theory, although there is some speculation today that neutrinos may actually have a very small mass, far less than the mass of an electron.

So in the early 1950s physics had enough particles and fields to explain how atoms behave. The weak field and the interactions it mediates are crucially important for the processes of nuclear fusion and fission, the manufacture of the elements in the stars, the fact that the Sun is hot, and the power of the atomic bomb. Electromagnetism remained its familiar self, and gravity refused, as stubbornly as ever, to be brought in to the quantum fold. Not all fields will succumb to the trick of renormalization, and every attempt to tackle the problems with infinities that had been tamed* with QED failed in the context of gravity. Just two leptons (and their antiparticle counterparts) were known, the electron and the muon, and each of them had associated with it its own type of neutrino. So attention focused on the particles that are governed by the strong force. But for a decade, the more physicists probed the nature of hadrons, the more confusing a picture they came up with.

In 1932, the material world could, it seemed, be explained in terms of three particles. In 1947, there were half a dozen (and their antiparticles). By the end of 1951, there were at least fifteen "fundamental" particles, and the list was just beginning to grow. Today, there are more particles in the list than there are elements in the chem-

---

*Or, as Dirac no doubt would have said, swept under the carpet.

ists' periodic table. The decade of the 1950s saw physicists manufacturing new kinds of hadrons every time they opened up new particle accelerators, creating more and more members of the particle zoo, not quite out of thin air, but out of pure energy. The energy came from machines, ever bigger and better machines, in which charged particles such as electrons and protons were accelerated by electromagnetic forces and smashed into one another, or into targets of solid matter—which means into atomic nuclei, since the accelerated particles brush through the electrons in clouds around atoms like a six-inch shell moving through sea mist. No material object can be accelerated to the speed of light, so as more and more energy went in to these experiments, the particles did not go faster and faster. Once their speeds were up to a sizable fraction of the speed of light, they increased in mass, instead. And when they were involved in collisions—interactions—all this extra mass was available to create other particles (almost invariably short-lived), which showed up as tracks in bubble chambers and other detectors. Generally, of course, each new particle made in this way is accompanied by an antiparticle partner; both lepton number and baryon number are conserved, although mesons can be manufactured at will.

Once again, I should stress that there is no sense in which these "new" particles could be thought of as being "inside" the protons, or whatever particles were being used in the colliding-beam experiments. The particles were being made out of the energy fed into the machines. The new particles were given names, and their family characteristics identified and labeled, sometimes with quixotic terms such as "strangeness." Particle physics was in a stage very similar to chemistry before Mendeleev, when the elements were identified and their properties determined and compared with one another, with no idea of how or why those properties and family relationships were produced. The step forward for chemistry came with the periodic table of the elements, and its later interpretation in terms of the structure inside the atom. The step forward for particle physics came in the early 1960s with the development of a "periodic table" for the particles, and a few years later with the interpretation of this new periodic table in terms of the structure within hadrons themselves.

THE EIGHTFOLD WAY:
ORDER OUT OF CHAOS

Field theories were not making much progress at the end of the 1950s toward an understanding of the multiplicity of hadrons. There were problems with infinities, like the ones that have to be renormalized in QED, and there was also some difficulty with the need to invoke a separate field for each particle—acceptable, perhaps when you have two or three fundamental particles, but more and more disquieting when the count rises to dozens, and then above a hundred. Most theorists abandoned field theory in the early 1960s, trying other approaches to the problem of the strong interaction. I won't discuss those approaches here, since in the 1970s it was field theory that triumphed. But although the impetus for finding patterns among the properties of hadrons came partly from ideas developed in the context of field theory in the 1950s, the "periodic table" of the particles stood on its own merits, as a classification system like Mendeleev's table, at the start of the next phase of development of particle physics.

The classification system was arrived at independently by two physicists, the American Murray Gell-Mann (born in 1929), and the Israeli Yuval Ne'eman, born in 1925. Ne'eman's education and career were interrupted by the fighting in the Middle East following World War Two, during which Israel emerged as a nation in the region that had previously been Palestine. Ne'eman stayed in the Israeli armed forces after this period of disturbance but found opportunities to study as well as to carry out his military duties. Although his first degree was in engineering, Ne'eman's interests led him toward problems in fundamental physics during the 1950s, when he served as a military attaché at the Israeli embassy in London and worked for a Ph.D., which was awarded in 1962 at the University of London. Gell-Mann's career followed a more conventional route, from Yale University to MIT, where he earned his Ph.D. in 1951, and then to Princeton, the University of Chicago (where he worked for a time with Fermi), and, in 1955, CalTech. Gell-Mann was responsible for the idea of "strangeness" as a quantifiable property of particles, an idea introduced into particle physics to account for some of the new phenomena being observed in high energy interactions in the early 1950s.

Strangeness is just a property that fundamental particles seem to have (or, rather, it is a property that we need to put into our models if we want to think of the world as being made of particles). It is no more and no less mysterious than electric charge. Some particles carry charge, some do not, and charge comes in two flavors, which we call $+$ and $-$. If we are being more precise and include zero charge, we have three choices: $+1, 0$, and -1. Strangeness varies from particle to particle, and there are more options than with charge, but the principle is the same. Strangeness can be $0, -1, +1, +-2$, or even bigger. And strangeness has to be conserved in strong particle interactions. Just as a neutron can turn into a proton only by an interaction that produces an electron to balance the electric charges (and an antineutrino to preserve the lepton number unchanged), so strangeness has to balance, by the creation of particles with the appropriate amount of strange "charge," during strong interactions. This restricts the number of interactions allowed, in line with the "strange" results physicists were obtaining in the 1950s; hence the name.

By using rules of this kind, Gell-Mann and Ne'eman were each able to group the new particles, together with the old familiar ones, into patterns according to their charge, spin, strangeness, and other properties. Gell-Mann called this the "eightfold way," in conscious tribute to the "eight virtues" of Buddhist philosophy, because some of the patterns he found initially involved particles in groups of eight. In fact, the system includes families with one, eight, ten, or twenty-seven members, in which each member of a particular family represents a variation on some basic theme. The system was proposed in 1961, and in 1964

Gell-Mann and Ne'eman, together acting as editors, produced a book, *The Eightfold Way,** in which their own original papers and other key contributions to the new understanding of the particle zoo were reprinted. By then, the classification system had made a triumphant prediction of the existence of a new particle, putting it on the same secure footing that Mendeleev's table had just before the development of quantum physics.

The pattern of the eightfold way, extended to group one family of baryons in a pattern of ten, had a gap in it. One particle was needed to complete the picture, and Gell-Mann called it the omega minus $\Omega-$), after the last letter of the Greek alphabet. The gap in the pattern "belonged" to a particle with negative charge, a strangeness of -3, and a mass of 1680 MeV. Just such a particle was found, in 1963, by researchers following up the prediction at Brookhaven Laboratory in New York, and at CERN in Geneva. It took sixty years for Mendeleev's table to be interpreted in terms of a complete theory of the structure of the atom. It took little more than ten years for the eightfold way to be interpreted in terms of a complete theory of the structure within hadrons, and it took as long as that only because many physicists were initially reluctant to accept the idea, put forward as early as 1964 by Gell-Mann and separately by George Zweig, that "fundamental" particles such as protons and neutrons are actually made up of peculiar particles called quarks, which come in threes and which have, heretical though it may seem, charges that are a fraction of the charge on an electron.

QUARKS

Looking back over a span of more than twenty years to the genesis of the quark model of matter, it is hard to tell just how seriously even the proponents of the model took it at first. The idea that protons and neutrons, and other particles, were actually made up of triplets of other parti-

*New York: Benjamin.

cles, some with a charge of ⅓ of the electron's charge, some with a charge of ⅔, ran so much against the grain of everything that had been learned since the closing years of the nineteenth century that it could be presented, at first, only as a device, a mathematical trick for simplifying some of the calculations and giving an underlying structure to the patterns of the eightfold way. In itself that was, and is, no bad thing. It reminds us that *all* our models of fundamental particles and their interactions are no more than artificial aids to help us to get a picture of what is going on in terms that seem familiar, or at least recognizable, from everyday life. But it is ironic that as the quark model has become increasingly well established, in recent years many accounts of particle physics seem to have lost sight of the fact that even the best of our models are no more than aids to the imagination, and those accounts have begun to present an image of protons, neutrons, and the rest as made up of "real" little hard lumps, the quarks, which rattle around inside what we used to think of as the "fundamental" particles. The image is beguilingly reminiscent of the earlier vision of the atom as being made up of little hard lumps, electrons, protons and neutrons—and it is just as inaccurate.

Whatever its basis in "reality," however, the quark model very neatly explains the interactions of the particle world.* The everyday particles, the proton and neutron and the pions that carry the strong force, can all be described simply in terms of two quarks, which are given arbitrary labels to distinguish them from one another. One is called "up" and the other is called "down." The names have no significance; physicists could just as well, if they wish, call one quark "Alice" and the other "Albert." The up quark has a charge of ⅔ and the down quark a charge of −⅓ in this picture, and a proton is made up of two up quarks and one down, giving a total charge of +1, while a

---

*There were rival ideas in the 1960s, of course. Indeed, right up to 1970, the line of attack I describe here constituted less than half of all the theoretical papers tackling the problems of high energy physics published each year. Once again, in the interests of brevity I have stuck to what turned out to be the main trail, and even left out most of the backtracking, blind alleys, and retracing of steps that took place with the development of the quark theory itself.

neutron is made up of two down quarks and one up, giving a total charge of zero. Pions are then "explained" as being formed of *pairs* of quarks, always with a quark and antiquark paired together. Up plus antidown makes the pi+, down plus anti-up makes the pi−, and up plus anti-up *and* down plus antidown together make the pi^0.

All of this, so far, is no more than an *aide-mémoire,* a mnemonic for constructing the fundamental particles. But the power of the mnemonic became apparent when Gell-Mann and Zweig invoked a third quark, the "strange" quark, to account for the property of strangeness. By successively replacing one, two, or three of the quarks in ordinary matter with a strange quark, they could build up particles with strangeness number of −1, −2, or −3 (the negative numbers are a historical accident of the way strangeness is defined). The proton and neutron have zero strangeness, because they contain no strange quarks; the omega minus has strangeness −3 because it is built up from three strange quarks, and so on. The whole of the eightfold way pattern fell naturally, in this way, out of the possible combinations of triplets of quarks and of quark-antiquark pairs. By assigning a definite mass to each quark, with the strange quark being about 50 percent heavier than the other two, it even gave the right masses for all the known particles. But did the quark model have any *physical* significance?

Even Gell-Mann, who coined the name "quark" from a line in *Finnegan's Wake,*[*] was almost coy about the concept in the paper in which he introduced it. He said:

> It is fun to speculate about the way quarks would behave if they were physical particles of finite mass (instead of purely mathematical entities as they would be in the limit of infinite mass) . . . a search for stable quarks of charge −1/3 or +2/3 and/or stable disquarks of charge −2/3 or +1/3 or +4/3 at the highest energy accelerators would help to reassure us of the non-existence of real quarks.[†]

---

[*]"Three quarks for Muster Mark," which, from context, gives the pronunciation to rhyme with "bark," not with "pork."
[†]From Gell-Mann's paper in *Physics Letters,* Volume 8 (1964), page 214; also quoted by Andrew Pickering in *Constructing Quarks* (Edinburgh: Edinburgh University Press, 1984), page 88.

Did Gell-Mann himself really believe in the reality of quarks, but try to slide the concept into the physics literature as if it were just an amusing trick? Or was he as doubtful about the whole business as these words suggest? There is no doubt that Zweig took the idea seriously—and, equally, there is no doubt that he got precious little in the way of praise, and plenty in the way of brickbats, as a result.

George Zweig was born in Moscow in 1937. But he moved to the United States in the 1950s and obtained a B.Sc. in mathematics from the University of Michigan in 1959. He moved to CalTech to begin his career in research, and spent three years struggling with a high energy experiment at an accelerator called the Bevatron, before he decided to concentrate on theory and began to investigate physicists' understanding of the nature of the material world, under the guidance of Richard Feynman. As a newcomer to the field, Zweig perhaps lacked some of the caution, or tact, of his elders, and when he realized that the eightfold way patterns of mesons and baryons could be explained in terms of combinations of two or three subparticles, he immediately treated these subparticles as real entities, which he called aces, and described them as such in his work. This bull-at-a-gate approach seems to have filled his superiors (not including Feynman) with horror—a horror only compounded by the success of what they saw as a naïve, unrealistic approach. In 1963, Zweig went on a one-year fellowship to CERN, where he wrote up his work for publication in the form of CERN "preprints," concluding, "in view of the extremely crude manner in which we have approached the problem, the results we have obtained seem somewhat miraculous."* But were these really his own views? Or did someone else put the remarks about crudeness into his mouth—or pen? For the appearance of these reports at all in 1964 was itself something of a miracle. When the student Zweig presented his first drafts to his superiors at CERN they were dismissed out of hand, and he recalled in 1981, in a CalTech publication, how:

---

*The CERN preprints both appeared in 1964 and are numbered 8182/TH401 and 8419/TH412. A more accessible but secondhand account is given by Pickering.

Getting the CERN report published in the form that I wanted was so difficult that I finally gave up trying. When the physics department of a leading university was considering an appointment for me, their senior theorist, one of the most respected spokesman for all of theoretical physics, blocked the appointment at a faculty meeting by passionately arguing that the ace model was the work of a "charlatan."[*]

Whatever the theorists thought in 1964, the quark model continued to provide at the very least a handy rule of thumb for calculating how hadrons ought to behave. And with the latest generation of particle accelerators, the experimenters had the means to test the hypothesis by shooting electrons at protons, with so much energy that they ought to scatter off individual quarks inside the protons. The experiments that in effect "X-rayed" the proton involved an accelerator two miles long, at Stanford in California (the Stanford Linear Accelerator, or SLAC), where electrons were accelerated to energies of more than 20 thousand million electron volts (GeV). The way the electrons scattered from the protons in the targets they were directed at clearly implied that there were concentrated regions of electrically charged mass-energy inside the proton, just as Rutherford's experiments, all those years ago, had shown that there is a concentrated nucleus inside every atom. At about the same time, in the late 1960s, experiments at CERN in which neutrino beams, instead of electron beams, were used to probe protons, showed that there must also be electrically neutral "matter" inside the proton. But no matter how hard the protons were

---

[*] Isqur (1981), page 439. In the same report, Zweig says that "Murray Gell-Mann once told me that he sent his first quark paper to *Physics Letters* for publication because he was certain that *Physical Review Letters* would not publish it."

It is interesting that Gell-Mann received the Nobel Prize in 1969 for his other contributions to particle physics, notably strangeness and the eightfold way. Even in 1969, quark theory was not the obvious way forward in understanding the particle world and ranked low on the list of achievements cited. Zweig has not yet received the Prize, even though quark theory is now fundamental to our understanding of the Universe, and his 1964 version was much more completely worked out, in detail, than Gell-Mann's. Is Zweig still paying a price for his youthful presumption? If not, perhaps the Nobel Committee will soon wake up to their oversight.

bombarded, and no matter what they were bombarded with, it proved impossible, as it has proved ever since, to knock one of the presumed quarks out of it.

The explanation of the neutral matter associated with quarks inside the hadrons was simple in principle, although it raised new questions about what kind of fundamental theory could be constructed to explain what was going on. Just as protons and neutrons are held together by the exchange of pions, the carriers of the strong force, so quarks must be held together in some way by an exchange of particles that were dubbed "gluons," because they glue the quarks together to make protons, neutrons, and so on. At first sight, this looks as if it means that we have a fifth force to worry about. But current thinking suggests that the glue force is the real "strong" force of nature and that the so-called strong interaction of nuclear physics is actually a side effect of the glue force, in a way that is crudely similar to the way in which residual traces of the electric forces that hold atoms together in molecules provide a kind of weak electromagnetic force between different molecules.

But alongside the experimental successes of the quark model in the second half of the 1960s, there were problems. *Why* did quarks come only in threes, or in quark-antiquark pairs? The most profound puzzle, ironically, concerned the omega minus, the crowning prediction of the eightfold way, and particles that shared one important property with it. The omega minus is viewed, on the quark model, as a particle composed of three strange quarks. But all these quarks have to be spinning the same way, so they are in identical states. Similarly, the experimenters had found a type of particle that could best be explained as a set of three up quarks spinning the same way, and one that consisted of three down quarks, all with the same spin. Yet the quarks are fermions, and the Pauli exclusion principle says that no *two* fermions, let alone three, can be in the same state. Is it possible that quarks don't obey the exclusion principle? Or is there some way in which the three quarks inside the omega minus (and in other particles built of three "identical" quarks) can be distinguished?

A good theory of quarks would have to answer all these questions, and more besides. The "good theory" that was needed turned out to be a field theory. But the revival of field theory in the 1970s, which led to a good theory of quarks and now, in the 1980s, to hope of a unified theory of all the fields, came from a breakthrough in the study not of hadrons but of leptons and photons—a new theory that combined the electromagnetic and weak forces into one description, the electroweak theory. But before we can look at how that new theory was developed, and how it in turn helped theorists to find a better model of the strong force, we need to delve once more into the mathematicians' box of tricks to find out how to apply one of their most useful conceptual tools.

GAUGING THE NATURE OF THINGS

The interactions of ordinary matter all involve, in the new picture, just four particles—the up and down quarks, and the electron and its neutrino. When a neutron decays into a proton, emitting an electron and an antineutrino in the process, what quark theory says is that a down quark inside the neutron changes into an up quark and emits a W −, which in turn produces the electron and antineutrino. Another way of looking at this kind of interaction is as an exchange in which a down quark gives a virtual W − to a neutrino, converting it into an electron and converting itself into an up quark. The electron and its neutrino are the leptonic equivalents to the up and down quark in the hadron world. These interactions are all described schematically by scattering diagrams like the one shown in Figure 7.3; mathematically, a particle traveling forward in time is the same thing as its antiparticle equivalent traveling backward in time, so one basic diagram can stand for any or all of the fundamental interactions.

Historically, of course, an understanding of the weak force began to be developed before the idea of quarks was mooted, so the equations and diagrams were, and often still are, expressed in terms of protons and neutrons rather than up and down quarks. It makes no difference to the

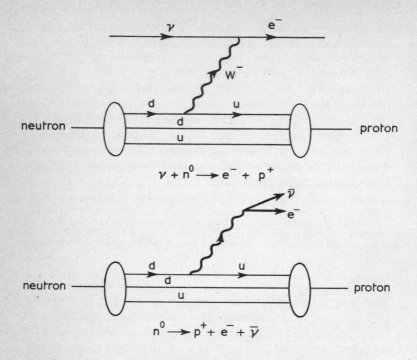

Figure 7.2 / The modern picture of particle processes shows that when a neutron decays, through the weak interaction, to produce a proton, at a more fundamental level a down quark is changing into an up quark. The W− released in the process can interact with a neutrino to produce an electron (top picture) or, in the exactly equivalent process, it can decay itself into an electron and an antineutrino.

general thrust of the argument, and I shall use both descriptions interchangeably. But it is worth remembering that at this level of description, dealing only with the common form of matter that makes up the Sun and stars, distant galaxies, interstellar matter, planets, and ourselves, we are dealing with a limited number of fundamental particles, just four. Almost all of the physics described in this book so far, and the evolution of the Universe, would be the same if these were, in fact, the only four types of particles that existed.

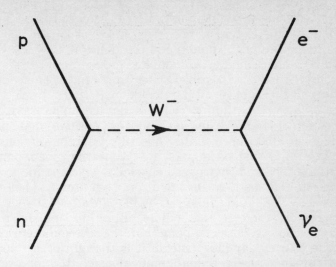

*Figure 7.3/*All fundamental particle interactions, like those shown in Figure 7.2, can be represented schematically by scattering diagrams like this.

When physicists attempted in the 1950s to construct a more complete field theory of the weak interaction, they naturally looked to the field theories they already had—gravity and, especially, electromagnetism—to decide what sort of properties a "good" theory ought to have. One of the most powerful concepts that can be used to describe these fields is the property of symmetry. The electric field is, for example, symmetric in terms of the forces between charged particles. If you were to lay out an array of charged particles, some positive and some negative, and to measure all the forces acting between them, and then if somehow it were possible to reverse the polarity of every charge, positive for negative and negative for positive, while keeping them all in place, you would find that the forces acting on each particle were exactly the same as before. Such a symmetry is called a global symmetry—*every* charge (strictly speaking, every charge in the Universe) has to be reversed at the same time to retain the original field of force.

Other laws of physics, or properties of particles, can be described in terms of symmetries. Positive and negative charge can be thought of as mirror image, opposite versions of some fundamental "state" of things. If we ignore electromagnetic forces, however, and look at the rest of the properties of the proton and the neutron, they are very similar to one another—so similar, indeed, that physicists regard them as two possible "states" of a fundamental entity they call the nucleon. What decides whether a nucleon is a proton or a neutron (leaving aside, as I have said, the question of charge)? Just as the terms "positive" and "negative" are introduced to describe the different versions of charge, and just as quarks are arbitrarily given names such as "up" and "down," so physicists give a name to the property that distinguishes neutron from proton. They call it isotopic spin and think of it as like an arrow, associated with each nucleon, that points either up and down or across. But it doesn't "point" in the three-dimensional space of everyday life. Instead, it is thought of as "pointing" in some abstract, mathematical space that represents the internal structure of the nucleon.

We can imagine changing the isotopic spin of every nucleon simultaneously so that every proton in the Universe became a neutron, and every neutron became a proton. That would be equivalent to rotating the orientation of the isotopic spin of every nucleon by 90 degrees, through a right angle. The point of all this is that the strong force is unaffected by such a transformation, just as the electric force is unaffected by reversing the sign of all electric charges. There is a fundamental symmetry between the two nucleon states, between the proton and the neutron—or, at a deeper level, between the up and down quarks. So when an individual neutron actually does change into a proton, the local symmetry, for that particular nucleon, is disturbed. There has been a *local* symmetry transformation. But the laws of physics stay the same, just as they did when the roles of every proton and every neutron in the Universe were swapped. How does the Universe take note of the local symmetry transformation? Through, in this case, the strong force itself. The fundamental forces of nature are therefore deeply involved with the basic symmetries—not just global symmetry changes, but also local ones.

neutron   proton

Figure 7.4 / The difference between a neutron and a proton can be represented by the direction in which a mythical "internal arrow" attached to each nucleon is pointing. This arrow is dubbed isospin.

There are many ways in which symmetry changes can occur, but it turns out that the symmetries that underlie the laws of physics are the simplest kind, mathematically speaking. They are called gauge symmetries, and they also have local symmetry, which, it turns out, restricts their properties and makes it possible to calculate their effects.

The term "gauge" is simply a label mathematicians use to describe a property of the field. The term was introduced in this context shortly after World War One by the German mathematician Hermann Weyl, who was trying to develop a unified theory combining electromagnetism (Maxwell's equations) and gravity (General Relativity). A gauge transformation is one that changes the value of some physical quantity everywhere at once, and the field has gauge symmetry if it stays unchanged after such a transformation. A good example is provided by the imaginary system of electric charges I have already referred to. If we set up such a system in a real laboratory and measured all the forces between the charges, we would find that it made no difference to these forces if we charged the whole laboratory to a high voltage.* The only thing that matters is the *difference* between the charges—and that is why a mouse can run quite happily along the live rail in the subway. All of the mouse is at the same voltage,

---

*And this isn't just an imaginary "thought experiment"; it can be and has been done.

and no currents flow. The problems arise for a person who touches the rail with one hand and the ground with some other portion of the body, allowing electric current to flow across the potential difference.

So the electric forces between particles are invariant if the potential (the voltage) on every charge is increased by the same amount at the same time. This gauge invariance is another kind of symmetry, one that is shared by the gravitational field. But what happens if only *part* of the system of charges is raised to a higher electric potential? Now electric currents begin to flow, just as when someone, or something, partially falls on a live rail in the subway. The moving electric charges create a new field, a magnetic field, which can be described in terms of a magnetic potential analogous to an electric potential. And *the magnetic field restores the symmetry of the equations describing the system.* If we imagine making any kind of complicated change in the electric potential anywhere in the lab, or in the Universe, raising it here and lowering it there, we can always cancel out the effects of these changes by making compensatory changes in the magnetic potential, lowering it there and raising it here. Electromagnetism, the theory that includes both electricity and magnetism, is therefore invariant under local gauge transformations. Indeed, Maxwell's equations describe the *simplest* kind of field that obeys both this symmetry invariance and the equations of special relativity.

This kind of symmetry is very deeply connected with the equivalence principle in General Relativity. Einstein taught us that accelerations could always be canceled out by gravity. Accelerations represent force. As Newton taught us, force is equal to mass times acceleration. In a laboratory moving at constant velocity through space, there is no change in the gravitational potential from one end of the lab to the other, and we have a situation like our electrical setup with a uniform base-line voltage. Experiments in such a laboratory obey Newton's laws perfectly. They show a symmetry similar to the symmetry shown by the system of charges in the earlier example. On Earth, there *is* a gravitational potential difference from the top of the lab to the bottom, because of the Earth's gravity. That is equivalent to our electrical setup with one end of the lab charged to a higher voltage than the other. The symmetry is no longer there.

If you keep the imaginary lab in space but jiggle it about by firing rocket motors from time to time, the effects show up in the laboratory as mysterious forces affecting the trajectories of particles. Those forces are exactly equivalent to the ones produced by gravity. To make the lab fly in a circle, for example, far from any large mass, you would have to apply a constant push, and an occupant of the lab could deduce that it was moving in a circle by measuring the forces inside. But if our space lab is in orbit around the Earth, the forces that "ought" to show up because it is moving in a circle, not in a straight line, are precisely canceled out by the force of gravity from the planet below. It is in free-fall. In principle, just as you could make the magnetic potential compensate for changes in the electric potential, so you could make a changing gravitational potential to cancel out even the most violent buffeting produced by the rocket motors. Putting it another way, you could, in principle, arrange lumps of matter (planets, stars, black holes, or whatever) around the spacecraft so that it followed the most bizarre wiggly line trajectory through space but was always in free-fall, just as a spaceship orbiting the Earth is in free-fall in a circular trajectory. It doesn't matter that this is not a practical proposition; the point is that the symmetry is built into the equations. The gravitational field is invariant under local gauge transformations.

But all we can ever "know" about the forces of nature is, indeed, the way in which they affect motion, deflecting an electron from its trajectory here, nudging a proton there, and so on. The other forces of nature play out the same role at the particle level that gravity does in the Universe at large, providing a means to cancel out disturbances caused by local symmetry transformations. In the quantum physics description of electromagnetism, QED, the force is equivalent to an exchange of photons between charged particles. And the changes in the particles and their associated fields cancel out to ensure local gauge symmetry if and only if the photon is a particle with one unit of spin and zero mass. The existence of the photon, with just these properties, is seen by physicists today as a requirement of gauge symmetry, or, depending on your point of view, as confirmation that the gauge symmetry approach is the key that will unlock the secrets of nature. What happens when that approach is taken over from QED into the description of the weak and the strong fields?

CHAPTER EIGHT

IN SEARCH OF SUPERFORCE

The idea of finding one mathematical description that would include all of the forces of nature has been the Holy Grail of physics from the moment Einstein came up with a field theory of gravity, the General Theory of Relativity. Early attempts started out by trying to unite gravity and electromagnetism into one theory—in the 1920s, after all, those were the only two fully worked out theories that physicists had to play with. Those attempts failed, although some of the techniques developed in the construction of those failed attempts at unified field theories have been revived, and are proving remarkably successful, in the context of physics in the second half of the 1980s. Gravity is the weakest of the four forces of nature and the hardest to reconcile with the other three. Although it has a very long range (the particle of the gravitational field, the graviton, is, like the photon, massless) and therefore dominates the Universe at large, gravity is easily overpowered by any of the other forces when they are working over a range where each can be effective. It takes the mass of the whole Earth to hold a scrap of paper on my desk down, with a weight of less than a gram. But I can lift that piece of paper up, against the gravitational pull of the whole Earth, simply by rubbing a plastic pen on my woolen sweater to build up an electric charge on the pen, and holding the charged pen over the paper. The electric force that the pen exerts on the paper then makes it jump off the desk. Gravity really is a *very* weak force indeed. The only reason electric forces don't dominate the Universe is that almost everywhere the positive and negative charges are in balance, so there is no net charge left over to influence distant stars and galaxies. The weak and strong nuclear forces are also much stronger than gravity but fortunately have only limited ranges, because they are mediated by particles (field quanta) with mass. In round terms, the strong force is 1,000 times stronger than the electric force and 100,000 times stronger than the weak force (so the electric force is about 100 times stronger than the weak force). But the strong force is 10^{38} times stronger than gravity, and it is therefore no surprise to find that developing a unified description of the strong, weak, and electric forces is far easier than trying to find a unified theory pairing up gravity with any one of the other three.

When physicists appreciated that they had four fundamental forces to deal with, not two, the problem of a unified field theory looked more daunting than it had in the 1920s. A few researchers, Einstein prominent among them, kept plugging away at developing sets of equations that might describe a unified theory that included gravity, electromagnetism, and the others in one package, but even Einstein had little success, although he spent most of the last thirty years of his life trying to unify electromagnetism and gravity. When success did begin to come, it came by starting from the opposite "end," as it were, to Einstein. He started out with the force of gravity, which dominates the Universe on the large scale. But today, adding gravity to the unified theory is seen by physicists as the *last* piece of the puzzle to tackle. Instead, they have proceeded piece by piece, starting with the forces that dominate atoms—indeed, starting with the two forces closest to each other in strength—and working outward into the Universe. The weak force was first given its own "proper" field theoretical model, then added to the electromagnetic force to provide a unified electroweak model. Today there is also a "proper" gauge theory of the strong force, and clear indications of how to add that strong force to the electroweak field as well, to provide a Grand Unified Theory, or GUT. There is no *unique* GUT that does unify the first three forces, but the family properties of the kinds of model that almost certainly include such a unified theory have been outlined. And there is real hope of bringing gravity within the fold before the end of the present century.

These ultimate developments involve an understanding of particle processes that go on at very high energies, energies that are equivalent to densities of matter far greater than the density of matter in an atomic nucleus. So the steps toward a unified theory of fields are also, in a real sense, steps back toward the moment of creation. The theories tell us what conditions in the Universe were like at times earlier than 10^{-35} second after the moment of creation, back to the moment when the concept of time itself first had any meaning. This is, perhaps, as clear an indication as any that these theories, involving quarks and leptons, really are reaching some fundamental level of physics. If the models can take us right back to the moment of creation itself, it becomes meaningless to ask if there is any deeper truth, just as it is meaningless to ask what happened "before" time began.

In the twentieth century, each great advance in understanding the Universe and probing back to the Big Bang has followed developments in physicists' understanding of the world of the very small. Spectroscopy and an understanding of atoms, developed in the late nineteenth and early twentieth centuries, led to quantum physics, which developed in the 1920s alongside the discovery of the distance scale of the Universe (itself dependent on an understanding of atoms) and the red shift. Nuclear physics developed during the 1930s and 1940s and led to Gamow's slightly premature version of the Big Bang in the 1940s, to the work of Hoyle and his colleagues on nucleosynthesis in the 1950s, and to the triumph of the standard model in the 1960s. Meanwhile, physicists had moved on to probe the nature of physics at higher energies, corresponding to interactions involving particles "within" the nucleons themselves. In the 1960s and, especially, the 1970s, this led to a new understanding of matter and to the beginnings of a unified field theory; in the 1980s this, in turn, is leading to a new understanding of the very earliest stages of the Big Bang. If the new theories stand up, as they seem to be doing so far, physics will soon have achieved its fundamental goal—indeed, the fundamental goal of *metaphysics*—of describing everything by one set of equations, and that will imply an understanding of the Big Bang itself from the moment of creation to the end of time. The one unified field—what the English physicist Paul Davies has called the "superforce"—is the key to understanding not only how the world works today, but also how it got to be the way we see it today. And the successful search for the superforce follows a trail that began in 1954, just one year before Einstein died, when a Chinese-born physicist working in the United States with an American colleague published a paper applying the idea of a local gauge theory to the problem of the strong force. Their model was not particularly successful as a description of the strong force but marked a conceptual breakthrough that encouraged other researchers to tackle other problems using similar techniques. Ironically, the first fruits of this attack on the *strong* force turned out to be a better understanding of the *weak* interaction.

ELECTROWEAK UNIFICATION

Chen Ning Yang had been born in Hefei, China, in 1922. His father was a professor of mathematics, and Yang himself studied at the Chinese universities in Kunming and Tsinghua, where he obtained an M.Sc., before moving to Chicago in 1945 to work for his Ph.D., which was awarded in 1948, under the guidance of Edward Teller. Yang then spent a further year at Chicago as an assistant to Enrico Fermi and in 1949 joined the staff at the Institute for Advanced Study, in Princeton, where he stayed until 1965. Yang was interested in the possibility of modeling a field theory of the strong interaction along the same lines as QED, and he worked intermittently on the problem, with only limited success, from the time he was in Chicago until 1954. Then he spent a year away from Princeton, at the Brookhaven National Laboratory, where he shared an office with the theorist Robert Mills.

Mills and Yang together were able to construct a gauge-invariant field theory of the strong interaction. The symmetry that is important in the Yang-Mills theory is the isotopic spin symmetry, which I have already mentioned. In such a description of nucleons, protons and neutrons are represented by vertical and horizontal arrows, respectively, in a mathematical space; and if there is a local symmetry, that means it is permissible to vary the isotopic spins of individual nucleons at different places in the Universe and at different times. In other words, there are interactions that change individual protons into neutrons, and vice versa. The simpler global symmetry, of course, "only" allows us, in imagination, to change *all* the neutrons into protons and all the protons into neutrons, and all at the same time.

Just as with other theories of this kind, the way the symmetry is preserved when we are allowed to make local changes in the field is by adding something else to counterbalance the changes we are making. In the Yang-Mills theory, the laws of physics can only be made to stay the same even when arbitrary changes in isotopic spin are made by including *six* vector fields. Two of these fields are mathematically equivalent to the ordinary electric and magnetic fields, and together they describe the photon, the carrier of the electromagnetic force. The other four fields, taken in two pairs, describe two new particles, which are similar to the photon but carry charge, one positive and one negative. And the interactions involving all these particles, as represented in the theory, were horribly complicated.

It was clear that this approach to an understanding of the strong interaction was, at the very least, incomplete. For a start, none of the "photons" had any mass, so they would have infinite range, whereas in fact the strong force is the one with the shortest range of the four classic forces, so its carriers ought to have relatively large masses. But the ideas underlying the model were, and are, very interesting indeed. At a simple level, two oppositely charged "photons" could be imagined binding together, like a proton and an electron, to make an "atom" of strong field. At a rather deeper level, one of the fundamental discoveries, which had important consequences in the development of later theories of the four interactions, was that because of the presence of the charged photons, the order in which a series of transformations is applied to a fundamental particle can make a crucial difference to the state it ends up in.

That sounds complicated, so let's take it step by step. The state of an electron, for example, can be changed by absorbing or emitting a photon of light. If the electron first absorbs and then emits the photon, it will end up in the same state as if it first emitted and then absorbed the photon (assuming it starts out the same in each case and that all the photons are identical). The order in which the interactions take place doesn't matter, and QED is therefore said to be an Abelian theory.*

Ordinary numbers work like this. We all know that 2×4 is the same as 4×2 and that $6 + 7$ is the same as $7 + 6$. The numbers are said to commute, and in general we can write $A \times B = B \times A$. But in quantum physics, this is generally not the case. It turns out that $A \times B \neq B \times A$, and the variables are said to be noncommutative, or non-Abelian. The same thing happens with the charged "photons" of the Yang-Mills theory. If a hadron is changed by a local rotation of the isotopic spin arrow and then is changed a second time by a second, different, isotopic spin rotation, the state it ends up in depends on the order in which the changes were made. The Yang-Mills theory is a non-Abelian local gauge theory, and it turns out that all of the fundamental fields are described by non-Abelian gauge theories—even electromagnetism, as we are about to see, is part of a bigger, non-Abelian theory.

All this may sound very deep and technical indeed. But you can demonstrate non-Abelian transformations simply by using the book you now hold (or another one). Place the book flat on the table in front of you, with the front cover showing and the right way up. If you rotate the book through 90 degrees by lifting the end farthest from you

---

*After Niels Henrik Abel, the Norwegian mathematician who lived from 1802 to 1829 and made major contributions to the branch of mathematics known as group theory. His early death was a great blow to nineteenth-century mathematics.

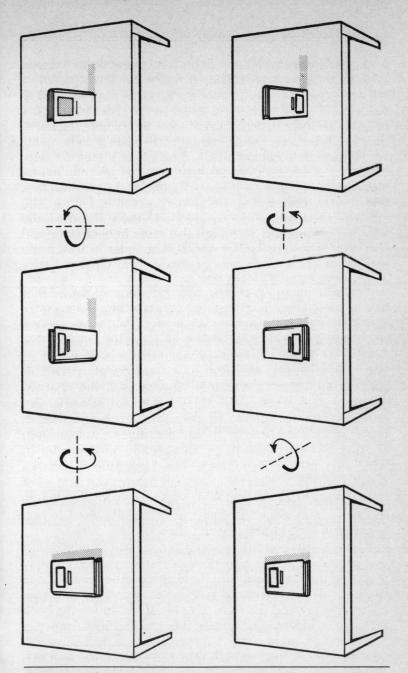

Figure 8.1 / If you rotate a book twice in two different directions, the position the book ends up in depends on the order of the transformations. Rotations are non-Abelian.

(the "top" of the book), the book will be standing upright, with the covering facing you. Now look down on the top of the book and rotate it by 180 degrees. It will be left upright, the right way up, with the *back* of the book facing you. Now try again, starting from the same place as before (book flat on the table, face up) and doing the same rotations in the opposite order. First, rotate the book 180 degrees, so it is flat on the table but the title is upside down. Now rotate it "upward" by 90 degrees, lifting the far end. You end up with the *front* of the book facing you, but with the book upside down. It is the same book with the same amount of energy, but it is in a different state. You have just carried out a couple of non-Abelian transformations of the book.

Although theorists in the mid-1950s knew full well that a little more work was needed on the Yang-Mills theory, basic ideas like these were interesting and encouraged new lines of thought—they were certainly interesting enough to justify the publication of the paper setting out the theory, in 1954.[*] It was to take twenty years for theorists to develop this approach into a satisfactory theory of the strong force, and they made very little progress until the late 1960s, when quarks were recognized as the fundamental entities involved in the interactions, and gluons as the carriers of the true strong force. But meanwhile the ideas were taken over into a theory of the weak interaction and then into the electroweak theory, uniting electromagnetism and the weak force.

Julian Schwinger was something of a child prodigy in mathematics. He was born in 1918, and entered the City College of New York at age fourteen, then transferred to Columbia University, where he gained his B.A. degree at age seventeen, and a Ph.D. three years later. He worked with Robert Oppenheimer (the "father of the atomic bomb") at the University of California, then at the University of Chicago and at MIT before joining the faculty of Harvard

---

[*]Incidentally, scooping another theorist who was thinking along similar lines independently. Ronald Shaw was a student working at the University of Cambridge under the supervision of Abdus Salam; Shaw came up with a model very similar to that of Yang and Mills, but after their paper appeared in *Physical Review* in October 1954 (Volume 96, page 191), he didn't bother to attempt to get his own version published.

University in 1945. A year later, at age twenty-eight, he became one of the youngest full professors ever appointed at that august institution. Schwinger made major contributions to the development of QED, and in 1965 he shared the Nobel Prize in Physics with Richard Feynman and Shin'ichiro Tomonaga, of Tokyo University, for this work.*

So Schwinger had the ideal background to pick up the Yang-Mills idea and apply it to the weak force and to electromagnetism. The rules of the game are slightly different with the weak interaction. In beta decay, for example, a neutron is converted into a proton, so the isotopic spin (isospin) symmetry is disturbed. But at the same time, in such an interaction, a neutrino is converted into an electron (or an anti-neutrino and an electron are created together, which is the same thing), so there has been a transformation in the lepton world analogous to the isospin change in the hadron world. This leads to the idea of "weak isospin," a quantum parameter like isospin but one that applies to leptons as well as to hadrons. In 1957, Schwinger took over the non-Abelian local gauge theory developed by Yang and Mills for the strong force and applied it to the weak force and electromagnetism (QED) together. Like the Yang-Mills theory, his version had three vector bosons, one without charge and the other two carrying charge. And, like Yang and Mills, he identified the uncharged field quanta with photons. But, unlike Yang and Mills, in Schwinger's treatment the two charged vector bosons were regarded as the W^+ and W^-, the carriers of the weak force. There was still the problem with masses. Masses had to be added in to the theory for the W particles more or less by hand, on an ad hoc basis. But this theory, in spite of its obvious flaws, again raised interesting new ideas. It implied that the weak force and the electromagnetic force were "really" the same strength as each other, in some sense symmetric, but that this symmetry had

*Tomonaga, who was born in 1906 and died in 1979, worked in isolation from the American scientists and published his results first, in 1943. Feynman and Schwinger made their independent contributions to QED just after the war, and Tomonaga's work became known to the English-speaking world in 1947. The three of them had arrived at the same model by three different routes, which was in itself a strong indication that the model they came up with described some fundamental feature of nature.

gotten lost, or was broken, because the W particles had mass (and therefore a limited range) while the photon had none (and therefore has infinite range).

This led to two lines of development in field theory. Sidney Bludman of the University of California at Berkeley took up the links with the Yang-Mills theory and pointed out in 1958 that the weak force *alone* could be described by a local, non-Abelian gauge theory with three particles, the W^+, the W^-, and a third vector boson, with zero charge, called the Z^0, or just Z. This left electromagnetism out of the picture for the time being but carried with it the implication that there ought to be weak interactions that involved no change in electric charge—ones that are mediated by the Z particle and are known as neutral current interactions. All these field quanta were still massless in Bludman's model, so the model was far from being realistic. But perhaps it was less far from the "answer" than earlier models had been.

Meanwhile, Sheldon Lee Glashow, a physicist who had been born in the Bronx in 1932 and graduated from Cornell University in 1954, had been studying for his Ph.D. at Harvard under the supervision of Schwinger. Glashow found a way to take Bludman's variation on the theme and combine it with a description of electromagnetism, producing a model, which he published in 1961, that included both a triplet of vector bosons to carry the weak field *and* a single vector boson to carry the electromagnetic force. The only immediate benefit of this approach was that it proved possible to ensure that the way the singlet and triplet mixed together produced one very massive neutral particle, the Z, and took all the mass away from the other one, the photon, instead of having two neutral particles that each had mass. But you still had to put the masses in by hand, to destroy the symmetry between electromagnetic and weak forces in the basic equations, and, worst of all, the theory did not seem to be renormalizable but was plagued by the kind of infinities that crop in in QED but are there removed by suitable mathematical sleight of hand. The mathematical sleight of hand needed to put mass into the early electroweak models made it impossible to carry out the renormalization trick as well.

At the same time, starting out in the late 1950s and continuing into the early 1960s, the Pakistani physicist Abdus Salam and his colleague John Ward were developing an electroweak theory very similar to the one proposed by Glashow. Salam was born in Jhang, in what is now Pakistan, in 1926. After attending Punjab University he went on to Cambridge, where he was awarded his Ph.D. in 1952, and taught in Lahore and at Punjab University until 1954, when he returned to Cambridge and, among other things, supervised the work of student Ronald Shaw. The subjects chosen by students for investigation usually reflect the interests of their supervisors, and Shaw's work was no exception. Salam was indeed interested in gauge theories of the basic forces of nature, along the lines of the Yang-Mills theory. In 1957 he took up a post as professor of theoretical physics at Imperial College in London, and in 1964 he was the moving force behind the establishment of the International Centre for Theoretical Physics in Trieste, an institute that provides research opportunities for physicists from the developing countries. Since then, Salam has been director of the Centre in Trieste and spends some of his time there and some at Imperial College.

The Salam-Ward variation on the electroweak theme (Ward, a British physicist, worked at several U.S. institutions in the 1960s, including Johns Hopkins University) suffered from the same defects as Glashow's version—the masses had to be put in by hand, and largely as a result of this, it was impossible to renormalize the theory. The first step toward solving this problem was taken in 1967, when Salam and, independently, American physicist Steven Weinberg found a way to make the masses of the weak vector bosons appear naturally (well, almost naturally) out of the equations. The trick involved spontaneous symmetry breaking, and once again it depended upon ideas that had been developed initially in the context of the strong field.

Actually, you can understand symmetry breaking quite easily in the context of the weakest field, gravity. Indeed, we have already come across such a broken symmetry. To an astronaut in free-fall in a space lab, there is no special direction in space. If the astronaut lets go of a pen, it floats off in any direction the astronaut pushes it. All directions are equivalent; there is a basic symmetry. On the surface

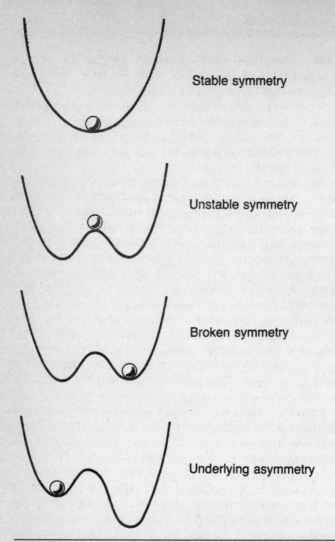

Stable symmetry

Unstable symmetry

Broken symmetry

Underlying asymmetry

Figure 8.2 / Symmetry breaking can be understood in terms of a ball in a valley. With only one valley to rest in, the ball is stable and the situation is symmetric. As soon as the ball has a choice of valleys to settle into, the situation is more complicated. Symmetry can be maintained, but such a state is unstable; it is more natural to find a state of stability, in which the symmetry is broken. In the real world, of course, things are often more complicated still, with an underlying asymmetry. Now, the ball is in a local stable state, but not the most stable *possible* state— rather like the alpha particle inside an atomic nucleus (Figure 4.6).

of the Earth, things are different. If you give a pen a slight push in *any* direction and let go of it, it always falls the same way, downward. "Downward" means toward the center of the Earth. Drop a pen at the North Pole and it falls downward; drop a pen at the South Pole and it falls downward. But the two "downwards" are opposite to one another. The basic symmetry is hidden, or broken, by the Earth's gravitational field.

Another form of hidden symmetry applies to a common bar magnet, which always prefers to line itself up pointing north–south, even though the basic equations of electromagnetism are symmetric. This form of hidden symmetry was discussed half a century ago by the physicist Werner Heisenberg, the same Heisenberg who derived the uncertainty relations for the first time. But the easiest example to understand involves gravity once again. Imagine a perfectly smooth, perfectly symmetrical surface shaped like a Mexican hat, with an upturned brim. If the "hat" is resting level on a horizontal surface, it is completely symmetrical in the Earth's gravitational field. Now imagine placing a small, round ball on top of the hump in the middle of the hat. Everything is still perfectly symmetrical as long as the ball doesn't move. But we all know what will actually happen in such a situation. The ball is unstable, balanced at the highest point of the hump, and soon will roll off and fall down one side of the hump to rest in the rim of the hat. Once this happens, the hat and ball together are no longer symmetrical. There is a special direction associated with the system, a direction defined by a line pointing outward from the center of the hat through the place where the ball rests on the rim. The system is now stable, in the lowest energy state that it can easily reach, but it is no longer symmetrical. It turns out that the masses associated with the field quanta in a Yang-Mills type of theory can arise from a similar symmetry breaking involving the abstract "internal space" in which the arrows of isospin point.

The idea gradually brewed up in the 1950s and 1960s from the work of several mathematical physicists, but it came into full flower with the work of Peter Higgs at the University of Edinburgh between 1964 and 1966. Higgs had studied at King's College in London from 1947 on-

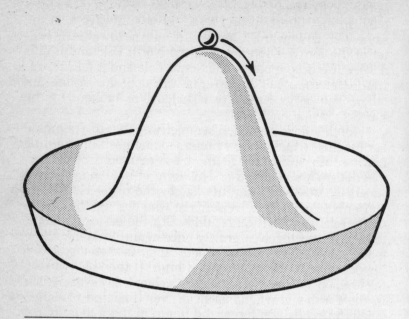

Figure 8.3 / "Mexican hat" symmetry. The ball on top of the "hat" represents an unstable symmetry, that can be broken by the ball rolling off in *any* direction.

ward and received his Ph.D. in 1954. He took up a post at Edinburgh in 1960. Although the line of thought behind the mechanism he proposed is too complex to detail here, its implications can be understood in terms of the same language we are now becoming familiar with. Higgs proposed that there must be an extra field added to the Yang-Mills model, one that has the unusual property that it does not have the least possible energy when the value of the field is zero, but when the field has a value bigger than zero. The electromagnetic field, and most other fields, have zero energy when the value of the field is zero, and the state in which all fields have minimum energy is what we call the vacuum. If all fields were like the electromagnetic field, that would be the same as saying that in the vacuum state all fields are zero. But the Higgs field has a nonzero value even in its state of minimum energy, and this gives the vacuum itself a character it would not otherwise possess. Reducing the Higgs field to zero would actually involve putting energy into the system.

The implications of this are profound. In terms of isospin, the Higgs field provides a frame of reference, a direction against which the arrow that defines proton or neutron can be measured. A proton can be distinguished from a neutron by comparing the direction of its isospin arrow with the direction defined by the Higgs field. But when the isospin arrow rotates during a gauge transformation, the Higgs arrow rotates as well, so that the angle stays the same. The angle that used to correspond to a proton now corresponds to a neutron, and vice versa. Without the Higgs mechanism, there would be no way to tell the difference between protons and neutrons at all, because there would be nothing to measure their different isospins against. All that can be measured is the relative angle between the isospin and the Higgs arrow, not any absolute orientation of isospin. And the Higgs field does this even though the field itself is a scalar, which has only magnitude and does not point in any preferred direction at each point of "real" space.

The effect of all this on the vector bosons is dramatic. There are four scalar Higgs bosons required by the field theory, and as we already know, the basic Yang-Mills approach gives three massless vector bosons. When the two elements are put together, three of the Higgs bosons and the three vector bosons merge with one another—in the graphic terminology used by Abdus Salam, the vector bosons each "eat" one of the Higgs particles. And when this happens, the vector bosons gain both mass and a spin corresponding to the spin carried by the Higgs bosons. Instead of having three massless vector bosons and four Higgs particles, the theory predicts that there should be three observable vector bosons that each have a definite mass, plus one scalar Higgs boson, which also has a large mass but whose precise mass cannot be predicted by the theory. The Higgs field breaks the underlying symmetry in just the right way to fit in with what we observe. At the cost of one extra undetected particle, mass appears naturally in all the variations in the Yang-Mills approach.

Higgs himself had been working in the context of the strong field. But soon his ideas were taken over into the developing electroweak theory. First off the mark was

Steven Weinberg in 1967. Weinberg had been an exact contemporary of Glashow (although six months younger, having been born in May 1933) at the Bronx High School of Science, from which Weinberg graduated in 1950, and Cornell University, where he graduated in 1954. But then he followed a different path to end up with a model very similar to Glashow's description of the electroweak interaction, but with the bonus of a Higgs-type mechanism included. By 1960 Weinberg had arrived at Berkeley, where he stayed until 1969 before moving on first to MIT and then, in 1973, to Harvard. Weinberg's approach to electroweak unification was largely his own, but drawing upon the same culture—the same background pool of knowledge in physics—that Glashow and Salam were drawing on. His interest in the weak interaction went back to his Ph.D. work in Princeton, and in the 1960s he worked toward an equivalent of the Higgs mechanism in his own way. His electroweak model, including masses for the vector bosons generated by spontaneous symmetry breaking, was submitted for publication in October 1967 and appeared in the journal *Physical Review Letters* before the end of the year.*

Salam heard about the Higgs mechanism, from a colleague at Imperial College, a few months before Weinberg submitted that paper for publication. Salam took the electroweak model he had developed with Ward and added the Higgs mechanism to it, giving essentially the same basic model that Weinberg developed, with masses now occurring naturally. He gave a series of lectures on the new model at Imperial College in 1967, followed by a talk at the Nobel Symposium in May 1968, later published in the symposium proceedings.

In due course, Glashow, Salam, and Weinberg jointly received the Nobel Prize in Physics for their roles in creating a unified electroweak theory, a step as important as Maxwell's development of a unified electromagnetic theory a century before.† But "in due course" was not until

---

*Volume 19, page 1264.

†Don't shed too many tears for Yang, left out of the 1979 award. He already had a share in the Nobel Physics Prize, awarded in 1957, for another key contribution to particle physics theory, which comes into the story of the early Universe in the next chapter.

1979. It took some time for even most theorists to appreciate fully the significance of the Weinberg-Salam model, because it wasn't until 1971 that a Dutch physicist, Gerard 't Hooft, showed that this version of the electroweak theory was, indeed, renormalizable. And then, in 1973, experiments at CERN came up with evidence of the elusive neutral current interactions that the theory predicted, interactions mediated by the neutral Z particle. It was the normalization of gauge theory by 't Hooft that led to the explosive development of field theory in the 1970s, to a theory of the strong interaction, and now to an understanding of the earliest moments in the life of the Universe itself.

GAUGE THEORY COMES OF AGE

The way I have told the story of the development of gauge theories in the 1950s and 1960s may seem logical and orderly, the onward, inexorable march of science. But that is true only to a point. The path followed by Weinberg, Salam, and the others in the 1960s, in particular, was then very much a byway of science. The theorists who dabbled in such things as non-Abelian local gauge theories were as much mathematicians as they were physicists, and they were often interested in the equations and the symmetries as much for their own sake as for their bearing, if any, on the real world. It is only with hindsight that we look back from the late 1980s and see this single thread of the whole tapestry of science as being particularly important and leading to greater things. And that is shown very clearly by the way in which Weinberg's paper on electroweak unification, published in 1967, was almost totally ignored for four years.

The fate of scientific papers published in the major journals, which Weinberg's was,* is monitored in the pages

---

*Salam's 1968 paper was not even published in a major journal of physics but in the more obscure pages of the Nobel Symposium proceedings, where

of a publication called the *Scientific Citation Index,* which lists, each year, the number of times that such a paper is referred to by the authors of other papers published in the major journals. In 1967, 1968, 1969, and 1970, *nobody* (not even Weinberg himself) referred to this paper in print. In 1970, there was just one citation; in 1971 there were four; in 1972, sixty-four; and in 1973 there were 162.† The sudden upsurge following 1971 was entirely due to the breakthrough achieved by Gerard 't Hooft when he showed that gauge theories in general, and the electroweak theory in particular, were renormalizable.

Progress toward such an achievement had been slow and painful, and there is no point here in recounting all the detours into blind alleys along the way. So, once again, the story may seem straightforward and uncomplicated; but remember, once again, that this is only because we have the benefit of hindsight.

This thread of the story begins with the work of another Dutch physicist, Martin Veltman, who was born in 1931 and studied at the University of Utrecht, then spent five years at CERN before taking up the post of professor of physics back at his old university. Veltman developed for himself, by a roundabout route, a set of gauge equations equivalent to the Yang-Mills model of fields, and although confused by a discussion with Richard Feynman in 1966, in which Feynman advocated a different approach to the problems of particle physics, he eventually decided to follow up a suggestion made by John Bell, a British physicist working at CERN, that the best way ahead would be through the development of a Yang-Mills model for the weak interaction. He tackled the problem in his own way, using the path integral approach pioneered by Feynman but which few physicists then (or, indeed, now) took very seriously as a practical tool.

The obvious major problem with all models of the Yang-Mills kind was the way in which infinities appeared and could not be canceled out. In the middle of the 1960s,

---

it didn't even fall within the net of the citation index. So we have no comparable figures for that paper, but since its publication was so obscure, it can hardly have received wider attention than Weinberg's paper in *Physical Review Letters.*

†Figures reported by Pickering, page 172.

it looked as if there might be no way of removing these infinities—that the theories were *in principle* not renormalizable. But with the aid of the electronic computers that were becoming increasingly important to such work as the 1960s wore on, Veltman was able to find ways in which many of the infinities could be canceled and to show that it might after all be possible, in principle, to renormalize the theory fully. He spent years laying the groundwork, backing and filling and covering an enormous amount of ground, but he never quite achieved his goal of the renormalization itself. That was left to the next person to pick up the torch.

Gerard 't Hooft was born in the Netherlands in 1946.* He joined the University of Utrecht as an undergraduate in 1964 and began full-time research for his Ph.D. under the supervision of Veltman in 1969. The problems 't Hooft chose to tackle, and the way in which he chose to tackle them, were both far from the mainstream of science. For a start, he was interested in gauge theories, which were completely out of fashion. And then, following Veltman's lead, he decided to tackle the gauge theory problems using Feynman's path integral approach. Taking over many of Veltman's techniques, 't Hooft was able to show, in a paper published in 1971, that *massless* gauge theories are indeed renormalizable. This was an excellent achievement for a student just starting out in research, but the really important problem, of course, was to renormalize the theories that included massive particles, the W's and the Z, the intermediate vector bosons that were thought to carry the weak force. Much later, Veltman told Pickering of a conversation with 't Hooft in early 1971, a conversation so striking that it was burned in his memory and could be repeated more or less verbatim more than ten years later. Translated into English, it went something like this:

> VELTMAN: I do not care what and how, but what we must have is at least one renormalizable theory with massive charged vector bosons, and whether that

---

*This happens to be the year I was born. There is an old saw that says that you know you are getting old when policemen start looking young. In my case, I feel my age when I notice that many members of the current batch of prospective Nobel laureates are younger than I am!

looks like nature is of no concern, the details can be fixed later.

'T HOOFT: I can do that.

VELTMAN: What do you say?

'T HOOFT: I can do that.

VELTMAN: Write it down and we will see.*

Gerard 't Hooft did write it down, and Veltman saw that he had indeed cracked the problem. The resulting paper was published in the journal *Nuclear Physics* before the end of 1971 (Volume B35, page 167), and 't Hooft was awarded his Ph.D. in March 1972. By then, the transformation of particle physics and the restoration of gauge theories to center stage were already occurring thanks to the way the word of this work by an obscure student tackling an obscure problem with an obscure technique was spread in the United States by physicist Benjamin Lee, who had been a visitor at Utrecht in the summer of 1971 and returned to the United States armed with copies of both of 't Hooft's 1971 papers. Lee both confirmed the validity of 't Hooft's work and translated it into more conventional mathematical language in his own paper, published in 1972. Lee's paper persuaded theorists such as Weinberg to take the work seriously and convinced them that gauge theories of the electroweak interaction involving symmetry breaking and the introduction of mass through the Higgs mechanism were indeed renormalizable. Gauge theory had come of age—at least as far as the theorists were concerned.

In 1973, experiments at CERN that involved shooting beams of high energy neutrinos through a huge bubble chamber called Gargamelle produced evidence of interactions involving the elusive Z particle. The tracks in the bubble chamber showed that an antineutrino or a neutrino could interact with an electron just as the electroweak theory predicted, with the Z^0 mediating the interaction. Further experiments confirmed the plausibility of this interpretation of events—after analyzing three million photographs of events occurring inside Gargamelle, the physicists found 166 examples of interactions best explained in terms of neutral currents. Now the experimenters, too, were

---

*Slightly paraphrased from Pickering, page 178.

persuaded that the electroweak gauge theory was the best theory of interactions involving leptons and photons.

The significance of the finds, coupled with 't Hooft's renormalization of the electroweak theory, was so profound that Weinberg, Salam, and Glashow were awarded the Nobel Prize in 1979, even though at that time there was still no direct evidence that the W's and the Z existed. But the theory had predicted not only that these particles must exist, but also the masses they should have. Each W ought to weigh about 92 GeV (a little less than 100 times the mass of a proton), and the Z^0 should have a mass of about 82 GeV. To make such particles and watch them decay, you need a particle accelerator that can put at least this much energy into collisions. Just such an accelerator was built at Geneva, by CERN, to smash a beam of protons head-on into a beam of antiprotons. And by the early months of 1983 the accelerator produced clear evidence for the existence of W and Z particles, with masses very close to the predicted masses, which are produced in the collisions and then decay into energetic electrons and other particles.* No doubt the discovery, confirming the basis of their 1979 award, came as a quiet relief to the Nobel Committee. Quick off the mark, they gave the 1984 Physics Prize to Carlo Rubbia, the head of the CERN team involved in the work.

The significance of these masses for the unification of the forces in the Big Bang is easy to see. When the energy density (temperature) of the universe was great enough, particles with masses of just under 100 GeV could appear spontaneously, in particle-antiparticle pairs. And instead of a carrier of the weak interaction being able to come into existence only for the brief instant of time allowed by the uncertainty principle, the supply of free energy around it could make any of these virtual particles real and give it an extended lifetime. As long as the mass of the particle was less than the energy available, it could live forever, like the photon, and the distinction between photons and

---

*Details of the search for these particles can be found in Christine Sutton's definitive book *The Particle Connection*, which describes how such energetic collisions are achieved (a saga in itself) as well as what the observations imply.

the W's and Z's would be dissolved away. At high enough energies, there is no distinction between the electromagnetic and the weak forces. The distinction appears only because we live in a cold Universe, where the symmetry is broken. The W's and Z's began to freeze out of our Universe when its temperature fell to 10^{15} K, about one thousand-millionth of a second after $t = 0$. And that is when the electromagnetic and the weak forces started to go their separate ways—until mankind intervened on a modest scale, re-creating for a tiny fraction of a second, in a tiny volume of space inside a machine near Geneva, the conditions that had existed everywhere in the Universe one thousand-millionth of a second after the moment of creation.

By 1985, the proton-antiproton collider at CERN was producing energies of 900 GeV, a new world record, and raising the prospect of making these intermediate vector bosons almost as a matter of routine. But there is no prospect of achieving the same kind of success by creating the particles required by higher order unified theories of the forces of nature. The new theories based on the triumphs of the electroweak gauge theory tell us that the masses of these particles are far beyond the range of any conceivable man-made accelerator. The only place such energies have been available was in the early stages of the Big Bang itself. So the Universe has become the testing ground of the latest ideas in particle physics, just as cosmologists had previously turned to particle physics for new ideas about the Big Bang. We are almost ready to resume our search for the Big Bang itself—once I have filled in some details about those theories of the strong force.

QUARKS WITH COLOR

In the middle of the 1960s, there were two families of leptons known, each made up of an electronlike particle and a neutrino. The pairs are the electron and its neutrino, and the muon and its neutrino. When the idea of quarks was introduced, only three were needed to explain all the known particles. The up and down quarks formed a pair, but the strange quark was out on its own. In fact, in the paper in which he put forward the idea of quarks, Gell-Mann did speculate that there might be a fourth quark, to pair up with the strange quark and make two quark pairs to match the two lepton pairs. But the idea was soon dropped because there was no evidence for the existence of particles incorporating the hypothetical quark. The problem of how three seemingly identical quarks could coexist in the same state to form a particle such as the omega minus was far more pressing, and it absorbed a lot of effort from those physicists who bothered to put much effort into quark theory in the middle and late 1960s, before it finally was cracked.

Walter Greenberg, a theorist working at the University of Maryland, was delighted by the idea of quarks when it was introduced in 1964, because it provided him with a practical application for some exotic field theory ideas he had been developing for several years. Greenberg was originally interested simply in developing mathematical versions of field theory, with little or no thought of practical applications. But one of his abstract ideas, called "parastatistics," turned out to be relevant to the quark problem. Greenberg quickly applied his abstract ideas to the new model of hadrons and came up with intriguing results. Although his approach was very technical, it boiled down to suggesting that there might be different varieties of "paraquarks" obeying the rules of parastatistics, and that the three seemingly identical quarks in the omega minus and some other hadrons were actually distinguished from one another by a previously unsuspected property that came in three different varieties. The idea was taken up by two Japanese theorists, Yoichiro Nambu at the University of Chicago, and M. Y. Han at Syracuse University. They collaborated in developing, in 1965, a version of Greenberg's approach that was rooted more obviously in the world of the experimenters and was therefore more accessible to more physicists than the elegant mathematics of parastatistics.

The idea underlying all this work was that each of the known quarks could come in three varieties, which are known as colors. The terminology is no more than a con-

venient labeling device, like the names "up" and "down."
But it enables us to understand that there is a difference
between a red up quark and a blue up quark, just as there
is between a red up quark and a red down quark. The
mathematical equations tell us how three kinds of quark
ought to interact, and they do so with elegant precision.
But the heart of what they tell us can be grasped in simple
color terms in the light of what the equations tell us. The
omega minus, for example, can be thought of as made up
of three strange quarks, each with the same spin, but one
"red," one "blue," and one "green," so that they are distin-
guishable and therefore not identical particles in identical
states. The color are just mnemonics, more mental crutches
to help us understand. But the mathematical physicists
assure us that the images conjured up by the analogy are
not too misleading.

At least they do today. This was regarded as little more
than a trick, with no profound meaning, in 1965. Nambu
and Han muddied the waters somewhat by elaborating
their model to include more triplets of quarks in an effort
to remove the need for fractional charges, but since few
people were taking the idea of quarks very seriously at the
time, none of this work caused much of a stir. But the idea
did offer new guidelines for the behavior of quarks, including a resolution of the puzzle of why they came only in
threes (as baryons) or in pairs (as mesons). Just by speci-
fying a single rule that the only "allowed" combinations of
quarks must be colorless, Nambu was able to explain the
division of hadrons into these two families. Each meson,
he said, must be composed of a quark of some particular
color and an antiquark of any variety but carrying the
equivalent anticolor. A red up, for example, might pair up
with an antired up, or an antired down, or an antired
strange; in each case the color and the anticolor "canceled
out" in a mathematical sense. The other way to achieve a
neutral state, he argued, was by mixing each of the three
colors in one particle—one red quark, one green quark,
and one blue quark, each of them being any of the flavors
up, down, or strange. Three antiquarks of different colors
would achieve the same objective. But single quarks, or
groups of four, for example, would carry a net color, which
seemed to be forbidden.

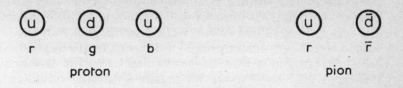

Figure 8.4 / Three quarks make up a proton—red/up + green/down + blue/up. A quark/antiquark pair make up a pion—red/up + antired/antidown.

By 1970, experimental results were coming in that seemed to be in line with this color model of quarks, and the concept began to gain ground. And at about the same time Glashow and two of his colleagues at Harvard, John Iliopoulos and Luciano Maiani, revived the idea of a fourth quark, which Glashow gave the name "charm" in order to tidy up the theoretical interpretation of some other puzzling experimental observations. In 1971, Murray Gell-Mann and Harald Fritzsch, who was born in Zwickau in 1943 and is now Research Professor of Physics at the Max Planck Institute for Physics in Munich, took up the idea of color and began to develop a field theory approach that would describe the behavior of interactions involving particles that came in three varieties. As early as the autumn of 1972, Gell-Mann and Fritzsch were proposing that the best description of the structure of hadrons was in terms of a Yang-Mills type of gauge theory in which the triplets of colored quarks interacted with one another through the mediation of an octet of gluons. The symmetry was more complicated, and the numbers larger, but the principles were the same as those of the successful theories of QED and the electroweak force.

Once again, the basic ideas can be understood in terms of symmetry. Now we have to imagine each baryon containing three quarks, and each quark as carrying within itself some means of selecting a color—an internal pointer, like the up or across pointer for isospin, but now with *three* settings, corresponding to the three colors. A symmetric global gauge transformation would be one that rotated every pointer clockwise (say) by 120 degrees, changing the color of every quark but leaving the laws of physics

the same. A local, symmetrical gauge transformation would
change the pointer setting (color) of just one quark inside
one baryon but still leave the world unchanged. And the
way to restore symmetry under local transformations is, as
before, to bring in new fields, corresponding in this case to
the eight gluons, that are all massless (in the original
version of the theory) and have one unit of spin—vector
bosons analogous to the photon.

The theory became known as quantum chromodynamics, a name given by Gell-Mann in conscious imitation of

*Figure 8.5/*The color of each quark can be thought of in terms
of a knob which rotates an internal pointer with *three* settings,
analogous to the isospin pointer that distinguishes protons and
neutrons (Figure 7.4).

quantum electrodynamics, and is usually referred to today
as QCD. It says that any quark is free to change its color
independently of all the other quarks, and does so by
emitting a gluon, which is promptly absorbed by another
quark, which suffers a color change of exactly the kind
required to cancel out the change in the first quark and
keep the hadron colorless. All hadrons are always colorless, even though the quarks within them may be undergoing kaleidoscopic changes of color every instant. Because
the gluons carry color, their behavior is very different from
that of photons, which do not carry charge and do not
interact with one another. Gluons *do* interact with each
other even while they are in the process of carrying the
force from one quark to another. Perhaps the strangest
result of this is that although the "strong" force is actually
quite weak over a short distance (inside the proton, for
example), the gluon interactions make the force stronger
at *larger* distances, so that over a range of 10^{-13} centimeters
it is strong enough to bind protons together in spite of the
repulsion between their electric charges. It is like a stretch-

ing piece of elastic, fastened to a quark at each end, that only holds the quarks loosely until you try to pull them apart. Then, the more you pull, the more the elastic stretches, and the harder it pulls back, trying to keep the quarks together. In this case, the "elastic" is a stream of gluons being exchanged between the two quarks.

If you stretch hard enough—put enough energy into a collision—then eventually the elastic will snap. But that still doesn't mean you will get a free quark emerging as a result. The energy from the interquark force goes into creating a new quark at each broken end, reminiscent of the way a bar magnet sawn in half "creates" a new pole on each side of the break. Instead of a *single* quark emerging, there are always at least two, joined by a stream of gluon elastic—a meson. And because the gluons carry color, they, too, are forced to travel in clusters, like quarks, and cannot exist in isolation—which is why, it is suggested, no isolated gluon has been detected. Even though they may be massless, gluons are unable to spread themselves about like photons. Perhaps, however, colorless bundles of gluons ("glueballs") might yet show up in experiments like those at CERN.

The turning point in physics in the 1970s came in 1974, when a team at Stanford and one working at the Brookhaven National Laboratory on Long Island each discovered, almost simultaneously, evidence of a new, massive particle (now generally referred to as the psi) that was best explained as one incorporating the fourth quark, "charm." The discoveries led to the award of the 1976 Nobel Prize in Physics to Samuel Ting, leader of the Brookhaven group, and to Burton Richter, his counterpart at Stanford. The discovery was so dramatic that the announcement of the experimental results, in November 1974, is referred to by physicists today as "the November revolution"; once *one* charmed particle had been found, the experimenters knew, in a sense, where to look for others, and soon they found a whole family of charmed particles. And that family of particles provided physicists with a testbed for QCD, which successfully predicted many details of the behavior of the "new" particles. With four quarks and four leptons identified, the particle world looked very neat. But there was still one (last?) step to be taken.

Table 8.1

Leptons	Quarks
e −	u
ν_e	d
μ −	c
ν_μ	s
τ −	t
ν_τ	b

*Table 8.1/*As far as we know, there are three kinds of matter in the Universe. Permanent matter is made up only of two types of lepton and two types of quark, shown at the top. For some unknown reason, this permanent world is duplicated by equivalent, but unstable, heavier particles—not once, but twice. All of everyday physics, and the world about us, would be unchanged if the only particles were the electron and its neutrino and the up and down quarks—and particle physics would be a lot easier.

In 1975, experiments at the Stanford Linear Accelerator suggested that there might be still another lepton, an "electron" twice as heavy as the proton, dubbed the "tau"; the hints were confirmed at Hamburg a year later. It is assumed (and there is very strong indirect evidence, although it is not yet proven) that an equivalent tau neutrino must also exist, making six leptons, which come in three pairs. So theorists argued that there "ought" to be two more quarks, as well, to restore the symmetry. These were called top and bottom, and evidence of bottom came through in 1977. The search for the top quark is now one of the main priorities at CERN, which has the highest energy colliding beams in the world. This really ought to be the end of the line, though, since there are compelling *cosmological* reasons for thinking that there can be no more than three or four sets of lepton pairs in the Universe. These reasons are featured in the next chapter. But remember that almost everything in the Universe would be the same as it is today if there were just two quarks, the up and down, and two leptons, the electron and its neutrino. The rest seems to be unnecessary triplication of effort, just one (or two) of those things that fell out of the equations and happened for no better reason than that they were not forbidden to happen.

The combination of the electroweak theory and QCD has proved so successful in describing the particle world that it is sometimes called the "standard model" of physics. But it is still incomplete. QCD has yet to be combined with the electroweak theory into one Grand Unified Theory, or GUT; and gravity isn't included at all. So there is plenty to keep the theorists occupied at present.* But the "experiments" of particle physics are now taking on a new complexion—for the best place to test the latest unified theories is in the Big Bang itself.

THE SEARCH FOR SUPERSYMMETRY

QCD is not yet as well established a theory as QED was even forty years ago. It took the hindsight of the 1980s to look back and point out what turned out to be the main thread of progress in physics in the 1960s, and it will no doubt require the hindsight of the year 2000, or later, to look back on the current confusion of theoretical developments around the search for superforce and pick out the main line. I shall not attempt to advocate any one path among those now being followed as the "best" or "true" path; anyone who had tried that in, say, 1961 would hardly have picked out the non-Abelian local gauge theories as the best candidates to keep an eye on, let alone the idea that protons and neutrons might be made of other particles. But I can briefly sketch in the outlines of some of the most interesting *fundamental* ideas, at the level of the fundamental concepts of symmetry and gauge invariance.

---

*There are also unresolved questions within QCD itself, for all its success so far. For instance, it may be possible, or necessary, to give the gluons mass, through the Higgs mechanism—although such a prospect is a daunting task for any theorist, faced with eight gluons to worry about and handle in one self-consistent package.

These ideas may underlie many different detailed theories, only one of which, we might hope, actually describes the real world. But if the recent past can tell us anything, it is that powerful, simple ideas like symmetry really do help us to select good theories from bad ones.

To put things in perspective, QED is an excellent theory, electroweak theory is very good indeed, and QCD is merely good, judging by the problems that have so far been resolved and those that remain as yet unanswered. The family resemblances among the theories are perhaps the best guide that the theorists are really on the track of something more fundamental that will unite all the forces of nature in one super theory of superforce. Electromagnetism is the simplest and involves just one charge. The weak field is characterized by a property that has two values, isospin, and relates doublets of quarks and doublets of leptons. Quarks come in triplets and are described by a field one step more complicated still. But the same common principles underlie the singletons of QED, the doubletons of the weak field, and the triplets of QCD, and that has enabled the first two to be combined into one successful unified theory. And the color of QCD is exactly analogous to the electric charge of QED, except that it comes in three varieties. Particles that do not carry charge cannot feel the electromagnetic field; particles that do not carry color, the leptons, cannot feel the field of QCD.

By pushing these ideas in the same direction, many theorists have attempted to construct Grand Unified Theories that encapsulate the electroweak theory and QCD in one package. Most of these GUTS are members of the same family of theories, following a line of research pioneered by Glashow and a Harvard colleague, Howard Georgi, in the mid-1970s. Such theories each deal with particles in families of five—one such family, for example, consists of the three colors of antidown quark, plus the electron and its neutrino. Members of these families can be changed into one another by the same kind of transformation that converts protons into neutrons and one color of quark into another color, equivalent to rotating a pointer that has five positions on its scale. But now we have the possibility of turning leptons into quarks, and quarks into leptons. The

GUTs describe a deeper symmetry than any of the simpler theories—but at a price.

The electroweak theory needs four bosons—the photon, two W's, and the Z. The fivefold GUTs—known in mathematical shorthand as SU(5) theories—require *twenty-four* bosons. Four of these are the four already needed by the electroweak theory; eight more are the gluons required by QCD. But that still leaves twelve "new" bosons, busy mediating new kinds of previously unsuspected interactions. Such hypothetical particles are collectively called X, for the unknown quantity, or Y. They can change quarks into leptons, or vice versa, and carry charges of $1/3$ or $4/3$. But they are very massive—so massive that their lifetimes are extremely restricted in the Universe today, and therefore they play very little part in the activity of the particle world.

According to these theories, the three forces (electromagnetism, the weak interaction, and the strong force of QCD) would have been equal to each other at energies as great as 10^{15} GeV—that is, 10^{13} (10 million million) times the energy at which the electromagnetic and weak forces were, or are, unified. That corresponds to a time when the universe was only 10^{-37} second old, at a temperature of 10^{29} K, and it means that the masses of the X particles themselves must be about 10^{15} GeV, a million million times more than the greatest energy yet reached in a collision at the new CERN proton-antiproton collider. There is no prospect of creating such conditions artificially, and that is why physicists have to look to the Big Bang for evidence that X particles ever existed. Surprisingly, though, there is a possibility of detecting a side effect of their existence here and now.

If a quark inside a proton could borrow enough energy from the uncertainty relation to create a virtual X boson and swap it with another quark, one of the quarks would become an electron (or a positron). The two quarks left over will form a meson—a pion—and the proton will have decayed. Because the X boson is so massive, its virtual lifetime is so short that it could cross from one quark to another only if they were closer than 10^{-29} centimeters, and this is seventeen powers of 10 smaller than the size of the proton itself (10^{-17} times the size of the proton). Such very close encounters between quarks must be rare indeed. But they will happen from time to time, and the likelihood of such events can be calculated. It turns out that for an individual proton such an event will occur once in more than 10^{30} years—probably, depending on which detailed theory you fancy, not for at least 10^{32} years. The Universe is only some 10^{10} years old, so it is no surprise to find that protons are still around and seem pretty stable. But if the chance of *one* proton decaying in *one* year is one in 10^{32}, if you have 10^{32} protons together, then there is a good chance that one of them (but you don't know which one) will decay in each year that you are watching.

Experiments have been designed to test just that—to watch large numbers of protons for months and years on end to see if any of them decay. A thousand tons of water contain about 10^{33} protons, and water is easy to come by. Several experiments in countries around the world have been watching for the products of proton decays in large tanks of water or lumps of iron. There is no conclusive evidence yet one way or the other, but as the years tick by, the limits being set on the lifetime of the proton are up to about 10^{32} years, where things start getting interesting as far as the theorists are concerned. Perhaps some definite news, one way or the other, will be published soon.

But all is not well with the GUTs. A line of research that started out with the simple idea of symmetry in gauge theory has become ugly and complicated, with a proliferation of bosons and with the problem of what renormalization really implies still swept under the carpet, forming a bigger and harder-to-hide lump with every new force that is incorporated into the models. More quarks and leptons can be happily accommodated every time you want one, which indicates a certain lack of restraint on the part of the theories. But, embarrassingly, all of the GUTs predict the existence of magnetic monopoles, none of which have yet been found in the world we inhabit. And, indeed, since there are an infinite number of possible gauge theories, it is a mystery why these particular ones should be the ones that tell us anything about the real world at all. So what might happen if we cut loose from this step-by-step approach, building a house of cards with one layer on top of another, and get back to the roots?

That is what Julian Wess of the University of Karlsruhe, and Bruno Zumino of the University of California at Berkeley did in 1974. GUTs surprise us by relating leptons to quarks but still leave bosons out on a limb as something different from material particles, merely the carriers of the forces. Wess and Zumino said, in effect, if symmetry is a good idea, why not go the whole hog with supersymmetry and relate the fermions to the bosons?

Stop to think about that for a minute. The distinction between fermions and bosons is *the* big one in quantum physics. Bosons do not obey the Pauli exclusion principle, but fermions do. The two seem far more unlike each other than the proverbial chalk and cheese. Can matter and force really be two faces of the same thing? Supersymmetry says yes—that every fermion in the Universe should have a bosonic partner, and every boson should have its own fermionic counterpart. What we see in our experiments, and feel the effects of in everyday life, is only half of the Universe. Every quark, a fermion, ought to have a partner, a boson called a squark; every photon, a boson, ought to have a partner, a fermion called a photino; and so on.* There is no problem in explaining where the partners have gone; at this early stage of the game, the theorists can wave their mathematical magic wands and invoke some form of (unspecified) symmetry breaking that gave the unseen partners large masses and left them out in the cold when the Universe cooled. Claiming that there is a symmetry between bosons and fermions sounds outrageous to anyone brought up to believe in the distinction between particles and forces. But is it so outrageous? Haven't we come across something like it before? Quantum physics, after all, tells us that particles are waves, and waves are particles. To a nineteenth-century physicist such

---

*In the same vein, there are winos, zinos, gluinos, and sleptons. You may take the idea with a pinch of salt if you wish. But, for the record, physicists at CERN were getting very excited late in 1984 and early in 1985 about some events they were monitoring in the colliding proton and antiproton beams, events that might just be explained most neatly in terms of gluinos or photinos. As I write (in May 1985), the initial burst of excitement has been followed by a tight-lipped silence. Maybe the early interpretation was wrong; or maybe the evidence is building up and will be announced to the world in detail soon. We'll just have to wait and see.

as Maxwell, electrons were particles, and light was a wave; in the 1920s, physicists learned that electrons are both particle and wave, while photons are both wave and particle. And these are the archetypal members of the fermion and boson families. Is supersymmetry really doing anything more outrageous to our common-sense view of things than taking wave-particle duality to its logical limit and saying that a particle-wave is the same thing as a wave-particle? It is only because we have gotten away from the roots of quantum physics in the past two chapters, and, for convenience, described events in the subatomic world in terms of collisions and interactions between tiny hard particles, that supersymmetry strikes us as very odd at all. If only our minds were equipped to handle the same concepts in a more abstract form, in keeping with the quantum equations, so that we could properly understand the nature of quantum reality, where nothing is real unless it is observed, and there is no way of telling what "particles" are doing except at the moments when they interact with one another, then supersymmetry would seem much more natural. The flaw lies in our imagination rather than in the theory. But even with our limited imaginations we can appreciate one feature of the new theory that makes it stand head and shoulders above most candidates for the title of "superforce." The most dramatic thing about supersymmetry (SUSY for short) is that the mathematical tricks needed to change bosons into fermions, and vice versa, automatically and inevitably bring in the structure of space-time, and gravity.

The symmetry operations involved in turning bosons into fermions are close mathematical relatives of the symmetry operations of general relativity. If you apply the supersymmetry transformation to a fermion, you get its partner boson. A quark, say, becomes a squark. Apply the same transformation again, and you get the original fermion back—but displaced slightly to one side. The supersymmetry transformations involve not only bosons and fermions but also space-time itself. And general relativity tells us that gravity is simply a reflection of the geometry of space-time.

Hardly surprisingly, a band of enthusiasts soon took up the ideas of SUSY, developing various lines of attack.

One describes GUTs in terms of SUSY—the theories are known as SUSY GUTs.* Another focuses on gravity—it is called supergravity and itself comes in various forms with family resemblances but different detailed constructions. One great thing about all the supergravity models is that each specifies a different specific number of possible types of particle in the real world—so many leptons, so many photinos, so many quarks, and so on—instead of the endless proliferation of families allowed by the older GUTs. Nobody has yet succeeded in matching up the specific numbers allowed in any of these supergravity theories with the particles of the real world, but that is seen as a relatively minor problem compared with the previous one of a potentially infinite number of types of particles to worry about. The favorite version of these theories today is called "N = 8" supergravity, and its enthusiasts claim that it could explain everything—forces, matter particles, and the geometry of space-time—in one package. But the best thing about N = 8 supergravity is that it seems not merely to be renormalizable but also in a sense to renormalize itself—the infinities that have plagued field theory for half a century cancel out of N = 8 theory all by themselves, without anyone having to lift a finger to encourage them. N = 8 *always* comes up with finite answers to the questions physicists ask of it. "Superforce" indeed!

But ironically, all this success in the 1980s in finding potential ways to bring gravity and space-time back into the fold of particle physics reminded physicists that way back in the 1920s there had already been attempts to explain all the forces of nature in terms of curved space-time, the way gravity is explained by Einstein's theory. This may or may not prove the best line of attack in the years ahead, but it seems appropriate, in a book about cosmology, to devote a little space to the line of attack on grand unification that most closely follows the lead set by Einstein more than sixty years ago.

---

*SUSY initially developed independently of, and a little before, the GUTs described earlier.

THE ELEVEN DIMENSIONS
OF REALITY

Early in 1919, Theodor Kaluza, a junior scholar at the University of Königsberg in Germany,* was sitting at his desk in his study, working on the implications of the new General Theory of Relativity, which Einstein had first presented four years before and which was about to be confirmed, in spectacular fashion, by Eddington's expedition. As usual, Kaluza's son, Theodor, Jr., age nine, was sitting quietly on the floor of the study, playing his own games. Suddenly, the older Kaluza stopped work. He sat still for several seconds, staring at the papers, covered with equations, that he had been working on. Then he whistled softly, slapped both hands down hard on the table, and stood up. After another pause while he gazed at the work on the desk, he began to hum a favorite aria, from *Figaro*, and started marching around the room, humming to himself all the while.

This was not at all usual behavior on the part of young Theodor's father, and the image stuck in the boy's mind, so that he was able to recall it vividly sixty-six years later, in an interview for BBC-TV's *Horizon* program.† The reason for the father's unusual behavior was a discovery that is now, after decades in the wilderness, at the heart of research into the nature of the Universe. While tinkering with Einstein's equations in which the gravitational force is explained in terms of the curvature of a four-dimensional continuum of space-time, Kaluza had wondered, as mathematicians do, how the equations would look if written down to represent five dimensions. He found that this five-dimensional version of General Relativity included gravity, as before, but also another set of field equations, describing another force. The moment that stuck in young Theodor's mind so vividly was the moment when Theodor, Sr., wrote out those equations and saw that they were

---

*The city is now Kaliningrad, part of the USSR.
†"What Einstein Never Knew," first broadcast in 1985.

familiar—they were, indeed, Maxwell's equations of electromagnetism.

Kaluza had unified gravity and electromagnetism in one package, at the cost of adding a fifth dimension to the Universe. Electromagnetism seemed to be simply gravity operating in the fifth dimension.

Unfortunately, although Einstein had had no problem in "finding" four dimensions (three of space and one of time) to put into General Relativity, there was no evidence that there really was a fifth dimension to the Universe. Even so, Kaluza's discovery was striking and looked important. In those days, a young researcher could not easily publish dramatic new discoveries out of the blue. Today, if you have a bright idea, you write a paper and send it to a learned journal. The journal editors then send it out to an expert (or several experts) to assess before they decide whether or not to publish. But in those days it was considered correct for the author to send the paper *first* to an eminent authority, who might then, if he approved, send the work to a learned society with his recommendation that it be published. So Kaluza sent his results to Einstein.

Einstein was initially fascinated and enthusiastic. He wrote to Kaluza, in April 1919, that the idea had never occurred to him and said "at first glance I like your theory enormously."* But then he began to pick at little points of detail. A perfectionist himself, he urged Kaluza, in a series of letters, to tidy up these details before publication. The correspondence, and what now seems nitpicking, continued until 1921, when Einstein suddenly had a change of heart (nobody is quite sure why) and sent Kaluza a postcard telling him that he (Einstein) was going to recommend publication. What Einstein recommended in 1921 no journal editor would argue with, and the article duly appeared in the proceedings of the Berlin Academy later that year under the title (in German) "On the Problem of Unification in Physics."

The obvious defect with the theory presented in that paper (apart from the absence of the fifth dimension) was that it took no account of quantum theory—it was, like General Relativity itself, a "classical" theory. Even so,

---

*Quoted by Abraham Pais in *Subtle Is the Lord*, page 330.

Theodor, Jr., recalls that there was a great deal of interest in his father's work in 1922—but then nothing at all. Even Einstein, who spent the rest of his life seeking a unified field theory, seems to have ignored Kaluza's idea from then on—in spite of the fact that in 1926 the Swedish physicist Oskar Klein, whom we have already met in connection with his later work, found a way to incorporate Kaluza's idea into a quantum theory.

The behavior of an electron, or a photon, or whatever, is described in quantum physics by a set of equations with four variables. A standard form of these equations is called Schrödinger's equation, after the Austrian physicist who first formulated it. Klein rewrote Schrödinger's equation with five variables instead of four and showed that the solutions of this equation could now be represented in terms of particle-waves moving under the influence of both gravitational and electromagnetic fields. All theories of this kind, in which fields are represented geometrically in terms of more than four dimensions, are now called Kaluza-Klein theories.* As early as 1926, they incorporated gravity and electromagnetism into one quantum theory.

One reason for overlooking, or neglecting, such theories in the years immediately following Klein's work was that there were now more forces to worry about, and so the model seemed unrealistic. The "answer" is to invoke more dimensions, adding more variables to the equations to include the effects of all the new fields and their carriers, all described by the same geometrical effects as gravity. An electromagnetic wave (a photon) is a ripple in the fifth dimension; the Z, say, might be a ripple in the sixth; and so on. The more fields there are, and the more force carriers, the more dimensions you need. But the numbers are no worse than the numbers that come out of standard approaches to the unification of the four forces, such as supergravity.

Indeed, the numbers are *exactly the same*. The front runner among supergravity candidates is the N = 8 the-

---

*In fact, Gunnar Nordström, working at what is now Helsinki University, had tried and failed to find a five-dimensional unification of gravity and electromagnetism in 1914, and in 1926 H. Mandel independently came up with the same basic idea as Kaluza, apparently in ignorance of Kaluza's 1921 paper.

ory. That theory describes a way to relate particles with different spins, under the operations of supersymmetry. The range of spins available is from $+2$ to -2, and spin comes in half-integer quanta. So there are eight steps (eight SUSY transformations) involved in getting from one extreme to the other; hence the name. But there is another way of looking at all this. Just as Kaluza tinkered with Einstein's equations to see how they would look in five dimensions, so modern mathematical physicists have tinkered with supergravity to see how it would look in different dimensions. It turns out that the simplest version of supergravity, the most beautiful and straightforward mathematical description, involves eleven dimensions—no more, no less. In eleven dimensions there is a unique theory that just might be the sought-after superforce. If there are eleven dimensions to play with, all the complexity of the eight SUSY transformations disappears, and we are left with just one fundamental symmetry, an $N = 1$ supergravity. And how many dimensions does the Kaluza-Klein theory need to accommodate all of the known forces of nature and their fields? Precisely eleven—the four familiar components of space-time, and seven additional dimensions—no more, no less.

The implications of all this have excited many physicists recently, and no less an authority than Abdus Salam has described this geometrization of the world of particles and fields as "an incredible, miraculous idea."[*] They are still a long way from producing a fully worked out theory of this kind, but the unification of Kaluza-Klein theories with supergravity looks like one of the most fertile areas of theoretical work today.

We lesser mortals, of course, may wonder why we don't "see" all those extra dimensions. But this is no problem to the mathematicians. Each of those extra dimensions may have, somehow, become curled in upon itself, becoming invisible in our three-dimensional (or four-dimensional) world. The analogy that is often made is with a hosepipe. From a distance, a hosepipe looks like a wiggly line, a one-dimensional object. But closer up you can see that it

---

[*]*Horizon*, op. cit.; see also Salam's paper with J. Strathdee in *Annals of Physics*, Volume 141, page 316.

is a cylinder, a two-dimensional object. Every "point" on the wiggly line is actually a circle, a loop around the point, and the cylinder is the string of all these circles, one behind the other. In the early Kaluza-Klein theory, every point of space-time is thought of as a little loop—a loop just 10^{-32} centimeters across, extending in a direction that is neither up, nor down, nor sideways. The modern version is a little more complicated. The "loop" becomes an object called a seven-sphere (actually a slightly squashed seven-sphere), the seven-dimensional analog of a sphere. But the principle is the same. And, mathematicians tell us, the seven-sphere is the *simplest* form of multidimensional structure that still allows for the Universe we see around us to be as complex as it is.

On the new picture, the Universe was born in an eleven-dimensional state, and there was no distinction between force and matter, let alone between different kinds of force, just some kind of pure state of eleven-dimensional energy. As the energy dissipated, some of the dimensions curled up upon themselves, creating the structures we think of as matter—the "particles"—as waves vibrating in the coiled-up dimensions, and creating the forces of nature as the visible manifestations of the distortions of the underlying geometry. To crack the seven sphere and unpeel it to reveal the ten dimensions of space in all their glory would require more than even the grand unification energy. It requires, indeed, the energy of creation itself.

It is all heady stuff, at the cutting edge of current research, and new ideas eddy around in profusion in the scientific journals of the 1980s.* One currently fashionable variation on the theme treats "particles" not as points but as one-dimensional strings that "move" in a many dimensional space-time. These are "string" theories. On the other hand, some theorists (including, surprisingly, Stephen Hawking (who is one of the biggest fans of $N = 8$ theory and who says that it might mark the end of physics by explaining everything that physicists set out to explain) see all of the Kaluza-Klein ideas as leading up a

---

*One current flurry of excitement concerns a *ten* dimensional theory, in which most of the dimensions are rolled up, or compactified, and particles are described as "strings." It is called "superstring" theory.

blind alley. The idea, in its modern form, is simply too new for us to be able to tell where it might lead. After all, it took nearly a decade and a half for the idea of non-Abelian gauge theory to be applied effectively to a unification of some of the fundamental fields. The revival of Kaluza-Klein theory is a child of the 1980s and dates back no more than to 1978. It is unlikely to bear full fruit until the 1990s, if it does prove to bear fruit at all.

The theorists who like the Kaluza-Klein version of supergravity and SUSY today like it not because of any experimental proof that it is correct, but because it is so beautiful and internally consistent. As Einstein once said of General Relativity, it is so beautiful that it *must* be true! Kaluza himself would have appreciated the point, for he was a theorist par excellence. His son tells how Theodor Kaluza, Sr., taught himself to swim—by reading a book. Having thoroughly absorbed the theory and convinced himself that it was true, he took the family off to a nearby lake, jumped in, and proceeded to swim, 50 meters out and 50 meters back. He proved that the theory worked. We don't have a suitable lake in which to throw the Kaluza-Klein theory to see if it will sink or swim. Like Salam, I can only say that I would like it to be correct.

But whether or not the Kaluza-Klein theories, or supergravity, or SUSY, prove correct, the success of the electroweak theory and the GUTs themselves is enough to give a new insight into the very early Universe. Having brought you to the farthest frontier of theoretical physics today, the time has come to fulfill the promise made at the start of this book and recount how these new ideas can account for the creation and very early evolution of the Universe itself.

CHAPTER NINE

THE VERY EARLY UNIVERSE

Particle physics and cosmology come together in the very early Universe, fractions of a second after the moment of creation itself. For me, the two branches of physics came together in November 1983, when I was able to attend, as an observer, the first scientific conference organized jointly by CERN, the European accelerator laboratory near Geneva, and ESO, the European Southern Observatory, which is administered from Munich, although its telescopes are in the southern hemisphere. The meeting was held at CERN, and the list of contributors included many of the most renowned authorities from both the particle physics and cosmology communities. Its subject was "Large-Scale Structure of the Universe, Cosmology, and Fundamental Physics." Although it covered a lot of ground, including such puzzles as the origin of galaxies and the ultimate fate of the Universe, for me the heart of the meeting was provided by the discussions of unified theories of physics and their application to the very early Universe. The theory of primordial nucleosynthesis, the grand achievement of cosmology in the 1960s and at the time of my own modest activities in astrophysical research, deals with events seconds and minutes after $t = 0$; the new generation was concerned not with how protons and neutrons got together to form helium, but with how protons and neutrons, and quarks and leptons, came into existence out of an energetic fireball in the first place. Instead of simply accepting the expansion of the Universe as an observational fact, they could offer at least the outline of a family of theories to explain how the expansion began and how it must have been almost unimaginably more rapid than it is today in the earliest moments of the existence of the universe. And one contributor to the meeting, Stephen Hawking, even suggested how the Universe came into being at the moment of creation itself.

It was this heady stuff that left me with a determination to write the book you now hold. We have come a long way, from Galileo's observations of the heavens with a telescope and Thomas Wright's speculations about the nature of the Milky Way. The two short chapters that complete this book may seem modest in terms of the length of the whole volume, but they represent the pinnacle of an achievement based firmly on three hundred years of research and refinement of both theories and observations. Newton wrote, "if I have seen further it is by standing on the shoulders of giants";* we can now see as far as the beginning of time itself, not because we ourselves are any more clever than our predecessors, but because we have been able to follow a trail up the tallest of scientific mountains, a trail blazed by generations of astronomers and physicists.

The great insight that the Geneva meeting provided for me was the very natural way in which the ideas of particle physics and cosmology now fall together. One simple example came in a presentation by Jean Audouze of the Institute of Astrophysics in Paris. He was describing the theoretical understanding of early nucleosynthesis—almost old hat, 1960s stuff, something I thought I was familiar with. But the precision of the numbers he tossed around, the intimacy of the links between cosmology and particle physics, and the casual way in which all of this was accepted almost took my breath away. The amount of helium in the Universe today, for example, depends on the

---

*Letter to Robert Hooke. See *Oxford Dictionary of Quotations*, page 362.

ratio of the number of neutrons to the number of protons. A standard parameter used in the calculations is defined as *twice* the number of neutrons/number of protons divided by one *plus* the number of neutrons/number of protons. That is:

$$2(n/p)/(1 + (n/p))$$

As well as depending on the rate at which protons and neutrons can be changed into one another by the weak interaction during the fireball era, this number is related to the expansion velocity of the Universe. The quicker the Universe expands, the less time there is to make helium during the fireball. But the reactions going on in the fireball don't just involve protons, neutrons, electrons, and the electron neutrinos. The other families of particles are also involved, and in particular the presence of extra neutrinos, apart from the electron neutrinos, affects the rate at which the helium is produced. Each neutrino family present, Audouze confidently stated, will increase the n/p ratio in such a way that the value of the parameter given above increases by 0.1. The standard model, with three types of neutrino, corresponds to a value of 0.25. If the number turned out to be as low as 0.23, that would imply the existence of no more than two types of neutrino in our Universe, while if it were as high as 0.26, there might be as many as four types of neutrino, but no more.

As I have mentioned, experimental physicists have found two types of neutrino and believe that a third, the tau neutrino, must exist to partner the tau particle itself. But according to Audouze (and the eminent cosmologists at the meeting were not inclined to disagree), our observations of the expansion rate of the Universe and of the amount of helium present in stars and galaxies are now so good that we can state confidently that there *cannot* be more than four types of neutrino and that most probably we have already identified the only three there are.

This relatively simple calculation, dealing still in the physics of temperatures below 10^{11} K and times later than one second after the moment of creation, says, by implication, that there are indeed just three lepton families and, if the symmetry between quarks and leptons is preserved, just three quark families for physics to investigate. In July

1984 the same CERN team that had found the W and Z particles reported finding evidence of the existence of the sixth quark, "top." More experiments are running now to confirm the detections; but if the cosmology is any guide and if the observations are borne out by further experiments, it may well be that all of the ultimate building blocks of matter are now known. And it is with triumphs like that behind them that the physicists now offer an explanation of where the protons and neutrons—the baryons—came from in the first place.

THE SOURCE OF MATTER

This is probably the moment to put things back in perspective in terms of the time scale of the Big Bang. The meaning of time itself becomes very uncertain if we deal with small enough intervals of time, just as the meaning of position and momentum become uncertain on the quantum scale. Max Planck himself pointed out, in 1913, that the fundamental constants of physics—G, c, and $\hbar$—can be combined in different ways to produce numbers that, in some sense, represent the smallest length, the smallest mass, and the smallest time that have any meaning. The Planck length, as it is known, is 2×10^{-33} centimeters; the Planck mass is 2×10^{-5} gram; and the Planck time is about 10^{-43} second. A "particle" with the Planck dimensions would be a quantum black hole. The Planck time is the time it takes light to travel across the Planck length, which is some 10^{-20} times the distance "across" a proton.

One way of interpreting the Planck time is that it defines both a time scale and a distance scale where the quantum effects of gravity dominate the structure of space-time. The distance scale of the Planck units is the distance scale at which gravity becomes the equal of the other forces of nature, corresponding to temperatures above 10^{32} K and energies in excess of 10^{19} GeV.

So the history of the first 10^{-43} second of the existence of the Universe is, as far as the notion of time has any meaning then, one dominated by quantum gravity. Since we have no satisfactory theory of quantum gravity, that moment of creation is at present unknowable; since the notion of time itself may have no meaning for such a short interval, it may always remain unknowable and marks the starting point for any description of the evolution of the Big Bang and of the later Universe. If the implications of Hubble's observations of the red shift and Einstein's General Theory of Relativity really can be pushed back that far, the quantum rules seem to be telling us that the Universe was "created" at an "age" of 10^{-43} second. The moment of creation itself is the subject of the next chapter.

Following the moment of creation, the next landmark occurred about 10^{-36} second after the moment of creation, when the grand unification of the other four forces ended at a temperature of 10^{28} K and energies of 10^{15} GeV; the interval from 10^{-43} second to 10^{-35} second is therefore known as the "GUT era." At 10^{-12} second (10^{16} K; 10^3 GeV), the electroweak unification was broken. This occurred when the whole Universe was at a temperature equivalent to the highest energies ever achieved in the record-breaking proton-antiproton collider at CERN. And at about 10^{-5} second the quarks all became locked up into baryons as the temperature of the Universe fell below 10^{13} K (about 1 GeV). From then on, the story is taken up by the standard model described in Chapter Six. But in a Universe initially full of energy, with particles existing only as a result of pair production in which a matter particle, such as a quark, is accompanied by its antiparticle counterpart, how come there was any matter left over to form neutrons and protons at all? Why didn't all the quark-antiquark pairs (and electron-positron pairs) annihilate when the universe cooled and no more pairs were being produced?

The explanation begins in 1956, with work by Chen Ning Yang (of Yang-Mills fame) and Tsung Dao Lee, a Chinese-American physicist born in Shanghai in 1926. Lee, at Columbia University, and Yang, at Princeton, had met several years before, when both were at Berkeley, and kept in touch to discuss problems in particle physics. At that time, the particle zoo was rapidly gaining new inmates, and the behavior of some of the newly discovered particles was baffling. One family, the kaons, did not seem to be acting as they should—their decay into stable particles such as electrons and neutrinos seemed to violate some of the rules of the particle physics game. Lee and Yang found a way around this, by proposing that in some weak interactions there is an occasional violation of a rule known as the conservation of parity. This rule holds that the laws of nature are unchanged if they are reflected in a mirror—that nature cannot tell left from right. But this was an assumption that had never actually been tested. Lee and Yang startled the physics community by pointing this out and suggesting that kaon decays violate parity conservation (P); within a few months, experiments had been carried out (by another Chinese physicist, Chien Shiung Wu, who had also been born in Shanghai, in 1912) that confirmed their prediction, and Lee and Yang shared the Nobel Prize in 1957, only a year after publishing their ideas. The speed with which the award was given indicates the dramatic impact of this overturning of a central idea in physics. It gave physicists a new way of

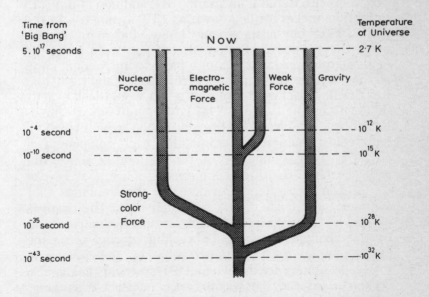

*Figure 9.1 / *Schematic representation of the way symmetry broke as the Universe cooled and aged, with one initial superforce giving rise to the four forces of nature known today.

looking at the particle world and took the blinkers of an old dogma away from their eyes.

In 1964, two American physicists, James Cronin and Val Fitch, working at Princeton, extended this work to include another form of nonconservation. They showed in their experiments that kaon decay also, very occasionally, allows particles to change into antiparticles. The process breaks a conservation "law" (really just dogma, based on "common sense") known as charge conjugation, or C. Cronin and Fitch showed that C sometimes is violated on its own and that a combination of C and P together, CP, can also be broken in some interactions. The changes in C do not always cancel out the changes in P. Cronin and Fitch duly received their Nobel Prize in 1980.* But this left physics with an interesting oddity. Apart from reflecting them in a mirror and swapping particles for antiparticles, the only other way to "reverse" a particle interaction is to make time run backward—or, if you prefer, to make a film of an interaction and then run the film backward. Together with C and P invariance, the addition of time (T) invariance makes a rule known as CPT symmetry. In the early 1950s, physicists already knew, and many experiments have since confirmed, that if you were to do the equivalent of making a film of a particle interaction, swap all the particles for antiparticles, reverse left and right, *and* run the film backward, the end result would look exactly the same as the original. The laws of physics *are* unaffected by a complete CPT transformation, which is why it had seemed natural to assume that each component of CPT was itself "symmetric" in the appropriate sense. But in fact each of the three components—C, P, and T—can be "broken" separately, provided that the combined CPT symmetry still holds in any particular case. The changes caused by C breaking, for example, may be canceled out by the changes involving P breaking during the same interaction; but if CP invariance is broken, the only way to restore symmetry for the whole CPT system is if T is also broken, in just the right way to cancel out the CP breaking.

---

*Why the delay, compared with Lee and Yang? Well, by the mid-1960s, the discovery of a violation of one of the conservation "rules" wasn't such a big shock as it had been in 1956!

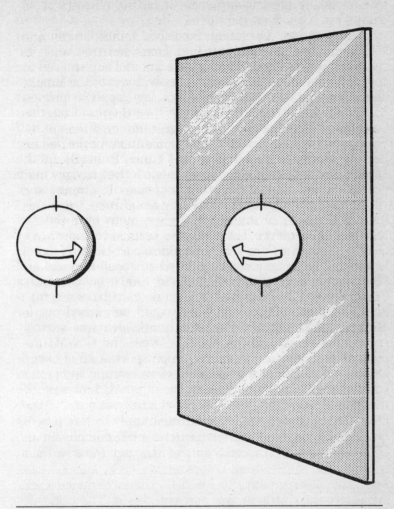

Figure 9.2 / In the mirror world, the original motion of the sphere
is restored if time runs backward. The mirror reflection and
the flow of time are both asymmetric, but put together they
produce symmetry—like the CPT symmetry, which is also made
up of pieces that need not be symmetric themselves.

What this means in practical terms can be seen by
looking again at the kaon, or specifically at one type of
kaon, called K^0_L. This is a neutral particle that, like

the photon, is its own antiparticle. It can decay in two important ways. One decay produces a negative pion, a positron and a neutrino. The other produces a positive pion, an electron, and an antineutrino. Don't worry about the pions—they are only bosons and are not subject to the conservation laws that seem to apply, most of the time, to fermions. But do those conservation laws apply to fermions *all* the time? If the laws of physics were symmetric, then we would find that out of a large number of kaons half would follow each mode of decay, maintaining the balance between electrons and positrons (anti-electrons) in the Universe. In fact, the first decay mode is very slightly more common. As kaons decay, they increase the proportion of positrons in the Universe by a tiny amount.

This was the first chink in the symmetry of the laws of physics at this level. The Universe seemed to show a very slight preference for left-handedness, at least as far as electrons were concerned. But what about baryons and the strong interaction? In the mid-1960s, nobody had a good theory of the strong force, so no calculations comparable to those of Lee and Yang could be carried out for protons and neutrons. And the quark idea was scarcely more than a glint in the eyes of Zweig and Gell-Mann— while there was, and remains, no prospect at all of experiments on Earth to test theories of the strong interaction directly. Against that unlikely background, however, the brilliant Soviet physicist Andrei Sakharov set out, in 1967, the underlying principles that must apply to any process that could produce matter particles preferentially in the early Universe.* To come out of the Big Bang with an

---

*Sakharov's name is familiar to a Western audience largely for political reasons, because of his position as a prominent "dissident" in the 1970s. But this publicity for his political activities as a campaigner for nuclear disarmament and human rights has, if anything, obscured the fact that he is one of the most brilliant physicists of his generation. Born in Moscow in 1921, Sakharov followed in his father's footsteps to become a physicist, graduating from Moscow State University in 1942 and joining the P. N. Lebedev Institute in Moscow in 1945. He was closely involved with the development of thermonuclear weapons in the Soviet Union, and in 1953 he became the youngest person ever, at age thirty-two, to be made a full member of the Soviet Academy of Sciences. He became a Hero of Socialist Labor and was awarded the Order of Lenin and many other honors. But by the late 1950s he was becoming interested in social issues.

excess of matter over antimatter, Sakharov said, three conditions must be satisfied. First, there must be processes that produce baryons out of non-baryons. Second, these baryon interactions—or, at least, the ones that matter— must violate both C and CP conservation. Otherwise, even if baryons are made by some process, there will be an equal number of antibaryons made in the equivalent antiprocess, and eventually the particles and antiparticles will meet and annihilate. And third, the Universe must evolve from a state of thermal equilibrium into a state of disequilibrium—there must be a definite flow of time so that CP processes together can be nonconserved, even though CPT remains conserved.

In physical terms, it is easy to understand this need for an "arrow of time" in the Universe. If radiation and matter are in balance at a uniform high temperature, then all the processes that turn radiation into particles and particles into radiation, or particles into other particles, are in balance and proceed equally happily in either direction. For matter to be left over in the Universe today, the particles that ultimately decay in such a fashion that a residue of matter is left over must be produced in such a hot state of the Universe. But as long as the temperature is high, the reactions that make matter are being balanced by the reverse reactions that use up matter and turn it back into those primordial particles. It is only if the temperature of the Universe falls that the balance of the equations is tilted in one direction, in favor of the lower energy state—it

---

At first his public comments were devoted to ideas for the reform of the Soviet educational system, which, while not following the Party line, were published in *Pravda*, and some of which became official policy in the early 1960s. During the 1960s, Sakharov's scientific research concentrated on cosmology and the initial stages of the Big Bang. In 1968, he published an essay calling for a reduction in nuclear arms, and in 1970 he was one of the founders of a committee for human rights. His increasing political activity during the 1970s led, among other things, to his being awarded the Nobel Peace Prize in 1975 and to his banishment to Gorky in 1980. It looked at that time as if his scientific career was at an end. But in 1984, following the development of new cosmological ideas that echoed some of Sakharov's theoretical work in the 1960s, papers from Sakharov taking up these ideas and discussing fundamental concepts related to the creation and early evolution of the Universe appeared in the Soviet *Journal of Experimental and Theoretical Physics*.

so happens, in the direction of decays that produce a surplus of matter—and at the same time the fact that the Universe is evolving from a hot state to a less hot state provides a direction for time. You need a high energy state to start with, plus a move toward lower energies, to get matter in the Universe.

Sakharov was able to state these conditions on the basis of fundamental physical principles alone, without knowing what forces or particles would be involved in the creation of matter, nor at what precise temperature the balance of the equations would tilt in favor of matter. He was far ahead of his time, and his paper was published in Russian; it made no great impact in the late 1960s. The

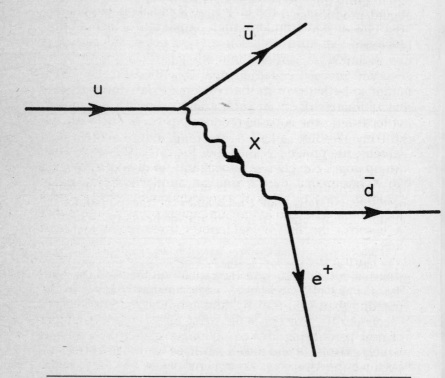

Figure 9.3 / Interactions involving an X boson can make baryons out of non-baryons, or vice versa. Quarks and leptons are interchangeable when there is enough energy available for X bosons to exist.

idea lay quietly for ten years. But it surfaced again in the work of a Japanese physicist, Motohiko Yoshimura of Tohoku University, in 1978. Yoshimura had been working on gauge theories and GUTs, and the single most solid prediction of all the GUTs is that there are X bosons that have masses of about 10^{15} GeV—10^{15} times the mass of the proton. With no hope of ever detecting such massive particles in accelerators on Earth, Yoshimura developed the idea that the X bosons might be revealed by their influence on the Universe during the GUT era, before 10^{-35} second, when they would have been the dominant constituent of matter. Following Yoshimura's lead—and only later rediscovering Sakharov's pioneering work and giving him due credit—theorists soon found that X bosons could produce an excess of baryons over antibaryons at the end of the GUT era, just as kaon decay can produce an excess of positrons over electrons today. The excess is small, but it is sufficient to do the job.

We have already seen how the X bosons can make protons decay today. Any process that can destroy protons has a counterpart that makes protons, and that is one way of looking at the X-boson interactions of the GUT era. Of course, all these interactions really involve *quarks* and leptons, not protons as such, but the principle is the same. An up quark can change into an anti-up quark by emitting an X boson that decays into an antidown quark and a positron. The GUTs specify a prescription for turning quarks into leptons and also for creating quarks *and* leptons out of X bosons—the first of Sakharov's three requirements is met.

During the GUT era, the X bosons themselves were in thermal equilibrium with the radiation that filled the Universe. Pairs of X and anti-X were constantly being made, meeting their counterparts, and annihilating. But by 10^{-36} second, or 10^{-35} second at the latest, after $t = 0$, the number of new pairs being created no longer matched the rate at which existing X and anti-X particles were being used up, because the Universe was cooling below 10^{15} GeV. If the using-up processes had consisted only of pair annihilation events, that would have been the end of the story. The Universe would have settled out as an expanding region of space-time containing nothing but cooling electromagnetic radiation. But, the GUTs tell us, the X particles can also decay into quarks and leptons, and many did so before they were annihilated.

An X boson can decay into other particles by two main routes. In one mode it produces two quarks, while in the other it produces an antiquark and a lepton (actually, of course, because of its huge mass energy even an *individual* X boson will decay into a shower of very many pairs of quarks and quark-lepton pairs, but let's take things one step at a time). Decay of anti-X, similarly, will produce either pairs of antiquarks or pairs made up of a quark and an antilepton together. But because the decay processes violate the C and CP symmetries, they do not work at the same rate for anti-X as they do for X, and Sakharov's second requirement is met. In very approximate terms, when anti-X decays to produce a billion antiquarks, the equivalent amount of X decays to produce a billion and one quarks. And that is the source of all the matter in the Universe today. As the Universe expanded and cooled (meeting Sakharov's third criterion), one quark in a billion (1 in 10^9) failed to find an antiquark partner after the GUT era and so never annihilated but instead stayed around to form the protons and neutrons that make up the bulk of the matter in the Universe today.* We owe our existence to a very tiny imbalance in the laws of physics, a preference for matter over antimatter in the decay of X bosons that amounts to no more than one extra quark for every billion antiquarks—an imbalance equivalent to one ten-millionth of one percent of all the matter that existed in the form of X and anti-X pairs in the GUT era.

The number 10^9 is not pulled out of the hat. It is the ratio of photons to baryons in the Universe today, calculated from the density of matter and the intensity of the cosmic background radiation. None of the GUTs is good enough to predict precisely what the imbalance between matter and antimatter "ought" to have been at the end of

---

*Sakharov's insight, explaining the requirements that had to be met in order for matter to exist in the Universe today, and made without the aid of the GUTs that were to come in the 1970s, surely deserves a Nobel Prize, which may yet be forthcoming. Perhaps, also, one may yet be forthcoming for Zweig, as well, since the Nobel Committee has not yet acknowledged the existence of quarks. It would be tidy if the awards were made jointly!

the GUT era, and estimates fall into a rather broad range for the photon/baryon ratio, anything from 10^4 to 10^{13}. At least the "required" value does lie somewhere in the middle of that range! But what matters most, of course, is simply that GUTs provide in principle a mechanism to make the matter in the Universe. It was this, as much as anything else, that encouraged cosmologists to embrace the new physics of high energies so warmly in the late 1970s and early 1980s. Perhaps, they thought, high energy physics could explain away some of the other remaining deep mysteries surrounding the standard model of cosmology. They were soon to be proved right.

THE PROBLEMS OF THE BIG BANG

The warmth with which cosmologists welcomed the news that GUT theory could explain the origin of matter was partly relief at the possibility of tackling some long-standing problems that had been neglected simply because there was no known way in which they could be tackled. The standard model of the Big Bang was certainly a triumph in its own right, and in a sense the problems it raised had seemed less important than the incredible fact that it gave any kind of insight at all into the origin of the Universe. But as time passed, those problems continued to gnaw away in the minds of some cosmologists, and by the end of the 1970s they looked far more significant than they had in 1965. As so often in the history of science, a major development in understanding achieved by one generation of researchers raised new difficulties that were tackled and resolved by the next generation.

There are several significant flaws with the standard model, apart from the puzzle of the origin of matter, which now seems to have been resolved. First, there is a difficulty known as the "horizon" problem. It arises because the Universe looks the same in all directions. Even if we look at the distribution of galaxies and clusters of galaxies on the sky, the Universe seems fairly uniform; but a true indication of the uniformity of the Universe comes from studies of the background radiation, which is isotropic (the same in all directions) to better than one part in ten thousand. How does radiation coming from one part of the sky "know" how strong it must be to match so precisely the radiation coming from the opposite part of the sky— and indeed from all points in between? The observations we make today are the first contact we have had with radiation from these opposite "sides" of the Universe, and these regions can never have been in contact with one another, according to the standard model, since they have always been farther apart than the distance light can travel during the age of the Universe, at every epoch of universal history to date. If the 3 K radiation was emitted 300,000 years after $t = 0$, as the standard model implies, then only regions of sky that are less than two degrees of arc across, as viewed from Earth, can have been in contact with each other at the time. So the background radiation "ought" to be patchy, with a grainy structure on a scale of two degrees or so. It looks as if the Universe was born out of the fireball era in a perfectly smooth state, with exactly the same energy density (the same temperature) "built in," even in regions that were too far apart for any signal, restricted to traveling at the speed of light, ever to have passed between them. But what built this uniformity of temperature into the Big Bang?

The horizon problem leads directly to the second problem, the existence of galaxies. If the Universe were created in such a perfectly smooth state, how could lumps the size of galaxies ever have formed? In a perfectly smooth Universe expanding uniformly, every particle of matter would be carried ever farther apart from every other particle, and there would be no seeds that could grow by gravitational attraction into bigger concentrations of matter. You don't need very big seeds. Just irregularities corresponding to regions with density 0.01 percent greater than the average, at a time 500,000 years after $t = 0$. But how could even such modest inhomogeneities be formed and emerge from a perfectly smooth Big Bang?

Then there is the monopole problem. The same GUTs that so successfully predict that there should be about the right amount of matter in the Universe also predict the existence of magnetic monopoles in the form of massive, very easily detectable particles. They ought to be found in cosmic rays—but they are not. In spite of several searches, only two experiments have ever shown up just two events that might possibly have been caused by the passage of a magnetic monopole through the apparatus, and nobody is going to accept them at face value without more evidence.

But the problem that triggered the new wave of research that led to a new theory of the evolution of the Universe at times prior to 10^{-30} second is called the "flatness" problem. It comes back to old-fashioned studies of galaxies, red shifts, and the expansion of the Universe, and it goes like this. We can calculate the expansion rate of the Universe, and we can estimate the amount of matter it contains—or rather, the *density* of matter, which is what is important—by counting the numbers of galaxies. Einstein's equations allow for the possibility that the Universe may be open, and destined to expand forever, or closed, and fated to collapse back into a fireball. Or, just possibly, it might be flat, balanced on a gravitational knife edge between the two possibilities, as I discussed in Chapter Four.

Observations show that the actual density of the Universe is definitely in the range from 0.02 to 10 times the critical density needed to make it closed, and cosmologists have argued for decades about which side of the critical value the density might lie. In the course of that argument, however, they slowly came to realize that the fact that there is scope for such arguments at all is one of the most remarkable features of the Universe. Why shouldn't the relevant parameter be 10^{-4} of the critical value, or a million times bigger than the density needed to close the Universe, or some other figure so different from 1 that it would be obvious from observations which side of the line it lay? The Universe today is actually very close to the most unlikely state of all, absolute flatness. And that means it must have been born in an even flatter state, as Dicke and Peebles, two of the Princeton astronomers involved in the discovery of the 3 K background radiation, pointed out in 1979.

Finding the Universe in a state of even approximate flatness today is even less likely than finding a perfectly sharpened pencil balancing perfectly on its point for millions of years; for, as Dicke and Peebles pointed out, any deviation of the Universe from flatness in the Big Bang will have grown, and grown markedly, as the Universe has expanded and aged. Like the pencil balanced on its point and given the tiniest of nudges, the Universe soon shifts away from perfect flatness. The state of perfect balance is in equilibrium, but it is an unstable equilibrium, and any deviation from perfection spells disaster for the balance. We can wind the clock back, in our imaginations, to calculate how flat the Universe must have been during the fireball era for it to have a density still so close to the critical value today. Dicke and Peebles, and others since, have done the calculations for us. If the density of the Universe is now one tenth of the amount needed to make it just closed (a figure that most astronomers would agree is a fair guide on the basis of the visible galaxies), that means that 1 second after the moment of creation the density of the Universe was equal to the critical value to within one part in 10^{15}. And if we go back to the time just after the GUT era, at 10^{14} GeV and 10^{-35} second the density must have been only one part in 10^{49} less than the critical value. This is hardly likely to be a chance occurrence and must mean that the laws of physics somehow require the Universe to be born out of the Big Bang in a state of extreme flatness.

In the spring of 1979, Dicke gave a talk at Cornell University in which he discussed the flatness problem and pointed out how closely the universe is balanced between runaway expansion and violent recollapse. One of the members of his audience was a young researcher named Alan Guth, a somewhat reluctant cosmologist who had been dragged into the subject by his friend and colleague at Cornell, Henry Tye, to tackle some aspects of the monopole problem. Guth was later to recall that he began working on cosmology only because he was pressured into it by Tye, who "had to do a lot of arm-twisting, because at that time I very strongly believed that cosmology was the kind of field in which a person could say anything he wanted, and no one could ever prove him wrong."* In spite of this initial distrust of the subject, Guth found the ideas fascinating and was slowly drawn deeper into cosmological studies. It took some months for the ideas presented by Dicke that spring day at Cornell to mingle with other ideas Guth was picking up from cosmology and particle physics— his original speciality—but by December 1979 they had begun to jell in his mind. In the course of the afternoon, evening, and part of the night of December 6, Guth put the pieces together in the first major new theoretical contribution to the cosmology of the early Universe since Gamow's work more than thirty years before. Guth introduced a completely new concept into cosmology, taking a step forward as profound as the idea of the cosmic egg itself.

THE ULTIMATE FREE LUNCH

Alan Guth followed a conventional route to become a research physicist in the 1970s. He was born in New Brunswick, New Jersey, in 1947, attended high school in Highland Park, New Jersey, where his family had moved when he was three years old, and entered MIT as a freshman to study physics in 1964. His bachelor's and master's degrees in physics were followed by a Ph.D. awarded in 1972—and then he ran up against the problems of finding a secure research appointment in physics. I know only too well what those problems were like in the early 1970s, since I completed my Ph.D. work in 1971. There were plenty of young physicists with fresh Ph.D.s in those days, most of them much brighter than I, and very few secure jobs were available. The only way to make the grade was to chase around from one short-term appointment to another, hoping one day to achieve the coveted position of a tenured scientist on a long-term appointment. I never even got on this treadmill, but quit research to take up

---

*Quote from Guth's contribution to *The Very Early Universe*, edited by G. W. Gibbons, S. W. Hawking, and S. T. C. Siklos, page 201.

writing instead; Guth, obviously a more persistent (and talented) character than I am, worked first at Princeton University before moving on to Columbia University and then Cornell University, where he heard Dicke talk about the flatness problem in the spring of 1979. In October 1979 Guth moved again, this time on leave from Cornell, to spend almost a year at the Stanford Linear Accelerator Center. It was there that the seed planted by Dicke's talk began to grow, fed by the input of all the pieces of information about cosmology and particle physics that Guth was taking in as the months went past.

Guth recalls the exact day that all the ideas, gathering in his head, suddenly seemed to come together in one fell swoop. It was Thursday, December 6, 1979, and the breakthrough started with an afternoon spent in conversation with a visitor from Harvard, Sidney Coleman, during which they discussed the latest ideas in GUTs. The idea of creating matter out of X bosons came up in the conversation, along with many other topics, and by evening Guth was aware of something trying to crystallize in his mind. At home, after dinner, he settled down with his current notebook and tried to give mathematical form to the ideas buzzing around in his head. He worked late into the night—long after his wife had gone to bed—filling page after page of the notebook with neat, meticulous calculations. When I was researching this book, Guth gave me photocopies of several of the pages from this and a later notebook. Toward the end of the section begun on December 6, 1979, and continued long after midnight into the small hours of December 7, there is a short, five-line passage at the top of a page, headed in capitals SPECTACULAR REALIZATION and carefully boxed around with a double line. It reads, "This kind of supercooling can explain why the universe today is so incredibly flat—and therefore resolve the fine-tuning paradox pointed out by Bob Dicke in his Einstein day lectures." Guth had found the basis of the description of the very early Universe that is now known as inflation—he gave the model that name very soon after making the discovery. A couple of weeks later, Guth, by no means an expert in cosmology yet, learned for the first time, in a conversation with SLAC physicist Marvin Weinstein, that cosmologists were also puzzled about the large-scale uniformity of the Universe—the horizon problem—and realized that his new model could explain that, too. Even though continued work on the model showed it to be flawed in at least one respect, he went ahead and published the paper in the hope, stated explicitly in the paper,* that someone else would find a solution to the flaw in it and carry the idea forward. And, in the wake of his work on inflation, Guth became first a Visiting Associate Professor and then, in June 1981, Full Associate Professor in the Department of Physics at MIT—the post he still holds.

What was the model, flawed or not, that had made him so excited and was to revolutionize cosmology in the 1980s? It jumps off from the idea, by now familiar to particle theorists, of the Higgs transition at the time GUTs were broken, the process by which symmetry is broken as the intermediate vector bosons "swallow up" Higgs particles and obtain mass. In many of the GUTs, symmetry is unbroken when the Higgs field (or rather, Higgs *fields*, since there are several of the beasts) is zero, but the symmetry is spontaneously broken whenever at least one of the Higgs fields is not zero. And there is a peculiarity about the Higgs field, which we met earlier. The state of lowest energy for the field is not necessarily the state corresponding to a zero value of the field. Guth gave the name "false vacuum" to a state in which the Higgs fields are zero, and "true vacuum" to a state with *lower* energy density in which the Higgs energy is at a minimum, but the field itself is not zero, symmetry is broken, and the vector bosons have acquired mass. GUT breaking, he suggested, corresponds to a transition from the false vacuum to the true vacuum, and when he put some numbers into his equations, some startling results emerged.

When the energy density is (or was, if we are thinking about the early Universe) very high, the exact value of the minimum and its position are of no great significance. It is only when temperature begins to fall that the field settles down into one or the other minimum states. The old analogy is with a marble in a large, smooth bowl. If the marble has a lot of energy—if it is rolled into the bowl,

---

around the rim, quite fast—it can orbit around the bowl high up near the rim, like a stunt motorcyclist on the "wall of death." The position of the minimum, or the depth of the bowl, has no effect on its behavior. But as its energy decreases, the marble slows and settles down into the bowl, eventually coming to rest at the bottom, in a state of minimum energy. Now, the position of the minimum is all-important. Something similar could have happened to the universe as it cooled from 10^{-43} second to 10^{-35} second (when the temperature of the universe was about 10^{27} K). The Higgs fields gradually settled down into a state of minimum energy. But which one? Suppose they settled into a state corresponding to the false vacuum, merely a *local* minimum, like the dip inside the crater of a volcano. In such a state, still with unbroken symmetry, the strong and electroweak forces still would be identical, and the energy density of the fields would be a colossal 10^{95} ergs per cubic centimeter, 10^{59} times the energy density of an atomic nucleus.

Such a state is likened to the way water can be supercooled, cooled below 0^0C without freezing. As the cooling continues, the water will eventually freeze quite suddenly, and give up its latent heat of fusion in the process. Below 0^0C, ice is a more stable state with lower

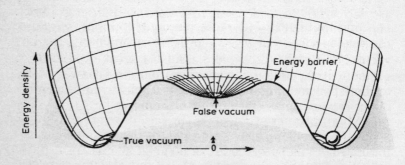

Figure 9.4 / In the first version of inflation, the universe is trapped in the "false vacuum" state of the Higgs field until it tunnels through the energy barrier, like the alpha particle escaping from a nucleus, and settles into the true vacuum. Energy released in the process drives the rapid "inflation" of the universe.

energy, but the transition into the more stable state, with accompanying release of latent heat energy, does not always happen at 0^0C. Guth said that the same sort of thing could happen to the Higgs fields. While the Universe continues to cool below 10^{27} K, where the symmetry ought to break, the fields stay for a time in the false vacuum state, like supercooled water staying liquid below its freezing point. Symmetry is broken only if and when the fields find a way to tunnel through the barriers around them and reach the deeper minimum of the true vacuum state, in which symmetry is broken.

The analogy with the volcano is a familiar one, of course. It is the one I used in describing the alpha particle trapped in an atomic nucleus. Just as the alpha particle can tunnel out of its captivity with the aid of the uncertainty principle, so the Higgs fields can tunnel out of the false vacuum with the aid of the uncertainty principle. But while the field is trapped in the false vacuum, or supercooled, state, its enormous energy density contributes, Guth found to his surprise, a huge outward push to the Universe, making it expand far faster than in the standard model. The effect, for a short time, is like that of a cosmological constant far more powerful than any that Einstein imagined. As a result, the Universe expands exponentially, doubling its size repeatedly with every 10^{-34} second that passes. This may sound like a modest expansion rate. But a doubling *every* 10^{-34} second means that in 10^{-33} second the region undergoes ten doublings and increases in size by a factor of 2^{10}, and in 10^{-32} second it increases in size 2^{100} times.* In far less than the blink of an eye, a region 10^{-36} times smaller than a proton itself can be inflated—hence the name for the model—into a region 10 centimeters across, the size of a grapefruit. Inflation takes

---

*Just as 10^2 is 100 (10×10), so 2^2 is 4 (2×2), and so on; 2^{100} means 2 multiplied by 2 one hundred times. Another way of writing this would be as $(2^3)^{33}$, and 2^3 is 8, so that would be 8^{33}, or 8 multiplied by 8 thirty-three times. If we fudge around the edges of the numbers a little to get a rough handle on what exponential inflation means, we can say that 8 is near enough 10 and that 2^{100} is near enough 10^{33}. In the same way, inflation by a factor of 10^{50} corresponds to doubling roughly 150 times—that is, growth by a factor of 2^{150}. And with one doubling every 10^{-34} second, that takes only just over 1.5×10^{-32} second (150×10^{-34} second) to complete.

the vastly submicroscopic world of the very early Universe and very suddenly brings it up to the sort of dimensions we are familiar with.

But once the Higgs field tunnels into the true vacuum state, the rapid exponential inflation stops. The energy of the field goes into the production of huge numbers of pairs of particles, which are reheated in the process almost to 10^{27} K. Virtually *all* of the matter and energy in the Universe as we know it could have been produced in this way out of the inflation. This possibility arises because the gravitational energy of the Universe is negative, and it is more negative the bigger the Universe is. As far as it is possible to talk about the way in which energy is conserved during the inflation, Guth says, the matter energy of the Universe increases, but the gravitational energy of the Universe gets more and more negative, so that the two together almost precisely cancel out—as Guth puts it, the Universe is "the ultimate free lunch." As the expansion of the Universe slows to the regular pace of the standard model of the Big Bang, X bosons produced by the Higgs energy decay to produce a tiny excess of matter over antimatter, and the rest follows as in the standard model described in Chapter Six. The inflation itself is over, still much less than 10^{-30} second after $t = 0$; but it has solved the horizon problem, the flatness problem, *and* the monopole problem.

The solution to the horizon problem is simply that the regions on "opposite sides" of the Universe today *were*, after all, "in contact" just after the moment of creation, before they were blasted apart from one another by inflation. The Universe we see is very uniform today because it has all been blown up from a tiny, tiny seed in which all of the energy was uniformly distributed. The solution to the flatness problem is only a little more subtle. When you blow up a balloon, the surface gets less and less curved the more you inflate it. It becomes a better and better approximation to a flat surface. The same thing happens to the curvature of space-time as space-time is expanded by inflation. Whatever curvature you start out with, by the time space-time has expanded by a factor of 10^{50} it is indistinguishable from a flat universe. Any curved universe becomes, as far as any of our observations could tell, a flat universe with density very close to the critical value by the time it has reached the size of a grapefruit. And the monopole problem is solved very simply indeed. Although there may have been many monopoles in the very early Universe *before* inflation, the region of space we can see has expanded from such a tiny volume that it is highly unlikely that there was even one monopole in that particular region of space-time to start out with.

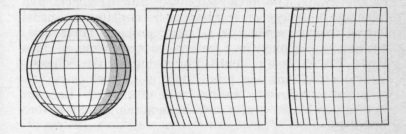

Figure 9.5 / Inflation makes the universe flat, no matter what curvature it starts off with. In this example, the radius of the sphere is multiplied by three in each frame as we move to the right. The total "flattening" is merely by a factor of 9; in the inflationary scenarios, the universe is flattened by a factor of 10^{50}.

This resolution of the monopole problem highlights a key feature of Guth's model and of later versions of inflation. By implication, there may indeed be *other* regions of space-time, beyond our visible Universe, that did not inflate at the same time or at the same rate as our "bubble" of the Universe. We may be living in a "local" region (the entire observable Universe) of some much bigger meta-universe. But *might* those other regions be observable? This prospect, indeed, was the fatal flaw with the original inflation model.

As Guth realized, the transition from the false vacuum to the true vacuum would take place at random all over (or all through) space-time. There would be many inflated bubbles of space-time, each with their own particular values of the Higgs fields, and each with slightly different laws of physics, because the symmetry would break in a slightly different way in each bubble. There was no graceful way for the inflation to proceed smoothly in the original inflation model, and instead bubbles of inflation would be going off all through space-time as different regions tunneled out of the false vacuum in different ways. The bubbles would form clusters, rather like clusters of frog spawn in a pond, or like the structure of a sponge, and the boundaries between the bubbles would be very energetic, clearly detectable features. Our Universe looks nothing like this. So this prediction of Guth's original model is clearly wrong. The model is flawed. But the exponential expansion that was a feature of the first inflationary model looked so good, and solved so many problems, that many cosmologists wanted it to be true in spite of its obvious flaws. The anguish of such a tantalizing but flawed possibility for resolving the prime puzzles of cosmology was summed up for me by Andrei Linde of the P. N. Lebedev Institute in Moscow, who took the next major step forward in 1981.

Linde was born in Moscow in 1948 and studied physics at Moscow University before moving on to research at the Lebedev Institute, under the direction, initially, of David Kirzhnitz. Linde was interested in the nature of the high-energy phase transitions involving the Higgs fields and was intrigued to learn of Guth's work. Linde was delighted that the topic he had worked on with Kirzhnitz might be of cosmological significance, but frustrated by the difficulty of explaining how to achieve a smooth transition from the false vacuum to the true vacuum. Writing in March 1985, Linde told me that "until the summer of 1981 I felt physically ill, since I could see no way to improve the situation and I could not believe that God could miss such a good possibility to simplify the work of creation of the Universe." But in the summer of 1981 he hit upon a solution to the problem. In simple terms, what Linde suggested was that there is no deep well, like the inside of a volcano, associated with the false vacuum state, but instead there is a shallow plateau of energy, very slowly sloping off at the edges and down into the true vacuum state. A Higgs field on such a plateau would very gently and smoothly "roll over" into the true vacuum without the confusion of a whole series of local quantum transitions associated with tunneling through the barrier.

The result is a universe that is smooth and uniform, one that has set like a mass of jelly instead of a handful of frog spawn. The idea became known as "the new inflationary scenario," and although it took a little time to catch on, it has gained wide popularity in the mid-1980s.

Linde's version of the theory was presented first at an international seminar in Moscow in October 1981. There, Stephen Hawking of Cambridge University responded with a "disproof" of Linde's scenario. On second thoughts, however, he found the idea more beguiling, and mentioned it during a seminar he gave in Philadelphia and wrote a paper on the subject with one of his colleagues, Ian Moss. Two Philadelphia researchers, Andreas Albrecht and Paul Steinhardt, were independently coming to much the same conclusions as Linde, and published their calculations in April 1982, referring in their paper to Linde's independent work; the "new" inflationary hypothesis became respectable about that time (scientists always like to be told something twice before they believe it), and Linde's variation on Guth's theme was the front-runner among inflationary models for the next couple of years.

The new inflationary hypothesis has been tinkered with further since 1982, in attempts to fine-tune it to produce a match with the observed features of the Universe. In one variation on the theme, the false vacuum state is sur-

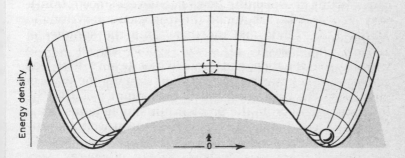

Figure 9.6 / In the second variation on the inflationary theme, the Universe slowly rolls off the top of an energy plateau into the true vacuum. Once again, the equations suggest that the accompanying release of energy can drive a brief phase of extremely rapid, exponential expansion of the whole universe.

rounded by a *small* barrier around the center of the "plateau" and tunnels out to form many bubbles, which each begin their life on the plateau and then each get involved, separately, in a steady roll over into the true vacuum. The accelerated expansion of each bubble of space-time continues as long as it is on the plateau, and each bubble can easily grow to the size of the observable Universe. At the time all this was happening, at the start of the phase transition, the distance that light could have traveled since $t = 0$ (the "horizon distance") would have been about 10^{-24} centimeters. After inflation by a factor of 10^{50}, the same region would be 10^{26} centimeters across, all derived from an almost perfectly uniform speck of space-time.* That volume of the inflated Universe would cover 100 million light-years. But the size of the region of space within that vast volume that grew to become our visible Universe today would still have been only 10 centimeters, the size of a grapefruit, at the end of the inflation, just under 10^{-30} second after $t = 0$. Everything we can ever see or know about fits way, way down inside just one bubble of the inflationary Universe.

Many details of the inflationary scenario, or scenarios, remain to be worked out. As Martin Rees pointed out at the ESO/CERN meeting in Geneva, the state of play today is rather like the state of play with standard Big Bang cosmology when Gamow was working on it in the 1940s. It is unrealistic to expect all of the answers to fall neatly into place just yet. Cosmologists now are working in two main directions. One line of attack seeks to explain how quantum fluctuations in the very early Universe can grow to become the seeds of galaxies a few minutes after the moment of creation. There is also the interesting question of just how important galaxies are in the Universe at all, gravitationally speaking; for, according to estimates of density based on counting the galaxies we can see, there is no more than 20 percent of the matter needed to make the

---

*A light-year is 9.5×10^{27} centimeters, but the expansion of the Universe can stretch space-time much "faster than light" because nothing is moving *through* space-time. So the exponential inflation of the Universe proposed by Guth and other cosmologists really can take a region of space-time much, much smaller than a proton and blow it up to a volume 100 million light-years across in a tiny fraction of a second.

Universe flat available in the form of galaxies. And the same calculations of the standard Big Bang that require there to be just three (or at most four) families of leptons in the Universe also tell us how much baryonic matter there should be around, and that figure ties in rather well with these counts of galaxies. So where is the other 80 percent (or more) of the matter needed to make space-time flat, as inflation says it must be? This is presumed to be nonbaryonic matter in the form of gauge particles, or inos, or some other seemingly exotic by-product of particle theory. And, lo and behold, when astronomers simulate the creation of galaxies in the Universe by modeling in a computer how gravity will pull clumps of matter together as the Universe ages and expands, they find that in order to match the observed clumpiness of matter they need a large amount of cold, dark matter in the voids between superclusters of galaxies. The particles in the cold, dark matter each have masses of 1 GeV or more; they make up the bulk of the gravitational mass of the Universe, and they are not baryons. But the gravity of all these particles pulling together explains why the baryons that make up the visible stars and galaxies (and ourselves) are distributed the way we see them.

The implications of inflation for an understanding of the Universe today, and of its ultimate fate, are fascinating and will keep cosmologists busy, and the bookshelves filled, for years to come. But that direction of research is the opposite of the one I have been following in this book, and reluctantly I must wrench myself away from it and back to the main line of the search for an understanding of the origin of the Universe itself; for the other recent development with inflation, which surfaced only in 1984, takes things back in time farther still, from the GUT breaking Higgs transition at 10^{-35} second to the time when quantum gravity only just ceased to be important, a mere 10^{-43} second after the moment of creation itself.

PRIMORDIAL CHAOS AND ULTIMATE ORDER

In spite of the conceptual breakthrough that Guth's work represented, the Higgs field that is so central to his model, and to the new inflationary scenario, remains its weak link. New inflation works only because the parameters of the Higgs field are adjusted very delicately—"fine tuning" that is permitted only because we don't really know how the Higgs field behaves and that smacks of special pleading. The trick works only if the field parameters are set up in just the right way in the first place, because we know the "answers" we want to get out,* and the inventors of the theory themselves accept that this is implausible. What they hope is that there may be realistic grand unified theories in which a smooth transition occurs naturally and that *automatically* give the "right answers" without any fine tuning. But since the details are intermeshed with details of the particle physics, and since the particle physics is not well understood, that remains only a pious hope as of 1985. Nothing daunted, some theorists have tried to resolve the difficulties by leaping off from a theory (GUT inflation) that is only poorly understood to another theory (SUSY inflation) that is even less well understood.

The approach favored at CERN, where particle physicists have become deeply interested in cosmology, avoids the difficulties of fine-tuning the symmetry breaking Higgs field at the end of the GUT era by going back to the symmetry breaking at 10^{-43} second, which split off gravity from the GUT forces. The idea is to provide the inflation first, before GUT breaking, and leave the settling out of the Universe into space filled with radiation, quarks, and the elusive particles of the cold, dark matter to come later. One of the principal spokesmen for the CERN team involved in this work is Dimitri Nanopoulos, a Greek particle physicist, who dubs the new scenario "primordial inflation" and refers to the various different models that make

---

*Shades of renormalization!

use of the trick as PRIMOs. He and his colleagues would like to use a version of $N = 8$ supergravity to describe an inflationary process in the very early Universe, but this is too complicated for them to handle at present. So they have used a simpler version of supergravity, an $N = 1$ theory, in the hope that either they will be able to extend their findings to $N = 8$ later, or that ways will be found to simplify $N = 8$ theory down to $N = 1$. This is very much work in progress, and it would be foolish to attempt to describe it in detail here, when it may be overturned by new developments before this book is in print. Indeed, as yet most of the work has been published only in the form of CERN preprints—"only," I should point out for fear of offending my friends at CERN, in the same form in which Zweig introduced his quark (ace) model to the world. But an important feature of this approach is that it is tackling the ultimate energies and densities that can be described at all by physics. Gravity is the last force to be included in unified theories and was the first to split off in the Big Bang. There is literally nothing else left to invoke in order to provide a mechanism to drive the inflation phase, and no earlier time left in which it could be squeezed in. So this research must end up telling us fundamental things about the nature of the Universe, even if those things it tells us turn out not to be what we expect.

Another approach, also pushing back to the moment of creation and forgetting about the Higgs fields (which have never been directly observed, and which have very peculiar hypothetical properties), has been followed by Linde and jumps off from work by other Soviet researchers. This line of attack is supported by many Soviet cosmologists, although it is not yet as popular as new inflation outside the Soviet Union. Linde abandons the idea of high temperature phase transitions providing the push behind the exponential expansion of the Universe in its inflationary state and has looked instead at how *all* the scalar fields that filled the Universe at its birth would have settled down into their stable, minimum energy states. At the moment of creation itself, he argues, each field will be created in a chaotic state and will have different values in different parts of the Universe. The field will try to "roll down" (using the marble in the bowl analogy) to the state of minimum energy, but the way in which it rolls down turns out to depend on the state in which it was created. In regions of the Universe where the field is almost uniform (almost homogeneous) and is very far from its equilibrium state, the state of minimum energy, it rolls down very slowly at first, like the field slowly rolling off the plateau in new inflationary models. But while the field is only slowly losing its energy, the energy density of the radiation and particles in the expanding Universe is falling rapidly as the Universe expands, and soon cools down to match the energy density of the slowly rolling field. At that point, the field energy dominates the expansion, and Einstein's equations tell us that as long as the energy density is either constant or changes only very slowly, the Universe must expand exponentially. In other words, the slow rolldown of *any* scalar field to its minimum is alone enough to ensure a burst of inflationary expansion without requiring either a phase transition or "supercooling." Some of these ideas are shared by the CERN PRIMO models and

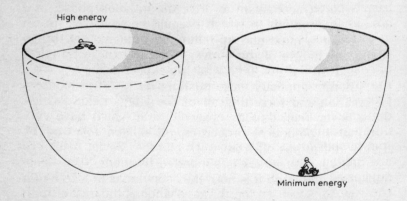

Figure 9.7 / The energy of the Universe can be likened to a wall of death motorcycle rider. When there is plenty of energy available, the rider can circle as high up the wall as he likes—this is equivalent to the creation of the Universe in a state of high energy density. When there is less energy, the motorcycle inevitably sinks down into the minimum. But in the case of the Universe, there may have been more than one minimum to choose from as it cooled and the energy density decreased (see Figure 9.9).

certainly seem simpler and more natural than the Higgs mechanism originally proposed by Guth.

Once the field reaches its minimum value, the conditions that have been driving the inflation no longer exist. The field oscillates to and fro about the minimum, like a marble rolling to and fro as it settles into the bottom of a bowl, and in the process all its energy is converted into pairs of particles. The marble slowly settles into the minimum energy state at the bottom of the bowl as friction converts its kinetic energy into heat; the oscillating field slowly settles into the minimum energy state as pair production converts the energy of its "roll" into particles. As in the earlier inflationary scenarios, the Universe is reheated to nearly 10^{27} K and filled with X bosons and the rest. Then it begins to cool rapidly as it expands in the more sedate fashion of the standard model. The largest "bubble" of the Universe is produced by exponential growth of the region that was farthest away from the equilibrium state at the moment of creation, and it may have inflated by the mind-boggling factor of $10^{1,000,000}$ times. If this picture is correct, the order we see about us today was created by inflation out of primordial chaos.

Linde calls his latest version of inflation "chaotic inflation" and he has suggested that the concept may also provide a link with Kaluza-Klein cosmologies. If space-time really did start out eleven-dimensional, then the process of compactification and rolling up of some of the dimensions of space-time may have occurred differently in different bubbles of the Universe—different "domains." It just happens that in our domain seven of the dimensions are hidden and four are manifest. Other theorists have suggested that it is the very process of compactification, the rolling up of seven of the original dimensions, that provided the push for the initial expansion of the Universe. But all of these ideas, including Linde's, are at least as speculative as the CERN group's thoughts on PRIMOs.

The proliferation of variations on the inflationary theme is a sign both of the richness of the possibilities opened up by the new idea and of the seriousness with which cosmologists and particle physicists take the fundamental concepts. The basic idea itself now seems powerful enough, and well enough established, to accept, with as much

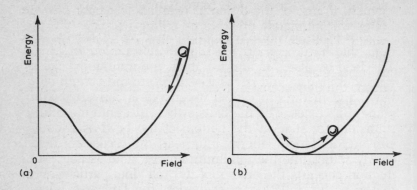

Figure 9.8/ As the Universe "fell" into a minimum energy state, for a time its field energy oscillated to and fro, like the oscillations of a marble settling into a bowl. It was during these oscillations that the remaining field energy was converted into particles by pair production.

confidence as Gamow accepted the idea of the Big Bang forty years ago, that there was indeed, early in the life of the Universe, a period of inflation that blew up everything we can see out of a seed no bigger than the Planck length, 2×10^{-33} centimeter, across. But it is far too early yet to say

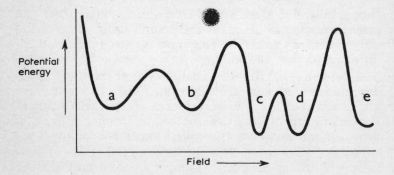

Figure 9.9/ Andrei Linde's idea of "chaotic inflation" envisages a universe in which there was a choice of minimum energy state to "fall into." Even this representation is simplistic, but it indicates how the extreme simplicity of the earliest inflationary scenarios may be made more complex to match more closely the real world.

which, if any, of the different detailed scenarios now on offer will ultimately prove to be telling us about the real world. I'll leave the last words on the subject to the two pioneers, Guth and Linde. Linde is confident that progress is being made in the right direction. "The old scenario is dead, the new scenario is old, and the chaotic scenario is in order," he told me. Guth, who once thought of cosmology as a field where you could say anything and nobody could ever prove you wrong, has a slightly different view of things today. "It now appears," he says, "that it is very easy to show that a cosmological scenario is wrong, and far more difficult than I had ever imagined to develop a totally consistent picture."

Perhaps the inflationary models are not yet "totally consistent." But they have already given us one powerful and all-important picture, an image of the moment of creation when the entire Universe as we know it was packed within the dimensions of the Planck length. And that makes it possible, at last, to develop a mathematical description of the moment of creation itself.

CHAPTER TEN

THE MOMENT OF CREATION

The puzzle of how the Universe as we know it came into being has been a major topic of religion and metaphysics for as long as there have been religions and metaphysicians. But it is also a puzzle for physicists, and one that began to feature in the discussions of physicists even before the idea of the Big Bang was put forward. The problem is best expressed, in its deepest and most fundamental form, in terms of the most basic expression of Olbers' Paradox: Why does a cold, dark Universe contain hot, bright stars?

All physical systems tend to operate so that heat flows from a hotter object to a cooler object. In the process, the systems become more disordered, and the ultimate stable state for any such system to be in is one in which there is a uniform temperature and all the particles in the system are moving about at random. It doesn't matter whether the temperature is high, as it was in the fireball of the Big Bang, or whether it is low, like the temperature of the background radiation today. What matters is that it should be uniform and that the system should contain no structure—no "information" of any kind.

Such a smooth, featureless system at a uniform temperature is said to have the greatest possible entropy, and it is a fundamental law of nature, revealed by experiment and derived by theory, that entropy—disorder—must always increase. The law can be bent, but not broken, in circumstances like those on the surface of the Earth today, where living things are able to feed off energy from sunlight and create structured *local* pockets of order, with decreased entropy. But this is always at the cost of increasing entropy elsewhere by an amount greater than it has been reduced locally. The Sun's nuclear burning represents a vast increase in entropy against which the growth of living things on Earth is producing an almost totally insignificant little decrease in entropy. If engineers on Earth build a bridge, or an aircraft, or a house, they are creating order and decreasing entropy locally, but only at the cost of creating disorder and increasing entropy where the raw materials are produced, and in conveying them to the manufacturing plant. Work can be done only if, somewhere along the line, heat is flowing from a hotter body to a cooler one. Entropy measures the availability of heat to do work—more entropy means less *available* heat, which means that there is less in the way of temperature *differences* to drive the flow of heat from a hotter body to a colder body, which is the ultimate source of all work and power. More entropy means less capacity to do work. If the temperature is the same everywhere, even if it is very high, no heat can flow and no work can be done. But even when work is done, it is never 100 percent efficient. Things wear out—that is the simplest way of expressing the inevitable increase of entropy, which is formally known as the Second Law of Thermodynamics. But the Universe is in a state of low entropy and disequilibrium, demonstrated by the lavish way in which stars pour out energy into the void. It is far from being "worn out" yet, and the analogy is made sometimes with a great clock, wound up and set ticking long ago, and slowly winding down today. So how was the clock wound up—how was the Universe engineered in the first place to have so little entropy, and so much order, that 15 billion years after the Big Bang we still see bright stars in a dark sky?

THE ORIGIN OF TIME

Our present understanding of the laws of thermodynamics and the role of entropy in the behavior of physical systems derives from the work of Ludwig Boltzmann in the nineteenth century. Boltzmann was an Austrian, born in Vienna in 1844, who among his many contributions to science worked out a mathematical description of the tendency of a gas to reach equilibrium, with all of the gas at a uniform temperature and with the molecules in the gas moving at random. It was Boltzmann who showed that entropy (a concept introduced by the German physicist Rudolf Clausius in 1865) is a measure of the disorder of a system.

Boltzmann's approach was statistical. The behavior of a gas could be explained, he found, by the random motions of very many molecules colliding with each other and with the walls of any container in which the gas was confined. The rules that describe such a system of many particles interacting at random are very accurate and reliable—they start out from simple probability calculations (like the chance of rolling two sixes on a pair of dice three times in a row) and give you the odds of certain possibilities occurring for the system of molecules that make up a gas, and they tell you what the most probable state for such a system is. The set of equations developed by Boltzmann and later refined by others is called statistical mechanics. This works extremely well—it is one of the most basic planks in the structure of modern physics. But it leads to some interesting and noncommon-sense predictions.

The room in which I work is, in effect, a box full of gas, and all the molecules in the air in my room are moving at random. That means that it is possible (although highly unlikely) that all the gas in the room will suddenly move off into the corners, leaving me with nothing to breathe. Or take another example. When I put an ice cube into a drink, the ice melts as it gets warmer, and the drink cools down as it gives up heat to the ice. But, say Boltzmann's equations, this is only a *statistical* law. It is possible, although highly unlikely, that one day I will put an ice cube into my drink and watch, astonished, as the ice cube gets even colder and the liquid around it begins to boil. It is conceivable, within the laws of physics, that entropy can decrease; but it is overwhelmingly improbable that such an event should occur.

To get a handle on just how improbable it is, consider how many molecules would have to work together to make my drink boil spontaneously in its glass, sucking in heat from the air around it, or from a handy ice cube, which would get colder while the water boiled. The number of atoms of hydrogen in one gram of the gas is 6×10^{23}, a 6 followed by 23 zeroes. Oxygen is 16 times heavier than hydrogen, and each molecule of water contains one oxygen atom and two hydrogen atoms. So in round terms we can ignore the mass of the hydrogen atoms in this rough calculation. Sixteen grams of water also contain just about 6×10^{23} molecules, and if we make the modest assumption that I am drinking only water, then a glass with 10^{24} molecules in it makes a pretty small drink—roughly one thirtieth of a pint. The probability that all those molecules will "work together" to make entropy decrease depends on the number of molecules involved, according to a strict statistical rule worked out by the French mathematician Henri Poincaré, who lived from 1854 to 1912. It is 1 in 10^n, where n is the number of molecules involved. Even leaving out of account the molecules of the air around the glass, which would also have to cooperate in this reversal of the normal flow of entropy, the chance of the water in my glass boiling spontaneously is 1 in $10^{10^{24}}$. These are very long odds indeed—1 in 1 followed by 10^{24} zeroes. For comparison, the age of the Universe in *seconds* is about 5×10^{17}, a 5 followed by a mere 17 zeroes. Don't bet on any ice cube you place in a drink doing anything except melting!

These probabilities for the occurrence of exotic and noncommonsense events are so tiny that they have no effect on our daily lives, or even on the most exotic experiments that physicists can dream up. But could they be relevant to the entire Universe? Boltzmann, puzzling over how we come to be living in such an ordered, low-entropy Universe, suggested that they might be. He speculated that the "real" state of the Universe must be one of thermodynamic equilibrium, a uniform sea of constant temperature and disorder that has lasted forever and will last forever, since time has no meaning when there are no differences in temperature that would allow heat to flow and work to be done.* If nothing ever changes, time does not exist, and it is always eternity. But within that infinite, eternal Universe there would be random processes, fluctuations which, for a limited time, created a region deficient in entropy in exactly the same way that a chance fluctuation might make the water in my glass boil. Perhaps our entire Universe represents such a statistical fluctuation away from the equilibrium state. The chance of such a fluctuation occurring is related to the number of atoms in the visible Universe, and it corresponds roughly to 1 such fluctuation in $10^{10^{80}}$ years.

This is extraordinarily unlikely. But, after all, if we are talking about an infinitely long existence for the larger meta-universe within which our fluctuation is simply a local freak, then there is literally all the time in the world to wait for such a freak event to occur. Alternatively, if we imagine the meta-universe as infinite in extent, then it is certain that anything that is possible, even if it is highly unlikely, will indeed happen somewhere within the infinite meta-universe.† Leave a uniform meta-universe alone for 1 followed by 10^{80} zeroes years, and, just by chance, in a part of that meta-universe as big as our Universe, all the heat will flow spontaneously into stars and raise their local temperatures to millions of degrees. What we are seeing

---

*British physicist Paul Davies has suggested, indeed, that inflation is what gave time a meaning in our Universe. The initial chaos represents a high entropy state, but the state of the Universe after inflation is one of very low gravitational entropy. Low entropy means that heat can flow and that therefore the Universe looks different as time passes, so that the concept of time passing has a meaning. As Davies puts it, the Universe is "wound up" by inflation. "The remaining history of the universe is the subsequent attempt to unwind by gravitational clumping (galaxies → stars → black holes) and nucleosynthesis (hydrogen → helium → iron). Together these two evolutionary chains account for all the observed macroscopic time asymmetry in the world and imprint upon our environment a distinct arrow of time." *Nature*, Volume 301, page 398; see also Volume 312, page 524.

†Indeed, in an infinite meta-universe anything that is possible will happen an infinite number of times in an infinite number of places.

today, on that picture, is simply a return toward the equilibrium that is the true, long-term state of the Universe.

Boltzmann's idea cannot be carried far in its original form, partly because of the difficulty of explaining why the Universe should be so uniform—why entropy should have decreased in just the same way over such an enormous volume of space-time. We are back to the horizon and flatness problems. But the concept of a statistical fluctuation creating the Universe was revived in a different format in the 1970s and suddenly began to look like a very respectable idea indeed, in its new form, when the inflationary scenarios began to receive attention in the 1980s.

THE QUANTUM UNIVERSE

It is quite astonishing how old ideas keep turning up in new guises as we probe back to the moment of creation. Boltzmann's picture of the Universe—his model—was very much a "steady state" model in which the overall features (or lack of features) are eternal and unchanging, and all of the action we see going on around us is just a temporary fluctuation. The Steady State model in its simplest modern form, originally put forward in 1948, is long since discredited, because we can see that the Universe is evolving, changing as it expands away from a superdense state. But in the 1960s, fighting a rearguard action against the advance of Big Bang cosmology, Fred Hoyle and his Indian colleague Jayant Narlikar developed a variation·on the theme. This involved an eternal Steady State universe in a state of high temperature and density, within which bubbles might sometimes be inflated to produce regions of expanding, evolving space-time just like the Universe we see about us. Shades of Boltzmann, indeed; but also a curious preview of the kind of inflationary model now so fashionable.

To provide a driving force behind this inflation, Hoyle and Narlikar had to invent a new kind of field, which they called the C field, because they designed it to be involved with the creation of matter. So they had a model of the

Universe, more than twenty years ago, in which a very
dense state was driven into a burst of rapid expansion by
the energy of a field that also made particles. Conceptu-
ally, there is very little difference here from the now fashionable idea of the inflation of the Universe out of a very
dense state by the action of a field or fields (perhaps the
Higgs field, perhaps not) that dumps its energy in the
form of particles. In 1984, Hoyle and Narlikar each separately published papers drawing attention to the similarities between their old C-field model and inflation. The
point they hope other cosmologists might pick up from
this idea is that the inflationary process, like the C field,
can operate quite happily against a steady state background, in the same way that a Boltzmann fluctuation can
create order out of chaos. Physicists have not, to be frank,
fallen upon this revival of the C-field idea with cries of
delight. *Any* variation on the steady state idea is unfash-
ionable. But credit where credit is due—the mathematics
of the C field *is* reminiscent of inflation (or, as Hoyle and
Narlikar would say, inflation is reminiscent of C-field theory), and it *is* important to keep in mind the possibility
that there may have been no actual singularity at what we
call the moment of creation, no state of literally infinite
density and temperature, but that there may have been
instead a transition of a local region of space-time, which
we call the Universe, from one state to another.

But one of the most dramatic implications of the idea
of inflation in its 1985 form is that the whole Universe
may have appeared out of literally nothing at all, created
as a quantum fluctuation in the same way that quantum
uncertainty allows a virtual pair of particles to appear and
to exist for a short time before annihilating.

The idea surfaced in *Nature* in December 1973, in the
form of a scientific paper from Edward Tryon of Hunter
College, City University of New York. Tryon proposed*
what he called "the simplest and most appealing" Big
Bang model imaginable, that "our Universe is a fluctuation of the vacuum." The jumping off point for his intro-

---

Nature, Volume 246, page 396. A similar idea was put forward independently
in the Soviet Union at about the same time by P. I. Fomin and circulated as a
"preprint"; but this work was not published until 1975.

duction of this model into cosmological debate was a calculation which showed that any closed Universe must have zero net energy.

Crudely speaking, we can understand this in terms of the negative gravitational energy the Universe possesses, which is so large (in a negative sense) that it cancels out all of the mass energy, mc^2, of the matter in the Universe. This is a consequence of a feature of gravity so strange that physicists scarcely seem to acknowledge it in public. If we try to describe the gravitational energy of a collection of matter in terms of the equations that describe gravity, we find that the only meaningful state which corresponds to a zero of energy from which we can measure is with all the matter dispersed to infinity. It doesn't matter if we think in terms of atoms, or planets, or stars, or galaxies as the building blocks of the material object under consideration. The zero of energy is when the building blocks are as far apart as it is possible to conceive. Now comes the strange thing. As the matter falls together under the influence of gravity, it gives up energy, so the gravitational potential energy gets less, and since it was zero to start with that means it becomes negative. So any object in the real Universe, like a planet, which is *not* spread out to infinity must have a negative energy to start with, and if it shrinks it releases energy and its own gravitational potential energy becomes more negative. Not something for nothing, but something for *less* than nothing. Using Newton's theory of gravity, there is no limit to how negative the potential energy of the planet can get. Every time it shrinks, energy is released and the gravitational energy becomes more negative.

In mathematical terminology, there is no "lower bound" to the energy state, in Newtonian physics, and that is one reason why we have to set zero as the energy of the dispersed matter. General Relativity does set a bound to the amount of negative gravitational energy associated with a body with mass m. If all of the mass m could be concentrated at a point in space, a singularity, then the negative gravitational potential energy associated with it would be $-mc^2$—equal and opposite to its Einsteinian mass-energy. But this is only a crude representation of a more subtle and sophisticated mathematical argument, which I can't go into here, which *proves* that a closed Universe has zero energy overall.* It is Guth's "free lunch" taken to its logical extreme; if the Universe contains zero energy, no wonder it is free. Not something for nothing, after all, but *nothing* for nothing. Tryon pointed out that the uncertainty relation $\Delta E \Delta t + \hbar$ allows anything with zero energy to exist for as long as you like, because if the energy is zero then the uncertainty in the energy ΔE is also zero. There would be no problem about "borrowing" energy from the vacuum to create the Universe, because you don't need any overall energy in the first place, and you don't have to hurry to pay it back, because there is nothing missing from the balance account!

---

*The basic idea of something for nothing goes back at least thirty years before Tryon's version appeared. In his autobiography *My World Line*, George Gamow tells about his role during World War Two as a consultant with the Bureau of Ordnance in the U.S. Navy Department in Washington, D.C. Gamow was not allowed to work on the atomic bomb, because he was a Russian by birth and delighted in telling all his friends that he had been a colonel in the Red Army at the age of twenty. Even allowing for Gamow's predisposition to tall tales and practical jokes, this wasn't to be taken lightly by those responsible for security on the Manhattan Project. So he spent the war years in Washington.

One of Gamow's jobs, however, was to deliver a briefcase full of papers to Albert Einstein, in Princeton, once every two weeks. Although officially secret, these papers had nothing to do with nuclear weapons. They described all kinds of ideas for new weaponry, which Einstein was expected to comment on for the navy. Einstein would almost invariably comment favorably, as Gamow tells it, no matter how weird and wonderful the new ideas for explosive devices. One day, while walking with Einstein from his home to the Institute for Advanced Study, Gamow mentioned that Pascual Jordan had come up with a new idea. Jordan was one of the pioneers of quantum physics, who made his name through work with Werner Heisenberg and Max Born that established the basis for the first version of quantum mechanics, called matrix mechanics, in 1925. His new idea didn't seem, in the 1940s, to be in that league. It was, indeed, just one of those crazy ideas physicists like to mull over during coffee time, or while walking through Princeton. What Gamow mentioned to Einstein on their walk was Jordan's idea that a star might be created out of nothing, since at the point zero its negative gravitational energy is numerically equal to its positive rest mass energy.

"Einstein stopped in his tracks," Gamow tells us, "and, since we were crossing a street, several cars had to stop to avoid running us down."

The idea that stopped Einstein in his tracks is the same idea, now applied to the whole Universe, not just a star, that researchers such as Ed Tryon are taking very seriously indeed in the 1980s.

This naïvely simplistic interpretation of the uncertainty rules made no great splash in the 1970s. It was just one of those passing comments that physicists often toss around during coffee time, and it clearly did not provide a precise description of our Universe. Taking the analogy with the creation of pairs of virtual particles literally, it would require, for example, that our Universe contained precisely equal amounts of matter and antimatter, which doesn't seem to be the case. And the whole basis of the argument was that the Universe is closed, whereas in the mid-1970s the well-established consensus among cosmologists was that the Universe was open. Finally, if a quantum fluctuation containing all of the mass of our Universe *were* created in a superdense state, why didn't it promptly collapse into a singularity under the influence of its own self-gravity?

The difficulties looked insurmountable. But the advent of inflation changed all that. Inflation requires that there must be enough dark matter to make the Universe so nearly flat that we cannot distinguish its curvature, and inflation doesn't "care" whether the Universe sits just on the closed side of flatness or just on the open side of the dividing line. And the GUT description of X-boson decay tells us that an energetic original universe created with equal numbers of X and anti-X still will evolve into a Universe with a slight residue of matter in it, in the fullness of time (the "fullness of time" being about 10^{-35} second). Hardly surprisingly, Ed Tryon himself revived his idea in the context of inflation in the 1980s, and in 1982 it was also taken up by Alexander Vilenkin of Tufts University.* Vilenkin, indeed, takes things a step further than Tryon did in 1973. Tryon talked about a "vacuum fluctuation," implying that some form of space-time metric ex-

---

*Vilenkin's unusual career development is worth a brief mention. He was born in Kharkov, in the USSR, in 1949, and obtained his B.Sc. in 1971 from Kharkov State University. But, he told me, he was unable to obtain a research post because he is Jewish, and he spent five years first in army service and then earning a living at various odd jobs (his favorite, he says, being night watchman in a zoo) before emigrating to the United States in 1976. During those five years, however, he had been studying physics in his spare time, to such good effect that in 1977, the year after he arrived in the States, his work earned him a Ph.D. from the State University of New York at Buffalo.

isted before the Universe came into being; but Vilenkin is trying to develop a model in which space, time, and matter are all created out of literally nothing at all, as a quantum fluctuation of nothing. "The concept of the universe being created from nothing is a crazy one," Vilenkin says in one of his papers (in *Physics Letters*, Volume 117B, November 4, 1982, page 26), but he goes on to show how it is mathematically equivalent to the creation of an electron-positron pair that then annihilate each other, and this is in turn equivalent to one electron being created out of nothing, traveling forward in time for a while, then turning around and traveling backward in time to meet up with its own creation. In this and other recent papers, Vilenkin puts a lot of respectable mathematical icing onto the basic cake baked up by Tryon, in more speculative form, in the early 1970s.

Hardly surprisingly, this revival of his speculation has meant a great deal to Tryon, especially since he has trodden a lone path in all his cosmological work. Born in 1940 in Terre Haute, Indiana, he obtained his bachelor's degree in physics from Cornell in 1962, then moved to the Berkeley campus of the University of California, where he was captivated by Steven Weinberg's courses in quantum field theory and General Relativity, and was lucky (and talented) enough to become one of Weinberg's Ph.D. students. After finishing his thesis, he then moved to Columbia University, carrying out calculations of the scattering amplitudes for collisions between pairs of pions, and earning the nickname "Pion Tryon" in the process. But he has never collaborated with anybody, and, possibly uniquely among his generation of particle theorists, is the sole author of all of his scientific publications. An interest in cosmology that went back to childhood had already led Tryon to speculate about the possibility of a closed Universe with zero net energy, but he recalls with amusement an incident at the end of the 1960s which, at the time, caused him acute embarrassment.

Cosmologist Dennis Sciama was visiting Columbia from Britain, and gave a seminar on the latest theories of the Universe. At a point in the presentation where Sciama paused for a moment, Tryon blurted out, to his own surprise as much as everyone else's, "maybe the Universe is a vacuum fluctuation!" The laughter that followed caused the junior researcher, who specialized in particle physics, not cosmology, to blot the incident from his mind. It was only after the *Nature* paper appeared that he was reminded of the occasion by a colleague, and realized that his subconscious had been prodding him towards completing that piece of work, even though the memory had been kept from his conscious mind for three years.

Tryon moved to Hunter College in 1971, and it was there that the image of the Universe as a quantum fluctuation appeared to him in mid-1972, in a flash, fully worked out. The subconscious had been absorbing all his reading on cosmology and working out the answer to that embarrassing laughter, only releasing it into his conscious mind when it was complete. And when it was published in *Nature*, the article drew some 150 requests for copies, even though the idea then fell into limbo until the concept of inflation made it timely. How did it feel to have an old idea, once literally laughed to scorn, made fashionable and referred to as a major conceptual advance? "All good scientists are dreamers," said Tryon when I asked him about this. "They dream of discovering some unknown phenomenon of major importance ... it would be difficult to exaggerate the satisfaction entailed."

Of course, the idea is still highly speculative, but it is now much more attractive. And its best feature is that there is no longer any need to create all of the matter in the present-day Universe at the moment of creation itself. All you need now is to create a region of closed space-time and energy, a self-contained microcosm much smaller than a proton, which has only a modest temperature and a slight tendency to expand. Without inflation, such a microcosm would soon collapse. But with inflation, says Tryon, there could have been a "cold big whoosh" (inflation) that blew the tiny speck of space-time up to an enormous size and ended in a burst of creation as the scalar field energy was dumped into pairs of Xs and other particles and created the hot Big Bang itself at $t = 10^{-35}$ second. Ever since, gravity has been at work to slow down the expansion, and eventually it will be first halted and then reversed. In the far distant future, the Universe will collapse back into a tiny singularity. Space-time itself, and everything it contains, will disappear into a single point and vanish. There will be nothing to show that our Universe ever existed. The proposal may remain speculative, but at least it now fits rather neatly into the overall framework of inflationary cosmology. If there really was a moment of creation, then the concept of quantum uncertainty, one of the strangest and most fundamental features of quantum physics, seems to provide the best hope of explaining how the Universe came into being. In that case, there may indeed have been a moment of creation marking the boundary of the Universe at the beginning of time. But there is an alternative view, one that is, if anything, even more deeply rooted in the basics of quantum physics. Stephen Hawking, of the University of Cambridge, has developed an approach based on the concept of defining a quantum mechanical wave function that describes the entire Universe, and dealing with this, as one could any other wave function in quantum physics, in terms of path integrals. And he says that there may be no boundary to the Universe, even at the moment of creation.

A SEEKER OF SINGULARITIES

Stephen Hawking is one of those rare scientists whose work captures the popular imagination and is often the subject of reports in newspapers and magazines. This is partly because he works on topics that seem to strike a chord with all of us—black holes, singularities in space-time, and the mystery of the origin of the Universe. But it is also because he suffers from a severely disabling disease called motor neurone disease. This is the disease that killed the actor David Niven; it attacks the nervous and muscular functions of the body, making it impossible for a severely afflicted sufferer—which Hawking now is—to walk, and extraordinarily difficult for him to talk. The image of a crippled genius struggling against overwhelming odds to achieve an understanding of the Universe far beyond most of us, and then struggling to communicate those ideas to his colleagues in spite of his handicaps, is one that obviously makes for "good copy," in newspaper parlance. But sometimes too much is made of this aspect of Hawking's life. Certainly his body is crippled. But his mind and intellect are totally unaffected by the disease, and his scientific achievements are of the first rank in themselves. It isn't that it is surprising that someone with his physical problems can make such progress in understanding the Universe; what is surprising is that any human being can achieve such understanding. And Hawking himself has commented on his great good fortune, as he sees it, of having a career that depends solely upon the ability of his brain to think, and in which his physical handicaps, severe though they are, rank as only minor distractions in his own eyes. Of course, these problems are of much greater significance to his life outside his work—but that is about as relevant to his scientific discoveries as the fact that Einstein played the violin is to the story of the search for the Big Bang.

Hawking was born on January 8, 1942—precisely, as he delights in telling people, three hundred years to the day after Galileo died. Hawking's father worked on research into tropical diseases at the National Institute of Medical Research and encouraged Stephen to follow an academic path aimed at entrance to Oxford University. The encouragement did not, however, extend to Hawking's decision to study mathematics—his father tried to talk him out of this, arguing that there were no jobs for mathematicians. Even so, Stephen entered Oxford University in 1959 to study mathematics and physics. His contemporaries and tutors recall today that he was a remarkable student with a mind unlike that of anyone else. He passed examinations with almost contemptuous ease, obtained a First Class degree, and moved to Cambridge to begin research on cosmology.

At this time, in the early 1960s, Hawking began his involvement with singularities, an involvement that lies at the heart of all his major contributions to science and that is the key to understanding the moment of creation itself. He was and is fascinated by the idea of a mathematical singularity, a point where not only matter but space and time as well are either crushed out of existence or, in the case of the Big Bang, created. The standard equations of relativity theory predict the existence of singularities, but in the early 1960s hardly anybody took this prediction seriously. Singularities were assumed to be an indication that the simplest version of Einstein's theory, with a smooth distribution of matter through space-time, was not a realistic way to describe the confusion of a superdense state, and that probably a better understanding of the equations would show that as a collapsing object approached a singularity, at some stage there would be a "bounce," making it expand again, or some other effect that halted the collapse short of a point of infinite density. Either that, or Einstein's theory was incomplete and would break down at very high densities—that is, in very strong gravitational fields. Hawking determined to find out if this were true. But it was to be several years before this determination bore fruit, because it was in his first year of graduate work, 1962, that the first symptoms of his illness appeared and were diagnosed. Given only a few years to live, he became depressed, took to drink, and virtually gave up his work.

But as the months passed it became clear that the progression of the disease had halted and stabilized. Hawking was slightly incapacitated physically, but he wasn't getting any worse. And at the same time he realized first that his intellect had been totally unaffected by the disease and would be unaffected whatever happened to his body, and also that his work was entirely brainwork, which could be carried on regardless of the deterioration of his physical condition. Since then, as far as a casual acquaintance such as myself can tell, Hawking has never looked back, either in his private life or in his work. He married in 1967, has two sons and a daughter, and leads as normal a life as possible. It was also in the late 1960s that he began to achieve recognition for his scientific work.*

---

*Not just his work on relativity theory, either. The first time I visited Cambridge was in 1967 to attend a presentation of the then new ideas on primordial nucleosynthesis from the Wagoner, Fowler, and Hoyle team. In a packed lecture room filled with some of the best physicists and astronomers in England, where the role of a research student such as myself was to keep quiet and take notes, the most penetrating questions from the audience were asked by a young man I had never seen before, a junior researcher who seemed to have a slight speech impediment but clearly had a first-class grasp of the subject under discussion. He was, of course, Stephen Hawking.

One of Hawking's major achievements at this time was carried out in collaboration with mathematician Roger Penrose, who was then working at the University of London. Together they proved that the equations of General Relativity in their classical form (that is, without allowing for quantum effects) absolutely *require* that there was a singularity at the birth of the Universe, a point at which time began. There is no way around the singularity problem within the framework of classical General Relativity. If singularities are to be avoided in the real Universe, the only hope is to improve relativity theory by bringing in the effects of quantum theory and developing a quantum theory of gravity. In the 1970s, Hawking's investigations of the mathematics of black holes led, through the introduction of quantum effects, to the startling conclusion that black holes can "evaporate" and must eventually explode. This work brought him into the popular limelight, at least in the science magazines. And in 1974, at the very young age of thirty-two, he was elected a Fellow of the Royal Society.

By then he was confined to a wheelchair following a further progression of his illness. For the past ten years, however, he seems to have remained much the same physically. He has only very limited control over the muscles of his body, and slumps rather than sits in his wheelchair; his speech is laboured and almost incomprehensible to anyone who does not know him well and has not become familiar with his voice. The honors Hawking has received include the Albert Einstein Award, in 1978,* and in 1980 he became Lucasian Professor of Mathematics in the University of Cambridge—a chair occupied previously by Paul Dirac and Isaac Newton, among others. These honors, and the honorary degrees heaped upon Hawking by universities around the world, are the sort of thing usually associated with a scientist who has completed his greatest work and can now settle down to a comfortable position of eminence as an administrator and teacher. Few mathematicians, in particular, achieve much in the way of new work after they reach age thirty; new ideas come

---

*This award is generally regarded by physicists as the ultimate accolade, ranking significantly above the Nobel Prize.

from young minds that are not hidebound by convention, or so we are told. But Hawking's mind is as sharp as ever, and he has now put forward a model of the Universe that attempts to combine the ideas of General Relativity and quantum physics and that not only removes the uncomfortable singularity at the moment of creation but that, in principle, explains *everything* in one package. Perhaps his disability is now actually an advantage as far as this work is concerned; for, unable to become a conventional committee man and figurehead, he continues to work in the only way he can, the way he has worked for twenty years, developing new mathematical descriptions of the world in his head. The astonishing thing about this latest work, which may well be remembered as Hawking's masterpiece, is not that it comes from someone with physical disabilities. The surprise is that it comes from a man who is now in his early forties, a remarkably late age for a mathematician to be achieving a new breakthrough. Even Einstein was still in his thirties when he completed his General Theory of Relativity, and he never achieved much of any significance in science after that.

The model Hawking proposes, and which is still being developed, has not yet won the kind of acceptance that his earlier work has achieved. But it strikes to the heart of the remaining puzzles about the origin of space, time and matter, and it is quite clearly the most complete, coherent account of the moment of creation that is on offer today.

HAWKING'S UNIVERSE

General Relativity tells us that there must be a singularity at the beginning of time—the moment of creation. But General Relativity, like all of our theories of physics, breaks down for times earlier than the Planck time, 10^{-43} second. Although a variation on the steady state idea, with either a smooth meta-universe or some sort of overall chaos, plus inflation, could provide a way to produce a local region of expanding space-time rather like the one we live in, it would be much more satisfying if we could develop a mathematical model, a set of equations, to describe our Universe in a self-contained way—especially if that model could avoid the embarrassment of a singularity at $t = 0$. This is the basis of Hawking's approach to the puzzle of our origins, and of his attempts to combine General Relativity and quantum theory, at least partially, in a good working model of the Universe.*

What version of quantum physics, however, is appropriate when we are describing the whole Universe? Remember that quantum theory tells us nothing about how a particle, or a system, gets from state A to state B. The conventional interpretation of quantum physics is the Copenhagen Interpretation. This says that when we are not looking at a system it exists in some sort of superposition of all the possible states it could be in, and that the act of measuring the system—or looking at it—causes a "collapse of the wave function" into just one of these possible states, a state selected solely on the basis of probability. When we stop measuring the system, or looking at it, it spreads out, in a quantum sense, from that certainty into a new superposition of states, only to collapse again, perhaps in a different way, the next time it is measured. This interpretation of the quantum math works very well as a practical tool for calculating how atoms and subatomic particles (and, indeed, molecules) will behave. But it is hardly common sense, and there is a real difficulty in trying to apply the Copenhagen Interpretation to the entire Universe.

We can imagine the Universe as being described by quantum mechanical wave functions, of course, even if we can never hope to write down the equations that would describe the "wave function" of the entire Universe. But since, by definition, the Universe includes everything of which we can have knowledge, including ourselves, there is nobody "outside" the Universe to observe it and thereby to cause it to collapse into one possible quantum state.

*It is only right to point out that very few physicists are entirely happy with Hawking's approach. He has to make a lot of simplifying assumptions, and they don't always approve of the way he handles the equations. But the underlying physical principles of the model are very clear and straightforward, and it is this that persuades me that Hawking is on the right track. The details of the equations may change; I doubt if the underlying physical principles will!

The correct way to calculate the probabilities that describe the behavior of the Universe (or of any system that includes the observer) is to use the alternative interpretation of quantum physics, the so-called Many Worlds Interpretation, in which the effects of all of the possible wave functions for the system can, in principle, be calculated and added together, using Feynman's path integral (or "sum over histories") technique to produce an overall mathematical description of the system and how it gets from state A to state B.

In most cases, these two approaches give the same answers to the problems of quantum physics, and few physicists bother with the Many Worlds Interpretation because they have grown up with the Copenhagen Interpretation and, having gotten used to one idea that conflicts with common sense, they find it hard to adjust to a second noncommon-sense idea. But as Hawking has pointed out on several occasions (including his contribution to the ESO/CERN symposium), a combination of the Many Worlds Interpretation and sum over histories is the *only* way to approach a quantum description of the Universe—and in this case the "sum over histories" is literally that, an adding together of all of the possible ways in which the Universe could evolve. Of course, we cannot even calculate one "history" of the Universe in detail. But we can choose a set of starting conditions for the Universe—boundary conditions—and we (or rather Hawking and his colleagues) can calculate the evolution of a simple version of the Universe, that contains just a couple fields (one representing gravity, one representing matter). The hope is that this simple model, which Hawking calls minisuperspace, will bear enough resemblance to the real Universe for him to deduce the broad features of the evolution of the Universe. And that hope seems to be fulfilled.

Hawking chooses as his boundary condition for the Universe a possibility that arises only when quantum physics is combined with General Relativity. General Relativity says that there must be a singularity at $t = 0$. But classical physics also said that there ought to be a kind of singularity in the atom—that an electron could not stay in orbit around the nucleus, but must fall into its center. Quantum mechanics explains why the atom can exist in a

stable form, and it also offers the prospect of removing the
singularity at $t = 0$ from cosmology. In physical terms, we
can think of the origin of time as being smeared out by
quantum uncertainty, over a time of 10^{-43} second, so that
there is no unique moment of creation. In terms of a
physical model, described by a proper mathematical combination of GR and quantum physics, this makes it possible to describe the *four* dimensions of space-time as a
closed surface like the surface of a sphere, or the surface
of the Earth.

Previously we met the idea of the *three* dimensions of
space forming such a closed surface, which expands as
time passes. But now we have to think of space-time, not
just space, in this way. Extending the analogy, space
would be represented not by a surface but by a line, which
we can choose to be a line of latitude circling around the
spherical surface that represents the fabric of space-time.
Time could then be represented by the "distance" from
the pole along a line of longitude, and if we start out from,
say, the North Pole and move toward the equator, the
great circles that represent space (lines of latitude) get
bigger as "time" passes and we approach the equator.
Such a model of the Universe is completely self-contained.
There are no edges, and there are no singularities in either
space or time. It is the simplest possible geometry that
could describe the Universe, and it is a geometry that can
exist only because quantum effects change the rules of
relativity theory, which on their own insist that there *must*
be a singularity at the beginning of time. Hawking stresses
that this proposed state of the Universe is just that—a
proposal. He suggests that the boundary condition of the
Universe is that "it has no boundary"—no edges, no singularities, no beginning or end of either time or space.
The astonishing thing is that this simplest of all possible
boundary conditions leads him to an entirely plausible
description of the Universe, indistinguishable from what
we see about us.

Hawking's tests of this model use the sum over histories approach to quantum physics. In principle, the idea is
to add up the effects of all the possible histories that
satisfy the boundary condition—all the possible universes
that are finite in size and have no boundaries. In practice,

he has to make many simplifying assumptions, boiling his model universes down to the basic two fields I mentioned. But when he does this and carries through the path integrals, he finds that most of the histories cancel out because of interference from neighboring paths, just as in the equivalent calculations of the orbit of an electron in an atom. Only a few of the possible histories are reinforced and therefore have a high probability. They form a family of high probability histories that share several important properties. One is that they expand uniformly in all three space directions; another is that each expands out to a definite size, then contracts back into a state of very high density like the state of our Universe at the Planck time, before expanding once again. And each cycle of expansion and collapse is exactly the same as the one before. The universe doesn't expand to a bigger or smaller amount in consecutive cycles, but always by exactly the same amount. Even better, the interaction of the two fields in Hawking's models produces an initial phase of very rapid expansion—inflation—before the matter begins to dominate the universe and causes it to switch over into the kind of sedate expansion we see in our Universe today.

Any one of these allowed universal histories would be a good description of our Universe, as a closed system with no boundaries and no singularities, eternally fated to carry out a cycle of expansion, collapse and expansion. It is easy to see why Hawking is excited by the possibilities thrown up by his model. The Universe, in such a picture, must be just closed, but an era of inflation will have carried it close to flatness and solved all the usual problems that are solved by inflation. But the model also throws up some strange and wonderful new ideas. The first is the implication that there are other universes in the family of allowed histories, going through their cycles of expansion and collapse in some sense alongside us (next door in superspace). But there is no way we could ever become aware of them, let alone communicate with them. Because of the way quantum physics works, whenever we make measurements or carry out experiments we will get results in line with one quantum state—the wave function that describes "our" Universe and everything in it, including ourselves. Intelligent beings who occupy a quantum state that corresponds to a second highly probable wave function of the Universe will make their own observations and always get answers appropriate for that wave function. Apart from canceling out some wave functions and reinforcing others, the quantum states do not interact—there is no interference, and the results of experiments are always in line with one or the other "classical" solution to the equations. Even so, restricted to knowledge of just one out of the many worlds that Hawking's model says exist alongside each other in superspace, we can gain new insights into the fate of our Universe, and into the nature of time.

Look again at Hawking's model of the four-dimensional Universe as a smooth sphere. The rings of constant latitude that expand outward from the North Pole represent the expanding universe of space, and the North Pole itself represents the Big Bang—the moment of creation. But there is no singularity at the pole. It is just a place from which we measure time. In the same way, the fact that the real North Pole of the Earth is a place from which we can measure latitude (in fact, we define the *equator* as latitude 0°, but we could just as easily measure from the Pole) doesn't mean that there is a singularity at the pole. There is nothing further north than the North Pole, but that doesn't mean that space has an edge there. And there is nothing earlier than $t = 0$, but that doesn't mean that time began then. The moment of creation, $t = 0$, is now just a convenient label against which to measure time.

Hawking first presented these ideas at a conference on cosmology in the Vatican in 1981. The physicists and mathematicians who attended that conference were granted an audience by the Pope, who told them that it was quite in order for them to study the evolution of the Universe after the moment of creation, but that the puzzle of the beginning of time itself was a matter for religion, not science, and represented the work of God.* Perhaps the

---

*In John Paul II's own words, addressing that meeting in 1981, "any scientific hypothesis on the origin of the world, such as that of a primeval atom from which the whole of the physical world derived, leaves open the problem concerning the beginning of the Universe. Science cannot by itself resolve such a question: what is needed is that human knowledge that rises above physics and astrophysics and which is called metaphysics; it needs above all

Pope's advisers had been too tactful to point out to him that Hawking's model of the Universe removed the singularity at the beginning of time and therefore removed the role assigned to God by the Pope. Or perhaps the full import of what Hawking had told the conference had not sunk in.

Hawking's model removes the embarrassing singularity at the "beginning" of the Universe. But, developing the analogy with lines of latitude drawn on a globe, what happens at the equator? If we continue to draw a series of lines of latitude around the globe further and further south, they get bigger—the Universe expands—until the equator, but after that they become smaller and smaller, eventually shrinking out of existence at the South Pole. This is equivalent to the contracting phase of Hawking's universe, and it has important implications for our understanding of the nature of time. Time exists because the Universe is evolving from a state of low entropy to a state of high entropy. The Universe expands from the ordered state of the Big Bang into the disordered state of the far future. It might seem natural to guess that during the collapse phase of its life, the Universe will be evolving from a state of disorder into a state of order—the flow of entropy is reversed, winding up the cosmic "clock" by exactly the right amount to ensure that the next cycle of expansion and collapse precisely follows the pattern laid down by all the previous cycles of that particular universal history. The three-dimensional Universe is ordered when it is small and disordered when it is large. Why should it be ordered when it is small? Why should entropy be forced to run backwards as the Universe contracts? Perhaps simply because there is no "room" for disorder in the smaller Uni-

the knowledge that comes from the revelation of God." And he went on to quote a predecessor, Pope Pius XII, who said in 1951, referring to the problem of the origin of the Universe, "we would wait in vain for a reply from the natural sciences, who on the contrary admit that they are honestly faced with an insoluble enigma." Less than forty years later, that "vain wait" is over. Many cosmologists no longer accept that the enigma is insoluble and there is a feeling now that science *can* resolve the metaphysical puzzle of the origin of the Universe. Hawking's universe, ironically presented at that very gathering where John Paul II claimed a still preeminent role for God, clearly points the way to an ultimate *scientific* solution to the greatest metaphysical puzzle of them all.

verse. A line of latitude around the equator, or close to it, can be quite wiggly and still be a reasonable approximation to a line of latitude. But a line of latitude drawn tightly around the North or South pole cannot wiggle without crossing over the pole itself. In the Planck limit, at $t = 10^{-43}$ second, the Universe is so small that it must be very uniform indeed. So if this picture is correct, that is why the arrow of time defined by entropy is the same as the arrow of time for which the Universe gets bigger as time passes. So are the two arrows of time out of step in the contracting Universe? Not necessarily, according to Hawking. In a series of lectures he gave in 1983,* he said, "Whether or not the arrow agrees with the direction of time defined by the expansion remains to be shown." The implication is that conceivably *both* arrows could reverse together but would still agree with each other. And that has some curious implications that were discussed by the astronomer Tommy Gold (one of the cofounders of the Steady State model) in the 1960s.

Gold's speculations were not based on anything so grand as Hawking's mathematical description of the Universe but simply on the possibility that our Universe might be closed and finite, so that it would one day recollapse. He attempted to describe the thermodynamics of a contracting universe with a reversed flow of entropy.† Instead of stars radiating heat out into space, they would be soaking up electromagnetic radiation—electromagnetic radiation coming in toward them from all directions in space, conveniently focused onto each individual star. Inside the stars, the incoming radiation would drive nuclear processes that converted helium into hydrogen, while on a planet like our own, ice cubes really would radiate heat and grow larger, while living things "grew" from old age to

---

*At the Les Houches summer school, in France; most of my discussion of Hawking's universe is based on the published version of these lectures, plus his contribution to the ESO/CERN meeting, and copies of several of his scientific papers that he gave me in 1984.

†A good, quick, and fairly accessible overview of Gold's model can be found on page 194 of *The Runaway Universe* by Paul Davies (London: Dent, 1978). The earliest version of the original work that I am aware of dates back to 1964, when Gold mentioned it at a Cornell conference, "The Nature of Time." Davies tells me he has now traced it back to a 1958 paper.

youth. It sounds bizarre, but it is no more than the world
we see about us described in time-reversed language. The
reality is that there is a change from one state to another;
the labels that define "forward" and "backward" with respect to that change are arbitrary. And if entropy is running backward, then, says Gold, so will the thought
processes that make intelligent creatures intelligent. Any
intelligent creatures living in what we call the contracting
phase of the Universe would think "backward" compared
with our way of thinking, and would still "see" heat flowing from hotter bodies to cooler ones, and would deduce
that the Universe was expanding but that it would ultimately switch over into a state of collapse—the phase of
the cycle that *we* think of as the expansion phase! As far
as intelligence is concerned, not only does Hawking's model
have no boundaries, but also each cycle of each quantum
history of the Universe has no end, just two distinct
beginnings.

There are problems, of course, about what happens at
the "equator," when the Universe switches from expansion to collapse. Paul Davies has conjectured that these
problems can be overcome in a model in which the arrow
of time is the same throughout one cycle of expansion and
collapse but then reverses in the fireball stage, where all
information is destroyed anyway, so that the arrow of time,
and the flow of entropy, is reversed in the next cycle of
expansion and collapse. This idea was put forward long
before Hawking's quantum model of the Universe (see
The Runaway Universe), but it suggested to me the neat
possibility that in Hawking's model one wave of expansion
and collapse could carry the Universe, in the form of
expanding and contracting "lines of latitude" out from the
North Pole to the equator and down to the South Pole, but
always with the same arrow of time and flow of entropy.
The next phase of the Universe would then be a cycle
starting out from the South Pole and running up past the
equator and collapsing onto the North Pole, with entropy
flowing in the opposite sense. But don't take my speculation too seriously just yet. I asked Hawking if it could
work that way, and he said, "No. The fact that the South
Pole is a regular point of space-time requires that the
Universe be smooth and homogeneous when it recollapses

into a small volume. This means that the disordered and inhomogeneous state at the point of maximum expansion has to become more ordered as the Universe recollapses. Thus the thermodynamic arrow of time *must* reverse in the contracting phase." And on this subject, for sure, he's the boss.

Speculation aside, though, Hawking's model of the Universe has important philosophical implications. Even though the details remain to be painted in and there is still scope for kite-flying speculation, he is telling us that it is possible in principle to develop a mathematical model that describes the Universe completely in terms of the known laws of science alone, without any need to invoke special conditions even at the moment of creation. Quantum physics is the key needed to unlock the last secrets of the Universe and to explain both its beginning and its end. If inflation today is in a state equivalent to the state of knowledge about Big Bang theory in the 1940s, then, extending the analogy drawn by Martin Rees, it might be fair to say that Hawking's model of the quantum universe is where quantum physics itself was in the early 1920s, before Heisenberg, Schrödinger, and the rest developed a complete, consistent theory. The kind of unified theories that physicists are now groping toward, and may discover (or invent) before the end of this century, ought to be able, combined with Hawking's universe, to explain every phenomenon that ever has happened or ever could happen in the Universe. Such a theory would be able to predict the probability of any event at all, at least in principle, although in practice the calculations would be too complex to make the equations solvable in all but the simplest cases.

Our search for the Big Bang, and back before the Big Bang to the moment of creation itself, is over. Hawking's universe holds out the prospect of combining General Relativity and cosmology in one grand theory of creation, and tells us that we already know all of the fundamental laws of physics. There is no need to invoke miracles, or new physics, to explain where the Universe came from. Hawking himself foresees an "end to theoretical physics" in the sense that a satisfactory unified theory of everything, perhaps based on $N = 8$ supergravity, may be in sight and could be reached before the end of this century. There would still, of course, be plenty of work for physicists left to do, such as filling in the details of the evolution of the Universe. Perhaps it would be more accurate to say that Hawking has already indicated an end, not to physics but to *metaphysics*. It is now possible to give a good scientific answer to the question "Where do we come from?" without invoking either God or special boundary conditions for the Universe at the moment of creation. As of the Vatican conference of 1981, it is the metaphysicians who are out of a job. Everything else shrinks into insignificance alongside such a claim, and the end of the road for metaphysics certainly seems to be a good place to end this book.

BIBLIOGRAPHY

These are the books I read and used during the preparation of the book you now hold. The list is not a complete guide to everything written about the Universe, but if you wanted to dive in anywhere here and follow up the references, and the references contained in those books, and so on, you could probably spend the rest of your life happily probing mankind's understanding of the mysteries of nature. Some of the books are like old friends; others are useful because they provide one particular insight into one particular puzzle. Most are accessible to anyone who has read my own book, but a few, each marked with an asterisk, might be intimidating either on the grounds that they contain extensive mathematical equations or because they assume a detailed background knowledge of physics or astronomy. With that warning, feel free to read and enjoy. And remember:

The true delight is in the finding out, rather than in the knowing.

Isaac Asimov

Abell, George. *Exploration of the Universe*, fourth edition. Philadelphia: Saunders, 1982.
A college text that covers everything from the Greeks to the Big Bang and sets in context just about all we know about the Universe as it is today. The book does not include anything on the inflationary cosmology, which is too new to have filtered into college texts yet, but it is an excellent place to find out more about the Universe at large than I have had space to deal with here.

Bernstein, Jeremy. *Three Degrees Above Zero: The Bell Labs in the Information Age*. New York: Charles Scribner's Sons, 1984.
This "profile" of Bell Labs is built around the story of Arno Penzias, Robert Wilson, and the discovery of the cosmic microwave background radiation. A lovely book, strong on people and places, and invaluable background to the science I have tried to describe here.

Bonnor, William. *The Mystery of the Expanding Universe*. New York: Macmillan, 1964.
Bonnor, himself a cosmologist, wrote this book in the early 1960s, not long before the accidental discovery of the cosmic microwave radiation, now generally accepted as the "echo of the Big Bang." His very clear account of the different models of the Universe allowed by General Relativity, and of rival ideas, sums up the state of cosmology in those days, when it was all very much still a mathematical game—just before the cosmologists were shocked, by the discovery of the cosmic background radiation, into the realization that the equations they scribbled so happily on their blackboards really did have a direct relevance to the origin and evolution of the real Universe in which we live. A lovely book—not so much dated as a period classic.

Chandrasekhar, Subrahmanyan. *Eddington*. Cambridge, Eng.: Cambridge University Press, 1983.
The subtitle of the book—*The Most Distinguished Astrophysicist of His Time*—gives you a feel for the

author's approach. Chandrasekhar studied under Eddington, and this little monograph is a tribute to the great man, in the form of lectures delivered at Trinity College, Cambridge, in 1982, the centenary of Eddington's birth. Full of anecdotal biography and a pleasure to read. Brief, but worth digging out simply for the description of the work leading up to the 1919 eclipse expedition that confirmed the prediction that light must bend as it passes near the Sun.

Davies, Paul. *The Forces of Nature*. Cambridge, Eng.: Cambridge University Press, 1979.
A very clear account of the concepts underlying the modern understanding of the world within the atom—particles, fields, and quantum theory. Light on math; strong on the "feel" of the subject. My favorite Paul Davies book, and a good place to find out more about symmetry and unification of the forces.

————.*Superforce*. London: Heinemann, 1984.
Davies's best "popular" book, covering much the same ground as *The Forces of Nature* but for an audience with less specialized knowledge of physics. Free from some of the constraints of writing textbook physics, Davies leaps off into more speculative realms in the later parts of the book and discusses subjects such as antigravity, the "holistic" view of nature, and even (in passing) astrology. If you read this and *The Forces of Nature* you'll get a good idea of what physicists are sure of, and also a glimpse of some of their wilder flights of fancy.

Ferris, Timothy. *The Red Limit*, revised and updated edition. New York: Quill, 1983.
Subtitled *The Search for the Edge of the Universe,* this book provides a graphic overview of the historical development of the observations that have established the nature of the expanding Universe. It has very little about the origin of the elements or the fireball era, "standard model" doesn't even appear in the index, and there is nothing on inflation, but Ferris provides a wealth of information and anecdote about the

characters involved in probing out as far as our telescopes can see. Beautifully written and a delight to
read.

French, A.P. (editor). *Einstein: A Centenary Volume*. Cambridge, Mass.: Harvard University Press, 1979.
A collection published to mark the centenary of Einstein's birth, this volume includes reminiscences from
his friends and colleagues, biography, outlines of Einstein's major contributions to science, and extracts
from his own writings. Literally something for anybody with an interest in science, and a delight to dip
into.

Fritzsch, Harald. *Quarks*. London: Pelican, 1984.
The author is a German physicist who worked with
Murray Gell-Mann on the theory that became known
as quantum chromodynamics, the "color" theory of
quarks. The book, first published in German in 1981,
provides a very clear introduction to the world of particle physics, with the new theories related to the experiments being carried out at high energy accelerators
in the 1960s and 1970s. It nods only briefly in the
direction of the electroweak unification and has nothing on GUTs, supersymmetry, or cosmology. But if
you specifically want to know about quarks, that is an
advantage, since you get an uncluttered view of the
main subject matter. An excellent book.

Gamow, George. *The Creation of the Universe*. New York:
Viking Press, 1952.
A very readable, entertaining account of the early
version of what became the Big Bang model of cosmology. As well as providing a fascinating insight into
Gamow's thinking, the book includes an equation for
the temperature of the Universe at any epoch. Although Gamow didn't bother, in the book, to put the
numbers into the equation, it does, in fact, "predict"
the existence of a cosmic background of radiation
today with a temperature of a few K—a prediction
published not just in some obscure technical journal
(though it was published in that form, too) but also in

a popular book that sold in large quantities throughout the 1950s. And yet when the predicted radiation was discovered in the 1960s, the pioneering prediction of Gamow and his colleagues had been forgotten by the experts.

————.*Mr. Tompkins in Paperback*. Cambridge, Eng.: Cambridge University Press, 1967.
Reprints of stories originally published in the 1940s, in which the mythical Mr. Tompkins explores the worlds of relativity (including cosmology) and quantum physics. Updated by Gamow to take account of developments in the 1950s and early 1960s. Still great fun, and a painless way to absorb some of the key concepts of modern physics.

————.*My World Line*. New York: Viking Press, 1970.
Autobiography from "Geo.," possibly the most versatile scientist of modern times, who participated actively in the three major scientific revolutions of the twentieth century—in quantum physics, cosmology, and molecular biology. All this without being able to spell or, literally, to get his sums right. Very enjoyable stuff from a master storyteller.

*Gibbons, G.W.; S.W. Hawking; and S.T.C. Siklos (editors). *The Very Early Universe*, Cambridge, Eng.: Cambridge University Press, 1983.
Definitely not for the mathematically fainthearted, this volume reports on a workshop on inflation and associated ideas held at Cambridge University in 1982. A very important landmark in the history of the search for the Big Bang, and a good place for the mathematically inclined to get a feel of the excitement raised by the idea of inflation in the early 1980s. Contributions from Guth, Hawking, Linde, Rees, and many others give you a ringside seat as new ideas unfold.

Gribbin, John (editor). *Cosmology Today*. London: New Science Publications/IPC Magazines, 1982.
A collection of articles from *New Scientist* rounding up cosmology as of 1982—which happens to have

been just *before* the inflationary scenario burst upon the astronomical community. Very good on Einstein and General Relativity; a useful snapshot view of the state of the art immediately prc-inflation.

————. *In Search of Schrödinger's Cat.* New York: Bantam; London: Corgi, 1984.
My account of the development of quantum physics. The bizarre world of the quantum is explained in more detail than I had space for in the present book, and it is fascinating to compare the development of the great ideas in astronomy and quantum physics as they progressed throughout the early part of this century. Great new ideas that seemingly had nothing to do with each other in the 1920s—that were literally at opposite ends of the physicists' spectrum of ideas— have come together in the 1980s to give the most complete description of the Universe yet.

*Harrison, Edward. *Cosmology.* Cambridge, Eng.: Cambridge University Press, 1981.
The author says his aim was to reach an audience "at a level that is understandable to a college student who is not necessarily majoring in a natural science," and he mostly succeeds in this aim. A very good jumping-off point if you want to investigate cosmology properly, because he also includes copious references to the books and other publications containing the key ideas. But also a good book to dip into, with many juicy tidbits tucked away as "reflections" at the end of each chapter. If you were to read just one book on cosmology (apart from my own!), then this is the one I would recommend.

Hoyle, Fred. *Galaxies, Nuclei and Quasars.* London: Heinemann, 1965.
Published just as the 3 K microwave background was being discovered, and mostly out of date, especially in terms of Hoyle's espousal of the Steady State theory. But worth seeking out for the last chapter alone, which summarizes the B^2FH scenario of the origin of the elements.

Hubble, Edwin. *The Realm of the Nebulae*. New York: Dover, 1958.

Originally published in 1936, Hubble's best-known book captures the freshness of the new discoveries about the nature of the Universe made in the 1920s and early 1930s. Very clear and well written, but remember that the distance scale of the Universe has been revised upward by several notches since Hubble's day.

Judson, Horace Freeland. *The Eighth Day of Creation*. London: Cape, 1979.

A massive book about the development of molecular biology in the twentieth century, including George Gamow's role in helping to crack the genetic code.

Layzer, David. *Constructing the Universe*. New York: Scientific American Books, 1984.

A very good, beautifully illustrated account of cosmological ideas from Aristarchus to Einstein, marred by one flaw. Layzer is an advocate of a minority interpretation of the cosmological equations called the "cold Big Bang" model. Instead of telling you this and offering the evidence for and against both his favored model and the standard model, he presents the cold Big Bang as gospel and dismisses the standard model as old hat. This is a somewhat misleading representation of how cosmology is viewed by most experts today. But if you treat this part of the book as a respectable minority view and remember that the standard model is much stronger and more widely accepted than Layzer leads you to believe, the rest can be taken very much as the received wisdom today.

In the last page of the text, the author comments that "the very early universe is a frontier where particle physics and cosmology meet." But he doesn't tell you anything about that meeting (and, of course, developments such as inflation *strengthen* the standard hot Big Bang model). So really, I suppose, you should have read *Constructing the Universe* before you read the book you now hold!

Narlikar, Jayant. *The Structure of the Universe*. London: Oxford University Press, 1977.
A very thorough account of the present understanding of the Universe (but written before the idea of inflation surfaced) that includes much more about the variety of possible universes and the observations that may decide which kind we inhabit than I have had space for here. More technical or mathematical items are set off from the main text in boxes, which helps the readability, but still this is not a book for the casual reader.

Novikov, I.D. *Evolution of the Universe*. Cambridge, Eng.: Cambridge University Press, 1983.
Novikov is one of the senior Soviet cosmologists, and he came close to discovering the cosmic background radiation. His guide to cosmology is doubly interesting as a Soviet view, which places the historical emphasis differently from most Western accounts. Unfortunately, the translation is not everything it should be, and the result doesn't always read smoothly. But well worth investigating if you want to know more about the standard model. Fairly accessible, but perhaps meriting half an asterisk.

Pais, Abraham. *Subtle Is the Lord*. London: Oxford University Press, 1982.
The definitive scientific biography of Einstein. Pais goes into a lot of scientific detail but also provides a wealth of biographical information. He is very good at providing insight into *how* Einstein arrived at his great ideas, such as General Relativity, and I strongly recommend the book. The "observer falling off a roof" quote from Einstein is taken from page 178 of this book.

Pears, D.F. (editor). *The Nature of Metaphysics*. London: Macmillan, 1957.
A collection of essays based on talks for the "Third Programme" (as it then was) of the BBC, this relatively slim and well-written volume provides the best basic introduction I know to metaphysics. Far more accessi-

ble and informative than many a weighty and learned academic tome.

*Pickering, Andrew. *Construction Quarks*. Edinburgh: Edinburgh University Press, 1984.
Subtitled *A sociological history of particle physics,* this book is aimed at specialists, both physicists and historians of science, but is quite accessible to anyone seriously interested in following up the saga of how high energy physics studies led to the idea of quarks as the building blocks of matter. Very thorough, with copious references and scarcely any mathematics, but pulling no punches when it comes to dealing with the basic concepts, such as gauge theory and symmetry.

Polkinghorne, J.C. *The Quantum World*. London: Longman, 1984.
A very neat little book—just a hundred pages, including a mathematical appendix and a glossary—that gets across most of the strangeness about quantum physics, and the philosophical discussions it has engendered. Especially interesting because the author was professor of mathematical physics at the University of Cambridge from 1968 to 1979, then resigned to train as a priest in the Church of England. He is now an assistant curate in Bristol. Recommended—not least to the army of physicists who use quantum physics today without ever pausing to wonder what it all really *means.*

Sciama, Dennis. *Modern Cosmology,* revised edition. Cambridge, Eng.: Cambridge University Press, 1973 (reprinted in paperback, 1982).
A good place to look if you want to go a little deeper into the equations of cosmology than I have gone here, with some discussion of the different models allowed by the theories. The equations are not *too* intimidating, and there are plenty of helpful diagrams—but nothing, of course, on inflation, which hadn't been thought of in 1973. Sciama also writes well on the philosophical side—Mach's Principle and Olbers's Paradox—but not, alas, at any length here. His older book

The Unity of the Universe, published by Faber & Faber, is better in that respect but is now, sadly, out of print. Worth looking out for in the libraries.

*Silk, Joseph. *The Big Bang*. San Francisco: W.H. Freeman, 1980.
A good introduction to the expanding Universe for anyone with a serious interest in the subject, including a great deal about how stars and galaxies form in the expanding Universe, and a chapter on "alternatives to the Big Bang"—the title is more than a little misleading and doesn't indicate the scope of the book. But you need some math and physics to get the most out of it.

Sutton, Christine. *The Particle Connection*. London: Hutchinson, 1984.
An excellent account of the work leading up to the discovery of the W and Z particles, which confirmed the predictions of the electroweak theory, written from an experimenter's point of view. This is the place to find out how the particle accelerators work, as well as to get a flavor of the excitement of particle physics in the late 1970s and early 1980s. Infuriatingly, the book has no index. Otherwise, its faults are few.

Weinberg, Steven. *The First Three Minutes*. London: Deutsch, 1977.
The best popular account of the standard model of the hot Big Bang, from a hundredth of a second after the moment of creation to the time when primordial nucleosynthesis came to an end and the hot fireball was left to expand into the Universe we know today.

Wright, Thomas. *An Original Theory of the Universe*. London: Macdonald, 1971.
A facsimile of the masterwork of the Durham philosopher, reprinted (with a new introduction by Michael Hoskin) in facsimile from the edition of 1750.

INDEX

ABOUT THE AUTHOR

JOHN GRIBBIN was born in 1946, in Maidstone, Kent, England. His Ph.D. in Astrophysics was awarded by the University of Cambridge in 1970, and after five years on the staff of the journal *Nature* and three with the Science Policy Research Unit at the University of Sussex, he became Physics Consultant to the weekly magazine *New Scientist* in 1978.

In Search of the Big Bang is his thirty-first book to be published so far, and completes a trilogy of major works on the most important scientific achievements of the twentieth century, which began with *In Search of Schrödinger's Cat* (1984) and continued with *In Search of the Double Helix* (1985). Gribbin's other main books include *Genesis* (1981), *Spacewarps* (1983), two novels written in collaboration with Douglas Orgill and, with Jeremy Cherfas, *The Redundant Male* (1984). He contributes on science topics to the *Guardian* newspaper, as well as to *New Scientist*, and to the domestic and world services of BBC Radio.

He has won several awards for science writing, including the top British award, a Glaxo Travelling Fellowship, in 1974. Current projects include a collaboration with Mary Gribbin on the sociopsychology of being human, a science fiction novel, and a major book on the ultimate fate of the Universe.

5649